CONVERGENCE AND DIVERGENCE OF PRIVATE LAW IN ASIA

There has been an increasing need for greater integration of many Asian economies, either within the confines of ASEAN or on a more geo-economically strategic scale including major Asian jurisdictions like China, Japan, and Korea. A number of key personalities within the regional legal fraternity have advanced views that such integration ought to occur through the harmonization of legal rules, arguing that in doing so, uncertainty and other transaction costs would be reduced and commercial confidence within the region concomitantly increased. This edited volume brings together eminent and promising scholars and practitioners to investigate what convergence and divergence means in their respective fields and for Asia. Interwoven in the details of each tale of convergence is whether and how convergence ought to take place, and in so choosing, what are the attendant consequences for that choice.

Gary Low is Vice-President (Legal & Regulatory Engagement) for e-commerce platform Lazada Group. He read for law at the LSE (LLB First Class Honours), Oxford (BCL, Distinction), and Maastricht (PhD). He was Justices' Law Clerk of the Supreme Court of Singapore, and shortly thereafter practised shipping and commercial law at Rajah & Tann LLP. Formerly on faculty at Tilburg, Maastricht and SMU, Gary has held visiting appointments at Cornell, Keio and CEU. Before becoming an in-house counsel, he was Deputy Senior State Counsel at the Attorney-General's Chambers.

Convergence and Divergence of Private Law in Asia

Edited by
GARY LOW
Lazada Singapore & RedMart

CAMBRIDGE
UNIVERSITY PRESS

University Printing House, Cambridge CB2 8BS, United Kingdom

One Liberty Plaza, 20th Floor, New York, NY 10006, USA

477 Williamstown Road, Port Melbourne, VIC 3207, Australia

314–321, 3rd Floor, Plot 3, Splendor Forum, Jasola District Centre, New Delhi – 110025, India

103 Penang Road, #05–06/07, Visioncrest Commercial, Singapore 238467

Cambridge University Press is part of the University of Cambridge.

It furthers the University's mission by disseminating knowledge in the pursuit of education, learning, and research at the highest international levels of excellence.

www.cambridge.org
Information on this title: www.cambridge.org/9781108475150
DOI: 10.1017/9781108566391

© Cambridge University Press 2022

This publication is in copyright. Subject to statutory exception and to the provisions of relevant collective licensing agreements, no reproduction of any part may take place without the written permission of Cambridge University Press.

First published 2022

A catalogue record for this publication is available from the British Library.

Library of Congress Cataloging-in-Publication Data
NAMES: Towards an Asian Legal Order: Conversations on Convergance (Conference) (2018 : Singapore Management University) | Low, Gary (Lawyer), editor.
TITLE: Convergence and divergence of private law in Asia / edited by Gary Low, Lazada Singapore & Redmart.
DESCRIPTION: Cambridge, United Kingdom ; New York, NY : Cambridge University Press, 2021. | Includes index.
IDENTIFIERS: LCCN 2021000359 (print) | LCCN 2021000360 (ebook) | ISBN 9781108475150 (hardback) | ISBN 9781108566391 (ebook)
SUBJECTS: LCSH: Commercial law – East Asia – International unification – Congresses. | Commercial law – Southeast Asia – International unification – Congresses.
CLASSIFICATION: LCC KNC242.A6 T69 2018 (print) | LCC KNC242.A6 (ebook) | DDC 346.5–dc23
LC record available at https://lccn.loc.gov/2021000359
LC ebook record available at https://lccn.loc.gov/2021000360

ISBN 978-1-108-47515-0 Hardback

Cambridge University Press has no responsibility for the persistence or accuracy of URLs for external or third-party internet websites referred to in this publication and does not guarantee that any content on such websites is, or will remain, accurate or appropriate.

To my children, Tobias William and Sophie Philippa, now six and four, respectively. One was born when I entertained the idea for this book, and the other was born just as I hosted the contributors at a conference. I should really stop at three.

Contents

List of Tables		page ix
List of Contributors		x
Acknowledgments		xv
List of Abbreviations		xvii

1   Introduction   1
    Gary Low

2   Uniform Law and the Production and Circulation of Legal Models   7
    Luca Castellani

3   Convergence, Divergence and Diversity in Financial Law: The Experience of the UNCITRAL Model Law and Cross-Border Insolvency   33
    Andrew Godwin

4   The New York Convention and the UNCITRAL Model Law on International Commercial Arbitration: Existing Models for Legal Convergence in Asia?   62
    Michael Hwang

5   Convergences and Divergences: Comparing Contractual and Organizational Models in International Regulatory Cooperation   81
    Fabrizio Cafaggi

6   Law as a Market Standard: Voluntary Unification in Contract and Company Law   105
    Andreas Engert

7	Is the Harmonisation of Asian Contract Law Possible? The Example of the European Union Mateja Durovic and Geraint Howells	135
8	The Presumption of Regularity in Chinese Corporate Contracting: Evidence and the Prospect of Regional Convergence Charles Zhen Qu	153
9	Mind the Gap: Studying the Implementation Discrepancy for the ASEAN Economic Community Sanchita Basu Das	180
10	The Rule of Law as Key to the ASEAN Legal Order: How Can It Be Ensured? Francis Jacobs	204
11	How Asian Should Asian Law Be? Ralf Michaels	227
Index		252

Tables

3.1	Convergence objects and methodologies	page 38
8.1	Patterns of cases: percentage of authorised transactions	156
8.2	Pattern of court decisions: Contract enforceability and company liability	157
8.3	The RTB approach: what the contractor is entitled to assume	161
8.4	Approaches to the determination of the validity of unauthorised corporate security contracts	163
8.5	Decisions based on (inter alia) the RTB approach: outcomes	165
8.6	Evidence on modes of executing security instrument: seal	173
8.7	Evidence on modes of executing security instrument: signature	174
9.1	State of development divide in ASEAN	190

Contributors

Editor

Dr. Gary Low is Head of Legal for e-commerce platform Lazada Singapore and RedMart. He read for law at the LSE (LLB First Class Honours), Oxford (BCL, Distinction), and Maastricht (PhD). He was Justices' Law Clerk of the Supreme Court of Singapore, and shortly thereafter practised shipping and commercial law at Rajah & Tann LLP. Formerly on faculty at Tilburg, Maastricht and SMU, Gary has held visiting appointments at Cornell, Keio and CEU. Before becoming an in-house counsel, he was Deputy Senior State Counsel at the Attorney-General's Chambers. He has published in the likes of the European Business Law Review, the European Journal of Law and Economics, and the European Review of Private Law. He also sits on the Central Committee of the Consumer Association of Singapore.

Contributors

Dr. Sanchita Basu Das is an economist at the South Asia Regional Department of the Asian Development Bank. She was the Lead Researcher (economic affairs) at the ASEAN Studies Centre of ISEAS-Yusof Ishak Institute (ISEAS), Singapore. She is a former ISEAS fellow and held concurrent duties as the coordinator of the Singapore APEC Study Centre and was coeditor of the *Journal of Southeast Asian Economies*. Prior to joining the Institute in 2005, she was an economist in the private sector, involved in infrastructure consulting, manufacturing, and banking. Sanchita holds an MBA from the National University of Singapore and an MA from the Delhi School of Economics. She has authored and edited numerous books and book chapters, policy papers, and opinion articles. Her research interests include economic regionalism in ASEAN and the Asia-Pacific Region, international trade, and economic development issues like connectivity.

Professor Fabrizio Cafaggi is a member of the Italian Council of State. He is concurrently Professor of Regulation at the School of National Administration and co-director of the Centre for Judicial Cooperation at the European University Institute (Florence, Italy). He also holds an appointment as Professor of Private Law at the University of Trento (on leave). He is a founding member of the

European Law Institute, a member of its executive committee, and an affiliate of the American Law Institute. Professor Cafaggi earned his JD *cum laude* at the University of Rome and his PhD in Law at the University of Pisa, Italy. He has been a visiting professor at the Columbia Law School, NYU School of Law, and the San Andres Law School in Argentina. Fabrizio Cafaggi's research activities are mainly focused on private regulation in its different forms (self-regulation, co-regulation, and standard setting), while he is also interested in comparative and transnational private law. His other research fields include law and economics, codes of conduct with a special focus on private law and regulatory techniques, NGOs, welfare systems, US contracts, tort law, and Italian law. He has taught courses on theories of regulation, transnational regulation, European contract law, and contract law in regulated markets. The current subjects of his research include transnational private regulation, European private law, regulation, and multilevel governance.

Dr. Luca Castellani is a legal officer in the Secretariat of the United Nations Commission on International Trade Law (UNCITRAL). After graduating in law at the University of Torino, he received a doctoral degree in comparative law from the University of Trieste and a master's in international law from New York University. He was admitted to the bar in Italy and has held research and lecturing positions in Italy (Università del Piemonte Orientale) and Eritrea (University of Asmara). He joined the Office of Legal Affairs of the secretariat of the United Nations in New York in 2001, working at its Treaty Section, and moved to its International Trade Law Division to discharge the functions of the UNCITRAL secretariat in Vienna, Austria, in 2004. While there, he was tasked with the promotion of the adoption and uniform interpretation of UNCITRAL texts relating to the sale of goods and electronic commerce. From March 2012 to November 2013, he was assigned as the first Head of the United Nations Commission on International Trade Law Regional Centre for Asia and the Pacific (UNCITRAL RCAP), located in Incheon, Republic of Korea. He has published in the fields of international trade law and comparative law, dealing, in particular, with the sale of goods, electronic commerce, and trade law reform in developing countries.

Dr. Mateja Durovic is Associate Professor at the Dickinson Poon School of Law, King's College London. Mateja holds PhD and LLM degrees from the EUI in Florence, an LLM (Cantab), and an LLB (Belgrade; valedictorian). Prior to assuming his current position, Mateja worked as a post-doctoral research associate at the EUI, the Legal Service of the European Commission, and as a legal consultant for the European Commission, BEUC (European Consumer Organisation) and the United Nations, and held a faculty position at the City University of Hong Kong. He has held visiting positions at Stanford, the Max Planck Institute of Private International and Comparative Law, as well as universities in Macau, Florence, Passau, and Belgrade. Mateja conducts research in the areas of contract law, consumer law, international commercial law, comparative law, and competition law. His work has been published inter alia in the *European Review of Private Law*, *European Review of Contract Law*, and the *Journal of Consumer Policy*.

Professor Andreas Engert is Professor of Law at the Freie Universitat Berlin, and a member of the European Corporate Governance Institute. Prior to this, he held the chair in Business Law and Tax Law at the University of Mannheim. He completed his undergraduate studies at the University of Tübingen and earned an LLM degree from the University of Chicago School of Law and a Doctorate in Law at the University of Munich. A law and economics scholar, Professor Engert has a particular interest in questions of regulatory competition, network effects, and the role of market-standards in private law. He has, among others, addressed these topics in writings on lender liability, corporate law, bankruptcy law, securities law, and tax law.

Dr Andrew Godwin is a Principal Fellow at Melbourne Law School. Prior to joining Melbourne Law School in 2007, Andrew was in legal practice for over 15 years, 10 of which were spent in Shanghai where he was a partner of an international law firm. Andrew researches in the area of finance and insolvency law, corporations and financial services regulation, property law and the regulation of the legal profession. Books that Andrew has published as an author or editor include *The Cambridge Handbook of Twin Peaks Financial Regulation* (Cambridge University Press, 2021), *Technology and Corporate Law: How Innovation Shapes Corporate Activity* (Edward Elgar Publishing, 2021), *Sackville & Neave Australian Property Law* (11th edition, LexisNexis, 2021) and *China Lexicon* (Vantage Asia, 2014). His PhD thesis examined traditional land-use rights in rural China and evaluated their relevance and suitability to reform today. Andrew has acted as a consultant to a broad range of organisations, including the World Bank and regulators and governments in Australia and abroad. In 2020, Andrew was appointed Special Counsel to the Australian Law Reform Commission to assist its inquiry into corporations and financial services regulation in Australia.

Professor Geraint Howells holds the Chair in Commercial Law at the University of Manchester. Prior to this, he was Dean of the School of Law at the City University of Hong Kong. He is an authority in the field of consumer law writ large, with a particular interest in product liability and product safety, and has produced a voluminous body of research on these issues. Professor Howells has held chairs at the universities of Sheffield and Lancaster and was offered visiting positions in Wurzburg, Munster, Paris XI, Tennessee, and Sydney. He is also a member of the Board, and former President, of the International Association of Consumer Law.

Dr. Michael Hwang, SC, a Senior Counsel of the Supreme Court of Singapore, and Chief Justice of the Dubai International Financial Centre Courts, received his undergraduate and postgraduate legal education at the University of Oxford where he was a College Scholar and Prizewinner. Dr. Hwang is active in international dispute resolution as an arbitrator (under the auspices of all the major arbitration institutions) as well as a mediator. Based in Singapore but associated with Chambers in London and Sydney, he is active both in commercial as well as investment treaty arbitration. He has conducted arbitrations in more than twenty-five cities and spoken at conferences in more than fifty cities. He has also conducted arbitrations under the auspices of the Permanent Court of Arbitration and ICSID. Dr. Hwang has served in various capacities, including as a Judicial Commissioner of the Supreme Court of Singapore; Singapore's Non-Resident Ambassador to Switzerland and Argentina; President of the Law Society of Singapore; Vice Chairman of the ICC International Court of Arbitration; Vice-President of ICCA; Court Member of LCIA; Trustee of DIAC; Council Member of ASA; Council Member of ICAS; and Commissioner of the United Nations Compensation Commission. In 2014, he was conferred an Honorary LLD by the University of Sydney.

Rt. Hon. Sir Francis Jacobs, KCMG QC, is Professor of Law at King's College London. He received his undergraduate legal education at Christ Church, Oxford, and obtained his MA and DPhil while in residence at Nuffield College, Oxford. Sir Francis's legal career spans more than four decades. At the Council of Europe in Strasbourg, he worked in the European Commission of Human Rights. He then worked in Luxembourg at the European Court of Justice (ECJ), starting just before British entry to the EEC. In 1974 he was appointed to the newly created Chair of European Law in the University of London. He has been one of the most distinguished Advocate Generals at the ECJ, a post that he held from 1988 to 2006, and in this capacity made numerous contributions to law reform across the expanse of EU law. He is the author or editor of myriad books and articles on EU law and human rights law. To celebrate his work, two Festschriften and a special issue of the *Fordham International Law Journal* were dedicated to him. Sir Francis was the first President of the European Law Institute and is a Bencher of the Middle Temple. He was appointed to the Privy Council in 2005 and knighted in 2006.

Professor Ralf Michaels is Director at the Max Planck Institute for Comparative and International Private Law, Global Law Professor at the Queen Mary University of London and Professor of Law at the University of Hamburg. He is a member of the American Law Institute and of the Academia Europea. Until 2019, he was the Arthur Larson Professor of law at Duke University. Ralf Michaels was a Visiting Professor at the Universities of Panthéon/Assas (Paris II), Princeton, Pennsylvania, Toronto, Tel Aviv and the London School of Economics; he was also Senior Fellow at Harvard Law School, Princeton University (Program in Law and Public Affairs) and the American Academy in Berlin. He studied law in Passau and Cambridge. His research focuses on questions of legal plurality, foundations of private international law, and decolonial comparative law.

Dr. Charles Zhen Qu is an adjunct professor of University of New England School of Law. He was conferred his PhD by the Australian National University and has been admitted to the New South Wales Bar. His research interests are in corporate law, corporate insolvency law, schemes of arrangement, and Chinese corporate law, and he is a prolific writer in these areas. Together with Stefan H. C. Lo, he is the author of *Law of Companies in Hong Kong* (2018), currently in its third edition.

Acknowledgments

I conceived of the idea for this book shortly after returning to Singapore from my sojourn in Europe, where, for some years, I had been an active participant in the discussion on the Common European Sales Law. My participation in drafting the Principles of Asian Contract Law allowed this to coalesce into something concrete. Then, unto Yeo Tiong Min (Singapore Management University, or SMU) and Geraint Howells (City University of Hong Kong), I posed this as a seed of opportunity for closer collaboration. That did not take long at all to germinate. I thank the two deans, as well as Chen Lei and Tang Hang Wu, along with the teams at both SMU's Centre for Cross-Border Commercial Law in Asia (CEBLA) and the City University of Hong Kong for backing this project, as well as the conference and book this has led to.

I single out Pamela Yap and Phyllis Yan for tireless and thankless work behind the scenes, making sure all administrative details were ironed out, all processes observed, and all the contributors kept happy.

Thanks go to Mark Fisher of the Asian Business Law Institute (ABLI) and Joao Ribeiro of the UNCITRAL Regional Centre for Asia and the Pacific (UNCITRAL-RCAP) for lending support and advertising the conference in their respective networks.

Maartje de Visser was active in the background, helping me with organizing the conference and reviewing a good number of the contributions, taking a backseat only recently and only because of additional university responsibilities she shoulders.

I also thank Naomi Lim and Soh Kian Peng, who as my one-time research assistants were involuntarily gang pressed (though adequately remunerated in accordance with the minimum requirements of any applicable laws) into the post-conference editorial process. I fear I may have scarred them for life from considering academia as a career.

Joe Ng, Gemma Smith, two anonymous reviewers, and the entire team at Cambridge University Press are the editor's editors. They've been tremendously patient, supportive, and professional in the face of my own sloth-like ineptitudes.

All fault is mine alone. But the credit is shared and justly so.

Abbreviations

ABLI	Asian Business Law Institute
ABs	accreditation bodies
AEC	ASEAN Economic Community
AFC	1997–98 Asian Financial Crisis
AFTA	ASEAN Free Trade Area
AICHR	ASEAN Intergovernmental Commission on Human Rights
AIMO	ASEAN Integration Monitoring Office
APLMA	Asia Pacific Loan Market Association
ARISE	ASEAN Regional Integration Support by the European Union
ASEAN	Association of Southeast Asian Nations
AUSAID	Australian Agency for International Development
B2B	business to business
BGB	German Civil Code
BRC	British Retail Consortium
CABs	conformity assessment bodies
CBs	certifying bodies
CEO	chief executive officer
CESL	Common European Sales Law
CISG	United Nations Convention on Contracts for the International Sale of Goods
CLMV	Cambodia, Laos, Myanmar, and Vietnam
CLOUT	Case Law on UNCITRAL Texts
COMI	center of main interest
CPOs	certification program owners
CPTPP	Comprehensive and Progressive Agreement for Trans-Pacific Partnership
CSR	corporate social responsibility
DCFR	Draft Common Framework of Reference
DIFC	Dubai International Financial Centre

DSU	Dispute Settlement Understanding
EASA	European Advertising Standards Alliance
EBRD	European Bank for Reconstruction and Development
ECHR	European Convention on Human Rights
ECJ	European Court of Justice
ECSC	European Coal and Steel Community
ECtHR	European Court of Human Rights
EEA	European Economic Area
EEC	European Economic Community
EFTA	European Free Trade Association
EU	European Union
EURATOM	European Atomic Energy Community
FAO	Food and Agriculture Organization of the United Nations
FDI	foreign direct investment
FLO	Fairtrade Labelling Organization
FSC	Forest Stewardship Council
FTA	free trade agreement
GDP	gross domestic product
GFSI	Global Food Safety Initiative
GLCs	government-linked companies
HCCH	The Hague Conference on Private International Law
HDI	Human Development Index
HKIAC	Hong Kong International Arbitration Centre
HPC	High People's Court (China)
HPMs	high-priority measures
IAF	International Accreditation Forum
IATA	International Air Transport Association
ICAO	International Civil Aviation Organization
ICC	International Chamber of Commerce
ICCA	International Council for Commercial Arbitration
ICoC	International Code of Conduct
ICSID	International Centre for Settlement of Investment Disputes
IEC	International Electrotechnical Commission
IFS	International Featured Standards
ILO	International Labor Organization
IMR	indoor management rule
INCOTERMS	International Commercial Terms
IO	international organizations
IOSCO	International Organization of Securities Commissions
ISDA	International Swaps and Derivatives Association
ISEAL	International Social and Environmental Accreditation and Labelling Association

ISO	International Standards Organization
ISO/GRI	International Standards Organization / Global Reporting Initiative
LCIA	London Court of International Arbitration
LMA	Loan Markets Association
LR	legal representative
ME	monitoring and evaluation
MNC	multinational corporation
MOU	memorandum of understanding
NGO	nongovernmental organization
NSW	national single window
NTBs	non-tariff barriers
NTR	national trade repository
OECD	Organisation for Economic Co-operation and Development
OHADA	Organisation for the Harmonisation of Business Law in Africa
P&C	parts and components
PACL	Principles of Asian Contract Law
PECL	Principles of European Contract Law
PEFC	Programme for the Endorsement of Forest Certification
PKDs	prioritized key deliverables
PPP	purchasing power parity / public-private partnerships
PRC	People's Republic of China
RA	Rainforest Alliance
RECEP	Regional Comprehensive Economic Partnership
ROO	rules of origin
RSPO	Roundtable on Sustainable Palm Oil
RTB	reason-to-believe approach
RTRS	Round Table on Sustainable Soy
SAARC	South Asian Association for Regional Cooperation
SADC	Southern Africa Development Community
SAFA	Sustainable Assessment of Food and Agriculture
SAN	Sustainable Agriculture Network
SAR	Special Administrative Region
SDG	Sustainable Development Goals
SME	small- and medium-sized enterprise
SOEs	state-owned enterprises
SPC	Supreme People's Court (China)
TPP	Trans-Pacific Partnership
TPR	transnational private regulation
UCC	US Uniform Commercial Code
ULF	Uniform Law on the Formation of Contracts for the International Sale of Goods

ULIS	Uniform Law on the International Sale of Goods
UNCITRAL	United Nations Commission on International Trade Law
UNCTAD	United Nations Conference on Trade and Development
UNFSS	United Nations Forum on Sustainability Standards
UNIDROIT	International Institute for the Unification of Private Law
UPICC	UNIDROIT Principles of International Commercial Contracts
USAID	US Agency for International Development
WHO	World Health Organization
WTO	World Trade Organization
WWF	World Wide Fund for Nature

1

Introduction

Gary Low

There have been increasing and stronger calls for greater integration of many Asian economies, either within the confines of ASEAN or on a more geo-economically strategic scale that would include major Asian jurisdictions like China, Japan, and Korea. A number of key personalities within the regional legal fraternity have advanced views that such integration ought to occur through the harmonization of legal rules, arguing among others that in so doing uncertainty and other transaction costs would be reduced and commercial confidence within the region concomitantly increased. That commercial law has come under the lens as a particularly suitable candidate for harmonization is, in a sense, unsurprising. It is for one ostensibly seen as a technical and relatively uncontroversial area of law, as opposed, for instance, to public law. For another, or probably for that precise reason, this area has been the historical choice for attempts at harmonizing substantive law – think of the CISG, the UCC in the United States, or the recently proposed CESL in the European Union.

This edited volume brings together eminent and promising scholars and practitioners to investigate what convergence and divergence mean in their respective fields and for Asia. Interwoven in the details of each tale of convergence is whether and how convergence ought to take place, and in so choosing, what are the attendant consequences for that choice. In an endeavour such as this, one finds familiar friends in the form of the West as a comparator for Asia (Engert, Durovic and Howells, Jacobs), although Michaels warns of the pitfalls of even this choice.

Castellani starts off the volume by recognising that the diversity of laws are a reflection of the differences across pluralistic societies. He then devotes the entire length and breadth of his contribution to examining how the model of uniform law has been used time and again to overcome these differences. His thesis, convincingly argued, echoes the beginning of this introduction: that uniform law's appeal (using the example of UNCITRAL) is that it is technical and pro-commerce, and at the same time, the inclusive process by which uniform law is drafted facilitates near-universal political acceptance.

To critics, this is the weakness that is uniform law – vague and ambiguous terminology borne of political disagreement. Castellani sees this same characteristic as one of synergy, a process which reflects consensus and compromise as and when needed. No stranger to the process, one's impression is that Castellani is not so much optimistic as he is pragmatic (perhaps the highest compliment a common lawyer can pay to his civilian colleague). This comes out in the way he highlights the deficiencies in uniform law and argues how to resolve them – or what he calls the 'adoption' gap. Scholars of uniform law have frequently lamented that this is a problem borne of unfamiliarity and suspicion. Castellani agrees and goes further, examining the problem using examples from the Vienna Sales Convention and the UNCITRAL Model Law on Electronic Commerce. For jurisdictions to accept uniform law, they must play a meaningful part in the process and they must be assured of sufficient technical assistance to help facilitate implementation. If one agrees with Menon's call for greater legal and economic integration within Asia, then Castellani's contribution is his roadmap on how to achieve it.

Godwin follows on and investigates convergence in financial law within ASEAN and the greater Asia region through the adoption of the UNCITRAL Model law on Cross-Border Insolvency as well as relevant UNIDROIT Principles. While it is generally accepted that this Model Law is an example of successful convergence in financial law, there is a significant degree of divergence between jurisdictions in terms of the modifications that have been made to the Model Law when it is incorporated into domestic legislation.

His contribution assesses the effectiveness of model laws as a methodology for legal convergence, identifies the reasons for divergence in the adoption of the Model Law and reflects on what those reasons reveal about the challenges facing legal convergence generally. Godwin's assessment harkens back to Castellani's opening statement – that diversity is the outcome of deliberate policy choices. This is evident where jurisdictions have differed in terms of the nature and extent of the relief that will be granted to assist in foreign insolvency procedures, the relevance of public policy in providing a ground on which recognition or relief should be refused and the significance of concepts such as the centre of main interests, or 'COMI'. In his words, the experience of the Model Law supports the comment by Bathurst CJ that it is 'undesirable to strive for uniformity in all areas of the law' and also the comment by Menon CJ that convergence must take account of the 'undulating legal terrain that results from differences in the national legal systems'. While Godwin sees merit in convergence (through adoption of the Model law), this does not mean he treats divergence as undesirable – there is value in deliberate choice and also the rigours of regulatory competition.

Hwang's is the last in this series of contributions investigating the role of Model Laws – in this case, the UNCITRAL Model Law on International Commercial Arbitration together with the 1958 New York Convention. Arguably the cornerstones of international arbitration. This chapter asks whether it would be prudent for Asian states to subscribe to these two instruments, reversing the current trend of a poor and slow take-up rate. Given the reality that corporations located in Asia will enter into arbitration agreements with counterparts both inside and outside that region, Hwang posits that ratification of the New York Convention and the adoption of the UNCITRAL Model Law is preferable to the path of fashioning a regional set of arbitration rules. At the same time, he acknowledges that criticism has been directed at various aspects of those instruments, such as the lack of a modernised, efficient, and universal enforcement procedure under the New York Convention. The chapter demonstrates how perceived shortcomings and concerns can be satisfactorily addressed through a clever exercise of discretion when Contracting States domesticate and courts are called upon to interpret the relevant legal provisions. Some of these solutions are in fact already being used to good effect by Singapore, Hong Kong, Malaysia, and Australia. Continuing and where necessary elaborating such national practices is salutary, as doing so obviates the need for revision and instead confirms the effectiveness of the Convention and Model Law as modern models for legal convergence in Asia.

In the chapter that follows, Cafaggi spotlights private actors and their incredibly important role in a scene where most rules are non-mandatory. He examines the different regimes at play in producing and enforcing voluntary standards: are they converging or diverging? Are the convergence or divergence regarding procedural or substantive standards? What are the determinative factors? In answering the questions posed, Cafaggi helps delineate the conditions upon which regulatory cooperation or integration contributes towards convergence or divergence of transnational standards.

Engert's chapter marks a turn from producers of uniform laws to that of the market at large. He applies a classic economic analysis to the question of legal convergence: he looks at standards competition or 'network effects' as a framework to evaluate the promise of voluntary law unification. As a complement to the much-discussed field of contract law, the analysis is extended to company law as another reference field. There, the European Union (EU) has to offer some mixed experience with voluntary unification in company law. The analysis of market standardization in private law leads to the following main conclusions: There is a strong case for voluntary law unification as opposed to any kind of mandatory standardisation. While the market can fail at achieving desirable standardisation, it provides some assurance against severe mistakes. Engert posits, on the balance, that the risk of serious error in forced unification would appear to be significantly greater. Promulgating an optional set of legal rules at the international or supranational level can help to promote desirable standardisation in the marketplace. At the same time, existing national laws can also serve as international standards and even have certain advantages over an additional international or supranational regime. Under suitable conditions, fostering jurisdictional competition can be a suitable alternative for advancing unification in private law. The reader would do well to contrast this view with that of Castellani's, in that

Engert does not presume the necessity of uniform law within the plurality that is the market for laws.

The conversation then returns to what some private lawyers might say is the crux of any legal marketplace – contracts. Durovic and Howells agree, and having been involved in the European debate, they see contract law as a *prima facie* obvious candidate for harmonization within Asia. Against that backdrop, this chapter holds up the European experience as a cautionary tale for the prospective 'Asianisation' of contractual rules. While rightfully considered as providing the most advanced example of regional harmonization in this domain, the chapter demonstrates that the EU has actually achieved relatively little over the course of a process spanning more than three decades as far as binding norms are concerned. Those pieces of legislation that have been adopted have a piecemeal character and primarily deal with selected aspects of consumer law. Repeated attempts to adopt a comprehensive settlement all were abandoned sooner or later, typically due to the difficulty of securing the requisite political agreement. Extrapolating to the Asian setting, Durovic and Howells recommend against over-ambitious projects for contract law convergence. The considerable variety in legal traditions, marked differences in the state of national economies, and the absence of a regional judicial body to help supervise and interpret common rules as compared to the EU setting all suggest that achieving even partial convergence will be an uphill task. The greatest chances of success, if any, are to be had in specialised or innovative areas of contract law such as consumer law or possibly digital content.

Qu's contribution takes us to East Asia, where, in late 2005, China adopted a new Company Law which sought to boost foreign investment. A problematic practice under the old regime consisted of companies investing profits in or guaranteeing debts of unrelated companies. The motivation to take on such liabilities was often found in personal financial interests or connections of directors, CEOs or controlling shareholders. This could make companies appear financially solvent while they could, in reality, be on the brink of bankruptcy. Worse, the existence of such unrestricted debt guarantees often would only become known once insolvency or bankruptcy proceedings were underway, to the detriment of the company's legitimate creditors. In response, the revised Company Law stipulates procedural limits that circumscribe the ability for companies to invest in or act as guarantors for third-party companies. Qu's contribution scrutinises whether the revised Company Law, through its Article 16, has been able to deliver the expected protection of company assets and has helped create a more secure climate for investors, in light of rapidly growing numbers of loan disputes that have resulted in adjudication in recent years. The chapter addresses how the language of parts of Article 16 has meant that there is considerable room for judicial discretion and the determinants that can account for decisional outcomes in surety contracts. It suggests that a case can be made for a further revision of this part of China's company law to achieve concordance with the approach under the common law as it stands in Hong Kong, Australia, Singapore, and the United Kingdom.

With economist Basu Das, we turn our sights to the ASEAN Economic Community (AEC). It is at a crossroads where policy implementation is a matter of crucial significance. At the end of 2015, though ASEAN announced a significant achievement rate of 93 per cent, effective implementation has remained patchy and there is growing concern among end users that ASEAN has fallen short of its aspiration of 'single market and production base'. This chapter postulates that economic conflicts among countries and firms within ASEAN states have resulted in regional policy documents that are too broadly framed, with flexibilities and loopholes, thereby negatively affecting the course of implementation. While some firms – such as foreign MNCs doing business in the region – firmly supported liberalisation, SMEs and other domestic-focused enterprises requested protection in the face of increased competition. The interests of ASEAN countries as regards extent of liberalisation and facilitation measures moreover differed, given their varied economic structures and uncertainties on the expected gains attendant on closer gains from economic integration. The national character of implementation has meant that organisational conflicts between government agencies and bureaucrats have to date further distorted the realisation of ASEAN policies and agreements on the ground. Basu Das concludes by offering some policy recommendations to reverse the current trajectory, including the need for improved communication between government agencies and end-users; more systematic matching between AEC objectives, headline commitments and concrete measures; and a rethinking of resource allocation among government agencies entrusted with implementation.

Although the fields of law within this book are clearly commerce-related, the successful adoption, implementation, and enforcement are entirely dependent on a robust adherence to rule of law. This is in terms of both institutions and attitude. But how to realise this? No less eminent a jurist than Jacobs tackles the issue of the rule of law in Asia head on. In his contribution, he first examines the composite elements of the rule of law, with reference works by leading constitutional theorists, and queries how far this normative concept has universal application. Next, Jacobs argues that the rule of law should be key to the legal order in Southeast Asia, and in particular to the market freedoms under ASEAN Economic Community. The chapter also discusses how respect for this concept is to be ensured. This, among others, requires a delicate balance to be struck between the importance of securing uniform interpretation of transnational legal rules, and their effective application and allowing States a necessary margin for manoeuvre. The chapter illustrates how the Court of Justice and the EFTA Court in Europe, the Caribbean Court of Justice and regional courts for transnational economic organisations in Latin America and in Africa have sought to do so and assesses the relevance or otherwise of those models for South-east Asia.

When the argument is made that laws of different jurisdictions or fields (should) converge, we concomitantly describe what the end result is or ought to be. As seen in the previous chapters, the EU provides an obvious example (or lesson) of what Asia is confronted with. Five decades of 'an ever closer Union' has informed the European discourse as to what European legal integration means. This common foundation is often referenced to Europe's common history, religion and culture. Ralf Michaels asks: What is meant by 'Asia'? And when we speak of Asian law, what makes law Asian? Is there an Asian identity comparable to European identity and therefore similarly useful as a justification for unification projects? If so, what does it look like? And if so, does this make Asia more like Europe, or less so? Or is this question itself already a mere European projection?

In what follows, noted comparatist Michaels attempts to shed light on what 'Asian' law means through meticulous detail and analysis of the major modern Asian unification projects in its post-war history – the UPICC inspired Principles of Asian Contract Law (of which this editor was once a member), the Studies in the Contract Laws in Asia (whose approach is akin to that of the Trento Common Core). Through this, Michaels ably unpacks the meaning behind 'Asian' laws: it could in truth simply be a Western import; or it is a call to recall and institutionalise values and attitudes that predate and survived Western colonialism; or it could be a vehicle for what is essentially propagation of the laws and values of an historically dominant Asian hegemon (like China or Japan).

And in his search for answers, he takes the reader down unexpected paths. He seems to find the erstwhile comparison between Europe and Asia (or East and West) too binary and unhelpful – so what if Asian law is European . . . or not? Drawing on Asian scholarship, he offers a novel injection into the legal discourse on convergence: Asian law as method. To Michaels, 'The West is neither dominant over nor absent from Asia'. He suggests a possibility 'to move beyond a focus on the West, and at the same time to overcome ideas of Asian homogeneity'. In other words, Michaels advocates a decentring of the West from studies into Asian legal convergence. The West and East are neither subject nor object but only method. They are 'no longer one but many parts that are in dialogue with each other, no longer recipient or opponent of Western law and instead co-producer of modernity and of modern law. In this, the West has at least as much to learn from Asia as Asia did from the West.'

It is in the spirit of these comments that the contributions within this book make the necessary steps towards engaging with the West, and in so doing, it is hoped, defining what it means to be East.

2

Uniform Law and the Production and Circulation of Legal Models

Luca Castellani[°]

1 INTRODUCTION: UNIFORM LAW AND LEGAL PLURALISM

The law constantly evolves in response to the needs of human societies. Legal evolution is seldom based on innovation (that is, the production of an original legal rule); more often, rules circulate from one legal system to another. To better understand the dynamics of the circulation of legal models, it is useful to identify the sources of those models.[1]

The diversity in human societies leads necessarily to legal pluralism – that is, the coexistence of different legal systems that give expression to the beliefs and values of a social group.[2] In particular, commercial law recognizes contractual agreements,

---

[°] The views expressed herein are those of the author and do not necessarily reflect the views of the United Nations.

[1] Among comparative lawyers, the Italian "School of Trento" has significantly contributed to discussing the circulation of legal models: R Sacco, Legal Formants: A Dynamic Approach to Comparative Law (1991) 39 American Journal of Comparative Law, 1, 1–34 (Installment I), 343–401 (Installment II). See also A. Watson, Legal Transplants: An Approach to Comparative Law, 2nd ed. (Athens: University of Georgia Press, 1993); M. Graziadei, Comparative Law as the Study of Transplants and Receptions, in M. Reimann and R. Zimmermann (eds.), The Oxford Handbook of Comparative Law (Oxford: Oxford University Press, 2006), pp. 441–475; M. Graziadei, Legal Transplants and the Frontiers of Legal Knowledge (2009) 10 Theoretical Inquiries in Law, 2, 723–743. D. Berkowitz, K. Pistor, and J. F. Richard, Economic Development, Legality, and the Transplant Effect, William Davidson Working Paper Number 410 (September 2001). For a discussion of legal transplants from the perspective of game theory, see N. Garoupa and A. Ogus, A Strategic Interpretation of Legal Transplants (2006) 35 Journal of Legal Studies 2, 339–363.

The 18th General Congress of the International Academy of Comparative law (Washington, DC, 2010) featured the topic "Legal Culture and Legal Transplants." An electronic edition of the national reports presented on that occasion, prepared by the Isaidat Law Review for the Società Italiana di Ricerca nel Diritto Comparato (SIRD), provides significant information on legal transplants in several jurisdictions: Special Issue 2: Legal Culture and Legal Transplants (2011) 1 ISAIDAT Law Review 2, available at www.isaidatlawreview.org/index.php/isaidat/issue/view/5.

[2] The literature on legal pluralism is significant. Early contributions include L. Pospisil, The Anthropology of Law: A Comparative Theory (New York: Harper & Row, 1971); J. Vanderlinden, Return to Legal Pluralism: Twenty Years Later (1989) 28 Journal of Legal Pluralism 149–158; P. S. Berman, Global Legal Pluralism (2007) 80 Southern California Law Review 1155–1237. On legal pluralism and the circulation of legal models, see W. Twining, Diffusion of Law: A Global Perspective (2004) 49 Journal of Legal Pluralism 1–45.

which are considered non-State law in a pluralistic perspective, as a particularly relevant source of rights and obligations.[3] Such recognition takes place through the principle of freedom of contract, which aims at accommodating traders' needs by addressing both legal predictability and legal flexibility.[4] The place of State law in commercial law may accordingly be residual.

At a first glance, uniform law may seem at odds with the pluralist nature of commercial law.[5] While uniform law ideally aims at establishing legal uniformity, legal pluralism denies that possibility.[6] However, it is necessary to frame realistically the goal of uniform law. Uniform law does not always or necessarily aim at universal legislative unification. On the contrary, it promotes the principle of freedom of contract by providing default rules while giving private parties the possibility to vary them.[7] Moreover, uniform law may enable free choice of the law governing the commercial relationship. As a result, the uniform law enacted by States[8] promotes legal diversity, especially when adopted in jurisdictions where the principles of freedom of contract and freedom of choice of the applicable law are less recognized.

This chapter discusses certain aspects of the production and circulation of uniform commercial law, including by providing examples relating to sales law and the law of electronic transactions. It is argued that uniform law has become increasingly important in the production and circulation of legal models. Hence it is desirable to make the uniform legislative process more efficient and effective.

---

[3] See, for example, S. Nystén-Haarala, Legal Pluralism and Globalising Business Contracts, in P. Wahlgren (ed.), *Law without State. Scandinavian Studies in Law* (Stockholm: Jure Law Books, 2016), pp. 297–315; F. Inocêncio, Direito do Comércio Internacional: a Emergência da Nova Lex Mercatoria (2017) 10 *Revista do Direito de Língua Portuguesa* 49–74, at 62–65.

[4] Recently, the principle of freedom of contract has been compressed by an emerging third need: the protection of the weak party. That need is paramount in consumers' law, and its extension to small- and medium-sized enterprises has been suggested in the proposal for a Common European Sales Law (Proposal for a Regulation of the European Parliament and of the Council on a Common European Sales Law, Brussels 11.10.2011 COM [2011] 635 final). That proposal was not adopted.

[5] Several definitions of uniform law have been suggested. Some focus on the lawmaking process and others on the outcome of that process. Reference is here made to a legislative text prepared in a dedicated forum for application across different jurisdictions. Because of its broad applicability, the law is considered "uniform" (as opposed to local). In particular, this chapter discusses modern commercial uniform law – that is, uniform law dealing with civil and commercial matters produced in the twentieth and twenty-first century.

[6] But see V. Mak, Globalization, Private Law and New Legal Pluralism, Jean Monnet Working Paper 14/15 (2015), available at http://jeanmonnetprogram.org/wp-content/uploads/JMWP-14-Mak.pdf; J. Coetzee, A Pluralist Approach to the Law of International Sales (2017) 20 *Potchefstroom Electronic Law Journal*, available at https://journals.assaf.org.za/per/article/view/1355.

[7] S. Gopalan, The Creation of International Commercial Law: Sovereignty Felled? (2004) 5 *San Diego International Law Journal* 267–322.

[8] Additionally, uniform law may be applied without connection to State law, especially in arbitral proceedings.

2 THE EVOLUTION OF UNIFORM LAW

Uniform law has undergone significant changes over the last forty years. It was originally conceived to operate at the international level so as to overcome barriers to trade arising from national legislation. The traditional justification for uniform law is based on the desire to facilitate international trade, which is considered an engine of economic growth and social stability. While knowledge of foreign legal systems may present challenges, all concerned parties may access uniform law on an equal footing. Increased legal predictability reduces transaction costs.[9] Legal uniformity should therefore be pursued by adopting uniform legislative texts with as few departures from the original as possible.[10] As a result, the negative effects arising from the coexistence of multifarious national commercial laws would be reduced or eliminated.

In that original conception, legal unification is pursued at the international level through the negotiation and adoption of treaties.[11] Early uniform law treaties include the Convention for the Unification of Certain Rules of Law relating to Bills of Lading (Brussels, 1924),[12] the Convention Providing a Uniform Law for Bills of Exchange and Promissory Notes (Geneva, 1930),[13] and the Convention Providing a Uniform Law for Cheques (Geneva, 1931).[14] Evidence of that original goal may be found in the mandate of the United Nations Commission on International Trade Law (UNCITRAL), which refers to "the promotion of the progressive harmonization and unification of the law of international trade,"[15] and in the name of the International Institute for the Unification of Private Law (UNIDROIT).

However, the influence of uniform law on State law was already present in those early days as legislators were often inspired by uniform models when embarking on domestic law reform. That influence highlights a second powerful argument in favor of uniform law: uniform law may improve the existing law.[16] That argument has become more evident as uniform lawmaking has shifted focus from international to national law reform.

In the early days, uniform law texts were prepared or, at least, finalized in ad hoc diplomatic conferences. The importance attributed to uniform law in facilitating trade suggested the establishment of dedicated intergovernmental bodies providing

---

[9] See e.g. C. P. Gillette, *Advanced Introduction to International Sales Law* (Cheltenham: Edward Elgar, 2016), pp. 5–6.
[10] Variations resulting from the operation of the principle of freedom of contract are, of course, excepted.
[11] On the drafting of treaties by experts (including in the commercial field), see J. E. Álvarez, *International Organizations as Law-Makers* (Oxford: Oxford University Press, 2006), pp. 304–316.
[12] League of Nations, Treaty Series, Vol. 120, p. 155.
[13] League of Nations, Treaty Series, Vol. 143, p. 257.
[14] League of Nations, Treaty Series, Vol. 143, p. 355.
[15] United Nations General Assembly Resolution 2205 (XXI), section I.
[16] S. Kozuka, The Economic Implications of Uniformity in Law (2007) *Uniform Law Review* 683–695, at 687–690.

a permanent negotiating forum for uniform texts as well as adequate secretarial support. The first session of The Hague Conference on Private International Law (HCCH) took place in 1893, and the HCCH became a permanent intergovernmental organization in 1955. UNIDROIT was established in 1926 as an auxiliary organ of the League of Nations,[17] and UNCITRAL was established by the United Nations General Assembly in 1966.[18] The availability of permanent fora and secretariats had a positive effect on expanding and preserving specialized expertise and on consolidating and improving working methods.

Core features of uniform lawmaking include a high level of technical expertise among uniform law drafters, and their supporting bodies; the use of the comparative method; inclusiveness through broad stakeholder participation; and decision-making by consensus or ample majority. Those features aim at facilitating the acceptance of uniform law by all States and other lawmaking bodies.

The comparative approach is used to assess and overcome the distance between national models. That approach allows identifying those common elements in national laws that may provide the basis for the uniform rule. Often, the identification is based on the legal rule's function, since apparently different rules may address the same socioeconomic problem in a similar manner, while rules that appear to be identical but for a minor detail, possibly contained in case law or in secondary legislation may lead to significantly different outcomes.

The principle of universal participation in the drafting process requires the representation of all world regions and types of legal and economic systems to ensure that relevant issues are taken into account so that the resulting legislative text is suitable for all jurisdictions and economic systems. Universal participation was particularly important in 1966 when UNCITRAL was established because uniform law drafting processes already in existence were not perceived as sufficiently inclusive by a number of countries, particularly Socialist and newly independent States.[19] UNCITRAL, which was set up at the suggestion of Hungary, then a Socialist country, could address the matter by adopting the United Nations' decision-making process, designed to take into consideration all States' views.

A turning point in uniform law drafting took place in 1985 with the completion of the UNCITRAL Model Law on International Commercial Arbitration, which quickly became a global success. Since then, work on soft law instruments such as model laws and guidance texts has greatly increased, shifting the focus of legislative

---

[17] A founding multilateral agreement was again concluded in 1940.
[18] United Nations General Assembly Resolution 2205 (XXI), Establishment of the United Nations Commission on International Trade Law. UNCITRAL is the only specialized intergovernmental body in the field of uniform law with universal participation.
[19] The drafting of the Convention Relating to a Uniform Law on the Formation of Contracts for the International Sale of Goods, 1964 (ULF; United Nations, Treaty Series, vol. 834, p. 169) and of the Convention Relating to a Uniform Law on the International Sale of Goods, 1964 (see section 3.4.1 below) may be cited as examples of only partially inclusive processes.

2 Uniform Law and the Production and Circulation of Legal Models

efforts from the unification to the harmonization of laws.[20] The rate of enactment of model laws soon outpaced that of treaties. This trend has become more pronounced over time.[21] Reasons explaining the success of model laws are related to their flexible nature, which may be more conducive to accommodating local needs and allow for the completion of projects in areas where consensus for a treaty would be difficult to achieve.[22] In short, the evolution of uniform law towards model laws has facilitated its diffusion since uniform law has become more flexible and may cater to a broader range of legislative needs.

Increased engagement in the preparation of uniform soft law instruments eventually opened the door to another role for uniform law: the modernization of laws (i.e., the preparation of texts to address matters not yet dealt with in national laws). The outcome of modernization work at the international level does not aim at facilitating the convergence of the few (if at all) existing legal texts, but at offering a uniform legislative model that will be the first set of rules available to address the issue in question.[23] In those cases, uniformity is therefore achieved ab origine.

The traditional use of the comparative method to assess existing laws is generally compatible with the preparation of model laws and other soft law texts. However, when few legislative precedents are available, the comparative method is used to compare suggestions, approaches, and policy choices, rather than actual legislative texts.

Legislative models are not the only ones relevant for the analysis of the circulation of legal models, including uniform ones, and ultimately legal convergence. At the operational level, standard contractual clauses may be even more significant in

---

[20] Broadly speaking, legal unification aims at promoting the adoption of the same legislative provisions in different jurisdictions, with few specified exceptions. This goal may be pursued with the preparation of treaties, and exceptions may be accommodated in reservations to those treaties. On the other hand, legal harmonization aims at introducing certain common elements in national laws, while leaving room for variation on details. This is typically pursued with model laws, but other tools, such as legislative guides, are also available. Of course, the enactment of a model law offers no guarantee that it will contain all provisions considered necessary to sufficiently comply with the model, and questions could be raised also with respect to which provisions are indeed considered essential for the model law.

[21] See, for example, S. M. Carbone, Rule of Law and Non-State Actors in the International Community: Are Uniform Law Conventions Still a Useful Tool in International Commercial Law? (2016) *Uniform Law Review* 1–7.

[22] See, generally, H. D. Gabriel, The Advantages of Soft Law in International Commercial Law: The Role of UNIDROIT, UNCITRAL, and the Hague Conference (2009) 34 *Brooklyn Journal of International Law*, 3, 655–672, available at http://brooklynworks.brooklaw.edu/bjil/vol34/iss3/3; H. D. Gabriel, Universalism and Tradition: The Use of Non-binding Principles in International Commercial Law, in J. Erauw, V. Tomljenović, and P. Volken (eds.), *Liber Memorialis Petar Šarčević: Universalism, Tradition and the Individual* (Munich: Sellier European Law Publishers, 2006), pp. 471–482. It has been suggested that soft law texts may be more easily enacted in common law jurisdictions: A. Efrat, Legal Traditions and Nonbinding Commitments: Evidence from the United Nations' Model Commercial Legislation (2016) 60 *International Studies Quarterly*, 4, 624–635.

[23] The examples provided later in this chapter illustrate both unification (in the field of sales law) and modernization (in the field of electronic commerce) initiatives.

achieving legal convergence than statutes. Those clauses are typically prepared by business organizations and not by intergovernmental bodies. For instance, even basic contracts for the international sale of goods typically refer to INCOTERMS.[24] It is therefore difficult to overstate the impact of INCOTERMS on harmonizing certain terms of the international sale of goods contracts. A similar example may be drawn from the standard terms and conditions contained in bills of lading issued by major maritime carriers.

3 SOME LIMITS OF UNIFORM LAW

The overall balance of a century of uniform law is positive. Certain texts became cornerstones of international trade law and provide a significant contribution to economic development through cross-border commerce. Reliance on or engagement with uniform law may be particularly appealing in Asia given the rapid rise in cross-border trade involving Asian countries and the need to find common legal ground to enable and further expand that trade. Moreover, no well-developed or comprehensive Asian regional economic integration process exists currently that allows for the production of uniform rules. It is therefore not only appropriate but also necessary for Asia to look at global models.

However, it is also important to recognize that uniform law texts have varying degrees of acceptance and actual use. A number of factors may explain this. These factors may intervene at the stage of drafting uniform texts as well as of promoting their adoption and uniform interpretation. Some of the factors touch upon legal or political issues, while others pertain to administrative matters. This section will discuss how some of those factors affect the production and circulation of uniform law.

3.1 At the Production Stage

3.1.1 Implementing Work Methods

A number of issues may affect the ideal core features of uniform law drafting.[25]

---

[24] J. Coetzee, INCOTERMS as a Form of Standardisation in International Sales Law: An Analysis of the Interplay between Mercantile Custom and Substantive Sales Law with Specific Reference to the Passing of Risk, unpublished PhD thesis, University of Stellenbosch (2010), at 282, and further references in footnote 2, available at http://scholar.sun.ac.za/bitstream/handle/10019.1/5222/coetzee_incoterms_2010.pdf. Challenges may, however, arise from national definitions of INCOTERMS, as well as from national variations in the interpretation of uniform INCOTERMS. The issue is relevant for all trade usages. For a summary of the discussion that took place during the preparation of the United Convention on Contracts for the International Sale of Goods in 1980, see G. Saumier, Trade Usages in the Convention on Contracts for the International Sale of Goods, in F. Gélinas (ed.), *Trade Usages and Implied Terms in the Age of Arbitration* (New York: Oxford University Press, 2016), pp. 125–144.

[25] In general, see J. A. Estrella Faria, Future Directions of Legal Harmonisation and Law Reform: Stormy Seas or Prosperous Voyage? (2009) *Uniform Law Review* 5–34; on UNCITRAL working

As a matter of principle, the use of a comparative approach in preparing uniform legislative texts is desirable for the reasons set out earlier. However, as a matter of fact, it is not always followed. Sometimes drafters may not fully master that method. They may also find challenges in accessing or fully understanding relevant legislative texts or even be unaware of their existence. Linguistic issues may also arise, especially at a regional level.

Moreover, the application of the comparative method should lead to a compromise result appealing to all legal and economic systems. However, familiarity with a national model may induce, explicitly or tacitly, to promote it as uniform law. The promotion of national models may in turn create challenges in reaching a consensus as those not familiar with the national model may not support it.

Similarly, the practice of broad participation and inclusiveness may depart from theory. Firstly, universal participation is available only in selected global fora.[26] In other cases, participation requires additional steps that may be time-consuming and costly.[27] Moreover, the actual participation of delegates and observers in the work sessions may vary in light of available resources and capacity. As a result, some States and organizations are more active in uniform lawmaking, while others may not participate despite membership. More active delegations may influence the drafting process at the expense of further discussion.[28] As a result, models influenced by national laws of more active delegations may be endorsed and promoted as uniform law.

Since the political process of production of uniform law is normally based on consensus or, at least, broad majority, which may be obtained only on matters that are not particularly controversial, uniform lawmakers look for a common denominator among legal systems. The need to ensure compatibility with all legal and economic systems may lead to adopting a compromise text that does not fully reflect the ideal rigorous construction that a specialist may imagine. While compromise shall not lead to contradictions in the resulting text, lack of clarity, if not ambiguity, remains possible.

Challenges may arise also from the proliferation of uniform texts, especially at the regional level. In some cases, regional and global texts are complementary, but priority is given to the adoption and implementation of regional ones since those are

---

methods, see S. Block-Lieb and T. C. Halliday, *Global Lawmakers: International Organizations in the Crafting of World Markets* (Cambridge: Cambridge University Press, 2017).

[26] Typically, those related to the United Nations, namely (but not only) UNCITRAL.

[27] It should also be noted that uniform law inter-governmental organizations predating UNCITRAL's establishment, such as UNIDROIT and the Hague Conference on Private International Law, have special membership: States need to become member of those organizations to participate in their work, and are not admitted automatically by virtue of their United Nations membership.

[28] T. C. Halliday, J. Pacewicz, and S. Block-Lieb, Who Governs? Delegations and Delegates in Global Trade Lawmaking (2013) 7 *Regulation & Governance*, 3, 279–298; C. Devaux, La fabrique du droit du commerce international: réguler les risques de capture, Thèse de doctorat, Sciences Po – Institut d'études politiques de Paris (Novembre 2016).

more directly relevant for the pursuit of the regional mandate.[29] As a result, global uniform texts may be neglected if not passively ostracized. In other cases, complementarity between regional and global levels is not sought; rather, the process of regional economic integration is pursued vigorously at the expense of extra-regional global integration. In such instances, regional harmonization of commercial law may become a barrier to trade with countries outside the regional market. Last but not least, regional initiatives may absorb the limited capacity of smaller jurisdictions and prevent their engagement in global texts.

3.1.2 Institutional Mechanisms

An additional set of issues may arise from the governance and administrative structure of uniform lawmaking bodies.

One challenge often evoked is the scarcity of available resources. Currently, three small-sized intergovernmental organizations share the mandate of dealing with uniform commercial law at the global level: UNCITRAL, UNIDROIT, and The Hague Conference on Private International Law.[30] In addition, some global non-governmental organizations and several regional organizations, specialized or not, are also active in the field.[31]

In light of the considerations expressed above, specialized organizations with a global mandate should take the lead in uniform law drafting. Among those, UNCITRAL is the only one offering universal participation and benefitting from the resources of the United Nations that, for instance, provide conference and linguistic support in six widely-spoken languages. Therefore, its formal meetings are particularly inclusive. However, the UNCITRAL process is costly and time-consuming, since a maximum of two meetings per year on the same subject is usually possible.[32] Calls for adopting a less formal approach have been made, but they need to take into account the desire of preserving universal participation.[33]

---

[29] See below for examples related to the United Nations Convention on Contracts for the International Sale of Goods, 1980 (CISG).

[30] The Hague Conference on Private International Law focuses on private international law issues. Its work is not limited to commercial and civil matters; for instance, it is prominent in the field of family law.

[31] For example: the Organisation pour l'Harmonisation en Afrique du Droit des Affaires (OHADA) is a regional inter-governmental organization specializing in uniform commercial law; the Organisation of American States and The Commonwealth, two regional non-specialized inter-governmental organizations, have prepared uniform commercial law texts; as did the United Nations Conference of Trade and Development, a global non-specialized inter-governmental organization; the International Chamber of Commerce and the Comité Maritime International provide examples of global nongovernmental organizations active also in uniform law drafting.

[32] However, this pace may be useful to support the progressive formation of consensus.

[33] UNCITRAL has held a discussion on its working methods where this issue has been raised. See e.g. United Nations Document A/CN.9/660, UNCITRAL rules of procedure and methods of work: Comments received from Member States, para. 5.

On the other hand, UNIDROIT's lack of a permanent structure for formal intergovernmental meetings has allowed developing an agile drafting practice. Building on the strong points of each organization, closer coordination between UNCITRAL and UNIDROIT has been advocated, including by States.[34] For instance, preparatory work for legislative texts could be carried out by experts at UNIDROIT but finalized in formal intergovernmental meetings at UNCITRAL. Such interaction would require a higher level of coordination in the work programs of the two institutions.

Standing institutional arrangements could represent a reasonable and feasible step toward closer cooperation, taking into consideration the overall coordination mandate given to UNCITRAL by the United Nations General Assembly.[35] Merging the two institutions to establish a single specialized inter-governmental organization for civil and commercial law reform may address scarcity of resources more effectively. However, that option would raise a number of complex political and administrative issues.

3.2 At the Circulation Stage

To be successful, legislative models should as a rule be economically efficient and effective, technically well-drafted, and politically acceptable. In practice, elements such as prestige, power, and chance are also relevant for the circulation of models of national origin as well as of uniform models.

Power may be exercised in different forms. During colonial times, legislative models were exported following military conquest. More recently, political and economic influence has become prevalent.[36] Commercial law reform measures included in the list of conditionalities agreed between States and international

---

[34] See e.g. M. J. Dennis, Modernizing and Harmonizing International Contract Law: The CISG and the UNIDROIT Principles Continue to Provide the Best Way Forward (2014), 19 *Uniform Law Review* 114–151 at 150. See also Estrella Faria, Future Directions of Legal Harmonisation and Law Reform: Stormy Seas or Prosperous Voyage?, p. 22.

[35] J. A. Estrella Faria, The Relationship between Formulating Agencies in International Legal Harmonization: Competition, Cooperation, or Peaceful Coexistence – A Few Remarks on the Experience of UNCITRAL (2005) 51 *Loyola Law Review* 253–285 at 254–259.

[36] See the various hypothesis formulated by F. Schauer, The Politics and Incentives of Legal Transplantation, CID Working Paper No. 44, April 2000. On the role of international financial institutions in law reform, see Kristen Boon, 'Open for Business': International Financial Institutions, Post-Conflict Economic Reform and the Rule of Law (2006) 39 *NYU Journal of International Law and Politics* 513–581; T. C. Halliday, Architects of the State: International Financial Institutions and the Reconstruction of States in East Asia (2012) 37 *Law & Social Inquiry*, 2, 265–296. On the operations of the World Bank, see S. Schlemmer-Schulte, The World Bank's Role in the Promotion of the Rule of Law in Developing Countries, in S. Schlemmer-Schulte and K. Y. Tung (eds.), *Liber Amicorum Ibrahim F.I. Shihata: International Finance and Development Law* (The Hague: Kluwer Law International, 2001), pp. 677–725; A. Santos, The World Bank's Uses of the Rule of Law Promise in Economic Development, in D. Trubek and A. Santos (eds.), *The New Law And Economic Development: A Critical Appraisal* (New York: Cambridge University Press, 2006), pp. 253–300.

financial institutions provide an example of the circulation of legal models based on economic influence.[37] In such cases, an external assessment of the legal system may highlight an opportunity for improvement, and the adoption of uniform texts may be among those measures whose adoption is conditional to receiving further assistance.

Trade agreements are increasingly relevant for the circulation of uniform legal models to the extent that they call for the adoption of those models as enabling legislative texts. For instance, their chapters on intellectual property, electronic commerce, and paperless trade facilitation may refer to an obligation of the parties to adopt or maintain legislation based on uniform texts.[38] However, commercial law reform at the national level does not always take into account trade agreement implementation: improved coordination could better clarify how enabling and regulatory texts can be mutually reinforcing and yield greater economic benefits.[39]

Chance, in its various shapes, may have a significant impact on the circulation of legal models, thus undermining the ideal model of the rational legislator who carefully surveys the offer of legal rules and arrives at a deliberate and well-thought choice of foreign law to transplant domestically.[40]

Prestige is a quality attributed to the legislative model by the recipients of that model, i.e. the enacting legislators. Traditionally, prestige has been based on subjective elements such as the perceived quality of the model or of the legal system of origin, which could coincide with the place of legal education of the legislators, or the teachers of the legislators. More recently, prestige has been associated with the proven positive impact of that model on the socio-economic issue it aims at addressing. Measuring the efficiency and effectiveness of legislative models has therefore become important for their promotion.

In general, empirical data helps in better measuring the frequency and actual impact of the circulation of legal models.[41] A number of increasingly complex

---

[37] In September 2015, OHADA adopted the Uniform Act on Insolvency (Acte uniforme portant organisation des procédures collectives d'apurement du passif), prepared with the assistance of the World Bank and the International Finance Corporation. One consequence of the adoption of that Uniform Act was the enactment of the UNCITRAL Model Law on Cross-Border Insolvency in seventeen African States.

[38] See, for instance, Article 14.5 of the Trans-Pacific Partnership, referencing UNCITRAL texts.

[39] For an example relating to international sale of goods, see B. Zeller, Facilitating Regional Economic Integration: ASEAN, ATIGA, and the CISG, in I. Schwenzer and L. Spagnolo (eds.), *Towards Uniformity: The 2nd Annual MAA Schlechtriem CISG Conference* (The Hague: Eleven International Publishing, 2011), pp. 255–267.

[40] G. Ajani, By Chance and Prestige: Legal Transplants in Russia and Eastern Europe (1995) 43 *American Journal of Comparative Law*, 1, 93–117. For a case study, see P. M. Nichols, Viability of Transplanted Law: Kazakhstani Reception of a Transplanted Foreign Investment Code (1997) 18 *University of Pennsylvania Journal of International Law* 1235–1279. Available at: http://scholarship.law.upenn.edu/jil/vol18/iss4/6.

[41] For an overview of that debate, see F. Parisi and B. Luppi, Quantitative Methods in Comparative Law, in P. G. Monateri (ed.), *Methods of Comparative Law* (Cheltenham: Edward Elgar, 2012), pp. 306–316. For a criticism of this approach (and of the "legal origins" theory), see U. Mattei, The Cold War and Comparative Law: A Reflection on the Politics of Intellectual Discipline (2017) 65 *American*

2 Uniform Law and the Production and Circulation of Legal Models

qualitative commercial law indicators have been developed, which seem to receive significant attention from policymakers.[42] Those indicators, which are regularly revised and improved, include the EBRD's Legal Assessment Web Tool and the World Bank Doing Business Annual Report. The EBRD Web Tool assesses national legislation against benchmark legislative standards, while the Doing Business Report evaluates the cost in money and time of certain business-related processes.[43] The EBRD Web Tool makes an explicit connection between expected benefits and commercial law reform based on the adoption of uniform texts. For instance, the EBRD 2012 PPP Legislative Framework Assessment uses the UNCITRAL Legislative Guide on Privately Financed Infrastructure Projects as a reference.[44] On the other hand, the Doing Business Reports data could be used to establish a correlation between the level of adoption of uniform texts and the existence of an enabling legal environment for business.

Views on the usefulness, reliability, and neutrality of the indicators vary.[45] Leaving aside any discussion of whether and how indicators should be designed

---

Journal of Comparative Law 567–607, at 604–606. Economists may assist in providing the relevant information: H. Rosenthal, E. Voeten, Measuring Legal Systems (2007) 35 *Journal of Comparative Economics*, 4, 711–728; C. Guerriero, A Novel Dataset on Legal Traditions, Their Determinants, and Their Economic Role in 155 Transplants (2016) 8 *Data in Brief* 394–398. See also H. Spamann, Large Sample, Quantitative Research Designs for Comparative Law? (2009) 57 *American Journal of Comparative Law* 797–810; and M. Berinzon and R. C. Briggs, Legal Families without the Laws: The Fading of Colonial Law in French West Africa (2016) 64 *American Journal of Comparative Law*, 2, 329–370, for a legal transplants analysis that takes into account statistical data.

[42] On the use of indicators in the legal field see S. E. Merry, K. E. Davis, B. Kingsbury (eds.), *The Quiet Power of Indicators: Measuring Governance, Corruption, and Rule of Law* (New York: Cambridge University Press, 2015).

[43] These are: Starting a Business, Dealing with Construction Permits, Getting Electricity, Registering Property, Getting Credit, Protecting Minority Investors Paying Taxes, Trading across Borders, Enforcing Contracts and Resolving Insolvency. For more information on the methodology used to compile the Doing Business Reports, see www.doingbusiness.org/methodology.

[44] A. Zverev, The Legal Framework for Public-Private Partnerships (PPPs) and Concessions in Transition Countries: Evolution and Trends, *EBRD Law in Transition Online*, at 1. Available at www.ebrd.com/downloads/research/news/lit112a.pdf.

[45] In general, see: K. E. Davis and M. B. Kruse, Taking the Measure of Law: The Case of the Doing Business Project (2007) 32 *Law & Social Inquiry* 4, 1095–1119; K. E. Davis, B. Kingsbury, and S. E. Merry, Indicators as a Technology of Global Governance, IILJ Working Paper 2010/2 (Global Administrative Law Series); S. Benedettini and A. Nicita, Towards the Economics of Comparative Law: The "Doing Business" Debate (2010) 1 *Comparative Law Review* 1, available at www.comparativelawreview.unipg.it/index.php/comparative/article/view/34/31; K. E. Davis, Legal Indicators: The Power of Quantitative Measures of Law (2014) 10 *Annual Review of Law and Social Science* 1 37–52; David Nelken, Contesting Global Indicators, in Engle Merry, Davis, and Kingsbury (eds.), *The Quiet Power of Indicators*; uncorrected version: King's College London Law School Research Paper No. 2015-18, available at http://ssrn.com/abstract=2465073; M. Versteeg and T. Ginsburg, Measuring the Rule of Law: A Comparison of Indicators (2017) 42 *Law & Social Inquiry* 1, 100–137. For a pluralistic perspective, see D. R. Amariles, Legal Indicators, Global Law and Legal Pluralism: An Introduction (2015) 47 *Journal of Legal Pluralism and Unofficial Law*, 1, 9–21.

A recent assessment of the usefulness of the World Bank Doing Business Reports may be found in D. Oto-Peralías, D. Romero-Ávila, *Legal Reforms and Economic Performance: Revisiting the Evidence* (Washington, DC: World Bank, 2017).

and used, preliminary remarks regarding the interaction between such indicators and the circulation of uniform models are warranted. Firstly, indicators are available only in certain legal fields. For instance, among the various areas of work of UNCITRAL, insolvency and security interests are those most directly captured by indicators. Secondly, the purpose of indicators is to highlight opportunities to improve the legal environment for businesses; the ranking of the performance of legal systems is not an end in itself but a means to an end. Indicators do not require as such the adoption of any legislative model, including uniform ones. Rather, indicators may incorporate diagnostic tools that may suggest adopting or implementing uniform texts to improve legal efficiency. Thus, diagnostic tools, especially if used in conjunction with conditionalities, may become a powerful vehicle for the circulation of uniform models, since a country wishing to improve the ranking of its legal system, as established by indicators, with respect to a specific area of the law, may adopt a uniform legislative model to do so.

To sum up, diagnostic tools may provide a valuable contribution to the promotion of uniform texts, in particular, by offering a standard methodology for legislative needs assessment. However, a comprehensive discussion on indicators and diagnostic tools, including in the broader framework of an objective assessment of the circulation of uniform law models, has yet to take place in uniform lawmaking organizations.

3.2.1 Addressing the "Adoption Gap"

Uniform law can be a powerful template for law reform. However, when compared to other branches of international law, the rate of adoption of uniform texts by States is limited. This is particularly true for developing countries, which could benefit the most from adopting uniform texts but have the least capacity to do so, and begs the question of how the promotion of uniform law can be cultivated and the "adoption gap" overcome.

The Convention on the Recognition and Enforcement of Foreign Arbitral Awards, 1958 (the "New York Convention")[46] is the only commercial law treaty featured among the world's most adopted treaties, having 159 State parties.[47] That achievement should not mislead: the average yearly adoption rate for the New York Convention stands at 2.6 per year. At that rate, it takes more than 70 years to achieve universal treaty participation. That adoption rate is surpassed in the international trade law field only by the Convention on International Interests in Mobile

---

A specific line of challenge to the World Bank Doing Business Reports came from French legal thinkers and led to the creation of an alternative set of indicators, the Index de la sécurité juridique. See B. Deffains, M. Séjean, "Index de la sécurité juridique: nouvelle étape" (2016) *La Semaine Juridique Edition Générale* 17, 519.

[46] United Nations, Treaty Series, vol. 330, p. 38.
[47] As of June 13, 2018.

Equipment, 2001 (the "Cape Town Convention"),[48] which has an adoption rate of about 4.5 States per year. The second most adopted commercial law treaty is the United Nations Convention on Contracts for the International Sale of Goods, 1980 ("CISG")[49], with an adoption rate of 2.3 States per year. All other uniform commercial law treaties lag behind. Several UNCITRAL treaties have managed to secure only low sign-up rates, although an assessment of the success of the most recent ones may be premature. Similar considerations apply to treaties prepared by UNIDROIT and, limited to the commercial field, by the Hague Conference on Private International Law. However, treaties in other fields — such as human rights, environment, transnational organized crime, and disarmament — are adopted at much faster rates. For instance, the Paris Agreement, 2015,[50] which is possibly the most successful treaty in the last decade, has attracted around 170 State parties in two years. The WHO Framework Convention on Tobacco Control, 2003,[51] received 168 signatures during its first year of existence and has now more than 180 State parties, most of which adopted the Convention at an early stage.

In addition, a trend may indicate that recent international trade law treaties are not as successful as older ones. For example, the most recent of the four most adopted UNCITRAL treaties is the CISG, concluded in 1980. Recent treaties were prepared amid high hopes, preceded by solid preparatory work and address topical matters. It is evident that the pace of adoption needs to accelerate if such treaties are to meet their intended objectives. It is therefore essential to explore further the reasons behind that trend.[52]

One explanation could be that prior texts addressed needs that were more urgent and therefore prompted states to swiftly ratify them. Another explanation may point at the preference for model laws, which, as noted above, are increasingly available.

Additional reasons may further explain the "adoption gap". One reason relates to the fact that the economic impact of uniform commercial law-based reform does not seem to attract much political attention. The matter is rather technical and does not attract headlines or otherwise influence immediately the opinion of electors. Hence, additional efforts are needed to illustrate the benefits arising from commercial law reform to legislators and decision-makers, especially in developing and least-developed countries. The fact that a number of government bodies may be involved in the consideration of uniform texts may add a layer of complexity that requires careful coordination and cooperation. Increased ability to separate value-based policy decisions, to be made by political bodies, and technical drafting, to be carried out by supporting offices, may help to ensure the success of the lawmaking process.

---

[48] United Nations, Treaty Series, vol. 2307, p. 285.
[49] United Nations, Treaty Series, vol. 1489, p. 3.
[50] United Nations Document A/AC.237/18 (Part II)/Add.1.
[51] United Nations, Treaty Series, vol. 2302, p. 166.
[52] See also Estrella Faria, Future Directions of Legal Harmonisation and Law Reform: Stormy Seas or Prosperous Voyage?, pp. 26–28.

Technical bodies may be more inclined to follow uniform legislative models as an expression of global consensus, rather than developing national solutions aimed at addressing local concerns whose effectiveness is yet untested.

Limited support from civil society is a significant contributing factor. The private sector may fail to appreciate that commercial law reform may be, and sometimes should be, a priority. In developed countries, this may be due to a general mistrust of all new legislation, which may be perceived as introducing regulatory measures. In developing countries, scarce capacity and the lack of a true market economy may inhibit the realization that commercial law reform is necessary. Exceptions do exist: nongovernmental organizations such as the International Chamber of Commerce are both active contributors to and leaders in uniform lawmaking.[53]

A broad issue affecting all stages of commercial law reform is whether jurisdictions have sufficient capacity to carry out commercial law reform processes successfully. This refers to the financial and human resources available to States and their relevant sub-national units. While some jurisdictions may have full capacity to draft and implement commercial legislation, others may have only limited capacity, and yet others – often, those who most need to reform the law – may have no capacity at all. This issue is obviously sensitive since legislative power is a core attribute of sovereignty, yet there is an acute need to ensure actual capacity to effectively exercise this function.

Technical assistance to legislative drafting and implementation may fill the resource gaps.[54] However, technical assistance to law reform is a legal services market built around core areas, such as human rights and environmental law, with established mechanisms for interaction between intergovernmental organizations, international and local nongovernmental organizations, and national stakeholders. Those actors have significant experience and expertise in highlighting the demand for, designing, and delivering technical assistance programs for law reform. Commercial law reform has a marginal place in such programs, and it is seldom featured in comprehensive projects, such as work on good governance and the reduction of poverty or post-conflict reconstruction efforts.[55]

Moreover, the United Nations system, which is the main promoter of the rule of law, focuses predominantly on public international law reform (human rights,

---

[53] The International Chamber of Commerce prepares the already mentioned INCOTERMS and participates in uniform legislative initiatives led by other organizations; see e.g. F. Grisel, Treaty-Making between Public Authority and Private Interests: The Genealogy of the Convention on the Recognition and Enforcement of Foreign Arbitral Awards (2017) 28 *European Journal of International Law*, 1, 73–87.

[54] For preliminary considerations on this topic, see L. A. Mistelis, Regulatory Aspects: Globalization, Harmonization, Legal Transplants, and Law Reform – Some Fundamental Observations (2000) 34 *International Lawyer* 1055–1069 at 1062–1064.

[55] Exceptions exist, for instance, in Haiti and Liberia the importance of commercial law reform in peace-building has been recognized (though not necessarily fully implemented). See J. Ford, *Regulating Business for Peace. The United Nations, the Private Sector and Post-Conflict Recovery* (New York: Cambridge University Press: 2015).

humanitarian law, environmental law, etc.). Initiatives originating from international financial institutions are more likely to have a commercial law reform component; however, coordination of those initiatives is far from straightforward given, inter alia, complex institutional structure and governance.

This is ironic given that uniform commercial law could particularly assist commercial operators in developing countries that lack local legal capacity and institutional support. Moreover, business law has been identified as one of the areas where the circulation of legal models occurs more often.[56] However, the international community does not consider supporting commercial law reform as a priority and, in particular, does not seem yet to appreciate in full the intimate nexus between an enabling legal environment for business, economic development, and social stability.[57]

Fortunately, technical assistance activities dealing with commercial law reform do exist. There is growing attention for security interests and insolvency law, reflecting the priorities of international financial institutions. Another budding area of work is alternative dispute resolution, possibly also because of the interest of local practitioners. UNCTAD's work on electronic commerce should be mentioned as an example of a technical assistance program supporting legislative drafting in developing countries.[58]

Technical assistance to law reform initiatives may however not be sustainable in the longer period due to lack of funds or political support. Moreover, national aid agencies engaged in commercial law reform projects are often disconnected from uniform lawmaking organizations.[59] Interestingly, even when those agencies promote neutral legislative models to avoid criticism of legal imperialism, they may not think of uniform models as the ideal solution. In addition, due to limited coordination, it is not uncommon to find contradictory texts at the regional and national levels, or even at the same level.[60] This may lead to the parallel preparation of different bills on the same topic funded by different donors. In some cases, the same bill may be redrafted with few variations, possibly drawing on different donors' funding.

---

[56] J. C. Reitz, Systems Mixing and in Transition: Import and Export of Legal Models, in J. Bridge (ed.), *Comparative Law Facing the 21st Century* (London: British Institute of International and Comparative Law, 2001), pp. 57–98, at 70–71.

[57] D. P. Stewart, Private International Law, the Rule of Law, and Economic Development (2011) 56 *Villanova Law Review* 607–630.

[58] See http://unctad.org/en/Pages/DTL/STI_and_ICTs/ICT4D-Legislation.aspx. That UNCTAD program is now included in the broader E-trade4All framework, which includes UNCITRAL as a partner.

[59] Estrella Faria, Future Directions of Legal Harmonisation and Law Reform: Stormy Seas or Prosperous Voyage?, pp. 28–30.

[60] Especially in cases when one law aims at reforming one specific issue and the other takes a more general approach: e.g. security law reform or land law reform vs. reform of the civil or of the commercial code. Estrella Faria, Future Directions of Legal Harmonisation and Law Reform: Stormy Seas or Prosperous Voyage?, at p. 23, refers to a possible deliberate decision of having competing legislative projects.

A significant push toward improving the availability of technical assistance to commercial law reform may come from a better understanding of its role as a component of the rule of law.[61] Moreover, modern commercial law may foster the development of a viable market economy, which, in turn, allows further refining and modernizing commercial law.

The acute need to expand technical assistance activities may be particularly appreciated in light of the progressive reduction of the resources available to the public sector, especially at the international level. More precisely, regular budget resources are constantly being reduced by States, as they represent a permanent non-disposable burden on national budgets. Additional resources may be available from donors on a project basis and may be used to open field offices, which are particularly useful in promotional activities, or to fund specific activities, including legislative drafting. However, it remains to be seen to what extent ad hoc contributions should support legislative and promotional activities. Excessive reliance on a limited number of donors may affect the definition of the work program as well as, in extreme cases, financial stability. Diversity of funding is therefore desirable.

Additional considerations on how to address the low pace of adoption of uniform texts pertain to more systematic use of the comprehensive approach to the preparation and management of uniform texts. That approach is based on four steps: the identification of a topic that warrants the adoption of a uniform rule, including an analysis of the expected impact of the resulting text; the preparation of the text; the promotion of its adoption and uniform interpretation; and monitoring its implementation with a view to reviewing, amending, and updating as appropriate.[62]

---

[61] R. McCorquodale, Business, the International Rule of Law, and Human Rights, in R. McCorquodale (ed.), *The Rule of Law in International and Comparative Context* (London: British Institute of International and Comparative Law, 2010), pp. 27–47.

UNCITRAL holds regular discussions on its role in promoting the rule of law at the national and international levels. For a recent summary of those discussions, see United Nations Document A/71/17, Report of the United Nations Commission on International Trade Law Forty-Ninth Session (27 June-15 July 2016), paras. 303–342. See also S. Musayeva and R. Sorieul, The Role of UNCITRAL in Fostering the Rule of Law, in L. Mooney (ed.), *Promoting the Rule of Law: A Practitioner's Guide to Key Issues and Developments* (Chicago: American Bar Association, 2013), pp. 99–109.

[62] UNCITRAL has already reviewed some successful model laws and contractual texts in the field of arbitration. However, that work mostly took place according to the workflow applicable to regular legislative activities.

Revision of treaties is not recommended since it may open the door to dual treaty regimes and other undesirable consequences. UNCITRAL has revised one treaty, the Convention on the Limitation Period in Contracts for the International Sale of Goods, when finalizing the United Nations Convention on Contracts for the International Sale of Goods, in order to ensure alignment between the two texts, which are complementary.

More recently, the United Nations Convention on the Use of Electronic Communications in International Contracts has been prepared with a view to updating, and de facto amending, other treaties with respect to the legal status of electronic communications. However, that convention is not considered as an amending treaty or protocol.

However, the current work program of uniform lawmaking bodies focuses on the initial production of texts rather than on ensuring their subsequent impact on business practice. This is particularly evident in the case of UNCITRAL, where the amount of human and financial resources devoted to legislative drafting is not comparable with that dedicated to the promotion of texts – partly because of the costs associated with formal intergovernmental meetings. The scarce budget available for promotional activities limits the ability to effectively promote the adoption of uniform texts.[63]

The establishment of more refined mechanisms for systematically monitoring uniform law implementation may also be useful. Uniform commercial law treaties mainly contain default obligations for traders engaged in cross-border commerce. Hence, such treaties typically do not lay down mandatory regimes, but rather consist of optional rules that contractual parties may derogate to or entirely opt out of by virtue of party autonomy. This may explain the absence in those treaties of a conference of the parties and of reporting and reviewing mechanisms that have proven to be useful in promoting treaty adoption and implementation.[64]

Moreover, treaty governance and implementation tools may assist in resource mobilization as they allow for a closer alignment of mandate and resources. This is particularly important in the international trade law field since the fact that the adoption of a new treaty does not explicitly entail additional costs may lead to overburdening organizations with multiple mandates. On the other hand, dedicated formal mechanisms for treaty implementation may greatly assist in accurately identifying each mandate and assessing related needs.

Last but not least, uniform law reform leadership plays an evident role in the circulation of uniform law models. Thirty years ago, commercial lawyers around the world – leaving ideological differences aside – looked to the free market economies in Europe and North America for inspiration.[65] The early acceptance of a new treaty by those jurisdictions paved the way to their global acceptance. In turn, those States were eager to engage in the early adoption of the uniform texts that they helped draft.

---

[63] In that respect, it should be noted that Strategic Objective No. 6 of the revised UNIDROIT plan for the organization's medium-term future (to cover the years 2012–2018) indicates that "Greater investment should be made in the promotion of UNIDROIT instruments. UNIDROIT should aim at doubling the resources available for the promotion of its instruments, through efficiency gains, reallocation, voluntary contributions or otherwise, within the coming years."

[64] While several treaties foresee a conference of the parties as governing body, peer review mechanisms have been introduced more recently. For a description and assessment of the peer review mechanism of the implementation of the United Nations Convention against Corruption, see A. K. Weilert, United Nations Convention against Corruption (UNCAC) – After Ten Years of Being in Force (2016) 19 Max Planck Yearbook of United Nations Law Online, 1, 216–240.

[65] It has to be acknowledged that the involvement of the United States of America in uniform lawmaking started only in the 1960s: H. S. Burman, The Second Window, in B. Ṣabāḥī, N. J. Birch, I. A. Laird, J. Rivas (eds.), A Revolution in the International Rule of Law. Essays in Honor of Don Wallace, Jr. (Huntington, NY: Juris, 2014), pp. 159–168, at 160, 162.

However, this does not seem to be the case anymore, at least in the uniform commercial law field.[66]

What could account for this development? The priorities of European jurisdictions have shifted to regional economic integration, namely consolidating European Union law and extending it to prospective European Union Member States.[67] Moreover, ensuring coordination of all concerned European Union stakeholders when negotiating or considering the adoption of a treaty is a time-consuming and resource-intensive process. As a result, the engagement of both the European Commission and the European Union Member States in global lawmaking is uneven. Issues may also arise with respect to compatibility between global and regional texts. In the United States, a general aversion to multilateral engagements, including commercial law treaties, is reinforced by increasing challenges from States' legislators to the adoption of uniform texts at the federal level.[68] While other countries may emerge as trendsetters, the "trailer effect" to new uniform texts erstwhile provided by early adoption in those European and American jurisdictions has greatly diminished.

3.3 At the Implementation Stage

An increased rate of adoption of uniform commercial law treaties does not per se assure increased familiarity with those treaties or help achieve their uniform interpretation.[69] The application and interpretation of legislative and contractual models open the door to variations. For instance, while the legislator may wish to introduce a new rule, judges may interpret it in light of preexisting law.[70] The challenge is particularly acute for uniform laws, which should be interpreted uniformly.[71]

---

[66] In the decade 2005–2015, only three EU Member States have adopted an UNCITRAL treaty. Namely, Belgium adopted the Limitation Convention, Cyprus adopted the CISG, and Spain adopted the Rotterdam Rules. The United States of America adopted no UNCITRAL treaty between 1994 and 2019. However, the treaty adoption rate of the concerned countries is higher with respect to treaties prepared by UNIDROIT and by the Hague Conference on Private International Law.

[67] See also Estrella Faria, Future Directions of Legal Harmonisation and Law Reform: Stormy Seas or Prosperous Voyage?, p. 24.

[68] On the relationship between federal law and the Uniform Law Commission, which is often tasked with internalizing uniform commercial law, see A. H. Boss, The Future of the Uniform Commercial Code Process in an Increasingly International World (2007) 68 *Ohio State Law Journal* 349–402; R. A. Stein, Strengthening Federalism: The Uniform State Law Movement in the United States (2015) 99 *Minnesota Law Review*, 2253–2272.

[69] M. Heidemann, International Commercial Harmonisation and National Resistance: The Development and Reform of Transnational Commercial Law and Its Application within National Legal Culture (2010) 21 *European Business Law Review*, 2, 227–244 (discussing European Union law).

[70] Sacco, Legal Formants, at 33.

[71] See e.g. T. T. Arvind, The "Transplant Effect" in Harmonisation (2010) 59 *International & Comparative Law Quarterly*, 1, 65–88 (discussing UNCITRAL texts on arbitration); F. Ferrari, Autonomous Interpretation versus Homeward Trend versus Outward Trend in CISG Case Law (2017) *Uniform Law Review* 244–257.

Certain uniform texts rely on a judicial mechanism, such as a common supreme court, to ensure their uniform interpretation. That approach is not always possible due to political and practical considerations. On the one hand, the mandatory jurisdiction of a supranational court is accepted by States only if there is strong political support, often in the framework of a regional integration process.[72] However, as noted, uniform law is often seen as a technical matter that does not attract much political attention. Acceptance of the mandatory jurisdiction of a transnational court requires a high level of political commitment and, if that commitment is not available, ultimately hampers the level of acceptance of the uniform text. Moreover, the introduction of a transnational court demands devising a mechanism to ensure its seamless interaction with national courts, which may pose jurisdictional and procedural challenges.

An alternative solution to the uniform interpretation problem is provided by the provision first formulated in article 7 of the Convention on the Limitation Period in Contracts for the International Sale of Goods, 1974 (the "Limitation Convention"),[73] and best known for its application in article 7, paragraph 1 CISG. That mechanism sets forth a duty incumbent on judges and arbitrators to take into account the international nature of the text and the need to promote uniformity in its application. This attributes persuasive value to foreign cases. The provision has been incorporated in several UNCITRAL treaties and model laws. Certain tools such as the Case Law on UNCITRAL Texts (CLOUT) case reporting system and the Digests of Case Law on UNCITRAL Texts have been developed to better disseminate information on the interpretation of uniform texts.

Despite dedicated legal provisions and tools, the goal of uniform interpretation remains particularly challenging as it requires targeted capacity-building activities to ensure adequate knowledge of the uniform law by concerned legal actors. However, as noted, few technical assistance initiatives aim to support the implementation of new laws. A comprehensive and structured strategy for technical assistance, which fully supports the capacity-building of legislators, judges, and other actors involved in drafting and implementing the law, is therefore desirable.

3.4 *Case Studies*

Two case studies provide further insight into the circulation of uniform law models. The first refers to the CISG, which is the most successful substantive uniform commercial law treaty but has a limited level of acceptance in Asia, with notable exceptions such as China, the Republic of Korea, and Vietnam.

---

[72] The European Union and OHADA provide relevant examples.
[73] United Nations, Treaty Series, vol. 1511, p. 3.

The second relates to the UNCITRAL Model Law on Electronic Commerce,[74] which has become the standard legislative text on electronic transactions in Asia and the Pacific.

3.4.1 Case Study 1: The CISG as a Model for National Law Reform

Since the sale of goods is a fundamental commercial transaction, each jurisdiction has a well-developed law to govern contracts for the sale of goods. Moreover, sales law is often used as a blueprint for other contracts. However, in modern legal history, only a few legislative texts on the sale of goods have functioned as leading models for other jurisdictions. In this select group are the French Civil Code (Code Napoléon, 1804), the German Civil Code (BGB, 1900), the English Sale of Goods Act (1893), and the US Uniform Commercial Code, Article 2 (1952). Although those models have been modernized[75] and are in permanent evolution through case law,[76] the CISG is the most recent of them and the only one with a uniform nature and transnational aspirations.

The drafting history of the CISG has been well documented, including with respect to the use of the comparative method in its preparation.[77] Compared to the preparation of the two predecessors of the CISG – that is, the Convention Relating to a Uniform Law on the Formation of Contracts for the International Sale of Goods, 1964 (ULF)[78] and the Convention relating to a Uniform Law on the International Sale of Goods, 1964 (ULIS)[79] – the inclusive method of work of UNCITRAL increased not only the number of participating States but also their geographic diversity and, ultimately, the sources of inspiration of the uniform text.[80] The resulting treaty is a success in terms of its technical quality, number of State parties, and increasing relevance for business.[81] The CISG should also be praised for an aspect that is not often highlighted, i.e. the fact that it upholds party autonomy in jurisdictions less familiar with that notion, and even when it is opted out of (by virtue of that very principle). This is particularly significant for Asian economies in transition.

[74] UNCITRAL, Model Law on Electronic Commerce with Guide to Enactment, 1996, with additional article 5 bis as adopted in 1998, New York, 1999 (United Nations Publication Sales No. E..99.V.4).
[75] Loss of international influence has been one of the reasons behind the recent reform of the French Civil Code: S. Rowan, The New French Law of Contract (2017) 66 *International & Comparative Law Quarterly* 805–831, at 808–809.
[76] However, the impact of case law may be limited to the jurisdiction of the court issuing the relevant decision.
[77] A. M. Garro, Reconciliation of Legal Traditions in the U.N. Convention on Contracts for the International Sale of Goods (1989) 23 *The International Lawyer* 443–483.
[78] United Nations, Treaty Series, vol. 834, p. 169.
[79] United Nations, Treaty Series, vol. 834, p. 107.
[80] On the position of the United States of America, see H. Landau, Background to U.S. Participation in United Nations Convention on Contracts for the International Sale of Goods (1984) 18 *The International Lawyer* 29–35.
[81] In that respect, it should be noted that the practice of blind opting out is morphing in a more selective and more professional approach based on the actual needs of the client and features of the contract.

The CISG, which was drafted as a treaty for cross-border transactions, has over time become a model law.[82] More precisely, the CISG has taken on three different roles: it is a treaty applicable to international transactions; a model for national and regional law reform; and an element of the lex mercatoria.[83]

China offers a good example of the use of the CISG as a blueprint for national law reform. With the adoption in 1978 of the "reform and opening up policy," the Chinese authorities decided to adopt a modern commercial legal framework to facilitate international trade.[84] The need for legislative reform led to importing uniform models to ensure legal predictability of commercial cross-border transactions.[85] During that process, China became more involved in uniform lawmaking, joining UNIDROIT in 1986 and the Hague Conference on Private International Law in 1987, as well as increasing its involvement in UNCITRAL.

The CISG and the Chinese Contract Law are largely similar.[86] The CISG was first enacted domestically in China with the Foreign Economic Contract Law of

---

[82] Significant literature is available: see e.g. A. Chianale, The CISG as a Model Law: A Comparative Law Approach (2016) *Singapore Journal of Legal Studies*, 29–45; J. Coetzee, CISG and Regional Sales Law: Friends or Foes? (2015) 2 *Journal of Law, Society and Development*, 1, 29–44; F. Ferrari, The CISG and Its Impact on National Contract Law – General Report, in F. Ferrari (ed.), *The CISG and Its Impact on National Contract Law* (Munich: Sellier European Law Publishers, 2008), pp. 413–480; K. Marxen, The Cycle of Harmonisation – From Domestic Laws to the CISG and Back? (2015) 132 *South African Law Journal*, 3, 547–565; S. A. Kruisinga, The Impact of Uniform Law on National Law: Limits and Possibilities – CISG and Its Incidence in Dutch Law (2009) 13 *Electronic Journal of Comparative Law*, 2, 1–20. Available from www.ejcl.org/132/art132-2.pdf; I. Schwenzer, Regional and Global Unification of Sales Law (2011) 13 *European Journal of Law Reform*, (3–4), 370–379; I. Schwenzer and P. Hachem, The CISG – Successes and Pitfalls (2009) 57 *American Journal of Comparative Law*, 2, 457–478, at pp. 461–463; B. Zeller, *CISG and the Unification of International Trade Law* (Abingdon: Routledge-Cavendish, 2008), in particular chapter 8, Transplantation of Laws; M. Wethmar-Lemmer, Harmonising or Unifying the Law Applicable to International Sales Contracts between the BRICS States (2017) *Comparative and International Law Journal of Southern Africa*, 3, 372–394; B. Zeller, Recent Developments of the CISG: Are Regional Developments the Answer to Harmonisation? (2014) 18 *Vindobona Journal of International Commercial Law and Arbitration*, 1, 111–128.

[83] For further illustration of this point, see L. Castellani, The Three Dimensions of the CISG, in A. Castro Pinzón (ed.), *360° de la Compraventa Internacional de Mercaderías. Memorias del II Congreso Iberoamericano de Derecho Internacional de los Negocios* (Bogotá: Universidad Externado de Colombia, 2016), pp. 308–339.

[84] D. Ding, China and CISG, in M. R. Will (ed.), *CISG and China: Theory and Practice* (Geneva: Faculté de droit, Université de Genève, 1999), pp. 25–37, at 25–26; K. Y. Zou, *Chinese Legal Reform: Towards the Rule of Law* (Boston: Martinus Nijhoff Publishers, 2006), pp. 73–86. With reference to contract law reform, Z. Mo, *Chinese Contract Law: Theory and Practice* (Boston: Martinus Nijhoff Publishers, 2006), pp. 7–15.

[85] H. Piquet, *La Chine au carrefour des traditions juridiques* (Bruxelles: Bruylant, 2005), p. 139. The relationship between this transplant and the movement in support of 法制化 ("rule by law") seems a relevant issue yet to be explored.

[86] However, some differences between the CISG and the Chinese Contract Law remain, which may lead to divergent interpretations of seemingly identical provisions.

Differences may also arise from the declarations to the CISG lodged by China: while the Chinese Contract Law allows freedom of form of the contract, the Chinese government withdrew its

1985.[87] The treaty itself was ratified in December 1986 and entered into force on 1 January 1988. In 1999, after the decision to unify the contract law applicable to foreign and to domestic exchanges, a new Chinese Contract Law was drafted, which further buttressed the influence of the CISG.[88]

Moreover, both the CISG and the Chinese Contract Law are taught in Chinese universities and were subjects of the National Judicial Examination (国家司法考试). The corollary is that Chinese lawyers are familiar with the provisions of the CISG and comfortable with using the CISG in contracts for the international sale of goods.[89] Chinese familiarity with the CISG and openness to its use has had important effects. For instance, the application of the CISG in cases involving Chinese and Japanese traders influenced Japan's decision to accede to the CISG.[90] In turn, Japanese scholars and policy makers advocated the inclusion of elements of the CISG in the reform of the Japanese Civil Code.[91]

The impact of the CISG on domestic law reform is on the rise.[92] Recent examples include the Civil Code of Hungary,[93] the Civil and Commercial Code of Argentina,[94] and the draft Commercial Code of Spain of 2014. Moreover, the adoption of the CISG may represent an important step toward contract law modernization. Accession to the CISG by Brazil and by Vietnam are examples of CISG adoption with a view to introducing and testing new contract law concepts.

---

declaration under articles 11 and 96 CISG, demanding that sales contracts must be in writing, only in January 2013. Moreover, China maintains a declaration under articles 1(1)(b) and 95 CISG, which excludes the application of the CISG when the rules of private international law lead to the application of the law of a Contracting State, despite the fact that the main rationale for that declaration lay in the existence of discrete legal regimes for domestic and international transactions. As seen above, that has not been the case in China since 1999.

[87] Y. Q. Zhang, J. S. McLean, China's Foreign Economic Contract Law: Its Significance and Analysis (1987–1988) 8 *Northwestern Journal of International Law and Business* 120–144, at 127–128; X. C. Tong, Le droit chinois des contrats: sa codification, ses sources, ses champs d'application et ses caractéristiques (1996) *Les Cahiers de droit*, 373, 715–738, at 723–725.

[88] J. G. Wang, L. A. DiMatteo, Chinese Reception and Transplantation of Western Contract Law (2016) 34 *Berkeley Journal of International Law*, 1, 44–99.

[89] Of course, room remains for improving the level of uniformity in the interpretation of the CISG: Qiao Liu and Xiang Ren, CISG in Chinese Courts: The Issue of Applicability (2018) 65 *American Journal of Comparative Law*, 4, 873–918.

[90] H. Sono, Japan's Accession to the CISG: The Asia Factor (2008) 20 *Pace International Law Review* 105–114 at 113. Interestingly, the use of the CISG in Japan is currently supported by small and medium-sized enterprises, as those enterprises lack established contractual practices and therefore are more open to building them based on uniform law rather than on national law.

[91] Details were provided by M. Okino at the conference that originated this volume.

[92] S. Grundmann, M. S. Schäfer, The French and the German Reforms of Contract Law (2017) 13 *European Review of Contract Law*, 4, 459–490.

[93] Act V of 2013. See A. Fuglinszky, The Reform of Contractual Liability in the New Hungarian Civil Code: Strict Liability and Foreseeability Clause as Legal Transplants (2015) 79 *Rabels Zeitschrift für ausländisches und internationales Privatrecht*, 1, 72–116; see also A. Kisfaludi, The Influence of Harmonisation of Private Law on the Development of the Civil Law in Hungary (2008) 14 *Juridica international* 130–136. Available at: www.juridicainternational.eu/?id=12711.

[94] Law 26994 of 1 October 2014.

Modernization may take place also through judicial reference to CISG provisions in support of novel interpretations of domestic law. Moreover, by referring to the general principles underlying the CISG, the influence of the CISG may extend to general contract law and beyond.

In other cases, legal concepts contained in the CISG are transplanted in national law through a regional model, at times without adoption of the treaty itself. For instance, the Civil Code of Azerbaijan, adopted in 1999, is modeled after the Model Civil Code of the Commonwealth of Independent States, which in turn was inspired by the CISG.[95] In fact, the presence of several CISG principles in domestic law was an argument in favor of the adoption of the CISG by Azerbaijan, which took place in 2016.[96] The OHADA Act on General Commercial Law, already inspired by the CISG in its original version,[97] has been revised in a manner that draws the two texts closer. However, as noted above, the adoption of a regional text based on a global uniform text does not provide any guarantee that the global uniform text will be adopted, too. Thus, only few OHADA member States, and the majority but not all of the CIS member States, have adopted the CISG as of this writing.

The draft Common European Sales Law[98] has been likewise influenced by the CISG, but that lineage was disguised by reference to more recent uniform texts based on the CISG such as the UNIDROIT Principles of International Commercial Contracts and its European descendants, namely the Principles of European Contract Law[99] and the Draft Common Frame of Reference.[100] A similar line of influence may be found in the recent reform of French contract law.[101]

---

[95] More liberal enactments of that Model Civil Code follow the CISG even closer.

[96] R. Knieper, Celebrating Success by Accession to the CISG (2005–2006) 25 *Journal of Law and Commerce* 477–481 at 478. Available from: www.uncitral.org/pdf/english/CISG25/Knieper.pdf. See also N. Vilkova, The Unification of Conflict of Law Rules in CIS Countries (2000) 26 *Review of Central and East European Law*, 1, 75–83.

[97] G. K. Douajni, La vente commerciale OHADA (2003) 8 *Uniform Law Review*, 1–2, 191–200.

[98] Proposal for a regulation of the European Parliament and of the Council on a Common European Sales Law, Brussels 11.10.2011 COM (2011) 635 final. The draft Common European Sales Law, though never adopted, has generated significant literature: ex multis, see U. Magnus (ed.), *CISG vs. Regional Sales Law Unification. With a Focus on the New Common European Sales Law* (Munich: Sellier European Law Publishers, 2012).

[99] O. Lando, H. Beale (eds.), *Principles of European Contract Law*, Parts I & II (The Hague: Kluwer Law International, 1999); O. Lando, E. Clive, A. Prüm, R. Zimmermann (eds.), *Principles of European Contract Law, Part III* (The Hague: Kluwer Law International, 2003).

[100] C. von Bar, E. Clive, H. Schulte-Nölke, *Principles, Definitions and Model Rules of European Private Law. Draft Common Frame of Reference (DCFR)* (Full Edition) (Munich: Sellier, 2009).

[101] Ordonnance n° 2016-131 du 10 février 2016 portant réforme du droit des contrats, du régime général et de la preuve des obligations. For a reconstruction of the interrelation of the various texts, see V. Rivollier, L'influence du droit européen et international des contrats sur la réforme française du droit des obligations (2017) 69 *Revue internationale de droit comparé*, 4, 757–777, at 769–770; R. Schulze, The Reform of French Contract Law – A German Perspective (2017) 6 *Montesquieu Law Review*. Available at https://montesquieulawreview.eu/pdfs_mlr6/schulze.pdf, at 1: "The national and model contract laws influenced by the CISG do not, however, exhibit all of these features [of the CISG]. Nonetheless, the overlaps are unmistakable and allow the CISG to be deemed

3.4.2 Case Study 2: The UNCITRAL Model Law on Electronic Commerce

UNCITRAL has prepared uniform legislative texts enabling the use of electronic means. UNCITRAL's foray into the field of electronic commerce started in the 1980s in two specific areas: payments and Electronic Data Interchange. When the need arose to prepare a general text, which eventually became the UNCITRAL Model Law on Electronic Commerce (the "Model Law"),[102] it was not possible to compare existing legislative models because few national laws existed, and those that did were in part technology-specific and provided only partial answers to the questions raised.[103] Thus the Model Law could not seek to achieve convergence of existing laws but was geared toward the harmonization of future legal regimes. For these reasons, legislative work proceeded by developing general principles and applying those principles to specific provisions.[104]

Today, the Model Law has been enacted in more than seventy States[105] and is considered a legislative benchmark in a number of regions, including most of Asia.[106] However, even this apparently sound success needs to be qualified.

First, some of the jurisdictions that claim to have enacted the Model Law have not reproduced its main provisions or, at least, implemented its core principles.[107] For instance, all but one Member States of the Association of Southeast Asian Nations (ASEAN) have indicated their intention to enact the Model Law when adopting legislation on e-commerce.[108] However, not all of those States have actually enacted the Model Law.[109] In some cases, the Model Law may have been one of the models taken into consideration, but other models were eventually chosen. In other cases,

---

as the most important common source of inspiration for the changes to the law of contract (at national and European level) over the past 25 years."
[102] UNCITRAL Model Law on Electronic Commerce with Guide to Enactment (New York, 1999), United Nations publication, Sales No. E.99.V.4.
[103] On the drafting process of the Model Law, see H. Gabriel, The New United States Uniform Electronic Transactions Act: Substantive Provisions, Drafting History, and Comparison to the UNCITRAL Model Law on Electronic Commerce (2000) *Uniform Law Review* 651–664.
[104] This may explain why comparative discussions of electronic commerce law are rare. For one exception, see W. Harry Thurlow, Electronic Contracts in the United States and the European Union: Varying Approaches to the Elimination of Paper and Pen (2001) *Electronic Journal of Comparative Law*, Vol. 5.3. Available at www.ejcl.org/53/art53-1.html.
[105] This count includes only jurisdictions that have enacted the text of the Model Law without significant variations or, at least, have fully respected its fundamental principles and have reproduced most of its provisions.
[106] United Nations Conference on Trade and Development (UNCTAD), Review of E-Commerce Legislation Harmonization in the Association of Southeast Asian Nations, United Nations Publication UNCTAD/DTL/STICT/2013/1 (Geneva: UNCTAD, 2013), pp. 7–8.

In certain regions (Europe, Central Asia, Western Africa), the Model Law has received few enactments due to the prevalence of regional models.
[107] The UNCITRAL Secretariat does not consider those as Model Law enacting jurisdictions.
[108] ibid.
[109] See the list of enactments of the Model Law compiled by the UNCITRAL Secretariat.

certain provisions of the Model Law may have been enacted, but the national law does not implement some of the fundamental principles of the Model Law and therefore may not be considered a faithful enactment of that Model Law.[110]

A second qualification regards the use of the comparative method in drafting the Model Law and its compatibility with all types of legal systems: Does the Model Law actually represent a balance between legal traditions or instead does it predominantly build on certain concepts, namely from the common law? For instance, article 9 of the Model Law is based on the "best evidence rule," which is familiar to the common law, and the Guide to Enactment of the Model Law cautions against the adoption of that provision in legal systems where the "best evidence rule" is not known, as the provision may interfere with the law of evidence.[111] Yet, some civil law jurisdictions have enacted article 9 of the Model Law, apparently regardless of their lack of familiarity with the "best evidence rule."

If the Model Law is indeed considered closer to the common law tradition, could this be because common law jurisdictions are at an advantage in legally enabling the use of electronic means?[112] One common assumption is that the contract law regimes in common law jurisdictions are generally more flexible with form requirements than those in civil law jurisdictions, while economies in transition are most concerned about formalism, possibly due to the enduring influence of Socialist legal systems.[113] Moreover, electronic commerce laws in common law jurisdictions tend to have a broad scope of application that encompasses transactions with public bodies unless otherwise specified as the common law supports the broader approach to the use of electronic transactions according to shared general principles.

4 CONCLUSIONS

As a social phenomenon, commercial law will continue to develop regardless of the creation and diffusion of uniform law and will retain its pluralistic nature. At the same time, this chapter indicates that uniform law may provide an important contribution to the evolution of commercial law, since it may offer a useful

---

[110] However, absent formal standards for assessing the level of conformity of a legislative enactment with a model law, this evaluation remains subjective.
[111] UNCITRAL Model Law on Electronic Commerce with Guide to Enactment, para. 70.
[112] The question is related to the much broader discussion on the inherent economic efficiency of legal systems or "legal origins theory": R. La Porta, F. Lopez-de-Silanes, A. Shleifer, The Economic Consequences of Legal Origins (2008) 46 Journal of Economic Literature, 2, 285–332. See also N. Garoupa, Carlos G. Ligüerre, L. Mélon, Legal Origins and the Efficiency Dilemma (New York: Routledge: 2017), at p. 14 ff.(discussing the efficiency of the common law).
[113] T. Mambetalieva and A. P. Beklemishev, E-Commerce Legal and Regulatory Systems in the Countries of Central Asia and the Caucasus, in United Nations Economic and Social Commission for Asia and the Pacific (ESCAP), in ESCAP, Harmonized Development of Legal and Regulatory Systems for E-Commerce in Asia and the Pacific: Current Challenges And Capacity-Building Needs, ESCAP Studies in Trade and Investment Series, No. 54, UN Sales Doc. ST/ESCAP/2348 (New York: United Nations, 2004), pp. 37–65.

inspiration when technically well drafted and politically acceptable. Suggestions have been made on how to improve uniform law production, circulation, and implementation. There is, however, no time for complacency: ever-increasing cross-border commerce calls for efficient and effective legal solutions.[114]

Many Asian States are deeply involved in world trade. It is highly desirable to ensure their familiarity with uniform law since uniform law could provide the legal environment necessary for economic cooperation.

Better understanding of uniform law, broader participation in drafting, and greater support for adopting uniform texts could accelerate legal convergence and ultimately provide a meaningful contribution to closer economic development and social stability.

---

[114] On the relationship between uniform commercial law and globalization, see R. Cranston, Theorizing Transnational Commercial Law (2007) 42 *Texas International Law Journal* 597–617.

3

Convergence, Divergence and Diversity in Financial Law: The Experience of the UNCITRAL Model Law and Cross-Border Insolvency

Andrew Godwin

It is no doubt impracticable to strive for uniformity in all areas of the law.... Not only would complete harmonisation be impossible, it is also undesirable. All courts in our region have spent many years developing their own legal systems and adapting the law to suit the particular needs of their countries. Any attempt to achieve uniformity between our systems would fail and in doing so would lead to perhaps increased national differentiation and parochialism.... What we should recognize is that convergence, if it is to occur, will probably occur incrementally. Further it is likely only to occur in areas where there is a genuine transnational interest.[1]

... even where harmonisation is desirable and practicable, the exercise must be approached with sensitivity towards the national legal systems which will have to implement these laws. Harmonisation without due regard to the idiosyncrasies of national legal systems will produce superficially uniform laws, which leave fundamentally unchanged the undulating legal terrain that results from differences in the national legal systems underpinning these laws.[2]

The author would like to thank Timothy Howse and Lachlan Sievert for their research and editorial assistance and the anonymous reviewers in the preparation of this chapter. The research for this chapter was supported by a project on Financial Regulation in Asia, which was funded by a grant from the Melbourne School of Government, the University of Melbourne.

[1] The Hon. T. F. Bathurst, Chief Justice of New South Wales, 'The Importance of Developing Convergent Commercial Law Systems, Procedurally and Substantively', Paper delivered at the 15th Conference of Chief Justices of Asia and the Pacific, 28–30 October 2013, Singapore, paras. 40–41.

[2] The Hon. Sundaresh Menon, Chief Justice of the Republic of Singapore, Transnational Commercial Law: Realities, Challenges and a Call for Meaningful Convergence, Keynote Address at the 26th LAWASIA Conference, 15th Biennial Conference of Chief Justices of Asia and the Pacific, 27–30 October 2013, Singapore, para. 46. Menon CJ continued in paragraph 50 as follows: 'Let me pause here to summarise the principal points thus far. First, generally, the harmonisation of commercial law is desirable as it reduces transactional costs for cross-border businesses and encourages trade and investment. Second, for certain areas of law, the harmonisation of commercial law may not yet be attainable for some time at least where national imperatives diverge or where the costs of harmonisation outweigh the benefits. Third, where harmonisation is desirable, possible and practicable, it should be undertaken but any such exercise should take into account the idiosyncrasies of the domestic legal systems which have to implement the harmonised law.'

1 INTRODUCTION

This chapter considers the experience to date of convergence in the area of financial law and, specifically, the UNCITRAL Model Law on Cross-Border Insolvency ('Model Law'). In particular, the chapter examines the factors that prevent convergence in the area of financial law or, to put it differently, the factors behind *divergence*. It is suggested that through an examination of these factors, or the reasons behind the 'undulating legal terrain that results from differences in the national legal systems' as described by Menon CJ in the above quote, it is possible to assess the practicalities – and the relative merits – of convergence. Such an examination also offers insights into the appropriateness of mechanisms that might be used to achieve convergence and the extent to which the mechanisms need to be tailored to the particular circumstances or legal terrain.

The experience of the Model Law shows that full convergence in law (in terms of absolute uniformity) is neither realistic nor practicable and that there is a need to accept a degree of divergence in law between jurisdictions as suggested by Bathurst CJ in the above quote. It also suggests that divergence in law is not a negative as it often leads to convergence in outcomes. Further, divergence – or diversity – is positive if it achieves convergence in outcomes that could not otherwise be achieved as a result of fundamental differences between national legal systems.

The structure of this chapter is as follows: Section 2 examines what is meant by convergence and the relevance of both the object of convergence and also the mechanisms that might be used to achieve convergence. It also provides a brief outline of the experience of convergence in the area of financial law generally. Section 3 outlines the Model Law and its adoption by enacting states in the Asia Pacific region. Section 4 analyses the factors behind divergence in the adoption of the Model Law by various jurisdictions and identifies four key explanatory factors: (1) legal institutions, as reflected in the courts and judicial practice; (2) policy choices in the adoption and interpretation of concepts and terminology; (3) the existing legislative architecture; and (4) the desire to align with benchmark jurisdictions or with an 'enhanced version' of the Model Law. Section 5 offers some insights into the benefits of diversity in the context of the Model Law. Section 6 considers whether there is a case for regional convergence in the Asia Pacific and offers some concluding comments.

2 WHAT IS MEANT BY CONVERGENCE, AND WHAT IS THE OBJECT OF CONVERGENCE?

Two threshold issues are relevant in any discussion about legal convergence: (1) first, what is meant by 'convergence'; and (2) second, what is the object of convergence; namely, what is it that we are trying to converge? Is it convergence in the text of law? Is it convergence in the application or interpretation of law? Is it convergence in the concepts and principles that underpin law? Or is it convergence in outcomes? These two questions are interrelated. It is suggested that the answers to the questions will inform the question of which mechanisms might be appropriate in order to achieve the desired convergence and the relevant degree of divergence that might be tolerated.[3]

First, what is meant by 'convergence'? Convergence is often used synonymously or interchangeably with harmonisation. As former Chief Justice French of the High Court of Australia has suggested, '[c]onvergence denotes movement along a spectrum of similarity which includes, but is not limited to harmonisation and uniformity of laws'.[4] Convergence is also sometimes understood to mean passive convergence, as distinct from harmonisation which involves active steps such as adopting legislation to achieve convergence. In addition, convergence is often used to refer to the move towards complete alignment or uniformity, whereas harmonisation sometimes implies the existence of consistent but different laws and does not necessarily involve uniformity. To put it differently, convergence may imply a move towards uniformity, whereas harmonisation may imply a move towards complementarity between divergent (or diverse) approaches.

Understood in this way, an example of convergence in the area of financial law is the OHADA[5] Uniform Act on Security Law and an example of harmonisation is the UNCITRAL Model Law on Cross-Border Insolvency. Although similar in terms of their aim to achieve uniformity in outcomes, they are different insofar as OHADA, being an international organisation created by treaty, does intend to achieve uniformity (to the extent possible) in the text of law,[6] whereas the UNCITRAL Model Law is, as its name suggests, a model law that is incorporated

---

[3] A related question that captures the imagination is whether there is anything about financial law that presents special or unique challenges and which requires a different approach from that which might be adopted in other areas. This may depend, to a large extent, on the answers to the above questions; namely, what do we mean by 'convergence' and what is it exactly that we are trying to converge? If, for example, we take convergence to mean uniformity and we take the object of convergence to mean concepts and principles, financial law is likely to prove more challenging than other areas because of the existence of fundamental differences between jurisdictions in terms of concepts and principles.

[4] Chief Justice Robert French AC, Convergence of Commercial Laws – Fence Lines and Fields (22 January 2016), paper delivered at the Doing Business Across Asia – Legal Convergence in an Asian Century Conference, 22 January 2016, 3, available at www.hcourt.gov.au/assets/publications/speeches/current-justices/frenchcj/frenchcj22Jan2016.pdf.

[5] OHADA is the acronym that stands for the Organisation for the Harmonisation of Business Law in Africa.

[6] Even this treaty, however, allows for a degree of divergence. Generally, according to Article 10 of the OHADA Treaty, the OHADA Uniform Acts prevail over national law and must be adopted as they are drafted, without modifications by adopting states. As noted by Anne-Catherine Hahn, Legal Harmonization in the OHADA Zone – An Introduction, in Baker and McKenzie Zurich, *Business in West and Central Africa: The Legal Framework – An Introduction to the Laws of the OHADA* (2015), 4: 'As has been held by the Common Court of Justice and Arbitration, national laws remain formally in force and continue to apply to matters not covered by the OHADA rules, but only to the extent that they are not in conflict with the harmonised law.' However, 'there is some limited built-in flexibility that [ensures] that concepts from common law or civil law can coexist with the new framework ... through the existence of many non-mandatory provisions in the uniform acts that apply only where the parties to an agreement have not provided for anything to the contrary'.

into domestic law by those jurisdictions that choose to adopt it and is often adapted or modified in the process.[7]

Professor Ralf Michaels has suggested a typology of convergence, which distinguishes between, on the one hand, formal (or hard) convergence as achieved through mechanisms such as uniform legislation,[8] treaties[9] and legal transplants[10] and, on the other hand, soft convergence as achieved through mechanisms such as model laws,[11] soft law (in the form of principles)[12] and harmonisation.[13] Professor Michaels also identifies what he describes as 'substantive convergence', which includes convergence in the application or interpretation of law.[14]

Standard documentation might be included in the category of soft law.[15] Unlike the other forms of soft law that come about through a top-down process, however, standard documentation can be described as a bottom-up methodology of convergence. This is because standard documentation is formulated by industry bodies and represents market practice.[16] As such, it is an example of transnational practice creating transnational form.

Although there will always be differences of opinion in relation to typology and categorisation, at the very least most people would probably agree that convergence involves a process by which the differences between the laws of jurisdictions become less pronounced, thereby facilitating cross-border transactions and activities and creating greater certainty and predictability.

It is likely that convergence in the text of law – as distinct from convergence in the application or interpretation of law or convergence in outcomes – is the main target for the various warnings against uncritical or superficial convergence, such as those

[7] The model law approach allows for divergences from the original text and often makes provision for divergence or optionality within the text of the model law itself. See further in Section 3 below for a discussion of this in the context of the UNCITRAL Model Law on Cross-Border Insolvency.
[8] Professor Michaels refers to federal law in a federal state as an example of this.
[9] An example in this regard is the Convention on the International Sale of Goods, Vienna, 11 April 1980, 1489 UNTS 3 (CISG).
[10] In the context of financial law, legal transplants have been particularly prominent in the area of insolvency or bankruptcy law.
[11] An example of a model law in the context of a federal framework is the Uniform Commercial Code ('UCC') in the US.
[12] An example of soft law is the UNIDROIT Principles on the Operation of Close-Out Netting Provisions, which were issued in 2013.
[13] In this context, harmonisation is often used to refer to the process of creating common standards or rules pursuant to instruments such as directives of the European Union.
[14] Examples that Professor Michaels gives in this regard are collections of case law (e.g. CLOUT; unilex. info and INCADAT); the duty to compare such as Art. 7(1) of the CISG; expert panels such as the CISG Advisory Council and Highest Courts such as the Court of Justice of the European Union. In a financial law context, an additional example would be the Common Court of Justice and Arbitration, which has jurisdiction pursuant to the OHADA Treaty to interpret the OHADA Uniform Acts.
[15] An example of standard documentation is the International Swaps and Derivatives Association (ISDA) Master Agreement and its related documents.
[16] Given that standard documentation embodies accepted usage and customs in the relevant market, it might be described as a form of *lex mercatoria*.

made by Bathurst CJ and Menon CJ in the quotes extracted above. In the context of financial law, the deficiencies of uncritical or superficial convergence have been particularly evident in legal transplants, such as those concerning substantive bankruptcy law, where laws have been transplanted from one jurisdiction to another with little regard to the national legal systems that have to implement the laws. This leads to a situation where the law is either not implemented in accordance with its letter or spirit, or is disregarded completely.[17] The result is like changing the dictionary meanings of words in an existing language – it may be possible to legislate for words to have new meaning, but the legislation will not have any effect at the practical or operational level.

The second question – concerning the object of convergence – is often the more critical question as it speaks to the effectiveness of convergence and the specific mechanisms that might be used to achieve convergence. It also speaks to the tolerance for divergence that might be acceptable in the relevant circumstances. For example, if the object of convergence is convergence in the text of law, a relatively low tolerance for divergence will be acceptable. On the other hand, if the object of convergence is convergence in outcomes, a relatively high tolerance for divergence in laws, rules and procedures will be acceptable, so long as the divergent approaches lead to the desired convergence in outcomes.

It might be said that drawing distinctions between the objects of convergence is somewhat artificial in view of the potential for significant overlap between the objects of convergence. For example, if there is convergence in the text of laws, it is very likely (indeed, it is expected) that there will be convergence in outcomes and also convergence in the concepts and principles that underpin the law. The purpose of drawing these distinctions, however, is to highlight that convergence or harmonisation of law does not necessarily require uniformity in the text of laws and, indeed, that convergence in outcomes through divergent approaches may be equally or more effective, particularly when convergence in the text of laws is not possible as a result of the 'undulating legal terrain' to which Menon CJ refers. This chapter argues that the experience arising out of the adoption of the Model Law on Cross-Border Insolvency is a good example of convergence in outcomes without full convergence or uniformity in the text of laws. It also exemplifies the need for those pursuing convergence to take into account the undulating legal terrain of local jurisdictions.

In short, the contention is that the effectiveness of convergence will inevitably be measured by reference to both the object of convergence and also the specific mechanism that has been used for the purpose of convergence. The different objects

---

[17] For a discussion about the perils of legal transplantation in the context of bankruptcy law, see N. Martin, The Role of History and Culture in Developing Bankruptcy and Insolvency Systems: The Perils of Legal Transplantation (2005) 28(1) *Boston College International and Comparative Law Review* 1.

TABLE 3.1 *Convergence objects and methodologies*

Object of convergence	Relevant mechanisms	Tolerance for divergence
Text of laws	• Uniform legislation (in a federal or supranational context) • Treaties • Legal transplants • Model laws	Low
Application or interpretation of law	• Collections of case law (e.g. CLOUT[1]) • Expert panels (e.g. CISG Advisory Council[2]) • Common courts[3] • Model laws[4]	Low
Outcomes	• Model laws and guides to their enactment and interpretation • Principles • Standard documentation[5]	Relatively high
Concepts and principles that underpin law	• All of the above	Relatively low

[1] CLOUT is the system established by the UNCITRAL Secretariat for collecting and disseminating information on court decisions and arbitral awards relating to the Conventions and Model Laws that have emanated from the work of UNCITRAL. According to the UNCITRAL website, the purpose of the system is 'to promote international awareness of the legal texts formulated by the Commission and to facilitate uniform interpretation and application of those texts'. See www.uncitral.org/uncitral/en/case_law.html.

[2] See www.cisgac.com: 'The [CISG Advisory Council] is a private initiative which aims at promoting a uniform interpretation of the CISG.'

[3] An example of a common court is the Common Court of Justice and Arbitration established pursuant to the OHADA Treaty, which 'ensures the consistent interpretation of the Uniform Acts, the OHADA Treaty and any regulations applying the latter'. See www.aict-ctia.org/courts_subreg/ohada/ohada_home.html.

[4] Model laws have been included as a methodology for convergence in the application or interpretation of law as many model laws contain a provision to promote convergence in this regard. See, for example, Article 8 of the Model Law, which stipulates that 'in the interpretation of this Law, regard is to be had to its international origin and to the need to promote uniformity in its application and the observance of good faith'.

[5] Although the use of standard documentation is a form of private ordering, it nonetheless represents market practice and influences the development of laws accordingly.

of convergence, the relevant mechanisms and their tolerance for divergence are represented in Table 3.1.

It is significant to note that model laws serve as a common mechanism for all of the objects of convergence; in other words, the use of model laws can assist in achieving all forms of convergence.

Financial law and regulation is an area in which there has been a relatively high degree of convergence, partly as a result of the interconnectivity and uniformity of financial transactions across borders and partly, of course, as a result of events such as the Global Financial Crisis.[18] In the context of financial law, soft law (as defined broadly to include model laws and principles) has been relatively successful in terms of the coverage that it has received across a range of areas. In addition, bottom-up forms of convergence as reflected in standard documentation, which influence legal convergence through uniformity in market practice, have had a significant impact as reflected in the widespread use of the ISDA Master Agreement and the Loan Markets Association (LMA) loan documentation.

That said, convergence of financial law has often been accompanied by a high degree of divergence, particularly in relation to the concepts and principles that underpin law. Examples of divergence in this regard include the divergent approaches to the validity of non-assignment clauses[19] and hybrid jurisdiction clauses,[20] and also the recognition and use of security trustees in secured transactions.[21] In addition, it is relevant to note that divergence does not just arise

[18] Convergence in the wake of the Global Financial Crisis has been particularly evident in the context of financial regulation and the initiatives of standard-setting bodies such as the Financial Stability Board (FSB).

[19] Non-assignment clauses are clauses that restrict or prohibit the assignment of contractual rights. In the context of financial transactions, they restrict or prohibit the assignment of debts. In some jurisdictions, such as the United States, they have been nullified by statute on the basis that they are inconsistent with the free trade of receivables and the promotion of commerce. § 2–210(3) of the Uniform Commercial Code ('UCC') provides that a prohibition of assignments is to be construed as barring only the delegation of performance (i.e. not the assignment of rights). In relation to the UNCITRAL Model Law on Secured Transactions, Kohn and Morse note that '[o]ne interesting difference between the Model Law and the UCC exists in the case of "anti-assignment clauses": contractual limitations contained in the documents governing receivables that purport to restrict the ability of the seller of goods or services to encumber or assign the receivables. In the United States, the UCC generally renders these clauses unenforceable for all purposes. The Model Law does not go that far. It provides that such clauses are unenforceable as between the owner of the receivables and the secured party (so that the security interest is enforceable notwithstanding the clause), but the account debtor retains its right to sue the owner for breach of the clause. The practical effect of the approach taken by the Model Law is that borrowers will be reluctant to grant security interests in their receivables in the face of an anti-assignment clause without obtaining the consent of the account debtor.' Richard M. Kohn and David W. Morse, UNCITRAL: The Model Law on Secured Transactions, *The Secured Lender*, November 2016.

[20] A hybrid jurisdictions clause, also referred to as a unilateral jurisdiction clause, is commonly seen in cross-border loan agreements, where the borrower agrees to submit to the exclusive jurisdiction of the courts in the jurisdiction of the governing law but the lender or lenders reserve the right to take action against the borrower in the courts of any other jurisdiction. For a UK case that considers the validity of such clauses as a matter of English law, see *Mauritius Commercial Bank Ltd v. Hestia Holdings Ltd* [2013] EWHC 1328 (Comm).

[21] In financial transactions, security trustees hold the benefit of security for the lenders or creditors. In jurisdictions that do not recognise the use of a trust for this purpose, the practice has been to appoint a security agent. For commentary on the operation of a security agent under the OHADA Uniform Act on Security Law, see Ashley Lee, African Security Enforcement Improves under OHADA, *International Financial Law Review*, 6 June 2013: 'A key part of the law was the introduction of a security agent, described as a hybrid between the civil law mechanism of agency and the common law's trustee. Previously individual lenders each took security, which then required an involved process whenever a lender transferred the loans. Under the revised law, all security or other guarantees for the performance of an obligation can be granted, registered, filed, managed and enforced by

between jurisdictions that have different legal traditions (e.g. common law and civil law jurisdictions) but also between jurisdictions that share the same legal traditions. An example of this is the divergence between English law and US law – both common law jurisdictions – in the validity of so-called flip clauses in structured finance and securitisation transactions. Flip clauses provide that the priority of payment obligations owed to two different creditors will flip following a specified event of default. Until recently, the US courts were unwilling to recognise the validity of flip clauses,[22] whereas the UK courts were willing to uphold them.[23] The example of flip clauses highlights the enduring divergence in the validity of contractual provisions and the reality that there will always be divergence in court interpretation, even between courts in common law jurisdictions, for a range of reasons that include differences in the statutory framework and differences in the concepts and principles that underpin the law.

The challenges of achieving uniformity in certain areas has led to the use of principles to achieve convergence in outcomes rather than the text of the laws themselves. The UNIDROIT Principles on the Operation of Close-Out Netting Provisions, which were issued in 2013, are a recent example. These Principles aim to provide guidance on national legislation relating to close-out netting, a critical element that underpins the effectiveness of derivative transactions and, in the case of banks, compliance with capital adequacy requirements. The use of the Principles is thus designed to encourage convergence, not in relation to the text of domestic laws but rather in relation to the outcomes that national laws are intended to achieve. Convergence in outcomes is appropriate where there is a high degree of divergence in the ways in which concept are expressed and interpreted and where the issues touch on fundamental differences in insolvency law policy and fundamental choices such as how risks between creditors should be allocated and how priorities between competing interests should be determined.

---

a national foreign financial institution or credit institution acting in its own name or for the benefit of creditors of the secured obligations that have appointed it.' It has been suggested that '[a]lthough this reform was inspired by the French security law, it is ahead of French law on various matters, especially concerning the security agent, so that some French lawyers now suggest that French law could be inspired by OHADA law in this respect': A. B. Epale, O. Fille-Lambie, and L. J. Lainsey, The Revised OHADA Uniform Act on Security Law, *Hogan Lovells Africa Newsletter*, December 2012.

[22] See *Lehman Brothers Special Financing Inc. v. BNY Corporate Trustee Services Inc.*, 422 BR 407 (Bankr SDNY 2010), 25 January 2010, in which Judge Peck of the US Bankruptcy Court held that a flip clause was an impermissible ipso facto clause in contravention of ss. 365(e)(1) and 541(c)(1) of the US Bankruptcy Code. In the 2016 case of *Lehman Brothers Special Financing Inc. v. Bank of America National Association* 553 BR 476 (Bankr. SDNY 2016), however, Judge Chapman of the US Bankruptcy Court ruled that not all flip clauses were ipso facto clauses; but, if they were, they were protected by the safe harbour provisions in the US Bankruptcy Code.

[23] See *Belmont Park Investments Pty Limited v. BNY Corporate Trustee Services Limited and Lehman Brothers Special Financing Inc* [2011] 1 AC 383, in which the Supreme Court of the United Kingdom upheld the validity of flip clauses under English bankruptcy law.

3 THE UNCITRAL MODEL LAW ON CROSS-BORDER INSOLVENCY

The UNCITRAL Model Law on Cross-Border Insolvency provides a template for enacting states to adopt for the purpose of establishing procedures for courts to grant recognition and assistance to foreign insolvency proceedings. This is an important area of convergence in view of the increasingly global nature of business activities and operations, and the benefits that accrue to debtors, creditors and other stakeholders in dealing with cross-border insolvency issues on a uniform (and universal) basis to the extent possible.

As noted by the UNCITRAL website, the Model Law 'focuses on four elements identified as key to the conduct of cross-border insolvency cases: access, recognition, relief (assistance) and cooperation'.[24] The access provisions give a foreign insolvency representative a right of access to the receiving court (i.e. the court in the enacting State from which recognition and relief is sought). The recognition provisions enable the receiving court to recognise a foreign insolvency proceeding as either a 'foreign main proceeding'[25] or a 'foreign non-main proceeding'. The relief provisions specify the different forms of relief that are available to assist a foreign insolvency proceeding, foremost of which is the automatic stay on actions against the debtor and its assets upon recognition of a 'foreign main proceeding'.[26] Finally, the cooperation provisions permit cooperation and direct communication between the receiving court and foreign courts or foreign insolvency representatives, and also establish the coordination that is required for the management of concurrent proceedings, the aim of which is to 'foster decisions that would best achieve the objectives of both proceedings, whether local and foreign proceedings or multiple foreign proceedings'.[27]

The Model Law is accompanied by a Guide to Enactment and Interpretation ('UNCITRAL Guide'). The UNCITRAL Guide 'is directed primarily to executive branches of Governments and legislators preparing the necessary enacting legislation, but it also provides useful insights for those charged with interpretation and application of the Model Law, such as judges, and other users of the text, such as practitioners and academics'.[28]

At the UNCITRAL 11th Multinational Judicial Colloquium, held in March 2015 in San Francisco, it was agreed that

> among the key benefits provided by the Model Law were streamlined, simple procedures, the provision of automatic relief that helped to move proceedings

---

[24] www.uncitral.org/uncitral/en/uncitral_texts/insolvency/1997Model.html.
[25] Under Art. 2(b) of the Model Law, a 'foreign main proceeding' is defined as 'a foreign proceeding taking place in the State where the debtor has the centre of its main interest'. The concept of 'the centre of main interest' is explored in Section 4.
[26] Article 20(1) of the Model Law.
[27] www.uncitral.org/uncitral/en/uncitral_texts/insolvency/1997Model.html.
[28] UNCITRAL, Model Law on Cross-Border Insolvency: Guide to Enactment and Interpretation ('Guide'), www.uncitral.org/uncitral/en/uncitral_texts/insolvency/1997Model.html.

along and preservation of the powers and integrity of ancillary jurisdictions. The Model Law is simply expressed, well understood, easily learned and retained; it can be applied consistently with appropriate discretions; provides a well-understood framework for foreign parties and reduces the need for foreign representatives to have to seek advice on domestic law.[29]

Writing in 2004, when only a handful of jurisdictions had adopted the Model Law,[30] Anderson argued that the model soft law approach had 'not achieved its promised harmonisation due to a failure in achieving extensive adoption and divergences in content'.[31] Anderson suggested, however, that the approach was 'nonetheless viable, because it may be on the threshold of widespread adoption and because model laws may still provide legal assistance and comparative law benefits'.[32]

This chapter suggests that the threshold of widespread adoption referred to by Anderson has now been reached.[33] As of today, legislation based on the Model Law has been adopted in forty-nine states in a total of fifty-three jurisdictions.[34] One notable exception in the Asia Pacific region is Hong Kong, although it is expected that Hong Kong will adopt the Model Law in due course.

[29] UNCITRAL, '11th Multinational Judicial Colloquium' (21–22 March 2015, San Francisco), www.uncitral.org/pdf/english/news/EleventhJC.pdf, para. 33.

[30] The statistics indicate that only eight jurisdictions had adopted the Model Law by 2004. See www.uncitral.org/uncitral/en/uncitral_texts/insolvency/1997Model_status.html.

[31] K. Anderson, Testing the Model Soft Law Approach to International Harmonisation: A Case-Study Examining the UNCITRAL Model Law on Cross-Border Insolvency (2004) 23 *Australian Year Book on International Law* 1. Anderson, 5, identifies the benefits of harmonisation as including (1) facilitating a common market; (2) simplifying legal compliance and planning; (3) simplifying cross-border litigation and dispute resolution; (4) simplifying, in practice, conflict of laws questions; (5) making applicable laws readily accessible in a variety of languages; and (6) providing a neutral and objective law.

[32] Anderson, Testing the Model Soft Law Approach, 5–6, identifies legal assistance benefits as including: (1) filling a domestic legal vacuum or undeveloped area of law, particularly in new market economies and developing states that have not had significant international trade; (2) creating a legal regime attuned to international transactions and thereby promoting foreign investment and trade; and (3) providing foreigners with confidence in the sophistication and objectivity of the domestic legal regime or rule of law. Anderson identifies the comparative law benefits of model laws as including (1) simplifying domestic legislation in the relevant area by consolidating the often disparate law; (2) providing a normatively better law than any domestic legislation given that it was drafted by international experts with the benefit of wide comparative experience; and (3) regardless of adoption, providing a well-reasoned comparative example to inform the domestic drafting process.

[33] Anderson, Testing the Model Soft Law Approach, 21, acknowledged that if the Model Law were adopted by the United Kingdom and the United States, 'that alone would assure the economic heft necessary to achieve the promised Harmonisation Benefits'. Those two jurisdictions have now adopted the Model Law.

[34] See www.uncitral.org/uncitral/en/uncitral_texts/insolvency/1997Model_status.html. There are some interesting statistics that relate to the adoption of the Model Law: in between 1997, when the Model Law was issued, and 2008, the onset of the Global Financial Crisis, only fifteen jurisdictions had adopted the Model Law; since the Global Financial Crisis, twenty-eight jurisdictions have adopted the Model Law. Accordingly, the second decade of the Model Law has seen a two-fold increase in the number of jurisdictions adopting the Model Law.

The Model Law has been a relatively successful example of convergence in the area of financial law as it relates to the procedures for recognition and assistance in cross-border insolvency proceedings.[35] That said, as discussed further in Section 4, there is a significant degree of divergence between jurisdictions in terms of the modifications that have been made to the Model Law when adopted into domestic legislation. For example, jurisdictions have differed in terms of the nature and extent of the relief that will be granted to assist in foreign insolvency procedures, the relevance of public policy in providing a ground on which recognition or relief should be refused and the interpretation given to concepts such as the centre of main interest as discussed in Section 4.2 below. Consequently, the Model Law is an example of how model laws are subject to modification and adaptation when they are adopted into domestic legislation. In some cases, the modifications are relatively minor; in other cases, they are more significant and increase the divergence in various areas.

The relative success of the UNCITRAL Model Law example can be attributed, in part, to its focus on procedural law as distinct from substantive law.[36] As noted in the context of domestic bankruptcy law, attempts to achieve convergence in the area of substantive law create challenges that figure prominently in the controversy surrounding the advantages and disadvantages of legal transplants.[37]

For the purpose of promoting the harmonisation of cross-border insolvency laws, UNCITRAL recommended in the UNCITRAL Guide that States make as few changes as possible to the text when enacting the Model Law:

> 20. In incorporating the text of a model law into its system, a State may modify or leave out some of its provisions. In the case of a convention, the possibility of changes being made to the uniform text by the States parties (normally referred to as 'reservations') is much more restricted; in particular trade law conventions usually either totally prohibit reservations or allow only specified ones. The flexibility inherent in a model law is particularly desirable in those cases when it is likely that the State would wish to make various modifications to the uniform text before it would be ready to enact it as a national law. Some modifications may be expected in particular when the uniform text is closely related to the national court and procedural system (which is the case with the UNCITRAL Model Law on Cross-Border Insolvency). This, however, also means that the degree of, and certainty about, harmonization achieved through a model law is likely to be lower than in the case of a convention. Therefore, in order to achieve a satisfactory degree of

---

[35] See G. McCormack and A. Hargovan, Australia and the International Insolvency Paradigm (2015) 37 *Sydney Law Review* 389, 409: 'The Model Law, in the countries where it has been implemented, has achieved a high degree of international uniformity, but it is not complete uniformity.'

[36] As Anderson, 'Testing the Model Soft Law Approach', notes, 8, 'the UNCITRAL Working Group limited its efforts to the discrete issue of the procedural aspects of cross-border cases. In doing so, they avoided the more controversial and diverging areas of substantive insolvency law and covered an area in which many domestic systems had a vacuum or only a minimal regime.'

[37] See the discussion in the text accompanying note 17 above.

harmonization and certainty, it is recommended that States make as few changes as possible in incorporating the Model Law into their legal systems.[38]

In addition, the importance of uniformity in the interpretation of the Model Law is underscored by Article 8 of the Model Law:

> In the interpretation of the present Law, regard is to be had to its international origin and to the need to promote uniformity in its application and the observance of good faith.

At the same time, UNCITRAL recognises that there will be divergence in substantive insolvency law:

> 3. The Model Law respects the differences among national procedural laws and does not attempt a substantive unification of insolvency law. Rather, it provides a framework for cooperation between jurisdictions, offering solutions that help in several modest but significant ways and facilitate and promote a uniform approach to cross-border insolvency.[39]

The Explanatory Memorandum to the Cross-Border Insolvency Regulations in the UK notes that the UK 'tried [to] follow UNCITRAL's exhortation to stay as close as possible to the original drafting in order to ensure consistency, certainty and harmonisation with other countries enacting the Model Law'.[40] There were, however, various areas of divergence from the original text of the Model Law, including 'references to Council Regulation (EC) 1346/2000 on Insolvency Proceedings (EU Regulation), section 426 of the Insolvency Act 1986, the British court systems, and the different forms of relief available under British insolvency law'.[41] McCormack cites the comments of the UK Insolvency Service that 'it had sought to stay as close as possible to the Model Law drafting, "to try and ensure consistency, certainty and harmonisation with other States enacting the Model Law and to provide a guide for other States who are considering enacting the law"'.[42]

Some jurisdictions in the Asia Pacific, including Australia, New Zealand, Vanuatu, and the Philippines, have adopted the Model Law with very little divergence from its text.[43] Japan and Korea, on the other hand, have diverged significantly from the original text. In the case of Japan, a query has been raised as to whether it

---

[38] UNCITRAL Guide, 19.
[39] UNCITRAL Guide, 19.
[40] Explanatory Memorandum to the UK Cross-Border Insolvency Regulations, para. 7.18.
[41] S. Shandro, *American Bankruptcy Institute Journal*, June 2006 European Update. See also S. E. Story, Cross-Border Insolvency: A Comparative Analysis (2015) 32 *Arizona Journal of International and Comparative Law* 431, 439, who notes that 'Great Britain adopted the UNCITRAL Model with the intention that it would operate in collaboration with, rather than supplant, the EU Council Regulation on Insolvency Proceedings and Britain's own Section 426 of the Insolvency Act of 1986'.
[42] G. McCormack, US Exceptionalism and UK Localism? Cross-Border Insolvency Law in Comparative Perspective (2016) 36(1) *Legal Studies* 136, 142.
[43] See the Explanatory Memorandum in Australia, para. 4: 'The Bill adopts the Model Law with as few changes as are necessary to adapt it to the Australian context.'

did in fact adopt the Model Law or, instead, whether it just borrowed from its principles.[44] As discussed further in Section 4.4 below, Singapore adopted what might be described as an 'enhanced version' of the Model Law, borrowing from both the UK experience and the US experience in this regard. The approach in Singapore is supported by the adoption by the Supreme Court of Singapore of the Guidelines for Communication and Cooperation between Courts in Cross-Border Insolvency Matters.[45]

4 FACTORS BEHIND DIVERGENCE

The analysis in this Section identifies and examines the factors behind divergence in the ways in which various jurisdictions have adopted the Model Law. Four key factors are identified and discussed by reference to selected examples:[46] (1) legal institutions, as reflected in the courts and judicial practice; (2) policy choices in the adoption and interpretation of concepts and terminology; (3) the existing legislative architecture; and (4) the desire to align with benchmark jurisdictions or with an 'enhanced version' of the Model Law. By surveying the undulating legal terrain in this regard, the analysis demonstrates that there are reasonable – and therefore legitimate – reasons as to why jurisdictions diverge in the text of laws and that this does not necessarily compromise convergence in outcomes. The jurisdictions examined in the analysis that follows include the UK and the US and those jurisdictions in the Asia-Pacific Region (other than Myanmar) that have adopted the Model Law – namely, Australia, New Zealand, Japan, Korea, the Philippines, Singapore and Vanuatu. The regional analysis is relevant for the purpose of considering whether there is a case for regional convergence; namely, whether there is a case either for

[44] Anderson, Testing the Model Law Soft Approach, 11–12, argues that 'while *consistent with* or *in principle based on* the Model Law, Japan's new cross-border insolvency is not *modelled on* the Model Law'. He further argues (p. 14) that the divergence between the Model Law and the Japanese law 'preclude[s] Japan from realising any of the Harmonisation Benefits of the Model Soft Law Approach. Furthermore, the promotion of the Japanese law as an example of adoption of the Model Law in fact harms the harmonisation movement by deceiving practitioners into either complacency or unnecessary scepticism.' For a contrary view, see K. Yamamoto, New Japanese Legislation on Cross-Border Insolvency as Compared with the UNCITRAL Model Law (2002) *INSOL International Insolvency Review* 67. Yamamoto argues (pp. 95–96) that the Japanese legislation 'adopts in principle the rule of the model law on cross-border insolvency' and that 'the most important differences, such as the provision that makes every relief upon recognition discretionary or that adopts the principle of "one proceeding running for one debtor", are not necessarily considered to conflict with the essential purpose of the model law'.
[45] The drafting of these guidelines arose out of the inaugural conference of the Judicial Insolvency Network (the 'JIN') on 10 and 11 October 2016. See Z. Mao, Heralding Protocols for Court-to-Court Communication and Cooperation in Cross-Border Insolvency Matters in Singapore, *Singapore Law Blog*, 21 November 2016, available at www.singaporelawblog.sg/blog/article.173.
[46] It should be noted that these examples have been selected to illustrate the relevant areas of divergence and do not purport to be comprehensive or exhaustive.

pursuing convergence initiatives on a regional basis or for achieving a regional form of convergence – an issue that is discussed in Section 6.

4.1 Courts and Judicial Practice

Given the focus of the Model Law on establishing procedures for courts to recognise and provide assistance to foreign insolvency proceedings, it is no surprise that one of the factors behind divergence should be courts and judicial practice.[47] As UNCITRAL has noted:

> 19. Some differences in approach to the interpretation of the terms of the Model Law (or any adaptation of its language) may arise from the way in which judges from different legal traditions approach their respective tasks. Although general propositions are fraught with difficulty, the greater codification of law in some jurisdictions may tend to focus more attention on the text of the Model Law than would be the case in other jurisdictions without the same degree of codification or in which many superior courts have an inherent jurisdiction to determine legal questions in a manner that is not contrary to any statute or regulation or have the authority to develop particular aspects of the law for which there is no codified rule.
>
> 20. These different approaches could affect a receiving court's inclination to act on the Model Law's principle of cooperation between courts and coordination of multiple proceedings. If the domestic law of the enacting State incorporates the cooperation and coordination provisions of the Model Law, there will be a codified recognition of steps that can be taken in that regard.
>
> 21. Without the explicit adoption of such provisions, there may be doubt as to whether, as a matter of domestic law, a court is entitled to engage in dialogue with a foreign court or to approve a cross-border insolvency agreement entered into by insolvency representatives in different States and other interested parties. The court's ability to do so will depend on other provisions of relevant domestic law. On the other hand, those courts which possess an inherent jurisdiction are likely to have greater flexibility in determining what steps can be taken between courts, in order to give effect to the Model Law's emphasis on cooperation and coordination.[48]

Japan is an interesting case in point. Yamamoto suggests that Japan's civil law tradition and judicial practice militate against adopting provisions in the Model Law that give courts too much flexibility or discretionary powers.[49] For example, Article 25 of the Model Law, which provides that 'the court shall cooperate to the

---

[47] One might refer to this as divergence in institutional design.

[48] United Nations Commission on International Trade Law, UNCITRAL Model on Cross-Border Insolvency: The Judicial Perspective (2013), available at www.uncitral.org/pdf/english/texts/insolven/Judicial-Perspective-2013-e.pdf.

[49] Yamamoto, New Japanese Legislation on Cross-Border Insolvency, 68–69, notes that 'the model law gives very broad scope of discretion to judges: this approach may be familiar to the common law judges, but it may cause confusion for the civil law judges. As we will explain later, most of the difference between the UNCITRAL model law and our new law results from such a technical reason'.

3 Convergence, Divergence and Diversity in Financial Law 47

maximum extent possible with foreign courts or foreign representatives', was not adopted in the Japanese legislation for the reason that such cooperation would only be relevant where a local Japanese proceeding had been commenced and concurrent proceedings were underway; in such circumstances, there would be a limit to the extent of cooperation that would be necessary.[50] Yamamoto also suggests that consistent with the trend of Japanese insolvency legislation, the courts are expected to perform a passive role in supporting cooperation between the insolvency representatives instead of an active role in cooperating and communicating directly with foreign courts.[51] By contrast, in its regulations adopting the Model Law, the UK in fact increased the discretion of the courts in this regard by replacing the words 'shall cooperate' with 'may cooperate'.[52]

> For a contrary view, see Anderson, Testing the Model Law Soft Approach, 13–14: 'the most commonly cited reason in Japan for the non-adoption of the Model Law (that it was inconsistent with civil law notions of judicial capacity) seems insincere in the face of other civil law countries' adoption of the act, the majority of civil law drafters in UNCITRAL, and mostly the fact that regardless of academic drafters' theoretical concerns Japanese judges have in practice been proactively managing cross-border insolvency cases for decades'.

[50] Yamamoto, New Japanese Legislation on Cross-Border Insolvency, 89–90. The Japanese legislation on cross-border insolvency provides that if a debtor has already commenced domestic insolvency proceedings, an application for recognition of foreign insolvency proceedings will be refused except where (1) the foreign insolvency proceeding is a main proceeding; (2) assistance would be in the common interests of creditors; and (3) it is unlikely that undue harm will be caused to the interests of creditors in Japan (see Art. 57(1)(i) to (iii) and Art. 59(1) of the Act on Recognition of and Assistance for Foreign Insolvency Proceedings 2000 ('Japanese Act'). In addition, if a petition is filed for recognition of a foreign insolvency proceeding and recognition orders have already been issued in respect of another foreign insolvency proceeding, the petition will be refused if the other foreign insolvency proceeding is a main proceeding or the foreign insolvency proceeding for which the petition is filed is a secondary proceeding and the provision of assistance would not be in the common interests of creditors (Art. 62(1)). This is consistent with the domestic Japanese law principle of 'one proceeding per debtor', which provides that 'where one proceeding is taking place in relation to a debtor, all other proceedings must be stayed': see B. Pogacar, The 1997 UNCITRAL Model Law on Cross-Border Insolvency – Ten Years After (2008) 2(1) *Insolvency and Restructuring International* 49. Anderson, Testing the Model Law Soft Approach, 13, writes that '[d]issimilarity is the rule when comparing how the Japanese and Model Laws treat concurrent cases as well. The Model Law provides for concurrent handling of recognised foreign insolvencies and local insolvencies. In contrast, the Japanese law mandates dismissal of the foreign insolvency whenever a local case is filed, even if the local case is filed after the foreign case has been recognised. The Japanese law does provide an exception to this rule for foreign "main" proceedings, but even in this case it requires that the court avoid a concurrent situation by dismissing the local proceeding.'

[51] Yamamoto, New Japanese Legislation on Cross-Border Insolvency, 89–90. Yamamoto, however, notes that Japanese law does not refuse such cooperation, that Japanese courts have the inherent powers to cooperate with foreign courts if such cooperation is considered necessary and that the internationalisation of the Japanese judicial system 'will in future make this type of cooperation much easier than today'. See also S. Takahashi, The Reality of the Japanese Legal System for Cross-Border Insolvency – Driven by Fear of Universalism, available at www.iiiglobal.org/sites/default/files/realityofthejapanese legalsystemforcrossborderinsolvencydrivenbyfearofuniversalism.pdf. Takahashi (p. 56) suggests that '[s]ince Japan is a civil law country, there might be a number of obstacles and resistance to introducing flexible and broad discretionary cross-border cooperation between Japanese courts and foreign courts'.

[52] See Ian Fletcher, *Insolvency in Private International Law: Supplement to Second Edition* (Oxford: Oxford University Press, 2007), 100. The US, on the other hand, adopted the text as written in the Model Law.

The influence of judicial practice is also evident in the reluctance in Japan to legislate for automatic effects, such as the automatic stay that arises upon the recognition of foreign main proceedings under Article 20(1) of the Model Law.[53] Interestingly, Yamamoto has attributed the refusal of the Japanese law to accept an automatic stay to the concern that courts would be excessively cautious in recognising foreign proceedings as a result of the automatic effect of recognition:

> New Japanese law does not provide automatic effects of recognition. That was a consequence of careful consideration after which we finally made a decision to refuse automatic effects upon the following grounds. The most important reason for our decision is that if recognition of a foreign proceeding accompanied several automatic effects, the recognizing court would be so prudent in deciding on recognition that simple and rapid recognition process requested by the model law would become very difficult. Differently from the convention or the treaty, it is inevitable for the local law of an individual State to deal with every sort of foreign proceeding. Accordingly, the recognizing court which must consider the interests of local creditors would judge very carefully whether conditions for recognition are so fulfilled as to recognize automatic effects on recognition. This prudence and delay of recognition process will be too much contrary to the purpose of the model law. In consequence, we decided not to introduce automatic effects of recognition into our law.[54]

The reluctance in Japan to confer discretionary power on courts in relation to areas such as cooperation and communications with foreign courts is also reflected in its adoption of the public policy ground for refusing recognition and assistance. Article 6 of the Model Law provides as follows:

Article 6
Public Policy Exception
Nothing in the present Law prevents the court from refusing to take an action governed by the present Law if the action would be manifestly contrary to the public policy of this State.

The corresponding provision under the Japanese legislation[55] provides that the court 'shall' dismiss a petition for recognition of foreign insolvency proceedings in

---

[53] Article 20(1) of the Model Law provides as follows: 'Upon recognition of a foreign proceeding that is a foreign main proceeding, (a) Commencement or continuation of individual actions or individual proceedings concerning the debtor's assets, right, obligations or liabilities is stayed; (b) Execution against the debtor's assets is stayed; (c) The right to transfer, encumber or otherwise dispose of any assets of the debtor is suspended.'

[54] Yamamoto, New Japanese Legislation on Cross-Border Insolvency, 83. Yamamoto goes on to say that despite the refusal of automatic effects, 'these systems as a whole will show our favourable attitude to international cooperation in the case of cross-border insolvency'. See also Barbara Pogacar, above n. 50, p. 51: 'So far all enacting states provide for a more or less extensive relief upon recognition. In Japan, however, the relief upon recognition is not automatic but left to the discretion of the court.'

[55] Japanese Act, Art. 21.

circumstances that are contrary to public policy in Japan, thus removing any discretion on the part of the court to determine whether any action should be refused in the circumstances. In addition, as is the case with some other jurisdictions, the word 'manifestly' has been removed from before 'contrary to public policy'.[56]

The above discussion about courts and judicial practice, particularly as it relates to Japan, highlights the extent to which differences in legal institutions and traditions affect: (1) the design of the legislation adopting the Model Law; and (2) the relative dependence by courts on the text of that legislation, including their ability to exercise discretion and flexibility in the determination of legal questions.

4.2 Policy Choices in the Adoption and Interpretation of Concepts and Terminology

This factor concerns differences in the ways in which concepts in the Model Law are incorporated into, and interpreted under, domestic law. This often involves policy choices and preferences in relation to terminology and language. Some of these choices are contemplated in the Model Law itself through drafting notes and alternative text. Other choices are made unilaterally by the enacting State. An overview of selected examples appears as follows.

(a) Statutory Exceptions

A threshold policy choice that States face when adopting the Model Law is whether certain entities should be excluded from its scope of application. This choice is expressly recognised by the Model Law in Article 1(2), which makes provision for the exclusion of 'entities, such as banks or insurance companies, that are subject to a special insolvency regime'. Many States have adopted this exclusion, including the UK, Australia and Singapore.[57]

(b) The Public Policy Exception

In relation to Article 6 of the Model Law, as extracted previously, the UNCITRAL Guide provides that the use of the word 'manifestly' as a qualifier of the expression

---

[56] See Section 4.2(b) for a further discussion of the public policy exception.
[57] Commenting on the legislation in Australia, McCormack and Hargovan, Australian and the International Insolvency Paradigm, 410, note that financial institutions 'invariably conduct business overseas and have as much, if not, greater, need for international cooperation in facilitating restructuring and liquidation' and argue that the exclusions should be reviewed, particularly in view of the number of cases under the Cross-Border Insolvency Act that have involved financial institutions. In the UK, the Explanatory Memorandum to the Cross-Border Insolvency Regulations noted that a number of respondents to the consultation had 'asked that [credit institutions and insurance companies] be included' and recognised the benefits in doing so. However, the Explanatory Memorandum noted that it had been decided not to include these entities in the Model Law for the time being, but their inclusion would be considered 'as soon as is practicable and possible.'

'public policy' 'is to emphasize that public policy exceptions should be interpreted restrictively and that article 6 is only intended to be invoked under exceptional circumstances concerning matters of fundamental importance for the enacting State'.[58]

In Japan, South Korea and Singapore, the legislation adopting the Model Law removed the word 'manifestly' from before the expression 'contrary to public policy'. Although recognising the inconsistency between the Japanese legislation and the Model Law in this regard, Yamamoto notes that the content of public policy is ambiguous anyway and expresses the hope that 'the Japanese court will not stick to trivial differences between an insolvency proceeding of Japan and that of a foreign State and that it will show its generosity in international aspects'.[59]

In a recent case in Singapore, the High Court considered the omission of the word 'manifestly' in the Singapore legislation and surmised that the omission was deliberate. Aedit Abdullah J stated the position as follows:

> What flows from the omission being deliberate is that the standard of exclusion on public policy grounds in Singapore is lower than that in jurisdictions where the Model Law has been enacted unmodified. That is, in Singapore, recognition may be denied on public policy grounds though such recognition may not be manifestly contrary to public policy. Whether this will lead to a significant divergence from other jurisdictions remains to be seen. I have noted that the commentaries to Article 6 of the Model Law suggest that Article 6, as originally worded, would be taken to exclude purely domestic public policy concerns (see Guide to Enactment of the UNCITRAL Model Law on Cross-Border Insolvency, UN Doc A/CN.9/442) If this were indeed so, then Singapore's version of Article 6 may not lead to the same conclusion.[60]

In Vanuatu, the word 'manifestly' has been replaced with 'clearly', highlighting the extent to which states have their own preferences about the terminology that is used to express certain concepts.[61]

---

[58] UNCITRAL Guide, para. 104.

[59] Yamamoto, New Japanese Legislation on Cross-Border Insolvency, 78. For a discussion about other jurisdictions that have removed the word 'manifestly', see S. Chandra Mohan, Cross-Border Insolvency Problems: Is the UNCITRAL Model Law the Answer? (2012) 21(3) *International Insolvency Review* 199, 211–212.

[60] Re: Zetta Jet Pte Ltd and others [2018] SGHC 16, para. 23. In this case, the Court held that recognition of a trustee under Chapter 7 proceedings in the US should be refused on public policy grounds for the reason that a Singapore injunction had been obtained to prohibit proceedings in the US and, accordingly, recognition would undermine the administration of justice in Singapore. Instead, in an approach that Aedit Abdullah J believed to be consonant with the promotion of uniformity under Article 8 of the Model Law, the judge granted limited recognition to the Chapter 7 Trustee for the purposes of applying to set aside or appeal the Singapore injunction. I am indebted to Professor Wan Wai Yee of Singapore Management University for drawing this case to my attention.

[61] Another interesting example of a preference for alternative terminology arises in the context of Art. 21(2) of the Model Law, which provides that upon recognition of a foreign proceeding, the court may entrust the distribution of all or part of the debtor's assets located in the enacting state to the foreign representative or another person designated by the court 'provided that the court is satisfied that the

(c) Exclusion of Foreign Tax Claims

Another policy choice – one that is expressly recognised by the Model Law – relates to Article 13(2) of the Model Law, which provides that the claims of foreign creditors should not be ranked lower than general non-preference claims, except to the extent that an equivalent local claim would have a lower rank. The Model Law provides that an enacting State may consider alternative wording that excludes foreign tax and social security claims from the requirement that foreign claims should not be ranked lower than general non-preference claims. Australia has opted for the alternative wording, as has New Zealand[62] and Singapore.[63] The UK Cross-Border Insolvency Regulations, on the other hand, adopt the original text, with the proviso that a foreign tax or social security claim may be challenged 'on the ground that it is in whole or in part a penalty' or 'on any other ground that a claim might be rejected in a proceeding under British insolvency law'.[64]

(d) The Concept of the Centre of Main Interest

The concept of the centre of main interest (COMI) is relevant to a determination of a 'foreign main proceeding', recognition of which triggers the automatic stay under Article 20 of the Model Law.[65] Article 16(3) of the Model Law provides as follows: 'In the absence of proof to the contrary, the debtor's registered office, or habitual

---

interests of creditors in [the relevant state] are adequately protected'. As noted by McCormack and Hargovan, Australia and the International Insolvency Paradigm, 412, Chapter 15 of the US Bankruptcy Code replaces the words 'adequately protected' with 'sufficiently protected', apparently because of the need 'to avoid confusion with a very specialised legal term in US bankruptcy law and not necessarily with an intention to bring about a different substantive result'. Terminology may also have an impact on the adoption of the Model Law on Secured Transactions, which was published by UNCITRAL in October 2016 and aims to 'help states, particularly those with developing and transitional economies, reform and modernise their secured transactions law so as to increase access to, and reduced the cost of, credit and thus to stimulate international trade'. As noted by Kohn and Morse, some of the terminology used by the Model Law on Secured Transactions may not be familiar to US readers: 'The term "security right" is used instead of "security interest" and the term "movables" is used to refer to "personal property." In addition, "secured creditor" is used instead of "secured party," "grantor" is used instead of "debtor," "debtor of the receivable" is used in place of "account debtor," "creation" of a security interest replaces "attachment," "effectiveness against third parties" is used instead of "perfection" and "acquisition security rights" replaces "purchase-money security interests."'. See R. M. Kohn and D. W. Morse, UNCITRAL: The Model Law on Secured Transactions, *The Secured Lender*, November 2016.

[62] Insolvency (Cross-Border) Act 2006, Schedule 1, Art. 13(2).
[63] Companies (Amendment) Act 2017, Fourteenth Schedule, Art. 13(2).
[64] Cross-Border Insolvency Regulations, Art. 13(3). In this regard, McCormack and Hargovan, Australia and the International Insolvency Paradigm, 410, note that 'Australia led the way over the UK with the abolition of the preferential status of tax claims, yet lags behind the UK with the refusal to recognise that foreign tax claims can be proved on a non-preferential basis as ordinary, unsecured claims. The time has come for Australia to move beyond the confines of narrow nationalism and to recognise that other countries have a legitimate interest in collecting taxes owing to them.'
[65] See n. 26 above.

residence in the case of an individual, is presumed to be the centre of the debtor's main interest.'

The concept of COMI was taken from the Convention on Insolvency Proceedings of the European Union 'for reasons of consistency'.[66] Although this convention was never ratified, the concept found its way into the European Council (EC) Regulation No. 1346/2000 of 29 May 2000 on insolvency proceedings. The UNCITRAL Guide notes that the concept 'corresponds to the formulation in article 3 of the EC Regulation ... thus building on the emerging harmonization as regards the notion of a "main" proceeding'.[67]

Apart from Article 16(3) as referred to above, the Model Law does not define 'centre of main interest'.[68] Instead, the concept of the centre of main interest is left to be determined by the courts in the enacting State.[69] This is an example of a concept in a Model Law that relies on court interpretations and will inevitably entail a degree of divergence between the enacting States.[70] In the case of Japan, the concept of the debtor's 'principal business office' replaces the 'centre of main interest' and is relevant only for the purpose of coordinating concurrent proceedings and not for the purpose of triggering the automatic stay.[71] The 'debtor's principal business office' is not defined under the Japanese legislation and is instead left to the courts to determine based on various factors, including the location of the debtor's registered office or headquarters.[72] Despite the different terminology and purpose, however, Yamamoto has suggested that the Japanese concept of the 'principal business office' 'coincides with the definition of the model law'.[73]

(e) Actions to Avoid Acts Detrimental to Creditors

Article 23 of the Model Law provides that upon recognition of a foreign proceeding, the foreign representative has the standing to initiate actions to avoid or otherwise

---

[66] UNCITRAL, UNCITRAL Model Law on Cross-Border Insolvency: The Judicial Perspective (2013), available at www.uncitral.org/pdf/english/texts/insolven/Judicial-Perspective-2013-e.pdf, para. 94.

[67] UNCITRAL Guide, para. 81.

[68] According to UNCITRAL, UNCITRAL Model Law on Cross-Border Insolvency, 'a deliberate decision was taken not to define "centre of main interests"'.

[69] As noted by UNCITRAL, UNCITRAL Model Law on Cross-Border Insolvency, a 'number of subtle differences in approach have emerged' between courts in enacting jurisdictions in terms of the factors relevant to rebutting the presumption in Article 16 and that 'courts in some jurisdictions might seek evidence of a greater quality or quantity to rebut the presumption than is the case in other States'.

[70] The challenges of determining COMI, and the potential need to rebut the presumption that it is the debtor's registered office, are reflected in case law. See, for example, the decision of Jagot J of the Federal Court of Australia in *Young, Jr, in the matter of Buccaneer Energy Limited v. Buccaneer Energy Limited* [2014] FCA 711, paras. 5–7. Similar challenges were acknowledged in *Re: Zetta Jet Pte Ltd and others* [2018] SGHC 16, paras. 16–20.

[71] See L. C. Ho, *Cross-Border Insolvency: Principles and Practice* (London: Sweet & Maxwell, 2016), p. 144; Yamamoto, New Japanese Legislation on Cross-Border Insolvency, 71.

[72] Yamamoto, New Japanese Legislation on Cross-Border Insolvency, 71.

[73] Yamamoto, New Japanese Legislation on Cross-Border Insolvency, 72.

render ineffective acts detrimental to creditors that are available in the recognising State to a person or body administering a reorganisation or liquidation.

Once again, Japan is an outlier in this regard. Ho notes that in Japan '[t]he drafters of the Recognition Law had hot and lengthy discussion on this issue and finally came to the decision "to remain completely silent about the issue" (even silent about standing)'.[74] Yamamoto suggests that the silence was due to several reasons, including the complexity of the conflict of laws issues that arise if a foreign representative is given standing to initiate such actions and the possibility that the existing law of civil procedure already provides a basis for this.[75] The provision was also deleted from the legislation in South Korea.[76]

(f) Reciprocity

Finally, reference could be made to the practice of some jurisdictions to include a reciprocity requirement in their laws adopting the Model Law, under which recognition and assistance will only be granted to insolvency proceedings in foreign states that have also adopted the Model Law.[77]

4.3 The Existing Legislative Architecture

This factor relates to differences between enacting States in terms of the extent to which areas covered by the Model Law are governed by separate laws and are therefore either superfluous or duplicative when viewed in the context of the Model Law.[78] UNCITRAL has noted that by adopting legislation based on the Model Law, States will need to amend their laws relating to insolvency 'in order to

---

[74] L. C. Ho, Cross-Border Insolvency, 146, who notes that under the Model Law the foreign representative is given full standing under the same conditions as domestic creditors.

[75] Yamamoto, New Japanese Legislation on Cross-Border Insolvency, 88–89.

[76] L. C. Ho, Cross-Border Insolvency, 250, notes that the reason for the deletion in the South Korean legislation is that 'the law on transaction avoidance is complicated and remains unsettled in South Korea'.

[77] Barbara Pogacar, The 1997 UNCITRAL Model Law, 50, notes that although the Model Law does not impose a reciprocity requirement, 'a number of states have included a reciprocity clause into their international insolvency law, such as Mexico and Romania'. The requirement of reciprocity was considered and rejected by the Singapore Insolvency Law Review Committee. See further below.

[78] It is also relevant to note that in some jurisdictions, such as the UK and Australia, there are multiple gateways for granting recognition and assistance to foreign insolvency proceedings, either pursuant to statute or the common law. In the US, however, Chapter 15 of the US Bankruptcy Code constitutes the sole gateway for such recognition and assistance. See G. McCormack, US Exceptionalism and UK Localism?, 142, who argues against such multiple gateways on the basis that 'the procedures overlap in a complex and confusing way, with cases potentially falling through gaps in the law and important provisions being overlooked'. The contrary view is that there is utility in having multiple gateways insofar as 'if there are gaps in the Model Law, the court can fall back on other statutory provisions' and that conflicts in Australia are avoided by having the Model Law prevail in the event of an inconsistency with the other legislation. See UNCITRAL, 11th Multinational Judicial Colloquium (21–22 March 2015, San Francisco), www.uncitral.org/pdf/english/news/EleventhJC.pdf, where it was

meet internationally recognized standards'.[79] Some States have achieved this through including a general provision in the enacting legislation concerning interaction with other legislation. For example, cl. 3(1) of the UK Cross-Border Insolvency Regulations provides that 'British insolvency law (as defined in article 2 of the UNCITRAL Model Law as set out in Schedule 1 to these Regulations) and Part 3 of the Insolvency Act 1986 shall apply with such modifications as the context requires for the purpose of giving effect to the provisions of these Regulations' and that the Regulations will prevail in the case of any conflict.[80] The equivalent provision in the Australian legislation provides that the Model Law (as adopted by the Cross-Border Insolvency Act) prevails over any inconsistency with the Bankruptcy Act 1966 and the Corporations Act 2001.[81]

On the other hand, the experience of some jurisdictions such as Japan demonstrates that instead of amending their laws to accommodate the international standards as embodied in the Model Law, the Model Law itself is modified in order to accommodate the existing laws on insolvency and to ensure that the enacting legislation operates on a stand-alone basis (i.e. without the need to consider how it might interact with other insolvency law and the associated requirement for the exercise of judicial discretion that this might entail).[82] Further, provisions of the Model Law are sometimes deleted to avoid duplication with the provisions of other legislation in the enacting State. Examples of this can be found in the legislation in both Japan and Korea.[83]

There are various reasons that might influence the approach adopted by a jurisdiction in this regard, including courts and judicial practice as outlined in Section 4.1 above. In civil law jurisdictions, for example, it is likely that coherence and consistency in legislation and codes will be preferred over the granting of discretion to courts to interpret or read down legislative provisions so that they are consistent with the Model Law.

---

also noted that '[o]ne consequence of the Australian approach is that while foreigners might know about the Model Law, they might be unaware of the possibilities provided by the other options'.

[79] UNCITRAL Guide, 19, para. 2.
[80] A similar position exists under s. 354C of the Singapore Act.
[81] Cross-Border Insolvency Act 2008, ss. 21–22.
[82] See S. Tagaki, Japanese Cross-Border Insolvency Law and Comments on US Chapter 15, paper delivered at the IBA Conference, SIRC Meeting, 18 September 2006, available at www.iiiglobal.org/component/jdownloads/finish/667/5809.html: 'The provisions of the LRAF [i.e. the Japanese Act] are not exactly the same as the Model Law in that they amend some of the provisions included in the Model Law, wherever necessary, to be compatible with the entire Japanese legal systems. However, I believe that the LRAF adopts the same concepts as the Model Law in substance so that the provisions of the LRAF are not contradictory to those of the Model Law. Rather, some provisions in the LRAF are more open to foreign insolvency proceedings than the Model Law.'
[83] For Japanese examples, see Look Chan Ho, Cross-Border Insolvency, 142 (Arts. 10, 11 and 12 of the Model Law), 144 (Art. 16(1) of the Model Law) and 146 (Arts. 26 and 27 of the Model Law); Takahashi, Reality of the Japanese Legal System, 43–44 (Art. 24 of the Model Law). For Korean examples, see L. C. Ho, Cross-Border Insolvency, 257 (Art. 13 of the Model Law).

4.4 The Desire to Align with Similar Jurisdictions or with an 'Enhanced Version' of the Model Law

This factor concerns the desire on the part of enacting States to align with other jurisdictions, either as a result of similarities in their legal systems or to reflect international practice, as implemented in major financial centres such as the UK and the US, even if this involves supplementing or expanding the Model Law to create an 'enhanced version' of the Model Law. As noted previously, one of the objectives of the drafters of the UK Cross-Border Insolvency Regulations was 'to provide a guide for other States who are considering enacting the law'.[84] One might refer to this as a form of gold-plating, a phenomenon that has also occurred in the area of financial regulation, such as the implementation of the Basel standards on capital adequacy.[85] The effect of this phenomenon is that after a model law is adopted by major financial centres such as the UK and the US, the legislation enacted in those states then becomes the gold standard for other jurisdictions and, in effect, a new version – the enhanced version – of the model law is created. This is an example of the influence of transnational interest as noted by Bathurst CJ in the quote extracted previously.

The legislation in Singapore is a good example of this type of divergence from the original text of the Model Law as it borrows from both the UK experience and the US experience. The provisions on cross-border insolvency are part of a broader package of reforms that were introduced to strengthen Singapore as a regional restructuring hub and to make Singapore's restructuring and insolvency procedures 'more accessible for foreign companies'[86] by making it easier for foreign companies to file for a scheme of arrangement and judicial management.

Singapore adopted the Model Law by inserting a new Division 6 – Adoption of the UNCITRAL Model Law on Cross-Border Insolvency into the Companies Act. Similar to the UK Regulations,[87] s. 354B(2) of the legislation provides as follows:

> In the interpretation of any provision of the Tenth Schedule, the following documents are relevant documents for the purposes of section 9A(3)(f) of the Interpretation Act (Cap. 1):

---

[84] See the text accompanying n. 41 above.
[85] For a discussion about gold-plating or 'over-compliance' in the area of the Basel standards, see A. Walter, The Political Economy of Post-Crisis Regulatory Response: Why Does 'Over-Compliance Vary?, unpublished manuscript, University of Melbourne, 2014, available at www.systemicrisk.ac.uk/sites/default/files/media/Walter-The%20political%20economy%20of%20post-crisis%20regulatory%20response%20(2).pdf.
[86] P. Apathy and E. Chua, Singapore Unveils Major Debt Restructuring Law Reforms, Herbert Smith Freehills Legal Briefings, 16 November 2016. According to this source, the reforms are 'consistent with some of the key recommendations arising from the recent Insolvency Service review in the United Kingdom' and reflect 'the tide of thinking regarding global restructuring law and the recognition in various jurisdictions that reform is necessary and desirable to stay globally competitive and to deliver better outcomes for distressed companies'.
[87] UK Cross-Border Insolvency Regulations, s. 2(2).

(a) any documents relating to the Model Law that is issued by, or that forms part of the record on the preparation of the Model Law maintained by, the United Nations Commission on International Trade Law and its working group for the preparation of the Model Law; and

(b) the Guide to Enactment of the UNCITRAL Model Law on Cross-Border Insolvency (UN document A/CN.9/442).

As noted previously, the legislation in Singapore modifies and supplements the UNCITRAL Model Law, borrowing significantly from the UK Cross-Border Insolvency Regulations 2006. Certain provisions in the legislation also borrow from the US Bankruptcy Code. Provisions that have been adapted from these two jurisdictions include the following:

1) Article 1(3), which has been adapted from the UK regulations and provides that the Court 'must not grant any relief, or modify any relief already granted, or provide any co-operation or coordination, under or by virtue of any of the provisions of this law if and to the extent that such relief or modified relief or cooperation or coordination would, in the case of a proceeding under Singapore insolvency law, be prohibited under or by virtue of [specified Singapore legislation]'.

2) Article 2, which contains definitions that have been adapted from both the UK Regulations (Article 2(a)-(c), (j), (l) and (m)) and also the US Bankruptcy Code (Article 2(d) and (h)).

3) Article 4(2), which has been adapted from the UK Regulations and provides that the High Court in Singapore has jurisdiction in relation to the functions mentioned in the Model Law if the debtor 'is or has been carrying on business' in Singapore, or 'has property situated in Singapore' or 'the Court considers for any other reason that it is the appropriate forum to consider the question or provide the assistance requested'.

4) Article 14(2), which has been adapted from the UK Regulations and refines the requirements for notification to be given to foreign creditors of a proceeding under Singapore insolvency law.

5) Articles 15(3) and (4), which have been adapted from the UK Regulations and relate to the content requirements of applications for recognition, including the requirement to provide an English translation of documents relating to the application.

6) Article 20(3), which has been adapted from the UK Regulations and detail the types of individual action that are unaffected by the automatic stay in Article 20(1).[88]

7) Articles 23(2)-(4) and (6)-(9), which have been adapted from the UK Regulations and deal with the circumstances in which a foreign representative may take action to avoid acts detrimental to creditors.[89]

---

[88] See also Arts. 20(4) and (6).
[89] See the discussion in section 4.2(e).

3 *Convergence, Divergence and Diversity in Financial Law* 57

Provisions that have been inserted or modified to adapt the Model Law specifically for application in Singapore, and which are either absent in the UK Regulations or diverge from the UK Regulations, include the following:

1) Article 1, sub-articles (4)–(6), which provide that the Model Law does not affect the operation of specified Singapore legislation[90] and represent an example of a modification or qualification to the Model Law to accommodate or preserve existing legislation.
2) Article 2(k)(iii), which includes the common law of Singapore in the definition of 'Singapore insolvency law', thus preserving the application of the common law of Singapore as it relates to recognising and providing assistance to foreign insolvency proceedings.[91]
3) Article 6, which diverges from the UK Regulations in removing the word 'manifestly' from the phrase 'contrary to the public policy of Singapore'. As discussed above, the removal of the word 'manifestly' lowers the public policy standard that must be met before a Court can refuse to take any action governed by the Model Law and may reflect a couple of considerations. First, in its 2013 Report, the Singapore Insolvency Law Review Committee reached a tentative conclusion that Singapore should not adopt a 'reciprocity' requirement (namely, that other jurisdictions must have adopted the Model Law in order to take advantage of its provisions under Singapore law). The removal of 'manifestly' may have been motivated by a desire to ensure equality of treatment for local creditors when granting specific relief.[92] Secondly, it may reflect regional developments and a desire to achieve consistency with other jurisdictions such as Japan and South Korea.

5 THE BENEFITS OF DIVERSITY

What does the experience of the Model Laws reveal about convergence? First, a truism: so long as there are different legal traditions and legal systems, there will always be divergence, whether in relation to legal institutions, policy

---

[90] Sub-article (5), for example, preserves the operation of ss. 46 and 47 of the Land Titles Act (Singapore), which provide that the estate of a registered proprietor of land is paramount (i.e. indefeasible), except in the case of fraud.
[91] The inherent power of courts in common law jurisdictions to recognise and provide assistance to foreign insolvency proceedings has been preserved in jurisdictions such as the UK and Australia, but not in the US where Chapter 15 of the Bankruptcy Code is the sole gateway for recognising and providing assistance to foreign insolvency proceedings. For a discussion of the inherent power, including its exercise in Singapore and Hong Kong, see A. Godwin, T. Howse and I. Ramsay, The Inherent Power of Common Law Courts to Provide Assistance in Cross-Border Insolvencies: From Comity to Complexity, (2017) 26(5) *International Insolvency Review* 5.
[92] See Report of the Insolvency Law Review Committee, Final Report 2013, available at www.mlaw.gov.sg/content/dam/minlaw/corp/News/Revised%20Report%20of%20the%20Insolvency%20Law%20Review%20Committee.pdf, paragraphs [33] and [35].

choices, the existing legislative architecture or the desire to align with an 'enhanced version' of the Model Law. Secondly, convergence needs to recognise the need for divergence, as reflected in the ways in which the Model Law has been adopted and modified. As suggested in Section 2, the Model Law is a good example of convergence in outcomes without full convergence or uniformity in the text of laws. Divergence does not need to be viewed as suboptimal or a negative element and, indeed, can be seen as healthy diversity – if you like, pluralism or multiculturalism in the law.[93] Thirdly, it is important to understand the reasons for divergence and the importance of achieving convergence in outcomes as much as convergence in the text of law. For this purpose, it must be acknowledged that convergence in outcomes can often be achieved through divergence in process or approach.

Diversity, as a positive element in legal convergence, reflects the need for states to make their own policy choices when adopting model laws and also the differences between states in terms of language and culture.[94] As Gotti has noted, 'even when cultural differences are not so evident, it is impossible to guarantee a perfectly homogeneous process, as the various legal patterns of the countries involved will re-emerge in some of the procedures described or in a few of the principles set out'.[95] Even where there is significant divergence from the original text of the Model Law, as we have seen in the case of Japan, it does not necessarily follow that this will compromise convergence in outcomes.[96] Indeed, some have argued that the modifications made by jurisdictions such as Japan exceed the standards in the Model Law.[97]

Diversity can also allow the flexibility that is required to facilitate the adoption of model laws and to allow model laws to evolve and be enhanced to suit local conditions, as we have seen in the case of the UK and Singapore, where there

---

[93] Even with formal or hard convergence, some provision should be made for flexibility.
[94] For a discussion about the impact of these differences in the context of the UNCITRAL Model Law on International Commercial Arbitration by way of comparison, see M. Gotti, Adopting and Adapting an International Model Law in a Multilingual and Multicultural Context [2014] *Semiotica* 201; A. Netzer, Incorporation of the UNCITRAL Model Law on International Commercial Arbitration in the Russian Federation (2010) 1 *Yearbook on International Arbitration* 29.
[95] Gotti, Adopting and Adapting an International Model Law, 49.
[96] Similar divergence has been seen in the adoption of the UNCITRAL Model Law on International Commercial Arbitration by the Canadian jurisdictions. As noted by H. C. Alvarez, N. Kaplan and D. W. Rivkin, *Model Law Decisions: Cases Applying the UNCITRAL Model Law on International Commercial Arbitration (1985–2001)* (New York: Kluwer Law International, 2003), p. 3: 'All the Canadian jurisdictions adopting the Model Law, except for BC [British Columbia] and Quebec, have done so by way of a short implementing statute which appends the Model Law as a schedule. BC has incorporated the text of the Model Law into a full statute in local legislative form while maintaining the same structure and section numbers of the Model Law. Quebec has not reproduced the Model Law nor has it adopted it into Quebec law itself. While the amendments Quebec has made to its Code of Civil Procedure and Civil Code essentially implement the Model Law, they do not use the structure nor, in a number of instances, the language of the Model Law.'
[97] See Tagaki, Japanese Cross-Border Insolvency Law and US Chapter 15, above n. 82.

3 *Convergence, Divergence and Diversity in Financial Law* 59

have been efforts to enhance the Model Law. Writing in relation to the US Uniform Commercial Code (UCC), Hisert has argued that even if one accepts a presumption in favour of uniformity, 'the desire for uniformity should not stultify a carefully considered experiment', and that the ability to experiment with different solutions 'has proven to be one of the greatest strengths of the UCC as compared to federal legislation', permitting the UCC 'to be a living and growing body of law'.[98] In the same way, it is reasonable to expect that the Model Law should be allowed to evolve and strengthen over time and that a balance should be struck between uniformity and flexibility.

6 IS THERE A CASE FOR REGIONAL CONVERGENCE IN THE ASIA PACIFIC?

Irrespective of the degree of convergence in relation to law, convergence between countries in the Asia Pacific region will inevitably occur in the area of market practice, which may differ from market practice in other regions. An example of regional convergence in market practice in the context of soft law is the standard loan documentation produced by the Asia Pacific Loan Market Association (APLMA), which includes provisions that reflect regional practice in areas such as terminology and procedures.[99] This might be referred to as a type of operational convergence, as distinct from legal convergence.

There is certainly a case for pursuing convergence initiatives on a regional basis in terms of discussing, and increasing the awareness of, the benefits and mechanisms of convergence in regional fora such as the Association of Southeast Asian Nations (ASEAN) and the South Asian Association for Regional Cooperation (SAARC).[100] There is also a case for pursuing regional convergence in some areas of substantive law.[101] By contrast, the experience of the

---

[98] G. A. Hisert, Uniform Commercial Code: Does One Size Fit All? (1995) 28 *Loyola of Los Angeles Law Review* 219. Hisert, 231 ff, argues that 'the UCC, by creating the ability to balance the competing interests of uniformity and local flexibility, maintains a strong substantive advantage over encroaching federal legislation'. Further, '[s]o long as nonuniform variations are carefully considered and maintained within appropriate bounds, it is possible to achieve most of the advantages of uniformity without creating rigidity'.

[99] According to APLMA's website, 'APLMA advocates best practices in the syndicated loan market, promulgates standard loan documentation and seeks to promote the syndicated loan as one of the key debt products available to borrowers across the region'. Its primary objectives include '[monitoring] legislative, regulatory and market changes for impact on the syndicated loan market'. See www.aplma.com/en/about-us.

[100] The conference that inspired this publication is a good example of pursuing convergence initiatives on a regional basis.

[101] An example of this is the Asia Business Law Institute (ABLI), which 'initiates, conducts and facilitates research and produces authoritative texts with a view to providing practical guidance in the field of Asian legal development and promoting the convergence of Asian business laws'. See http://abli.asia/ABOUT-US/Introduction. Another example is the efforts to promote harmonisation of contract law in Asia and to formulate Principles of Asian Contract Law along similar lines to the Principles of

UNCITRAL Model Law on Cross-Border Insolvency suggests that regional convergence is less relevant in this area as a result of the factors behind divergence as outlined in this chapter. Indeed, in place of a 'regional' form of convergence, we are perhaps more likely to see sub-regional convergence between jurisdictional groups that share similar legal traditions and legal systems, such as Japan-Korea and Australia–New Zealand. Accordingly, it is difficult to argue the case for achieving a 'regional' form of convergence in this area. The difficulties are compounded by the fact that demarcating the boundaries of the Asia Pacific region are challenging as compared with other regions such as Europe (and the EU) or Africa (and OHADA). Singapore's proposed adoption of the UNCITRAL Model Law, and the global convergence that this represents, is a case in point.

The experience of the Model Law supports the comment by Bathurst CJ that it is 'undesirable to strive for uniformity in all areas of the law' and also the comment by Menon CJ that convergence must take account of the 'undulating legal terrain that results from differences in the national legal systems'. This chapter has argued that in addition to considering the different mechanisms of convergence, it is important to consider the different objects of convergence as this will inform the question as to which mechanism might be the most appropriate and the degree of divergence that might be tolerated. For example, if the object is convergence in the text of laws and regulations, model laws will have a role to play. If it is convergence in the underlying concepts and philosophies, principles and standards might be more appropriate. Convergence in one respect does not necessarily lead to convergence in other respects. In addition, in a regional sense, it may be more important to understand the factors behind *divergence* than to try to achieve regional convergence, at least insofar as it implies uniformity. This is because the diversity between legal systems in terms of legal origins, traditions and the political and institutional context is significant and tends to overwhelm the factors that might promote convergence on a regional basis. In addition, as this chapter has shown, legal convergence between jurisdictions in the Asia Pacific tends not to occur along regional lines. At the same time, an understanding of the factors behind divergence will help identify the potential for convergence and the particular form that convergence might take.

Finally, it is important to consider how we conceive of convergence and whether we should look at it as uniformity or, instead, as a process that accommodates diversity and a pluralism of approaches and ultimately achieves convergence in outcomes. In a regional sense, the second approach is likely to prove more effective. In line with Menon CJ's comments at the beginning of this chapter,

---

European Contract Law. See M. Chen-Wishart, A. Loke and B. Ong (eds.), *Studies in the Contract Laws of Asia I – Remedies for Breach of Contract* (Oxford: Oxford University Press, 2016), pp. 1–2.

uniformity without due regard to the idiosyncrasies of national legal systems is likely to produce superficially uniform laws and may even prove counter-productive. Encouragingly, the experience in the area of financial law suggests that although full convergence in law may be unrealistic, convergence in outcomes is possible and is well underway.

4

The New York Convention and the UNCITRAL Model Law on International Commercial Arbitration: Existing Models for Legal Convergence in Asia?

Michael Hwang

1 A BRIEF HISTORICAL BACKGROUND OF THE NEW YORK CONVENTION AND THE UNCITRAL MODEL LAW ON INTERNATIONAL COMMERCIAL ARBITRATION

Globalisation has seen an evolution in the business world, such that 'international arbitration does not stay within national borders'.[1] A number of questions arise when disputes occur between corporations in two different countries to be settled by arbitration in a third country. First, if a dispute arises, and one of the parties refuses to arbitrate, where is such an arbitration agreement to be enforced? Second, which court will have such jurisdiction? Third, if there is an arbitration that leads to an award of damages and costs, how is that award to be enforced against the losing party if the losing party refuses to voluntarily implement the award? Fourth, again, which court has such jurisdiction?

It was in these circumstances that various international rules, treaties, and conventions were enacted. The position at common law already allowed (and continues to allow) for the recognition by each common law court of any foreign arbitral award, on the basis that the action to enforce the award is an action on the award and not on the contract to which the award gives effect, nor on a foreign judgment.[2] In spite of this position at common law, these international rules, treaties, and conventions serve a different purpose, 'linking national laws together and providing ... a system of worldwide enforcement, both of arbitration agreements and of arbitral awards'.[3]

Out of these international rules, treaties, and conventions, the 1958 Convention on the Recognition and Enforcement of Foreign Arbitral Awards (New York Convention) and the 1985 United Nations Commission on International Trade Law Model Law on International Commercial Arbitration (with amendments as

---

[1] N. Blackaby and C. Partasides QC, with A. Redfern and M. Hunter, *Redfern and Hunter on International Arbitration*, Student Edition, 6th ed. (Oxford: Oxford University Press, 2015).
[2] J. Fawcett, J. M. Carruthers, and Sir P. North, *Cheshire, North & Fawcett: Private International Law*, 14th ed. (Oxford: Oxford University Press, 2008), Chapter 17, pp. 652–653. For the award to be enforceable, it must, like a foreign judgment, be final and conclusive.
[3] *Redfern and Hunter*, p. 6.

adopted in 2006; UNCITRAL Model Law) are widely recognised as the 'landmarks' of international arbitration.[4]

This essay will be divided into two parts. First, we will discuss the success of the New York Convention which has been adopted by 156 countries. Second, we will look at the success of the UNCITRAL Model Law which has been adopted by 83 States in 116 jurisdictions at the time of writing.[5]

2 SUCCESS OF THE NEW YORK CONVENTION

The New York Convention replaced the 1927 Geneva Convention and the 1923 Geneva Protocol,[6] and is said to constitute a substantial improvement from the Geneva Convention and Geneva Protocol because it provides for a simpler and more effective method of obtaining recognition and enforcement of foreign awards, giving much wider effect to the validity of arbitration agreements.[7] It was prepared by the United Nations in 1958 prior to the establishment of the UNCITRAL in 1969, and seeks to achieve two goals:

a. To provide common legislative standards to ensure that agreements to arbitrate are respected; and
b. To provide common legislative standards to ensure that foreign and non-domestic arbitral awards will be recognised and enforced.[8]

The New York Convention has been largely successful in creating common legislative standards in the international arbitration system to promote the recognition and enforcement of arbitral agreements and awards. In 1998, twenty years after the New York Convention entered into force, efforts by the late Pieter Sanders and Albert Jan van den Berg to collate judicial developments revealed that courts already exhibit a 'pro-enforcement' bias,[9] consistent with the aims of the New York Convention.

The New York Convention is also recognised to have significantly reinforced the concept of legal certainty in international arbitration.[10] As a convention that sets a minimum standard for international arbitration, it provides a minimum degree of legal certainty in arbitration, which is necessary for the stability of business transactions that have an international dimension. Also, it ensures that foreign arbitral awards

---

[4] Ibid.
[5] Official UNCITRAL website, https://uncitral.un.org/en/texts/arbitration/modellaw/commercial_arbitration/status, accessed 9 September 2020.
[6] 1958 New York Convention on the Recognition and Enforcement of Foreign Arbitral Awards, Article VII(2).
[7] Redfern and Hunter, p. 61.
[8] Official UNCITRAL Website, www.uncitral.org/uncitral/en/uncitral_texts/arbitration/NYConvention.html.
[9] A. J. van den Berg, Striving for uniform interpretation, Enforcing Arbitration Awards under the New York Convention, 10 June 1998.
[10] E. J. Cardenas, Benefits of Membership, Enforcing Arbitration Awards under the New York Convention, 10 June 1998.

can be recognised and enforced even outside the State in which those awards are pronounced, preventing vulnerability of a State's traders and enterprises when they do business on an international scale. These qualities of the New York Convention comport with UNCITRAL's object of promoting harmonisation and unification of the law of international trade by promoting ways and means of ensuring a uniform interpretation and application of international conventions and laws.[11]

To date, the New York Convention has been ratified by 165 states.[12] It is hailed as 'the single most important pillar on which the edifice of international arbitration rests'[13] and as a convention that 'perhaps could lay claim to be the most effective instance of international legislation in the entire history of commercial law'.[14] This could be attributed to the advantages of ratifying the New York Convention described above. To this extent, the New York Convention appears to be suitable as a model for legal convergence in international arbitration.

3 NON-UNIFORMITY OF THE NEW YORK CONVENTION AND ITS ANALYSIS

3.1 *Non-uniformity of the New York Convention*

Despite its widespread acceptance, the New York Convention is commonly criticised for lacking a modernised, efficient, and universal enforcement procedure.

One common argument is that the recognition and enforceability of foreign arbitral awards is largely subject to where the seat of arbitration is located. Article V(1)(e) of the New York Convention provides that recognition and enforcement of a foreign arbitral award may be refused if the award has been 'set aside or suspended by a competent authority of the country in which, or under the law of which, that award was made'.[15] This makes it possible for courts to refuse to recognise or enforce foreign awards if they have been set aside by the courts in the country where they were rendered. The implication of this is that the reliability of an award is subject to the local peculiarities where the award was rendered, which is inconsistent with the aim of the New York Convention to harmonise the legal regime of international transactions.

Additionally, the written form requirement of the arbitration agreement under Article II(2) of the New York Convention is generally regarded as too stringent. Article II(1) provides that the New York Convention only recognises an 'agreement

---

[11] Official UNCITRAL Website, www.uncitral.org.
[12] Official New York Convention Website, www.newyorkconvention.org/countries, accessed 9 October 2020.
[13] J. Gillis Wetter, The present status of the International Court of Arbitration of the ICC: An Appraisal (1990) 1 *American Review of International Arbitration* 91, p. 93.
[14] M. J Mustill, Arbitration: History and Background (1989) 6 *Journal of International Arbitration* 49; S. M. Schwebel, A Celebration of the United Nations' New York Convention on the Recognition and Enforcement of Foreign Arbitral Awards (1996) 12 *Arbitration International* 823.
[15] 1958 New York Convention, Article V(1)(e).

in writing', and this phrase is clarified to include 'an arbitral clause in a contract or an arbitration agreement, signed by the parties or contained in an exchange of letters or telegrams'.[16] On a plain reading, it appears that the arbitration agreement must be in written form. In light of modern advancements in telecommunications, a broader reading of 'in writing' should be applied by the courts to find that there is a valid arbitration agreement as long as there is *consensus ad idem* between the parties. Otherwise, many arbitration agreements would not be recognised as valid under the New York Convention. This would be contrary to the purpose of the New York Convention to ensure that agreements to arbitrate are respected.

Also, there are shortcomings regarding the procedure for enforcement of a foreign arbitral award. At present, such enforcement largely depends on the country where enforcement of the award is sought. Depending on the country, a number of differences will arise. First, there will be a different number of courts that may adjudicate on a request for enforcement. Second, the limitation period for enforcement differs between countries. For instance, in China this is six months after the award, while in the Netherlands, this is twenty years.[17] Third, the applicability of the New York Convention depends on two reservations – the 'reciprocity' reservation and the 'commercial' reservation.[18] To date, only 74 out of 156 State parties to the New York Convention have adopted the 'reciprocity' reservation,[19] meaning that only these 74 States restrict themselves to applying the New York Convention to awards rendered in other States when such other States are also parties to the Convention. This is to be contrasted with the common law position, in which any foreign arbitral award is enforceable by each common law court based on an action on the award at common law.[20] As for the second reservation on 'commercial' legal relationships, relationships that are regarded as 'commercial' by one State may not necessarily be so regarded by others.[21] It is important to note that whilst the New York Convention is silent on the definition of 'commercial',[22] the UNCITRAL Model Law clarifies this at footnote 2 of Article 1(1) of the UNCITRAL Model Law. Hence, this might lead to the conclusion that States that ratified the New York Convention

---

[16] 1958 New York Convention, Article II(1) and II(2); The New York Convention was of course drafted before the age of electronic communications.

[17] Van den Berg, Striving for Uniform Interpretation.

[18] 1958 New York Convention, Article I(3) and Article XIV.

[19] 1958 New York Convention website, www.newyorkconvention.org/countries.

[20] Fawcett, Carruthers, and North, *Private International Law*, 14th ed., pp. 652–653; *Dalmia Cement Ltd v. National Bank of Pakistan* [1975] QB 9.

[21] *Indian Organic Chemical Ltd v. Subsidiary 1 (US), Subsidiary 2 (US), and Chemtex Fibres Inc (Parent Co) (US)* (1979) IV YBCA 271 (agreement is not commercial 'under the law in force in India'); *Union of India and ors v. Lief Hoegh Co (Norway)* (1984) IX YBCA 405 ('commerce' is a word of the largest import; disagreed with *Indian Organic v. Chemtex*).

[22] Pursuant to Article I(3) of the New York Convention ('It may also declare that it will apply the Convention only to differences arising out of legal relationships, whether contractual or not, which are considered as commercial under the national law of the State making such declaration'), the New York Convention allows 'commercial' to be interpreted in accordance with the national law of the State making such reservation.

but did not adopt the UNCITRAL Model Law will still have the leeway to interpret 'commercial' in the manner they deem fit.

To this end, it may be argued that these shortcomings of the New York Convention reduce its effectiveness as a modern model for legal convergence. First, since State parties to the New York Convention may recognise and enforce arbitral agreements and foreign arbitral awards to varying degrees, the commonality of the legislative standards prescribed by the New York Convention is arguably doubtful. Second, the recognition of such shortcomings has given birth to a Hypothetical Draft Convention[23] to stimulate reflection on the subject, and the adoption of such a convention would possibly render the New York Convention obsolete.[24]

3.2 Analysis of Non-uniformity of the New York Convention

Nevertheless, such non-uniformity cannot be conceived of as inconsistent with the spirit of the New York Convention. The New York Convention merely serves as a minimum standard[25] and gives room for States to adopt alternative interpretations of the provisions in the Convention. Ultimately, the purported inconsistencies in interpretation and application mentioned above do not depart from the purpose of the New York Convention.

In spite of criticisms against the Convention and calls for its modernisation, it has been noted that no convention since 1958 has had the same impact as that of the New York Convention,[26] and that the New York Convention still remains 'the cornerstone of international arbitration'.[27] To date, there is no record of any nation denouncing the New York Convention pursuant to Article XIII of the Convention. Diversity is not divergence,[28] and countries are allowed variance in their rules for enforcement. This is also reflected in Article VII(1) of the New York Convention, which will be further elaborated on in the reasons we are about to set out. Hence, it is submitted that the New York Convention is a suitable model for legal convergence for the reasons set out below.

With regard to the Draft Convention put forward by Albert Jan van den Berg, Emmanuel Gaillard is of the view that there is 'no need, no danger and no hope'.[29]

---

[23] A. J van den Berg, 'Hypothetical Draft Convention on the International Enforcement of Arbitration Agreements and Awards, Text of Draft Convention', AJB/Rev06/29-May-2008.
[24] The chances of such an amended Convention is at present unlikely.
[25] M. Paulsson, The 1958 New York Convention in Action (Kluwer Law International BV, 2016).
[26] J. Lew, L. A Mistelis, and S. M Kroll, Comparative International Commercial Arbitration (Kluwer Law International, 2003).
[27] UNCITRAL, UNCITRAL Secretariat Guide on the Convention on the Recognition and Enforcement of Foreign Arbitral Awards (United Nations, 2016).
[28] P. Sanders, Unity and Diversity in the Adoption of the Model Law, *Arbitration International* (Kluwer Law International, Volume 11, Issue 1, 1995) pp. 1–38.
[29] E. Gaillard, The Urgency of Not Revising the New York Convention, Enforcing Arbitration Awards under the New York Convention, 10 June 1998.

4 THERE IS NO REAL NEED TO REVISE THE NEW YORK CONVENTION

4.1 *The Shortcomings of Article V(1)(e) May Be Circumvented*

Article V(1)(e) of the New York Convention provides:

> 1. Recognition and enforcement of the award may be refused, at the request of the party against whom it is invoked, only if that party furnishes to the competent authority where the recognition and enforcement is sought, proof that:
> (e) The award has not yet become binding on the parties, or has been set aside or suspended by a competent authority of the country in which, or under the law of which, that award was made.

Jan Paulsson has recognised that the power conferred on courts by virtue of Article V (1)(e) of the New York Convention poses an 'obvious danger to the harmonisation of the legal regime of international transactions'.[30] To this, he suggested three solutions.

The first solution is to ignore Article V(1)(e) entirely, on the basis that the Convention allows (or even mandates) each country under Article VII to adopt a more liberal regime in favour of enforcement.[31] This solution completely displaces the control function of the enforcement jurisdiction or jurisdictions, meaning that the judge in the enforcement jurisdiction would not be required nor entitled to give any weight to what a foreign court may have done to an award, as long as the award meets the criteria of the enforcement jurisdiction. This would encourage enforcement of foreign arbitral awards despite local peculiarities.

The second solution is to understand that some countries cannot be relied upon to apply international standards, and to recognise that the most important trading countries abide by the contemporary international consensus – hence there is no need for concern. However, this creates a class of 'trustworthy' countries, which by its very nature goes against the notion of legal convergence.

The third solution is to recognise that Article V of the New York Convention is discretionary through its use of the word 'may' rather than 'shall'. Thus courts also have the discretion to accept enforcement, even when an award has been annulled in the place where it was rendered. This solution is also consistent with Article VII of the New York Convention, which provides that the New York Convention does not

---

[30] J. Paulsson, Awards Set Aside at the Place of Arbitration, Enforcing Arbitration Awards under the New York Convention, 10 June 1998.

[31] *Hilmarton Ltd v. Omnium de Traitement et de Valorisation* (OTV) (1994) Rev Arb 327 (award was enforced by Cour d'Appel even though it was set aside in the country in which it was rendered i.e. Switzerland); *In Re Chromalloy Aeroservices and the Arab Republic of Egypt*, 939 F Supp 906 (DC Cir 1996) (United States court enforced award rendered in Egypt even though it was set aside in Egyptian court); *Societe PT Putrabali Adyamulia v. Societe Rena Holding et Societe Mnogutia Est Epices* [2007] Rev Arb 507 (French courts enforced an award set aside in England); *Corporación Mexicana De Mantenimiento Integral, S De RL De CV v. Pemex-Exploración Y Producción*, No. 13-4022, 2016 US App LEXIS 13991 (2d Cir 2016) (United States District Court enforced a Mexican award despite being set aside at the seat of arbitration).

'deprive any interested party of any right he may have to avail himself of an arbitral award in the manner and to the extent allowed by the law or the treaties of the country where such award is sought to be relied upon'. In fact, this was the case in the *Hilmarton*[32] and *Chromalloy*[33] decisions. In the former case, the Paris Court of Appeal enforced an award rendered in Geneva even though it was set aside by the Court of Justice of the Canton of Geneva. In the latter, the District Court for the District of Columbia enforced an award rendered in Egypt even though it was set aside by the Cairo Court of Appeal.

The question would then be how this discretion should be exercised. Jan Paulsson was of the view that the enforcement judge should determine whether the basis of the annulment by the judge in the place of arbitration was consonant with international standards. This interpretation would make the New York Convention a suitable model for legal convergence.

4.2 Courts Already Adopt a Liberal Interpretation of the 'In Writing' Requirement

Articles II(1) and II(2) of the New York Convention provide:

1. Each Contracting State shall recognize an agreement in writing under which the parties undertake to submit to arbitration all or any differences which have arisen or which may arise between them in respect of a defined legal relationship, whether contractual or not, concerning a subject matter capable of settlement by arbitration.
2. The term 'agreement in writing' shall include an arbitral clause in a contract or an arbitration agreement, signed by the parties or contained in an exchange of letters or telegrams.

In practice, there is a widespread trend to apply the 'in writing' requirement under Articles II(1) and II(2) of the New York Convention liberally.[34] This is reflected in Article 7 of the UNCITRAL Model Law, which broadens the definition of 'in writing' to suit modern circumstances.[35] Such an intention is also reflected in numerous national arbitration laws.[36] Hence, while it would be helpful to make it clear that the term 'in writing' covers all means of communication which can be evidenced by text, it is not necessary to do so.

---

[32] *Hilmarton Ltd v. Omnium de Traitement et de Valorisation* (OTV) (1994) Rev Arb 327.
[33] *In Re Chromalloy Aeroservices and the Arab Republic of Egypt*, 939 F Supp 906 (DC Cir 1996).
[34] International Council for Commercial Arbitration, ICCA's Guide to the Interpretation of the 1958 New York Convention (International Council for Commercial Arbitration, 2011).
[35] 1985 UNCITRAL Model Law on International Commercial Arbitration (with amendments as adopted in 2006), Article 7.
[36] European Convention on International Commercial Arbitration 1961, Article I(2)(a); Swiss Federal Act on Private International Law 1987 (as amended until 1 July 2014), Article 178.

The UNCITRAL Model Law further provides (at Article 2A) that 'regard is to be had to its international origin and to the need to promote uniformity in its application and the observance of good faith' in interpreting the UNCITRAL Model Law. This is indicative of UNCITRAL's intention to afford a broad interpretation of 'in writing', both in the UNCITRAL Model Law and the New York Convention, so that the phrase would be consistent with the modern liberal approach adopted by many States today. An inflexible application of the New York Convention's writing requirement would contradict the current and widespread business usages and be contrary to the pro-enforcement thrust of the Convention. The current view is that an arbitration agreement will be valid as long as there is a meeting of the minds between the parties in that the offer to arbitrate has been accepted.

Hence, criticisms of the New York Convention premised on its archaic 'in writing' requirement cannot render the New York Convention an unsuitable model for legal convergence.

4.3 There May Be More to Lose than to Gain in Embarking Upon a Revision Process

As mentioned above, the fact that the language of the Convention is sometimes outdated or could be fine-tuned does not warrant a revision of the Convention, because this would have a broad-brush impact on all 156 State parties.

Emmanuel Gaillard is also of the view that the revision of the New York Convention would not solve the pertinent issues raised by the New York Convention. As for the issue of recurring instances of bias in favour of local companies by the courts in certain jurisdictions at the place of enforcement, a rewording of the New York Convention will not hinder the court from taking advantage of the broad 'public policy' exception under Article V(2)(b) to achieve the same result. As for the issue of States that lose in arbitrations and never satisfy the award, these difficulties are unrelated to the New York Convention and are instead a result of the State's ability to invoke its immunity from execution to resist enforcement. Thus it would be ineffective and indeed disruptive to allow a revision of the New York Convention.

4.4 There Is No Danger in Leaving the Current Convention Untouched

Moreover, there is no danger in leaving the New York Convention unrevised because the New York Convention sets only a minimum standard.[37] States are

---

[37] 1958 New York Convention, Article VII; Albert Jan van den Berg, Hypothetical Draft Convention on the International Enforcement of Arbitration Agreements and Awards, Explanatory Note, AJB/Rev06/

free to recognise and enforce foreign arbitral awards more liberally, so long as they do not fall below the standard required of them under the New York Convention. Examples of States that exercise such discretion include France and the United States.[38] They may also fall back on the common law position on recognition and enforcement of foreign arbitral awards, or on converted judgments. Thus the Convention merely serves as a safety net and will do no harm, even if it is not used.

It is also important to note the roles of the authoritative bodies behind the New York Convention – the International Council for Commercial Arbitration (ICCA) and UNCITRAL. ICCA aims to 'promot[e] the use and improv[e] the processes of arbitration, conciliation and other forms of resolving international commercial disputes'.[39] UNCITRAL aims to 'further the progressive harmonisation and unification of the law of international trade'.[40] Given the express aims of these authoritative bodies to harmonise and improve the New York Convention, State parties to the New York Convention need not be concerned that leaving the New York Convention unrevised would result in stagnation of the development of international arbitration.

Therefore, to the extent that States have ratified the New York Convention, the development of arbitration will never deteriorate. Indeed, to date, there is no record of any nation denouncing the New York Convention pursuant to Article XIII. This may be contrasted with several States' denunciation of the ICSID Convention pursuant to Article 71 of the ICSID Convention. Examples of such States include Indonesia, Bolivia and Ecuador.[41] Hence, leaving the New York Convention unrevised will not result in grave repercussions. The New York Convention is unlikely to be revised, and will remain relevant as a model for legal convergence.

4.5 There Is No Hope to Achieve a Better Instrument than the Existing Convention

Additionally, the pro-arbitration bias of most of the 156 State parties, coupled with the dramatic development of arbitrations based on investment protection treaties, has led to States developing a defendant's mind-set. As of 12 April 2016, 163 States

---

29-May-2008; Lew, Mistelis and Kroll, Comparative International Commercial Arbitration; M. Paulsson, The 1958 New York Convention in Action.

[38] E.g. *Hilmarton Ltd* v. *Omnium de Traitement et de Valorisation* (OTV) (1994) Rev Arb 327 (award was enforced by Cour d'Appel even though it was set aside in the country in which it was rendered, i.e. Switzerland); *Societe PT Putrabali Adyamulia* v. *Societe Rena Holding et Societe Mnogutia Est Epices* [2007] Rev Arb 507 (French courts enforced an award set aside in England); *Corporación Mexicana De Mantenimiento Integral, S De RL De CV* v. *Pemex-Exploración Y Producción*, No. 13–4022, 2016 US App LEXIS 13991 (2d Cir 2016) (United States District Court enforced a Mexican award despite being set aside at the seat of arbitration).

[39] Official ICCA Website, www.arbitration-icca.org/about.html.

[40] Official UNCITRAL Website, www.uncitral.org.

[41] C. Schreuer, Denunciation of the ICSID Convention and Consent to Arbitration, The Backlash against Investment Arbitration: Perceptions and Reality, pp. 353–368, 2010.

have signed the ICSID Convention,[42] while 155 States have ratified the ICSID Convention.[43] Thus it is unlikely that they would be willing to enhance the effectiveness of the enforcement process, given that they are increasingly in a position to resist enforcement of awards. By extension, it would be unlikely that there will be a majority in the UN General Assembly to agree to any changes to the New York Convention.

Since the revision of the New York Convention is both unnecessary and disruptive, the New York Convention appears to be a laudable international convention that has largely succeeded in harmonising the recognition and enforcement of foreign arbitral awards today.

5 SUCCESS OF THE UNCITRAL MODEL LAW ON INTERNATIONAL COMMERCIAL ARBITRATION

After the New York Convention came into force in 1958, UNCITRAL was established by the United Nations General Assembly in 1966.[44] UNCITRAL then prepared a Model Law with the purpose of improving the overall framework of international commercial arbitration.[45] As the Introduction to the UNCITRAL 2012 Digest of Case Law on the Model Law explains, the 'form of a Model Law was chosen as the vehicle for harmonisation and modernisation in view of the flexibility it provides to States in preparing new arbitration laws'.[46] The UNCITRAL Model Law was designed to be compatible with the New York Convention[47] and was adopted by UNCITRAL on 21 June 1985. Together, they are viewed as a 'unified legal framework for the fair and efficient settlement of disputes arising in international commercial relations'.[48]

To date, the UNCITRAL Model Law has been (to a greater or lesser extent) been adopted by 83 States in 116 jurisdictions at the time of writing.[49] According to Professor Gary Bell, these include 31 countries or jurisdictions in the Asia-

---

[42] Official ICSID Website, https://icsid.worldbank.org/about/member-states/database-of-member-states, accessed 9 September 2020.
[43] Official ICSID Website, https://icsid.worldbank.org/resources/rules-and-regulations/convention/overview, accessed 9 September 2020.
[44] United Nations, General Assembly Resolution 2205(XXI) of 17 December 1966, Establishment of the United Nations Commission on International Trade Law.
[45] H. M. Holtzmann and J. E. Neuhaus, *A Guide to the UNCITRAL Model Law on International Commercial Arbitration: Legislative History and Commentary, Part I* (Kluwer Law International, 1995).
[46] United Nations, UNCITRAL 2012 Digest of Case Law on the Model Law of International Commercial Arbitration (United Nations, 2012).
[47] Holtzmann and Neuhaus, A Guide to the UNCITRAL Model Law on International Commercial Arbitration.
[48] Ibid.
[49] Official UNCITRAL website, https://uncitral.un.org/en/texts/arbitration/modellaw/commercial_arbitration/status, accessed 9 September 2020.

Pacific.[50] There have been some deviations in interpretation and application of the provisions in the UNCITRAL Model Law, which will be further elaborated on below. However, having compared 22 versions of adoptions of the UNCITRAL Model Law by nations all around the world (as of 2005), the late Pieter Sanders concluded that 'the success of the Model Law as a whole may be seen in the fact that there is no one particular Article which generally has been deviated from. Nor has this been the case with additions … there is no particular addition which has been generally made'.[51] Hence, the UNCITRAL Model Law may also be a suitable model for legal convergence in Asia and elsewhere.

5.1 Non-uniformity of the UNCITRAL Model Law and Its Analysis

5.1.1 Non-uniformity of the UNCITRAL Model Law

The non-uniformity of the UNCITRAL Model Law is reflected in areas where States have adopted the Model Law differently, as well as in additions that some States have adopted.

5.1.2 The Definition of Public Policy in Article 34(2)(b)(ii) of the UNCITRAL Model Law

Article 34 is arguably one of the most important provisions in the Model Law as it is this Article that details the limits of a court's intervention with an arbitral award.

Under Article 34(2)(b)(ii), an arbitral award may be set aside by the court if the award is in conflict with the public policy of the State which is the seat of arbitration. This 'public policy' requirement also appears in Article 36 of the UNCITRAL Model Law and Article V(2)(b) of the New York Convention.

Australia was the first country to insert provisions referring explicitly to fraud and corruption. These provisions were inserted via the Australia International Arbitration Amendment Act 1989 as follows:

> Without limiting the generality of subparagraphs 34(2)(b)(ii) and 36(1)(b)(ii) of the Model Law, it is hereby declared, for the avoidance of any doubt, that, for the purposes of those subparagraphs, an award is in conflict with the public policy of Australia if:
> The making of the award was induced or affected by fraud or corruption; or
> A breach of the rules of natural justice occurred in connection with the making of the award.

---

[50] Gary F. Bell, The UNCITRAL Model Law on International Commercial Arbitration in Asia, National University of Singapore, Faculty of Law website, www.law.nus.edu.sg/clb/projects/clb_projecto09.html, accessed 9 September 2020.

[51] P. Sanders, Unity and Diversity in the Adoption of the Model Law, pp. 1–38.

This was subsequently adopted by New Zealand, Singapore, and Malaysia, with minor changes to the text that do not appear to be significant. However, this was not followed by Hong Kong and Canada.

Logically, specific references to fraud, corruption, and breaches of natural justice would seem unnecessary, as there is universal agreement (even among civil law countries) that these are vitiating factors for any award, wherever the seat may be located and most civilian lawyers would probably say that these factors would be vitiated either under Article 34(2)(b)(ii) (unable to present his case) or public policy.

Article 34(6) of the New Zealand Arbitration Act 1996 includes an extension to the provision on breach of natural justice in that for the purposes of that Act, a breach of natural justice can be a ground for setting aside not just if it occurs 'in connection with the making of the award' but also if there is a breach of natural justice generally 'during the arbitration proceedings'.

Section 37(2) of the Malaysian Arbitration Act 2005 (revised 2011) leaves out the phrase 'for the avoidance of doubt', but still remain elaborations on public policy.

Section 24 of the Singapore International Arbitration Act (Cap 143A) frames fraud and corruption as additional grounds for setting aside. This could possibly reflect Singapore's hard stance against fraud or corruption.

Since the UNCITRAL Model Law leaves open the issue of what constitutes 'public policy', and this subsection does not limit the generality of Article 34(2)(b)(ii), it is evident that this subsection is not exhaustive, and serves as a clarification rather than an addition to the UNCITRAL Model Law. Each State is free to determine what constitutes 'public policy'. Thus this cannot be said to be a deviation from the UNCITRAL Model Law.

5.2 The Parties' Right to Present Their Case under Article 18 of the UNCITRAL Model Law

Article 18 of the UNCITRAL Model Law states that 'the parties shall be treated with equality and each party shall be given a full opportunity of presenting his case'.

This has given rise to concerns that the phrase 'full opportunity' is too extreme and may not accurately describe the appropriate balance to be drawn between efficiency and due process. Some counsel may also attempt to argue that the requirement of a 'full opportunity' is higher than that of reasonableness.[52]

Accordingly, Hong Kong and Australia amended the text of Article 18 of the UNCITRAL Model Law in the relevant provision in their own arbitration statute by replacing 'full opportunity' with 'reasonable opportunity'.

---

[52] This appears to have been attempted by the applicant in a setting aside proceeding in Hong Kong (*Pacific China Holdings Limited (In Liquidation)* v. *Grand Pacific Holdings Limited* (HCCT 15/2010), though it was rejected by Saunders J, who held that 'full opportunity' under the Model Law and 'reasonable opportunity' under the ICC Rules was a distinction without a difference.

Properly viewed, however, these changes may not be as significant as they first appear. Holtzmann and Neuhaus explain this as follows:

> [T]he terms 'equality' and 'full opportunity' are to be interpreted reasonably in regulating the procedural aspects of the arbitration. While ... the arbitral tribunal must provide reasonable opportunities to each party, this does not mean that it must sacrifice all efficiency in order to accommodate unreasonable procedural demands by a party.[53]

Hence, while it may be seen as preferable to clarify this via amending the text in the statute rather than waiting for case-law to develop, the result is undeniably consistent with the spirit of the Model Law. It is also notable that other States, such as Singapore and South Korea, did not see the need to make any amendments to the text of Article 18 and adopted it wholesale.

5.3 Confidentiality Provisions

The UNCITRAL Model Law is notably silent on the issue of confidentiality, leaving the position up to each Member State. The confidentiality provisions may be in relation to the arbitration in general, or of the court proceedings arising out of arbitration. Unsurprisingly, the approach taken has differed from country to country.

Most arbitration statutes do not expressly touch on the general confidentiality of the arbitration.[54] In the circumstances, unless there are express provisions in a country's national arbitration law, it usually falls to the courts to decide whether or not this should be implied. For instance, Singapore, following the English position, has recognised an implied undertaking of confidentiality in arbitral proceedings.[55]

Prior to the 2010 Amendments, Australian legislation, too, was silent about the confidentiality of arbitration, although the Australian courts chose not to recognise such an implied undertaking in the interests of transparency.[56] However, this decision was not well-received. Amendments were thus introduced in 2010 to provide for an 'opt-in' confidentiality regime.[57] This was supplemented by legislative amendments in 2016, which essentially changes the default position from 'opt-in' to 'opt-out'. This is also the position in Hong Kong, where Section 18 of the Hong Kong Arbitration Ordinance (Cap. 609) provides:

---

[53] Holtzmann and Neuhaus, A Guide to the UNCITRAL Model Law on International Commercial Arbitration.
[54] E.g. England, Singapore, China, Japan, Indonesia, India.
[55] AAY v. AAZ [2011] SLR 1093 applying *John Forster Emmott v. Michael Wilson & Partners Ltd* [2008] EWCA Civ. 184.
[56] *Esso Australia Resources Ltd v. Plowman* [1995] HCA 19. (The Court held that even if a contract provided for confidentiality, this was subject to the public interest, and in certain cases could be overridden if there was a sufficiently strong need for transparency.)
[57] Australia International Arbitration Act 1974, Articles 23C to 23G.

4 Existing Models for Legal Convergence in Asia?

(1) Unless otherwise agreed by the parties, no party may publish, disclose or communicate any information relating to – (a) the arbitral proceedings under the arbitration agreement; or (b) an award made in those arbitral proceedings.

Australia, Hong Kong, New Zealand, and to a lesser extent, the Dubai International Financial Centre (DIFC), have introduced comprehensive confidentiality provisions in their respective legislations. Evidently, various States take different approaches in their amendments to the UNCITRAL Model Law when it comes to confidentiality. However, continuing the trend that has been observed previously, this does not change the spirit of the UNCITRAL Model Law. The UNCITRAL Model Law is deliberately silent on confidentiality, which has given individual States the freedom to chart their own course.

5.4 Immunity of Arbitrators

The UNCITRAL Model Law is silent regarding the immunity of arbitrators. However, the Singapore International Arbitration Act (Cap 143A) provides for the immunity of arbitrators for certain situations at Sections 25 and 25A:

25. An arbitrator shall not be liable for –
   (a) negligence in respect of anything done or omitted to be done in the capacity of arbitrator; and
   (b) any mistake in law, fact or procedure made in the course of arbitral proceedings or in the making of an arbitral award.
25A. – (1) The appointing authority, or an arbitral or other institution or person designated or requested by the parties to appoint or nominate an arbitrator, shall not be liable for anything done or omitted in the discharge or purported discharge of that function unless the act or omission is shown to have been in bad faith.
   (2) The appointing authority, or an arbitral or other institution or person by whom an arbitrator is appointed or nominated, shall not be liable, by reason only of having appointed or nominated him, for anything done or omitted by the arbitrator, his employees or agents in the discharge or purported discharge of his functions as arbitrator.

Singapore is not the only country that has provided for immunity of arbitrators. This is also the case in Hong Kong and the UK, for instance.

Section 104 of the Hong Kong Arbitration Ordinance (Cap 609) provides that an arbitral tribunal or mediator is liable in law for an act done or omitted to be done 'only if it is proved that the act was done or omitted to be done dishonestly'.

Section 29 of the English Arbitration Act 1996 provides that 'an arbitrator is not liable for anything done or omitted in the discharge of purported discharge of his functions as arbitrator unless the act or omission is shown to have been in bad faith'.

This is also reflected in various Arbitration Rules.

The Hong Kong International Arbitration Centre (HKIAC) Administered Arbitration Rules 2013, Article 43.1 states:

> None of the Council of HKIAC nor any committee, sub-committee or other body or person specifically designated by it to perform the functions referred to in these Rules, nor the Secretary General of HKIAC or other staff members of the Secretariat of HKIAC, the arbitral tribunal, any Emergency Arbitrator, tribunal-appointed expert or secretary of the arbitral tribunal shall be liable for any act or omission in connection with an arbitration conducted under these Rules, *save where such act was done or omitted to be done dishonestly.*

The London Court of International Arbitration (LCIA) Arbitration Rules 2014, Article 31.1 states:

> None of the LCIA (including its officers, members and employees), the LCIA Court (including its President, Vice-Presidents, Honorary Vice-Presidents and members), the Registrar (including any deputy Registrar), any arbitrator, any Emergency Arbitrator and any expert to the Arbitral Tribunal shall be liable to any party howsoever for any act or omission in connection with any arbitration, *save: (i) where the act or omission is shown by that party to constitute conscious and deliberate wrongdoing committed by the body or person alleged to be liable to that party; or (ii) to the extent that any part of this provision is shown to be prohibited by any applicable law.*

The International Chamber of Commerce (ICC) Arbitration Rules 2012, Article 40, indicates:

> The arbitrators, any person appointed by the arbitral tribunal, the emergency arbitrator, the Court and its members, the ICC and its employees, and the ICC National Committees and Groups and their employees and representatives shall not be liable to any person for any act or omission in connection with the arbitration, *except to the extent such limitation of liability is prohibited by applicable law.*

To this extent, the presence of add-ons cannot be said to be a deviation from the UNCITRAL Model Law, but rather an appreciation of modern needs in international arbitration that the drafters of the 1985 UNCITRAL Model Law could not possibly have contemplated at the time of drafting.

5.5 *Other Add-Ons*

Other add-ons to the UNCITRAL Model Law include Sections 20 and 21 of the Singapore International Arbitration Act (Cap 143A), which provide for an award of interest on awards and taxation of costs directed by an award respectively. The UNCITRAL Model Law is silent on these points.

To provide another example, Sections 16 and 17 of the Singapore International Arbitration Act (Cap 143A) provide that an arbitrator may act as a conciliator. This is also the case in Sections 32 and 33 of the Hong Kong Arbitration Ordinance (Cap 609), which provides that an arbitrator may act as a mediator.

Again, these additions merely address modern needs, and cannot be said to be a deviation from the Model Law.

6 ANALYSIS OF NON-UNIFORMITY OF THE UNCITRAL MODEL LAW

As can be seen from the examples above, while it is possible to identify certain areas where States have differed in their implementation of the UNCITRAL Model Law, these differences tend not to be significant in the sense that they typically do not depart from the overall thrust of the UNCITRAL Model Law. Furthermore, while there were differences in implementation of the UNCITRAL Model Law, many of these differences were subsequently amended for greater clarity.

The UNCITRAL Model Law is a form of 'soft law' and is only a foundation for a comprehensive arbitration law. Hence, additions and relatively minor omissions are permissible, expected, and not inconsistent with convergence.

In Singapore, Chan Leng Sun SC has written that 'Singapore adopted the Model Law in 1994 because it was an internationally accepted model. Singapore believed that it must adopt a world view of international arbitration if it were to be an international arbitration centre'.

In South Korea, the learned authors of 'Arbitration in Korea',[58] in their introduction, noted that 'the [Korean] Arbitration Act substantially adopts the language and structure of the Model Law, and has served to promote international arbitration in Korea and to support international arbitrations abroad'.

In Hong Kong, a Law Commission Paper on the Arbitration Practices Adopted by Hong Kong's Major Competitors specifically included 'extent of adherence to Model Law' as one of the factors in its comparison table, highlighting the significance of association with the UNCITRAL Model Law.

Even in countries such as Indonesia that are not currently adopters of the UNCITRAL Model Law, the importance of the UNCITRAL Model Law as a basis for international commercial arbitration is increasingly being recognised. For instance, in Indonesia, Husseyn Ummar, then Vice Chairman of the Board (and now Chairman) and Arbitrator at the Indonesian National Board of Arbitration, stated the following in a Q&A section of the *Indonesia Arbitration Quarterly Newsletter* No. 12/2013:

> There is indeed an urgent need for Indonesia to consider to perceive the application of the Model Law by reviewing and adjusting the current law with respect to international arbitration. This will attract parties of diverse nationalities in the cross border trade and foreign investment to arbitrate in Indonesia. It will also benefit Indonesia in promoting the country as one of the attractive venues for international arbitration.

Indeed, as UNCITRAL commented, 'as a rule, relatively few deviations from this [the Model Law] have been made by States adopting enacting legislation, suggesting that the procedures it establishes are widely accepted and understood as forming

---

[58] Shin & Kim, *Arbitration in Korea* (a pamphlet published by Shin & Kim), p. 4.

a coherent basis for international commercial arbitration'.[59] Since the UNCITRAL Model Law, unlike the New York Convention, is not a treaty obligation, States that adopt it are free to amend it to suit their own requirements, and this cannot be seen to hinder its suitability as a model for legal convergence.

What Asia needs now is for the big Asian countries missing from the UNCITRAL Model Law family to sign up. These countries include China, India, Indonesia, and the Middle East.[60] The UNCITRAL Model Law will be an effective model for legal convergence in Asia when more countries in Asia adopt the UNCITRAL Model Law.

7 CONCLUDING REMARKS

As noted by Julian Lew QC et al., 'the New York Convention constitutes the backbone of the international regime for the enforcement of foreign awards'.[61] Indeed, the New York Convention is to be lauded for having provided a minimum standard for international arbitration applicable to all State parties, in spite of the difficulties of achieving perfect convergence in a world with various local peculiarities.

By building on the New York Convention, the UNCITRAL Model Law is also prominently viewed as the 'gold standard' in international arbitration. It has been said that 'as a rule, relatively few deviations from [the UNCITRAL Model Law] have been made by States adopting enacting legislation, suggesting that the procedures it establishes are widely accepted and understood as forming a coherent basis for international commercial arbitration'.[62]

Thus, given the difficulties of achieving perfect convergence, the New York Convention and the UNCITRAL Model Law should be seen as exemplary documents that have largely succeeded in their goal to harmonise and improve arbitration laws. To the extent that more States ratify the New York Convention and adopt the UNCITRAL Model Law, they are rightfully viewed as suitable models for legal convergence in today's modernised and globalised world.

8 POSTSCRIPT: DIFFERING INTERPRETATIONS OF MODEL LAW PROVISIONS

Aside from variations in how the UNCITRAL Model Law is adopted in individual jurisdictions, there is another avenue by which the implementation of the UNCITRAL Model Law could, in practice, result in diverging outcomes: the interpretation of Model Law language by national courts.

---

[59] United Nations, A Guide to UNCITRAL: Basic Facts about the United Nations Commission on International Trade Law (United Nations, 2013).
[60] The new UAE Federal Arbitration Law, which entered into force with effect from 16 June 2018 and is largely based on the UNCITRAL Model Law, is a promising start.
[61] Lew, Mistelis, and Kroll, Comparative International Commercial Arbitration.
[62] United Nations, A Guide to UNCITRAL: Basic Facts about the United Nations Commission on International Trade Law.

Recently, this issue has come into sharp relief in respect of Article 34(3) of the UNCITRAL Model Law. This Article states that an application to set aside an arbitral award 'may not' be made after three months has elapsed since the award was rendered. The courts in an overwhelming majority of common law Model Law jurisdictions have taken the position that this three-month time limit is strict and cannot be extended.[63] As clear as the language may appear to be on the surface, courts in several Asia-Pacific jurisdictions have differed in their conclusions on whether Article 34(3) (or its equivalent provision in national arbitration statutes) leaves the courts any residual discretion to extend the three-month limit within which a setting-aside application must ostensibly be brought.

The Singapore courts have consistently refused to allow a setting-aside application to be made after the three-month time limit has elapsed, regardless of whether there is good reason for the delay. In the 2003 case of *ABC v. XYZ*,[64] the Singapore High Court held that the words 'may not' in Article 34(3) had to be interpreted as 'cannot', to give effect to the intention to limit the time during which an award can be challenged.[65] Further, Article 34(3) was silent on the issue of time extension and therefore did not confer on the courts any power to extend time. The Singapore courts in subsequent cases, such as *BXS v BXT*,[66] have followed this position.

In this connection, the recent case of *Bloomberry Resorts and Hotels v. Global Gaming Philippines*[67] provides a useful case study demonstrating that even relatively significant extenuating circumstances will not move the Singapore courts to allow a setting-aside application to be brought after the time limit has elapsed. In this case, the claimants asserted that they had come into possession of evidence of fraud and/or corruption that were material to the findings in the arbitral award that was being challenged, but this new evidence only came to light after the three-month time limit had expired. Belinda Ang J took the position that even alleged fraud did not give the courts discretion to extend the time limit in Article 34(3), notwithstanding the presence of the aforementioned extenuating circumstances that prevented the setting-aside application from being brought earlier. However, the authors must caveat that at the time of writing, this case has been heard by the Singapore Court of Appeal and is pending its final decision.

The Malaysian position is less settled, although recent decisions have favoured the strict interpretation of the domestic Malaysian equivalent of Article 34(3). In *Government of the Lao People's Democratic Republic v. Thai-Lao Lignite*,[68] the

---

[63] For Australia, see *Sharma v. Military Ceramics Corporation* [2020] FCA 216. For New Zealand, see (inter alia) *Kyburn Investments v. Beca Corporate Holdings* [2015] NZCA 290. For Ireland, see *Moohan v. S. & R. Motors [Donegal] Ltd* [2009] IEHC 391. Finally, for Canada, see *Ontario Inc. v. Lakeside Produce Inc.*, 2017 ONSC 4933.

[64] [2003] SGHC 107.

[65] Ibid., at [9].

[66] [2019] SGHC(I) 10.

[67] [2020] SGHC 1.

[68] Civil Appeal No: W-02(NCC)-1287-2011.

Malaysian Court of Appeal held that notwithstanding the Arbitration Act 2005 (the domestic statute through which Malaysia adopts the UNCITRAL Model Law), the Malaysian courts retained their general discretion to extend time even for arbitration-related matters.[69] This position was not in line with the broad consensus among common law Model Law jurisdictions that the setting-aside time limit should be strict.

The *Thai-Lao* case has, however, been doubted by at least three subsequent Malaysian High Court cases. In *JHW Reels* v. *Syarikat Borcos Shipping*,[70] the Malaysian High Court, looking favourably on the Singapore decision of *ABC* v. *XYZ*,[71] held that the words 'may not' in Section 37(4) of the Arbitration Act 2005 (which is *in pari materia* with Article 34(3) of the UNCITRAL Model Law) had a mandatory effect, and therefore that the time limit for a setting-aside application should be strictly construed.[72] Shortly afterward in *Kembang Serantau* v. *Jeks Engineering*,[73] Mary Lim J (as she then was) agreed with the reasoning in *JHW Reels* and also adopted a strict interpretation of Section 37(4). Finally, this approach was also followed in the case of *Triumph City Development* v. *Selangor State Government*.[74] Malaysia thus appears to be realigning itself with the orthodox position in respect of Article 34(3).

Unfortunately, Hong Kong does not yet appear to be as eager to fall into step with the broad consensus. In *Sun Tian Gang* v. *Hong Kong & China Gas (Jilin) Limited*,[75] an arbitration had been commenced and an arbitral award rendered against the claimant, while the claimant was incarcerated in mainland China. In the circumstances, the claimant was only able to apply to set aside the award some eight years after it had been issued. Mimmie Chan J held that the phrase 'may not' in Article 34(3) conferred discretion on the courts to extend the three-month time limit. However, the authors would note that this decision is now an outlier in view of the case law emanating from the other common law Model Law jurisdictions as earlier mentioned.

It is surprising, to say the least, that the time period within which a setting-aside application can be made, is a matter of some uncertainty in certain prominent arbitration jurisdictions, especially considering the practical significance of setting aside an award. The above cases serve as a useful reminder that while legal convergence and harmonization still remain common goals in Asia, there remain some problem areas where there is still progress to be made, which are all the more jarring for their potentially serious consequences.

---

[69] *Thai-Lao Lignite*, at [31].
[70] [2013] 7 CLJ 249.
[71] Ibid., at [22].
[72] Ibid., at [21].
[73] [2016] 2 CLJ 427; [2016] 1 AMR 261.
[74] [2017] 8 AMR 411.
[75] [2016] HKEC 2128.

5

Convergences and Divergences: Comparing Contractual and Organizational Models in International Regulatory Cooperation

Fabrizio Cafaggi

1 INTRODUCTION

Transnational private regulation (TPR) includes a large number of private regimes that regulate the behaviour of multinational firms and their interaction with investors, consumers, local communities.[1] It consists of regulatory regimes designed and implemented by private actors, often in collaboration with international organizations.[2] TPR standards are voluntary. TPR's legitimacy is linked to and partly based on its effectiveness. TPR's effectiveness differs from that of public regulation: its metric for evaluation both in terms of adhesion and effectiveness is the response of regulated entities to the recommended standard and its governance. Supply and demand of private standards are determined by market-like dynamics. This differs

---

This chapter was written for a Conference in Singapore organized at SMU in December 2016. I am grateful to Maartje De Visser for very useful comments. The chapter has benefitted from several interviews and conversations over the past years. I would particularly like to thank Daan de Vries and Dirk Straathof (UTZ), Jeanne Stampe (WWF), Daniele Gerundino, and Sean McCurtain (ISO) for their time and their insightful comments about private regulatory competition and cooperation. For useful exchanges, I would also like to thank Celine Cauffman and Nick Malyshev of OECD. The responsibility for any errors the text is mine alone.

[1] See J. Braithwaite and P. Drahos, *Global Business Regulation* (Oxford University Press, 2000); W. Mattli and T. Büthe, *The New Global Rulers – The Privatization of Regulation in the World Economy* (Princeton University Press, 2011); F. Cafaggi, New foundations of transnational private regulation (2011) 38 *Journal of Law Society* 1:20–49; A. Marx, M. Maertens, J. Swinnen, and J. Wouters (eds), *Private Standards and Global Governance – Economic, Legal and Political Perspectives* (Edward Elgar, 2012); F. Cafaggi, The many features of transnational private rule making, unexplored relationships between custom jura mercatorum, and transnational private regulation (2015) 36 *Penn Journal of International Law* 875; P. Delimatsis, *The Law, Economic and Politics of International Standardization* (Cambridge University Press, 2016); G. Shaffer, Theorizing transnational legal ordering of private and business law (2016) 1 *UC Irvine Journal of International, Transnational and Comparative Law* 1.

[2] On the role of IOs in relation to transnational private standards and the different types of transnational regulations, see K. Abbott and D. Snidal, The governance triangle: Regulatory standards institutions and the shadow of the state, in Walter Mattli and Ngaire Woods, eds., *The Politics of Global Regulation* (Princeton University Press, 2009), pp. 44–88.

from public standards where States play a dominant role,[3] and which are usually mandatory and compliance is binding,[4] The incentives of regulated entities to comply play an important role but are not the only determinant of the standard's effectiveness. Despite these differences private and public regulation at the transnational level are intertwined and the international organizations play a significant function in making TPR effective.[5]

The chapter examines these regimes and tries to identify determinants of regulatory convergence and divergence. Convergence may concern procedural and/or substantive standards. Do private transnational regulatory models vary? Are they converging towards common characteristics? What are the factors determining divergences or convergences?

Differences across private regulators concern standard setting, implementation, monitoring compliance, and assessing conformity, enforcement, and sanctioning. The models of TPR are sector specific and generally tailored to the particular market structure of regulated entities. These variations relate to both governance and regulatory activities.[6] How can differences be explained beyond sectoral distinctions that certainly contribute to variation? They concern the content of the standards: private regulators engaged in financial regulation differ from those addressing e-commerce or sustainability. Differences are driven by market structures and trade flows where regulated entities operate. But differences can also be based on specific regulatory objectives and, in particular, whether regulators aim at increasing efficiency by removing barriers to trade or protecting interests and values that are not internalized in market prices (negative externalities, global bads) or are undersupplied (global public goods). These variations when excessive may produce regulatory fragmentation, increasing regulatory costs without additional benefits. Furthermore, differences can generate a race to the bottom and undermine the

---

[3] This is not to deny that private actors do not play an indirect paramount role in influencing states' decisions about international standards.

[4] Even in the field of public international standards, there is an increasing number of voluntary standards based on soft law. These standards are often addressed to firms as the OECD Guidelines on Multinational Enterprises or the Multinational Enterprise Declaration issued by ILO. Both soft law and private standards are voluntary, but the incentives to adopt and comply with them significantly differ.

[5] See B. Kingsbury and R. Stewart (eds.), *Global Hybrid and Private Governance* (Oxford University Press, 2017). K. Abbott, International organisations and international regulatory co-operation: Exploring the links, in *International Organizations and International Regulatory Cooperation* (OECD, 2014), p. 17: 'The UN Environment Program (UNEP) has been a particularly active orchestrator, helping to create and support the Global Reporting Initiative (the most widely used standard for corporate sustainability reporting), the Principles for Responsible Investment and other transnational schemes. The International Finance Corporation (IFC), part of the World Bank Group, helped launch the Equator Principles; the two organisations meet regularly to keep their standards aligned.'

[6] On the interplay between governance and regulatory activities by private regulators, see F. Cafaggi, Transnational private regulation. A comparative analysis, legitimacy, effectiveness, quality and enforcement. EUI Working Paper 2014/15, available at www.eui.eu.

credibility of the entire field. Reputation in private regulation is a key feature to legitimacy and accountability. Regulatory cooperation can represent one possible response to fragmentation. The issue addressed in the chapter is upon which conditions regulatory cooperation or integration contribute to divergence or convergence?

A satisfactory comparative methodology for transnational private regimes is still missing. The objective of the chapter is, however, more limited. The main question concerns the impact of international regulatory cooperation on the divergence or convergence of transnational regulatory models. The chapter demonstrates a correlation between forms and instruments of cooperation and modes of convergence. Firstly, the analysis shows that the conventional comparative methodology used for state laws is unsuitable to compare transnational private regimes. Secondly, the determinants of convergence or divergence of transnational regulatory models differ from those affecting the evolutionary patterns of State legal systems.

The thesis developed in this chapter is that conflicts in the private sphere generate divergences in regulatory models, whereas the alignment of interests produces cooperation and convergence[7]. Conflicts trigger institutional responses, which may promote different degrees of convergence in regulatory models. Various forms of regulatory cooperation may bring different types and degrees of regulatory convergence. We distinguish between contractual and organizational forms of cooperation and describe the type of convergence that results from each family of cooperative instruments. Firstly, contractual cooperation among regime owners is examined. Secondly, the role of private meta-regulator as drivers of cooperation is considered. Thirdly, organizational cooperation is analysed up to the most extreme form of regulatory integration. Thereafter, a comparative analysis of the different forms describes the correlation with convergence of regulatory models. Concluding remarks follow in the final portion of the chapter.

2 TRANSNATIONAL PRIVATE REGULATION AND THE PRIVATE SPHERE: FROM CONFLICTS TO COOPERATION, THE DRIVERS OF REGULATORY CONVERGENCE

Unlike conventional self-regulatory regimes, where there is a coincidence between regulators and regulated entities, TPR presents a different composition and architecture.[8] On the one hand, it includes interests and organizations other than those of the industry (regulated entities); on the other hand, it takes fully into account the conflicts of interest within industries. Even within the same industry, interests may significantly diverge and the distribution of regulatory power among enterprises (large, medium, and small) can be uneven. Firms with different size and

---

[7] See B. Eberlein, K. Abbott, J. Black, E. Meidinger, and S. Wood, Transnational business governance interactions: Conceptualisation and framework for analysis, 8:1 *Regulation and Governance* 1 (2014).
[8] On the distinction between conventional self-regulation and transnational private regulation, see F. Cafaggi, Transnational private regulation, new foundations, (2011) 38 *Journal of Law and Society* 20, p. 21 ff.

geographical scope may have divergent regulatory objectives, depending on how close to the market of destination they are. Firms that are closer to supply may be more sensitive to the needs of local communities, whereas firms closer to consumers may privilege the final product and have less interest in the process. A key divergence concerns the distribution of costs of regulatory compliance along the global chain.

Private actors include trade associations, global labour unions, NGOs, multi-stakeholder organizations encompassing industry, trade unions, and NGOs. NGOs are engaged in regulatory activities when they design and implement standards and principles to be applied by enterprises along their global supply chains.[9] Within the term *NGOs* we include single and multi-stakeholders representing various interests affected by the economic activities. A well-known example of multi-stakeholder organization is the Forest Stewardship Council (FSC), with the three chambers that represent environmental, social, and economic interests.[10] A similar multi-stakeholder structure is that of the Roundtable on Sustainable Palm Oil (RSPO) or the Roundtable on Sustainable Soy (RSS), with many constituencies represented in different chambers.[11] Multi-stakeholder organizations have emerged in other fields like defence and military service, international code of conduct for private security service providers (ICoC) or in the area of advertising with EASA.[12]

A second factor of differentiation from conventional self-regulation is related to the interaction between the transnational, regional, and national levels. In some organizations, the model is a federation of pre-existing national entities; in other organizations, the birth is transnational and then national chapters are created for purpose of standards implementation and enforcement. The different approaches reflect power allocation between levels and across regions, and may have an impact on the intensity and degree of convergence.[13]

TPR differs also from industry customs and jus mercatorum.[14] The inclusion of NGOs as independent standard setters or as members of multi-stakeholder organizations marks a major difference with self-regulatory models. This difference initially represented a major factor of divergence in transnational rule making. Later, the proliferation of standards and toolkits to monitor compliance forced forms of cooperation between conventional self-regulatory bodies and transnational private regulators.[15]

---

[9] I use the term *non-governmental organizations* interchangeably with the term *civil society organizations* (CSO).
[10] See the FSC statute available at www.fsc.org.
[11] See the RSPO statute available at www.rspo.org, and the RSS statute available at www.rss.org.
[12] See IcoC at www.icoc-psp.org.
[13] See F. Cafaggi, A comparative analysis (n. 6).
[14] See F. Cafaggi, The many unexplored features of transnational private rule making (n. 1).
[15] Marx and Wouters distinguish between different functions and modes of cooperation. According to their analysis, meta-regulation addresses the credibility gap while mutual recognition is directed at cost reduction. See A. Marx and J. Wouters, *Competition and Cooperation in the Market of Voluntary Sustainability Standards* in P. Delimatsis, the *Law, Economic and Politics of International Standardization* (Cambridge University Press, 2016), p. 215.

In a recent line of research, the notion of regulatory intermediaries has been used to identify the many entities standing between rule makers and rule takers engaged in the implementation process, affecting not only effectiveness but also the accountability of the regulatory chain.[16] Whereas this characterization seems to be appropriate and useful in the field of public regulation, it raises some conceptual questions in transnational private regulation. Clearly, the definition of *intermediaries* can change, depending on the one held by rule makers. If rule making coincides with standard setting, then all those involved in monitoring compliance and enforcement can be considered intermediaries.[17] If rule making encompasses also monitoring and enforcement the space for regulatory intermediaries is radically reduced, many entities participate in the same regulatory process as players and not intermediaries.[18]

Even in the latter case, however, the role of intermediaries can be meaningful and their influence on convergence of regulatory models and practices remarkable.[19] Hence we shall consider the role of regulatory intermediaries taking a narrow definition, as those who do not play one of the three traditional functions (e.g. standard setting, monitoring, enforcement).

Empirical research across different sectors shows that there is substantial isomorphism in relation to the organizational forms.[20] Private regulators select their legal forms according to the national law of the place of incorporation. Most of the organizations incorporate in Switzerland, Belgium, England, and the United States. The structures reflect the differences among not-for-profit forms in national legal systems where incorporation takes place. An additional factor of differentiation is related to organizational choices. Heterogeneity of legal forms is increased by different procedural choices about the relationship between standard setting, monitoring, and enforcement.[21] Some organizations choose to separate them into

[16] See D. L. Faur and S. M. Starobin, Transnational politics and policy. From two-way to three-way interactions. Jerusalem Papers in Regulation & Governance Working Paper No. 62, The Hebrew University, 2014; Kenneth W. Abbott, David Levi-Faur, and Duncan Snidal, Theorizing intermediaries in regulatory governance, (2017) *The Annals of the American Academy of Political and Social Science* 14.

[17] See A. M. Loconto, Models of assurance: Diversity and standardization of modes of intermediation, (2017) *Annals of the American Academy of Political and Social Science* 112; T. Havinga and P. Verbruggen, Relationships in food safety regulation: The RIT model as a theoretical lens, (2017) *Annals of the American Academy of Political and Social Science* 59.

[18] See F. Cafaggi, A comparative analysis (n. 6).

[19] See G. Auld and S. Renckens, Rule making feedback through intermediation and evaluation in transnational private governance, (2017) *Annals of the American Academy of Political and Social Science*, 93 and 97, distinguishing between intermediation and evaluation feedback. Their contribution focuses on the role of intermediaries which participate in the regulatory process and those which are not technically regulators like the media which, nevertheless, provide information about (non) compliance with standards. This distinction results into a difference between co-regulation and intermediation.

[20] See F. Cafaggi, A comparative analysis (n. 6).

[21] Global administrative law (GAL) produces differentiations of legal forms in TPR. That is, two associations whose legal form are very similar may have important governance difference, depending on how they apply stakeholders' participation, transparency, and duty to give reasons.

different entities; others simply build internal divisions with functional rather than structural separation.[22]

In the former case, functional separation is combined with structural differentiation; in the latter, the organization remains unitary while the various functions are played by different units. Clearly, structural separation ensures higher independence. If the monitoring system is entrusted in a different organization or at least an independent entity, it is more likely that they will evaluate the compliance more objectively and will report whether the standard achieves or not its objectives. When the same entity performs all the functions, coordination costs are lower but the risks of capture and conflict of interest are higher. The example of certification bodies and their independence from the standard setters is a good illustration of the structural separation between setting standards and monitoring compliance.[23] Similarly, in the case of military service providers, the decision of creating a separate grievance mechanism was driven by the necessity to increase accountability. Variations concerning governance are significant when considering the organization of the regulatory process. The degree of differentiation increases even more if one considers the adoption of global administrative standards related to transparency, participation, duty to give reasons, and the establishment of a separate and independent enforcement mechanism.[24]

Stakeholders' participation in the activities may significantly modify the balance between conflicting interests, even if the organizational models are identical. The same associational model with different instruments favouring stakeholder participation in the regulatory process may diverge on their regulatory outputs and their level of accountability.[25] Hence there is a strong correlation between organizational governance and procedural rules that affects the degree of convergence or divergence.[26] Differences concern – in particular – monitoring and auditing. This is probably the area where variations are most significant, and they reflect the different approaches to accountability. The move from auditing to more structured conformity assessment; the distinction between first-, second-, and third-party verification generates a high degree of divergence on how to measure effectiveness. The consequences of non-compliance and the use of grievance mechanisms between the scheme owner and regulated entities and among regulated entities vary, depending on the organizational model. These features represent important variations across

[22] Sometimes separation is required by common principles, as is the case when ISEAL requires independence of certifiers from standard setters. See the ISEAL Assurance Code Standard below (n. 66).
[23] Different views on how independence should be achieved are reflected in the conformity assessment standards produced by ISO and ISEAL, which determined the creation of different rules by the latter after adhering to the standard issued by ISO (17065).
[24] See B. Kingsbury, N. Krisch, and R. Stewart, The emergence of global administrative law, (2005) *Law and Contemporary Problems* 33; S. Cassese, *Research Handbook in Global Administrative Law* (Edward Elgar, 2016).
[25] See R. Stewart, Remedying disregard in global regulatory governance: accountability, participation, and responsiveness (2014) 108 *American Journal of International Law* 211.
[26] See F. Cafaggi, A comparative analysis (n. 6).

transnational private regulators. It is contended that organizational features affect the degree and the modes of convergence.

These dimensions are partly and occasionally related to conflicts between the regulators and the regulated, and among the latter, about regulatory objectives and instruments. This is the main topic of the chapter, to which we now turn.

3 CONFLICTS IN THE PRIVATE SPHERE: A BRIEF CONCEPTUAL MAP

Private regulatory regimes are voluntary, and regulated entities choose to subscribe to them.[27] The degree of voluntariness may vary across global chains, depending on how the contractual power is concentrated. It is often the case that small suppliers are forced to comply with private standards on the basis of a decision to join, exclusively made by the chain leader. Private regimes are sector specific, and their variations are significant across industries. Within industries (electronics, agri-food, textile, extractive, etc.), conflicting interests explain variations of regulatory regimes related to the institutional design and to the content of standards.[28] We identify three conflict dimensions: (1) conflicts among regulated entities, (2) conflicts between regulated entities and intermediaries, and (3) conflicts between intermediaries.

Firstly, conflicts within industries among regulated entities occur between large enterprises and small suppliers often located in different countries. SMEs often find it difficult to meet the standards because of low capabilities, partly associated with the socio-economic and institutional environment they operate in.[29] Not only do these conflicts concern the objectives of the standards; they also concern their distributional consequences. Compliance with private standards requires costs that are not evenly distributed along chains between various regulated entities.

Secondly, conflicts arise between industries and NGOs about the targets and the compliance methods. NGOs require rigorous compliance and effective monitoring and enforcement. When they own certification schemes, NGOs influence not only the activity of the supply chain but also their governance. For example, sustainable supply chains require a traceability system that may force information sharing along the chain beyond the level that would otherwise be chosen in ordinary commercial relationships. A classical conflict in the forest sector between FSC and PEFC has evolved from fierce competition into an informal process of mutual learning.[30]

[27] See F. Cafaggi, The many unexplored features of transnational private rule making (n. 1).
[28] On the variations among private regulators and their explanations, see in relation to sustainability Marx and Wouters, *Competition and Cooperation* (n. 15). For a comparison between technical and financial standards, see Buthe and Mattli, *The New Global Rulers* (n. 1).
[29] See OECD and the World Bank's report on inclusive value chains, 2015.
[30] See C. Overdevest, Comparing forest certification schemes: The case of ratcheting standards in the forest sector, (2010) 8 *Socio-Economic* 47–76; C. Overdevest and J. Zeitlin, Assembling an experimentalist regime: Transnational governance interactions in the forest sector (2014) 8 *Regulation and Governance* 22.

Whereas conflicts persist, increasingly cooperation has developed to integrate different approaches that combine efficiency (reducing costs and increasing benefits of TPR) and effectiveness (achieving the objectives of regulatory standards).

Thirdly, conflicts exist among NGOs. Conflicts may occur when NGOs pursue different objectives in the same industries or similar objectives with different strategies. In the field of crop certification related to sustainability in agriculture, different scheme owners coexist: some focus more on the protection of smallholders and local communities, some on the protection of the environment, others on the working conditions of employees and their families. Not only differences but also the relationships with transnational corporation affect regulators' objectives. Some prefer to engage in dialogue or even in cooperation with common projects; others privilege a more adversarial perspective and jealously preserve their independence. As the palm oil example shows, these differences may translate into conflicts among NGOs over compliance with labour standards.[31]

We suggest that conflicts within the private sphere may be one of the drivers of cooperation that can promote transnational regulatory convergence. Hence there is a relationship between conflicts-cooperation-convergence.

4 INTERNATIONAL REGULATORY COOPERATION AND CONVERGENCE

There is an increase of regulatory cooperation at the international level that involves states, international organizations, and private actors.[32] In their famous governance triangle, Abbott and Snidal provided the first taxonomy of different typologies of interactions between states, industry, and NGOs.[33] Since then, the debate on the public/private interactions and the drivers of conflicts and cooperation has bloomed, providing deeper and more comprehensive analyses.[34]

International regulatory cooperation can take various forms and deploy different instruments.[35] In addition to the traditional forms of treaty-based and international

---

[31] See below on the conflict between Amnesty and RSPO concerning the compliance by WILMAR with international labour standards. See Amnesty International, The great palm oil scandal: Labour abuses behind big brand names, Amnesty International, November 2016, available at www.amnestyinternational.org.

[32] See OECD, *International Regulatory Co-operation: Addressing Global Challenges* (OECD Publishing, 2013). For a pioneering account, see G. Bermann, M. Herdegen, P. Lindseth, *Transatlantic Regulatory Co-operation, Legal Problems and Political Prospects* (Oxford University Press, 2000), and Vogel and Swinnen, *Transatlantic Regulatory Cooperation: The Shifting Role of EU, US, and California* (Edward Elgar, 2011).

[33] From a wider perspective, see Abbott and Snidal, Governance triangle (n. 2).

[34] B. Eberlein et al., Transnational business governance interactions: Conceptualisation and framework for analysis (2014) *Regulation and Governance* 1; Kingsbury and Stewart (eds.), *Global Hybrid and Private Governance* (Oxford University Press, 2017).

[35] The OECD identifies eleven forms of IRC based on more than forty case studies. OECD, *International Regulatory Co-operation: Case Studies, Vol. 3* (OECD Publishing, 2013). This taxonomy has been revised by Abbott, International organisations and international regulatory co-operation

organizations, multiple 'informal' or semiformal instruments have emerged, like networks, associations, memorandum of understanding, and agreements. There has been a shift from intergovernmental organizations to transgovernmental networks.[36] The latter do not need the formal step of state ratifications and are considered more flexible and effective.[37] Transgovernmental formal and informal networks are generally created by independent administrative authorities and central banks; they do not follow the conventional paths of Intergovernmental organizations.[38] However, IGOs increasingly act as institutionalized forums to orchestrate regulatory cooperation among public and private actors.[39] Variations occur between intergovernmental organizations and transgovernmental networks but also within each category.[40] The instruments differ, but the focus on coordination and the promotion of collaboration to define and implement international standards is similar to IGOs. International regulatory cooperation (IRC) can be driven by multiple factors: (1) harmonizing sector-specific regulation that may impair free trade and increase regulatory burdens without additional benefits, (2) solving policy conflicts and trade-offs among diverging objectives (e-commerce and data protection, trade and environmental protection, environmental and consumer protection), (3) supplying global public goods when market incentives may lead

---

(n. 5), pp. 31–32: 'They include treaties; legally binding Council Decisions; model conventions, which shape inter-state negotiations; diverse and nuanced forms of "soft law," including declarations, Council Recommendations, principles and guidelines; and statements of good practices and other forms of agreed policy guidance.'

[36] See A. M. Slaughter, *The New World Order* (Princeton University Press, 2004).

[37] See K. Abbott, International organisations and international regulatory co-operation: Exploring the links, in *International Organizations and International Regulatory Cooperation* (OECD, 2014), p. 17, part 23: 'Transgovernmental institutions are seen as having several advantages. They can adopt rules without ratification by states. They may reach cooperative agreements more easily because all participants share common experiences and understandings. And they may be more flexible than formal IOs in responding to changing conditions. On the other hand, transgovernmental rules are not binding under international law, although participating agencies typically face strong pressures to adopt and comply with those rules.'

[38] See J. Pawelyn, R. Wessel, and J. Wouters, *Informal Law Making* (Oxford University Press, 2013).

[39] See K. Abbott, P. Genschel, D. Snidal, and B. Zangl, *International Organizations as Orchestrators* (Cambridge University Press, 2015), and before, K. W. Abbott and D. Snidal, International regulation without international government: Improving IO performance through orchestration, (2010) 5 *Review of International Organizations* 315–334.

[40] See K. Abbott, International regulatory cooperation (n. 37), p. 32: 'Importantly, however, there appears to be wide variation among IOs in the procedures and instruments they employ. In contrast to the OECD, for example, the WTO acts almost exclusively through multilateral treaties; as a result, WTO negotiations over IRC are highly formalised and almost always inter-state. The case study of the International Maritime Organization (IMO) in this volume suggests that it too relies primarily on treaties. The ILO embodies international labor standards in treaties, but these are frequently supplemented with recommendations on implementation. The ILO has also adopted some prominent soft law declarations, notably the Declaration of Philadelphia and Declaration on Fundamental Principles and Rights at Work – as well as the Tripartite Declaration on Multinational Enterprises. The WHO, in contrast, has adopted only a single treaty, the Framework Convention on Tobacco Control; it is, however, empowered to adopt "regulations" in specified areas, most quite technical. The WHO has recently invoked the broadest of its regulations, the International Health Regulations 2005, in response to the Ebola outbreak in West Africa.'

to undersupply, and (4) tackling global bads.[41] The focus of this chapter is on the relationship between conflicts and IRC: Conflict avoidance and mitigation can lead to forms of regulatory cooperation between public actors, public and private actors, and private actors. Clearly, this is only one driver of regulatory cooperation. Complementarity of activities may be another factor leading to regulatory cooperation. They may have different effects over the convergence of transnational regulatory models.

Cooperation between public and private actors in the definition of standards and implementation has become very frequent;[42] IOs have modified their toolkit to define collaborative modes with different private actors.[43] FAO, for example, identifies six instruments to collaborate with civil society organizations (memorandum of understanding, exchange of letters, letters of agreement, formal relations, partnership committees for review of financial and other agreements, multi-door trust funds to support civil society organizations) and three instruments to collaborate with the private sector (memorandum of understanding, partnerships agreements, exchange of letters).

MOUs and agreements have proliferated. A powerful illustration of public/private cooperation aimed at avoiding or at least mitigating conflicts in the field of corporate social responsibility is the MoU between the International Labor Organization (ILO) and the International Standard Organization (ISO). ISO wanted to enter the field of social and labour standards. Mindful of the strong presence of ILO and other intergovernmental organizations, ISO decided to enter the field with a cooperative attitude and proposed MoUs to ensure the respect of existing international standards. The MoUs with ILO and with the OECD have had a specific procedural focus, defining the consultation over the content of the standard and the procedure to solve disagreement in the case of conflicting views.[44] ISO had a duty to ILO to respect their conventions and consult with ILO; ILO had the right to participate in the standard-setting process and provide comments and suggestions. ILO could express its disagreement, which ISO had a duty to take into account. In

---

[41] See I. Kaul, I. Grunberg, and M. Stern, *Global Public Goods: International Cooperation in the 21st Century* (Oxford University Press, 1999); K. Abbott, *International Organisations and International Regulatory Co-operation: Exploring the Links*, in *International Organizations and International Regulatory Cooperation* (OECD, 2014), p. 17, part. p. 22 ff.; S. Battini, The proliferation of global regulatory regimes, in *Research Handbook of Global Administrative Law* (n. 24), p. 45 ff; I. Kaul (ed.), *Global Public Goods* (Edward Elgar, 2016).

[42] Such cooperation is changing the nature of the public/private distinction, giving rise to hybrids that do not easily fit with the conventional description of international public and private standards. This change does not eliminate the distinction but forces us to reconsider its features. See B. Kingsbury and R. Stewart, The structures and problems of global hybrid and private governance, in Kingsbury and Stewart (eds.), *Global Hybrid and Private Governance* (Oxford University Press, 2017).

[43] IOs distinguish between instruments of collaboration with for-profit entities like multinationals and non-profit entities like non-governmental organizations (NGOs).

[44] See ISO/ILO MoU; J. Diller, Private standardization in international law making, (2012) 33 *Michigan Journal of International Law* 481.

5 Convergences and Divergences

case of persisting disagreement, ISO could go ahead but should make ILO's observations publicly available and circulate them among the stakeholders.[45]

This specific instrument of collaboration has been followed by a wider agreement in the area of health and safety at work related to the issuance of the new ISO standard 45001.[46] The agreement broadens the scope of collaboration to all subject matters that concern ILO's mandate. It specifically provides for an obligation to respect ILO's standards in case of conflict.[47]

Similar forms of collaboration between ISO and international organizations have developed in different areas. But ISO is also involved in cooperative activities with private organizations.[48] Cooperation serves multiple objectives: it avoids conflicts between ISO and international organizations and promotes the implementation of international standards by enterprises subscribing to ISO standards, making them more effective.

There are examples of flourishing cooperation in many other fields. Take for instance IOSCO and ISDA, in the field of financial regulation. In civil aviation, think of the long-standing collaboration between ICAO and IATA. Consider SAFA, which was the product of collaboration between FAO and many private actors. In sustainability and CSR, consider the United Nations Forum on Sustainability Standards (UNFSS), the collaboration between OECD and trade associations, and the UN Global Compact giving rise to the Agenda 2030 Sustainable Development Goals.[49]

5 PRIVATE TRANSNATIONAL REGULATORY COOPERATION

No comprehensive studies have classified the forms of transnational private regulatory cooperation.[50] The exponential growth of private schemes is not homogenous across sectors. In some areas, the number is growing exponentially; in other areas, it remains quite stable, with some schemes playing a dominant role in the market. Schemes' proliferation can produce adverse selection. On the demand side, users

---

[45] See ISO/ILO MoU.
[46] See the agreement between the International Labour Organization (ILO) and the International Organization for Standardization (ISO); hereinafter Agreement ILO/ISO.
[47] See Agreement ILO/ISO: '3. To date the ILO and ISO have cooperated on a case-by-case basis, such as through the Memorandum of Understanding (MoU) on social responsibility and liaison arrangements with ISO committees. This Agreement between the ILO and ISO provides the following framework for cooperation on any proposed new work in the ILO or ISO that may be of mutual interest as specified below. 4. Given the broad mandate and action of the ILO to promote social justice and decent work, and ISO's broad mission, ISO standards that relate to issues within the ILO's mandate (ILO issues) should respect and support the provisions of ILS and related ILO action, including by using ILS as the source of reference with respect to ILO issues in case of conflict.'
[48] See the ISO case study within the OECD project on international regulatory cooperation, available at www.oecd.org.
[49] See the SAFA guidelines, available at www.fao.org.
[50] See F. Cafaggi, A comparative analysis (n. 6).

may not be able to distinguish between good and bad schemes; such inability can drive to a race to the bottom. Fragmentation can also increase the costs of compliance, forcing enterprises to engage in double or triple certification without additional benefits for the environment or consumer protection.

Transnational private regulators are under pressure to reduce fragmentation, to harmonize standards, to implement them according to comparable logics, and to enforce them on the basis of common principles.[51] Drivers to cooperation are based both on cost evaluation and on the increasing complementary nature of different forms of private regulation. Cooperation is often deployed to reduce the differences or at least to reduce those differences that may impair the achievement of regulatory objectives. The example of sustainability – where environmental and social regulations once perceived as different if not conflicting are now integrated into a single standard – is illustrative of a process of integration taking place in other areas like data protection and e-commerce.[52] While in this chapter conflicts as causes of divergences and drivers to cooperation are the main focus, the causes of variations and determinants of cooperation are many-fold.

Cooperation can take place at different stages of the regulatory process. It can concern standard setting, reporting, auditing, and enforcement. When one regulator only performs a single function, cooperation with other private regulators is necessary. This is the case for private standard setters, which cooperate with other regulators by defining standards for reporting and auditing. The joint guidelines ISO/GRI on corporate social responsibility is a case in point. Bilateral cooperation can link standard setting and reporting, standard setting and auditing, and more generally monitoring compliance and standard setting.[53] These forms of cooperation integrate regulatory activities performed by different entities at various stages of the regulatory process. These are instances where cooperation is not only the response to conflict between regulators with different approaches but also the result of regulatory specialization and an appropriate institutional response to conflicts of interest. In other instances, the monitor is an independent organization and provides either at the individual or collective level information about the compliance with a standard or with multiple standards. This is the case for the WWF scoreboard on palm oil, used to evaluate regulatory performance in the field of sustainability by multinational enterprises engaged in agri-food.[54] A different interesting example in the field of palm oil concerns violations of labour standards. An important agri-food enterprise, subject to RSPO monitoring for sustainability standards, has been found

---

[51] See F. Cafaggi, The many unexplored features of transnational private rule making (n. 1).
[52] See A. Marx and J. Wouters, Competition and cooperation in the market of voluntary sustainability standards, in P. Delimatsis, *The Law, Economic and Politics of International Standardization* (Cambridge University Press, 2016), 215.
[53] See GRI G4 Guidelines and ISO 26000:2010, How to use the GRI G4 Guidelines and ISO 26000 in conjunction; available at www.iso.org.
[54] See the WWF Palm Oil Scoreboard available at www.wwf.org.

in violation by Amnesty International.[55] In its report, Amnesty not only described the violations committed by the enterprise but also passed negative judgments on the adequacy of RSPO standards and their monitoring practices. RSPO responded constructively to the criticisms and engaged in an internal review of its practices.

Auditing and reporting focus on practices and provide the standard setter with feedback about the causes of non-compliance and possibly the solution when they are rooted in the design of the rules.[56] Reporting when addressing the differences in compliance among regulated entities can explain the divergences in action in spite of convergences, as described in the books.

Regulatory cooperation may focus only on the activity or include some organizational dimensions. The former is usually softer and operates via contract: agreements and MoUs. The latter is usually stronger and may deploy both agreements and organizational devices. Cooperation may result in integration when the cooperating entities decide to create a single organization by merging the existing ones. We examine each form and suggest that they might have a different impact on regulatory convergence.

5.1 Agreements

Transnational private regulatory cooperation deploys agreements with different degrees of binding commitments. Even within memoranda of understanding, there are various levels of commitments resulting in different modes of enforceability (legal and non-legal). Despite the fact that legal enforceability may not be a feature entirely in the hands of the signatories, parties' expression of their willingness to make legally binding commitments is relevant to defining legal enforceability and the boundaries with non-legal modes of enforceability.

MOUs can either be specific and focus on one standard or one activity (auditing, reporting, grievance mechanism) or be general and include various activities performed by the regulator. Even in the latter case, they do not involve organizational changes but focus on the regulatory process.

Contractual cooperation among private regulators via MOUs is aimed at avoiding conflicts and increasing effectiveness but does not change either the identity or the structure of transnational private regulators. It focuses on the standards and their implementation but does not impact the organizational features and the relationships with stakeholders. Exit costs from the agreement are relatively low, and the degree of cooperation can change over time. The influence on convergence relates

---

[55] See Amnesty International, The great palm oil scandal: Labor abuses behind big brand names, November 2016, available at www.amnestyinternational.org.
[56] G. Auld and S. Renckens, Rule-making feedbacks through intermediation and evaluation in transnational private governance, (2017) 670 *Annals of the American Academy of Political and Social Science* 1:93–111, and G. Auld, *Constructing Private Governance* (Yale University Press, 2014).

to the standards but does not influence the organizational structure. It is usually deployed for mutual recognition of standards, which leads to limited convergence

5.2 Private Meta-regulation

A more intense form of cooperation results in the establishment of meta-regulators.[57] The creation of meta-regulators whose members are individual regulators may pursue different objectives: to strengthen legitimacy, to prevent or solve conflicts among standard setters, to ensure uniform compliance, to promote mutual learning, to define best practices.[58] We focus on one particular objective: conflict avoidance and the mitigation of the consequences when they arise.

Meta-regulation is an intermediate form of regulatory cooperation between agreement and organization because a new entity is created but the participants preserve their independent and autonomous existence and their mission. It does not give rise to full organizational integration. Private meta-regulators encompass individual entities engaged in regulation in the same field or in a particular type of standards (e.g. sustainability or food safety). Each regulator maintains its independence and autonomy and the freedom to exit the meta-organization at any time, with limited exit costs. Some meta-regulators are composed of entities coming from different constituencies within the private sectors; others belong to either industry or NGOs. Private meta regulators can differ from multi-stakeholder organizations on two different grounds: firstly, they focus on regulation and not on the operational side; secondly, they are not necessarily multi-stakeholders. The key feature is represented by a multiplicity of private regulators aimed at creating common principles or a regime of mutual recognition.

We examine here membership-based meta-regulators where various private regulators decide to create/join a meta regulator and commit to comply with its principles.[59] The members are often competitors and their market shares are contested[60]. Clearly, a prominent role of meta-regulators is to ensure that competition is not disruptive and does not lead to a race to the bottom.[61] But divergences and potential conflicts may arise from different regulatory objectives even beyond competition. Private meta-regulation can contribute to address divergences and steer towards cooperation, mitigating conflicts.

---

[57] C. Coglianese and E. Mendelson, Meta-regulation and self-regulation, in R. Baldwin, M. Cave, and M. Lodge (eds.), *The Oxford Handbook of Regulation* (Oxford University Press, 2010), at 146.
[58] See F. Cafaggi, Transnational private regulation: Regulating global private regulators, in S. Cassese, *Research Handbook on Global Administrative Law* (Edward Elgar, 2016), p. 282.
[59] Private meta-regulators can be membership or non-membership based. The latter is an organization that provides principles or rules for private regulators, but it is not composed by the regulated entities. See F. Cafaggi, Regulating private regulators (n. 2).
[60] For example, consider the Rainforest Alliance and Fair Trade within ISEAL, or the different firms within GFSI.
[61] See F. Cafaggi, Transnational private regulation: Regulating global private regulators (n. 58).

5 Convergences and Divergences

Private meta regulation can result in mutual recognition or the definition of common principles. Mutual recognition is one institutional response to differences arising out of the proliferation of private standards. The Global Food Safety Initiative (GFSI) is a foundation that encompasses many food safety certification program owners, mainly retail driven. The desire to ensure standards of participants (certification program owners or CPOs) are mutually recognized motivated retailers to group together (the British Retail Consortium or BRC) to define common principles.[62] It represents a form of collaboration between trade associations in the agri-food business and certification schemes that define minimum requirements and monitor compliance along supply chains. These are primarily B2B schemes with no involvement of consumer organizations in the regulatory process. Mutual recognition favours a process of convergence over standards and their monitoring; at the same time, it contributes to reducing costs for large enterprises that source from suppliers linked to different certification schemes across the world. GFSI defines benchmarks that CPOs have to comply with in order to be members.[63] Both the process of setting the benchmarks and that of monitoring are participatory, but the involvement of external stakeholders is very limited.

Another example of regulatory cooperation aimed at mutual recognition in the private sphere is represented by the International Accreditation Forum (IAF). IAF has produced a mutual recognition arrangement that ensures signatories' compliance with ISP conformity assessments. The objective of the arrangement is to create common rules among accreditation bodies when accrediting Certifying Bodies (CBs). IAF membership grants the licensee the right to use the IAF mark when accrediting the certification bodies.[64] IAF controls the ABs and should ensure that they have appropriate criteria to control certification bodies that must certify compliance of regulated entities.

Private meta-regulators can create common rules that members need to abide by.

Competition and/or complementarity between regulatory activities may give rise to forms of organizational integration between two or many private regulators. Historically there are examples of programs initiated by the cooperation of large enterprises and NGOs giving rise to new entities. The classical examples are Marine Stewardship Council, created by Unilever and WWF, and UTZ Certified, created by an NGO (Solidaridad) and two enterprises: a coffee grower and a coffee roaster.[65] MSC then became a member of ISEAL.

---

[62] See T. Havinga and P. Verbruggen, Relationships in food safety regulation (n. 17).
[63] See F. Cafaggi, Transnational private regulation: regulating global private regulators (n. 58); T. Havinga and P. Verbruggen, Relationships in food safety regulation (n. 17).
[64] See the General Principles on the Use of the IAF MLA Mark, available at www.iaf.org.
[65] UTZ was founded by Nick Bocklandt, a Belgian-Guatemalan coffee grower, and Ward de Groote, a Dutch coffee roaster, with the goal of implementing sustainability on a large scale in the worldwide market. Solidaridad (www.solidaridadnetwork.org) was another co-initiator of UTZ Certified and helped UTZ to become a global standard through financial support and field implementation'

The International Social and Environmental Accreditation and Labelling Association (ISEAL) is an organization encompassing a large number of scheme owners in the field of sustainability.[66] ISEAL is a membership-based organization that has recently moved to a broader objective to reach out also to non-members. With the issuance of the Credibility Principles, ISEAL is trying to influence the entire sustainability field beyond its membership.[67] ISEAL goals range from 'enhancing the livelihoods of people living in poverty, to supporting workers' rights and gender equality, to addressing water and energy use, to minimizing negative impacts on the climate, biodiversity and ecosystems'. It has a full commitment to contributing to the Sustainable Development Goal (SDG), Agenda 2030.[68] ISEAL is steering its members towards alignment of their objectives with SDG and focuses on impact by encouraging them to measure their effectiveness based on changes they produce.[69]

The codes produced by ISEAL define general principles that members have to comply with during their activities. This is mainly a form of procedural convergence. The codes concern how to produce, monitor, and implement rules enacted by individual organizations.

The standard-setting code has produced radical changes in codes' drafting procedures, imposing stakeholders' consultation and duty to periodically revise the code after a thorough analysis.[70] The impact code has generated remarkable changes in the organizational culture, shifting the focus from rule-making to effective implementation. ISEAL's members have to engage in both ex ante and ex post impact analysis on the basis of objective indicators. Their impact assessment requires monitoring and evaluation (ME). To implement the Code, each member has created an internal ME division responsible for assessing the impact of the standard. This is a clear illustration of how the structure of the regulatory process influences the organizational structure of the members.

ISEAL's codes have an influence not only on members' activities but also on their internal organizations. Hence, they strive to organizational convergence of private regulation in the field of sustainability. In particular, ISEAL requires its members to have independent compliance monitoring regimes.[71] This requirement has driven important governance changes in ISEAL's members, steering towards

---

[66] See Loconto and Fouilleux, Politics of private regulation: ISEAL and the shaping of transnational sustainability governance, (2014) *Regulation and Governance* 165.
[67] Currently it has twenty-two full members and three associate members.
[68] See the WWF-ISEAL joint report, 2017, and ISEAL, Sustainability standards and the SDGs: Evidence of ISEAL members contribution, 2017, both available at www.iseal.org.
[69] See, for example, UTZ Impact Reports.
[70] On the differences between standard setting practices before and after ISEAL membership, see F. Cafaggi, Regulating private regulators (n. 2).
[71] See A. Loconto, Models of assurance (n. 17): 'From 2005, then, member schemes needed to separate their standard-setters and certifiers into independent legal entities; standard-setters were required to comply with ISEAL's code for setting standards, and certifiers had to be accredited according to the ISO guide 17065 by a national accreditation body.'

organizational convergence within ISEAL and via the Credibility Principles also outside ISEAL members.[72]

ISEAL provides its members with a conflict resolution mechanism which has recently been reformed and been made independent from ISEAL itself deploying structural separation.[73] The mechanism solves conflicts between members and between ISEAL and individual members. GFSI also has an internal dispute resolution mechanism.

Private meta regulation produces procedural and organizational convergence. Not only does ISEAL impose convergence among its members, but it also promotes cooperation with other public and private regulators. ISEAL has also cooperated with other private regulators to make sustainability standards effective. In relation to conformity assessment, ISEAL refers to ISO accreditation standards and to other standards like IEC.[74] Even if outside a formalized cooperation, ISEAL – by making reference to ISO and imposing compliance to its members – contributes to the diffusion and implementation of the ISO model, operationalizing transnational regulatory cooperation.[75]

GFSI and ISEAL reflect two models of private regulatory cooperation. Whereas GFSI defines principles aimed at benchmarking different standards, ISEAL requires its members' compliance with the three codes whose content is procedural rather than substantive. GFSI is concerned primarily with substantive standards, whereas ISEAL focuses on procedural standards. In both cases, the definition of the common rules is the result of a collaboration of the individual regulators and the organization monitors its compliance. But the benchmarking model is more interactive and mainly reflects the existing common features of the schemes. To oversimplify, ISEAL is more proactive with respect to its members; GFSI is more reactive.[76] This difference is partly related to the independence of the management.

A case of private meta-regulation that deserves special attention is ISO.[77] ISO produces technical standards for enterprises. Recently it entered the field of certification and has issued a conformity assessment standard (ISO 17065) adopted by many certification schemes, often upon the request of national legislation. The ISO 17065 standard addresses both governance and procedural issues and is a powerful driver of regulatory convergence of certification models.

---

[72] See www.iseal.org.
[73] Ibid.
[74] ISEAL members have to comply with the ISO/IEC 17011:2004 guide for accreditation bodies.
[75] Ibid.
[76] This is indeed an oversimplification, since in many respects GFSI benchmarking guidance has introduced new rules and principles, rather than simply mirroring the state of the art. See F. Cafaggi, Regulating private regulators (n. 2).
[77] See P. Delimatsis, *The Law, Economic and Politics of International Standardization* (Cambridge University Press, 2016); F. Parisi and V. Fon, *The Economics of Lawmaking* (Oxford University Press, 2008).

Private meta regulators have a significant impact on the convergence of regulatory models through different and often complementary instruments. They deploy mutual recognition and common codes or principles related to procedural and substantive standards. Their impact varies, but it often includes not only standard but also relevant features of the organizational models, including forms of participation aimed at increasing effectiveness and accountability.

5.3 International Regulatory Integration of Private Regulators: Mergers and Acquisitions

Transnational private regulators may decide to cooperate when their activities are complementary to increasing their market share (e.g. the number of firms subscribing to their regimes). But regulatory cooperation may also arise out of competition when competing for market shares increases the costs without adding benefits to the regulated entities (the firms) and even more to the final regulatory beneficiaries (consumers, investors, environmental organizations, human rights NGOs). In this analysis, we focus more on the integration between existing regulators as a radical form of regulatory convergence.

Patterns of integration may concern only the activity (e.g. designing common standards, conducting joint auditing, creating a single enforcement mechanism). Or it can involve the organizational dimension of the creation of common entities to the more radical organizational integration giving rise to a single entity. Mergers in the field of TPR have been rare thus far. More common is the opposite phenomenon of splitting.

Regulatory integration can follow different pathways. We distinguish between incremental and radical integration to identify ideal models that can present many variations in between.

Incremental integration follows a step-by-step logic where two or more private regulators decide to have common standards and/or common compliance monitoring and then might create a single entity to jointly perform part of their activity to integrate part of the activity. The new entity does not replace the old ones. This process could eventually end in a merger. Even after the merger, the degree of integration can differ, with the two or more entities preserving some or even a high degree of independence when, for example, the types of certifications differ (e.g. one related to product safety and the other to sustainability).

Radical integration occurs when two or more separate entities that have had soft forms of cooperation decide to merge without intermediate steps like agreements to cooperate or joining standard setting. It results in the creation of a new organization and the disappearance of the old ones.

The decision between incremental and radical integration may depend on several factors related to the costs and benefits of cooperation. One strategic variable is the control of opting out by some of the participants and the costs that exit can generate for those which remain. Opting out of an incremental process of integration may have disrupting consequences on one or both sides, giving rise to an unravelling of the entire process. Radical integration reduces the risks of opting out by increasing the level of common stakes, making exit a costly option since the very beginning. What is relevant in incremental integration is the strategic use of the opt-out option to renegotiate the terms of the process. Therefore the risks of opportunistic behaviour in renegotiating the process of integration are lowered by selecting the radical integration option. However, the advantages of incremental integration may be significant. Especially when the level of reciprocal trust is initially low, engaging in radical integration may be perceived as risky and even dangerous.

The number of players and their respective 'weight' may have a relevant impact on the decision to integrate and the modes of integration. When the number of parties willing to integrate is small (two) the opt-out is extremely costly and the entire process may unravel. When the number is relatively large, the exit of one player may undermine the integration project only if its participation is considered to be essential by the other players. The difference in regulatory shares held by participants influences both modes of cooperation and the quality of regulatory convergence.

Even when radical integration is chosen, the process of regulatory convergence may be slow. The creation of a single entity still requires a transition process towards regulatory convergence.

In practice, we observe different degrees and various paths towards regulatory integration in the world of private regulation. The area of sustainability provides interesting examples of integration. We have seen that the creation of ISEAL has promoted common procedural rules related to standard setting, implementation and impact assessment, assurance, and enforcement.

UTZ and the Rainforest Alliance, together with Fair Trade, represent the three most relevant market players in the field of certification of coffee, tea, and cocoa. They are all members of ISEAL. Hence they all have to comply with the Credibility Principles and with the three ISEAL codes. Their origin is different but their standards have become increasingly similar. The Fair Trade Labeling Organization (FLO) is a certification scheme owner with a strong focus on distributional issues.[78] Rainforest Alliance is part of the Sustainable Agriculture Network

[78] See A. Loconto, Models of assurance (n. 17): 'FLO is one of the best-known sustainability standards. emerging from a charity shop movement, the fair trade concept was first established in 1988 under the label Max Havelaar in the Netherlands; it quickly spread through national labeling initiatives across europe and North America (Raynolds, Murray, and Wilkinson 2007). In 1997, FLO was established as the Fairtrade Labelling Organizations International (a nongovernmental organization) and developed the first international standards for Fairtrade, which included a label and a certification scheme. FLO now operates a suite of standards that differ by type of producer (e.g., smallholder organizations, hired workers) and also apply to traders. Its standards cover production practices, treatment of workers, and terms of trade. FLO also has product-specific standards that define minimum prices for producers and a "social premium" that must be paid to producers and/or farm workers (t+B). *FLO retains control over the implementation, interpretation, and monitoring of its standards.* FLO provides direct support

(SAN) and also a member of ISEAL. It has been focusing on environmental issues and has entered the certification market of agricultural commodities, bringing closer the relationship between environment and agricultural quality and efficiency.[79] Its primary area of activity has been the United States. UTZ was born with an agreement between two enterprises and an NGO. Its focus has been single agricultural commodities (first coffee and then tea and cocoa), and the final market is primarily though not exclusively Europe. In time, UTZ has become a global organization with an impact in many countries located across various continents.

Despite their similarities, the three organizations differ on a number of dimensions. FLO targets primarily cooperatives and small farmers, whereas UTZ and RA include also large estates. FLO determines the premium to be paid to farmers, whereas UTZ and RA promote negotiations between farmers and buyers to determine the amount and modes of payment. FLO and RA have their own certification bodies, whereas UTZ relies upon an independent certifier. UTZ and RA are primarily funded by farmers' contributions, whereas FLO also raises funds from consumers. While they have all integrated the environmental and agricultural aspects, RA still has a stronger focus on the environmental dimension.

UTZ and RA are merging toward a single organization. As a result, there will be two major players in the sector: Fair Trade Labeling Organization International

to producer organizations to strengthen their operational capacity. FLO trainers work directly with producers (t+B) to interpret the standards and develop implementation strategies. FLO also monitors and evaluates its standards. through its audit and producer support processes, FLO collects monitoring data on twelve key indicators; it also commissions impact and evaluation reports by external experts. Following initial ISEAL rules, FLO separated its standards-setting and enforcement activities, putting it in compliance with the ISO model.'

[79] See A. Loconto, Models of assurance (n. 17): 'SAN and RA jointly regulate in this scheme. Rainforest Alliance, Inc. is an international nonprofit organization, founded in 1986, dedicated to the conservation of tropical forests. It owns the rainforest Alliance certified seal, which is awarded to farms that meet the environmental, social, and economic standards of SAN, a coalition of conservation organizations (including rA) that had set the first standards for sustainable farming in rainforest areas in 1992. Over the years, SAN has consolidated numerous crop standards into one whole-farm standard for sustainable agriculture and one standard for sustainable livestock production. It also maintains a standard for group certification, a chain of custody standards that ensures traceability along the supply chain, and an optional module on climate change. SAN standards cover ecosystem conservation, worker rights and safety, wildlife protection, water and soil conservation, agrochemical reduction, and education for farm children. In addition, rA manages other standards systems, which can carry the rA Verified mark, related to forestry, carbon, and tourism, but unlike the rA certified seal, this mark cannot be used on product packages. While SAN is clearly the regulator, rA plays a major role as a secondary regulator in implementing and monitoring its standards. Implementation is done through the creation and enforcement of rules regarding the use of rA labels, collaborations with the private sector to train producers (t+B) to meet the standard, and work on ecosystem-focused community projects (Loconto 2015). Since the creation of ISEAL's impacts code in 2010, all ISEAL members have begun to collect monitoring and evaluation data. rA is at the forefront of these efforts, with a research and evaluation program that includes three levels of monitoring. through local interpretation guidelines that are country-, product- and standard-specific, rA guides the interpretation of its standards instead of delegating this task to certifiers (SAN 2015). Feedback in this model occurs through research, interpretation guidelines, and conformity assessments, where producers (t) communicate their concerns to certifiers (I).'

(FLO) and the new organization complementing the 'business-like' approach of UTZ and the environmental focus of RA. The decision to merge has arisen out of a relatively soft cooperation in the field of joint auditing. The merger will result in the creation of a holding incorporated in Delaware and two entities: one foundation operating according to Dutch law and one non-stock corporation operation under New York law. The Foundation will mainly deal with supply chain certification; the non-stock corporation with landscapes and livelihood. Both will engage in advocacy. The stability of the organization will be guaranteed by the composition of the boards. The board of the holding and those of the two operating entities will be composed of the same people.

This is a case of radical integration where the two managements decided that there was room for integration and selected the fast-track option rather than incremental. An important reason was to avoid negotiations over policy during the transition period. The merger will precede the definition of the content of the standard, which will be defined by the management of the new organization. The objectives of the merger are regulatory simplification, which should reduce costs along the supply chain and harmonize standards, strengthening the influence of certification, providing farmers with wider market opportunities. At the moment, a substantial amount of farmers (around 180,000) have double certification both with UTZ and RA. With the merger, those farmers with double certification (UTZ and RA) will incur less costs. Those who were only certified by one organization (i.e. UTZ) will be able to supply also to buyers which were certified by the other organization (also RA).

The two organizations will issue a single standard in 2020. Until then, they will keep the current different standards and administer them according to the current rules. Hence, after the merger, there will be two years of transition with a single organization but different standards reflecting the current practices. The auditing model will be that currently adopted by UTZ – independent auditing. Interestingly, ISEAL has not played a major role in promoting and defining the terms of integration. The decision to merge has followed a bottom-up process. Clearly, ISEAL will play a role in the new scenario, with the two big players being both members. The market for certification will become a duopoly.

It is not easy to predict the impact of the merger on the market and the regulatory arena of crop certification. On the one hand, it is likely that the merger will contribute to creating larger markets for certified agricultural commodities. On the other hand, it is likely that competition between the two main certifiers will increase. However, given that the share of the market for certified products is still limited, both organizations will try to increase the size of certified products rather than compete over the existing one.[80]

---

[80] See A. Marx and J Wouters, Competition and cooperation in the market of voluntary sustainability standards, Leuven Centre for Global Governance Studies Working Paper 135/2014.

Different forms of regulatory cooperation lead to different forms of regulatory convergence. Unlike international regulatory cooperation, where the dominant form is agreement, transnational private regulatory cooperation deploys different models that lead to various forms of convergence. Agreement provides the softer forms, meta private regulation provides the intermediate form, and organizational integration provides the hardest form of convergence.

6 THE IMPACT OF TRANSNATIONAL REGULATORY COOPERATION ON DIVERGENCES AND CONVERGENCES OF TRANSNATIONAL REGULATORY MODELS

We have identified three main forms of transnational regulatory cooperation: agreements, meta private regulation, and organizational integration. This chapter links regulatory divergences within the same policy field, cooperative responses by private regulators, and examines the resulting convergences. The causes of divergences are manifold and conflicts within the private sphere are only one of them. Conflicts within the private sphere generate regulatory divergences. Such divergences can create barriers, increase costs for regulated entities, and eventually undermine the regulatory objectives. Cooperation is one potential response to divergences and may occur via various instruments. Each instrument can determine the intensity of cooperation and have an impact on regulatory convergences. The chapter shows that there is a conceptual correlation between the choice of cooperative instrument and the quality and degree of convergence. The findings based on a limited number of policy areas suggest that the impact of cooperative instruments varies. Agreements essentially affect the content of the standard. Meta regulation both in the forms of mutual recognition and membership-based organizations also includes some influence on the procedural dimensions of standard setting, monitoring, and enforcement. The creation of multi-stakeholder organizations and the occurrence of mergers also affects the governance of the organization. Given the strong link between the 'who' regulate (governance) and 'how' the process is regulated (the nature of the standard and the legal instrument deployed to adopt and implement it), the latter forms of cooperation are the most inclusive.

When regulatory cooperation is in place, partial or limited convergence may be the objective, but divergences may still occur. It is important to distinguish between divergences in the design and divergences in practices. Here we are considering multiple regulators that decide to have some degree of common principles to orient their activities. The former occurs by design; the latter by failure to properly implement the rules. Both may need to be governed, but the governance tools differ.

Divergences by design are meant to promote choice by regulates among alternative regulatory regimes. Governance, in this case, serves the purpose of limiting the scope and number of different regimes so that the scope of choice is sufficiently wide but not too broad to excessively increase the costs of regulated entities. It should also ensure that differences are mainly about means rather than ends.

Divergences in practice may occur because the standards are not correctly implemented. Divergences may in this context be seen as an undesirable effect that should be addressed and reduced. TPR often deploys monitoring and reporting mechanisms to address divergences in practices and provide the standard setter with the necessary information to deal with them.

7 AN AGENDA FOR FUTURE RESEARCH

The empirical evidence suggests that Southeast Asia is deeply influenced by transnational private regimes whose origins and developments occur outside the region. The example of the Roundtable of Sustainable Palm Oil (RSPO), located in Kuala Lumpur, Malaysia, seems to be the exception rather than the rule. These regimes influence financial regulation, product safety regulation, data protection, e-commerce, climate change, and cultural heritage, to name a few areas. Clearly, a very relevant role is also played by ISO standards, although technical standardization in ASEAN countries follows various patterns.

The importance of regional regulatory integration is confirmed in the increasing work on comparative regional integration and the attempt to identify differences and similarities across the models. What are the factors that determine the scope and pathways of regional regulatory integration? How does the public/private interaction influence both the if and the how of regional cooperation to achieve regulatory convergences?

Interesting questions on regional regulatory regimes and the interplay between private and public actors arise in relation to ASEAN and more broadly East Asia. The role of 'local' private actors, including trade associations and NGOs, seems to differ from that played in Europe and North America, which are themselves quite different.[81] In abstract terms, the influence of private actors seems less relevant in East Asia. In practice, it is simply less apparent and transparent, but private actors, not only economic players, exercise significant influence in the implementation of private standards.

8 CONCLUSIONS

This chapter links transnational governance and comparative law by filling a gap in comparative methodology. Traditional comparative law based on the state as a unit

---

[81] A useful yet incomplete account of comparative models organized around both states and regions is provided by F. Fukuyama, *Political Order and Political Decay* (Farrar, Straus and Giroux 2014), p. 386 ff., comparing Latin America, sub-Saharan Africa, and Asia. Some comparative analysis between EU and ASEAN is included in several volumes of the series integration through law edited by Tan Hsien-Li and J. H. H. Weiler and published by Cambridge University Press. See, for example, J. Pelkmans, *The ASEAN Economic Community* (Cambridge University Press, 2016).

of analysis is unsuitable for examining the drivers and consequences of convergences and divergences at the global level when transnational private regulators dominate the scene. The unit of comparative analysis to identify convergences and divergences in transnational private regulation is the single regime or a cluster of regimes identifiable by their common features. It is a functional unit whose jurisdiction does not have any territorial stability, unlike the States. Legal variations in transnational private regulation may depend on the conflicts of interests within the private sphere. These conflicts affect mainly the regulatory activity, but to a limited extent, they also explain the variations and divergences of organizational models. Divergences may generate high costs for regulated entities and require mitigation. This can occur via institutional responses leading to regulatory cooperation. We have examined different forms of regulatory cooperation, ranging from contractual to organizational. It has been shown that the nature of the institutional response (e.g. the form of cooperation) affects the type of convergence. The use of regulatory agreements leads to soft and unstable regulatory convergence. The creation of private meta-regulators can offer a system of shared principles or common rules, reducing conflict while increasing legitimacy and effectiveness. It may influence both procedural and substantive convergence. The deployment of organizational responses via regulatory integration brings more stable and stronger convergence. It generally unifies procedural standards and brings substantive standards closer together. In this framework, the role of meta-regulators is significant and likely to increase. Symmetrically, an important role will be played by international organizations to promote regulatory cooperation among private actors and with states and steer towards different forms of regulatory convergence.

6

Law as a Market Standard: Voluntary Unification in Contract and Company Law

Andreas Engert[*]

6.1 INTRODUCTION

Global commerce faces a dazzling and at times lavish manifoldness of private laws. Each country and many more jurisdictions maintain their own sets of rules for the various kinds of commercial transactions. Why a need should exist for hundreds of different contract laws capable of regulating a sale of goods is far from obvious. At all times, attempts have been made to cut back the proliferous branches of law and to tackle the incongruities among different legal regimes. Examples include the national codifications in Europe in the eighteenth and nineteenth centuries as well as endeavors for uniform laws within the United States as well as at the international level. Regional international or supranational organizations may also pursue the harmonization or unification of private laws to facilitate cross-border economic activity. The European Union (EU) has adopted so many measures in contract law, company law, and other fields that "European private law" has become a well-established term.[1] By contrast, international organizations in Asia such as the Association of Southeast Asian Nations (ASEAN) have been far less active in promulgating harmonized or unified law.[2]

---

[*] The contribution builds on an earlier article in German: A. Engert, Regelungen als Netzgüter, Eine Theorie der Rechtsvereinheitlichung im Vertragsrecht (2013) 213 *Archiv für die civilistische Praxis* 321. David Haubner has provided a very helpful translation of the original article into English, parts of which have entered the present text.

[1] See only the "Draft Common Frame of Reference," a broad comparative and consolidating study in the form of a general codification of private law commissioned by the EU Commission, C. von Bar, E. Clive, and H. Schulte-Nölke, *Principles, Definitions and Model Rules of European Private Law: Draft Common Frame of Reference (DCFR)* (Berlin: De Gruyter, 2009).

[2] See, e.g., J. Wong, On Legal Harmonisation within ASEAN (2013) *Juris Illuminae* 5, available at https://singaporelawreview.com/juris-illuminae-entries/2015/on-legal-harmonisation-within-asean (last visited September 27, 2021). On the initiative to create "Principles of Asian Contract Law" similar to corresponding work in Europe (such as the one mentioned in n. 1), see S. Han, Principles of Asian Contract Law: An Endeavor of Regional Harmonization of Contract Law in East Asia (2013) 58 *Villanova Law Review* 589. For the rather modest progress in e-commerce law, see United Nations Conference on Trade and Development, *Review of e-commerce Legislation Harmonization in the Association of South East Asian Nations* (New York and Geneva, 2013).

This contribution offers a conceptual framework for thinking about the variety of private laws, the potential need for unification, and ways to achieve it. The economics of network effects explain why standardization is often beneficial and how it can be accomplished – or missed. Network effects occur when the value of a good for the individual user grows with the number of other users. Popular examples are means of communication, such as telephone networks but also languages. The law likewise serves human interaction. Aptly, it has been called the "language of cooperation,"[3] and, as such, it exhibits network effects. The rationale for law unification then is to benefit from stronger network effects through standardization: Parties "speak the same tongue" when it comes to law.

The economics of network effects highlight that standardization need not be the responsibility of lawmakers. With free choice of law, markets themselves produce their own degrees and patterns of standardization. The paper makes several predictions about the scope of market standardization in two particularly important areas, contract law and company law; it also adduces some empirical evidence. One policy implication is that international standardization does not depend on crafting uniform law. The laws of national jurisdictions can also be suitable as market standards for cross-border transactions. This adds a new perspective to the continuing debate about regulatory competition between jurisdictions: The winners of the race are decided as much by network effects as by differences in the substantive quality of their laws. Better law standardization can be a desirable outcome of jurisdictional competition. This is especially relevant in Asia where the prospect of government-led law harmonization or unification appears rather dim. It deserves careful consideration whether striving for international uniform law promises a significant improvement over jurisdictional competition that justifies the cost.

The chapter proceeds in three steps: Section 6.2 introduces the economic theory of network effects. Section 6.3 analyzes the character of laws as networks and uses it to assess the scope of voluntary market standardization under free choice of law in contract and company law. Section 6.4 takes a normative perspective leading to a comparative evaluation of jurisdictional competition and international uniform law as policy approaches. A short outlook in Section 6.5 concludes.

---

[3] L. Fuller, Human Interaction and the Law (1969) 14 *American Journal of Jurisprudence* 1, 2; B. Druzin, Buying Commercial Law: Choice of Law, Choice of Forum, and Network Externalities (2009) 18 *Tulane Journal of International and Comparative Law* 1, 18–19 (citing Fuller in connection with network effects of laws). See also S. Sanga, Choice of Law: An Empirical Analysis (2014) 11 *Journal of Empirical Legal Studies* 894, 923 (comparing laws to languages in terms of network effects).

6.2 NETWORK EFFECTS: THE ECONOMICS OF STANDARDIZATION

The economics of network effects originated in the analysis of markets in information technologies.[4] But these technologies are only one conspicuous example. The ambit of the theory reaches much further.[5]

6.2.1 Network Effects as Advantages of Standardization

In the traditional economic view, the value of a good depends on its inherent quality.[6] Personal preferences and the good's properties determine which car, dessert, or piece of music we value most. Network goods exhibit an additional characteristic – network effects. Such an effect arises when the value of a good for the individual user increases with the number of other users of the same good or an equivalent, compatible one.[7] Physical communication networks illustrate the idea: A single telephone is useless. It becomes valuable in connection with other telephones, and its value grows as more users are added to the network. To connect oneself to the telephone network generates a network effect for other users by

---

[4] Seminally, yet without using the term "network effects," J. Rohlfs, A Theory of Interdependent Demand for a Communications Service (1974) 5 *Bell Journal of Economics* 16; the more recent debate started with M. L. Katz and C. Shapiro, Network Externalities, Competition, and Compatibility (1985) 75 *American Economic Review* 424; M. L. Katz and C. Shapiro, Technology Adoption in the Presence of Network Externalities (1986) 94 *Journal of Political Economy* 822; J. Farrell and G. Saloner, Standardization, Compatibility, and Innovation (1985) 16 *RAND Journal of Economics* 70; J. Farrell and G. Saloner, Installed Base and Compatibility: Innovation, Product Preannouncements and Predation (1986) 76 *American Economic Review* 940; an early precursor is H. Leibenstein, Bandwagon, Snob, and Veblen Effects in the Theory of Consumers' Demand (1950) 64 *Quarterly Journal of Economics* 183. For useful overviews, see J. Farrell and P. Klemperer, Coordination and Lock-in: Competition with Switching Costs and Network Effects in M. Armstrong and R. Porter (eds.), *Handbook of Industrial Organization*, vol. 3 (Amsterdam: Elsevier, 2007), p. 1967; D. Birke, The Economics of Networks: A Survey of the Empirical Literature (2009) 23 *Journal of Economic Surveys* 762. For the competition law literature on network effects, see the survey article by M. A. Lemley and D. McGowan, Legal Implications of Network Economic Effects (1998) 86 *California Law Review* 479; D. Spulber, Consumer Coordination in the Small and in the Large: Implications for Antitrust in Markets with Network Effects (2008) 4 *Journal of Competition Law and Economics* 207; D. Spulber and C. Yoo, Antitrust, the Internet, and the Economics of Networks in R. D. Blair and D. D. Sokol (eds.), *Oxford Handbook of International Antitrust Economics* (Oxford: Oxford University Press, 2014), p. 380.

[5] Consider the interpretation of globalization as an increase in network effects: D. S. Grewal, *Network Power: The Social Dynamics of Globalizatuon* (New Haven, CT: Yale University Press, 2008). For application of the theory to social norms, see M. Adams, Norms, Standards, Rights (1996) 12 *European Journal of Political Economy* 363; A. Aviram, Regulation by Networks (2003) *Brigham Young University Law Review* 1179, 1194–1203; A. Engert, Norms, Rationality, and Communication: A Reputation Theory of Social Norms (2006) *Archiv für Rechts- und Sozialphilosophie* 335, 341–343.

[6] See G. Debreu, *Theory of Value: An Axiomatic Analysis of Economic Equilibrium* (New Haven, CT: Cowles, 1959), pp. 29–30 (describing a "commodity" in the case of a physical good as being defined by physical characteristics and availability in space and time).

[7] According to "Metcalfe's law," the value of a network results from possible links and therefore rises quadratically with the number of users; see C. Shapiro and H. R. Varian, *Information Rules: A Strategic Guide to the Network Economy* (Cambridge, MA: Harvard University Press, 1999), p. 184. The real growth rate likely is much lower as most users connect only with a limited number of others.

increasing the value of the network for them. However, network effects do not depend on physical connections. Economically, the "network" can consist in any benefits from the use of compatible network goods by others.

The literature commonly differentiates between direct and indirect network effects. Direct network effects result from the ability to enter into direct exchange with other users of the same network.[8] By contrast, indirect network effects arise through third parties who are not themselves users of the network good, especially when a larger user base attracts more suppliers of complementary goods. Human languages provide an example.[9] The benefit from learning a language correlates with the number of people who can communicate in the language. There are – from a global perspective – stronger *direct network effects* of the English language than, say, the Romanian language (but the reverse is true in Romania). The usefulness of a language also increases with the amount of literature, media, and technologies that make use of it. The more a language is used in literature, politics, science, and the economy, the richer and better its means of expression. Whether a language offers such benefits also depends on the number of people speaking and understanding it. This constitutes an *indirect network effect*.

6.2.2 Network Effects as a Cause of Market Failure

In choosing between network goods, users have to consider two aspects: the inherent quality, which can differ like in any other type of good (e.g., the speech quality of telephone networks), and the network effects. Network effects cause a drive toward standardization: users prefer as few networks as possible with as many members as possible. Ignoring for a moment the quality aspect, the strongest network effects – and hence the greatest use – would be achieved with a single network as all-encompassing standard. A rational choice can then be made for a network good of lesser intrinsic quality if in exchange it offers greater network effects. For example, while an instant messenger service (such as ICQ, WhatsApp, or WeChat) may provide more advanced features, it could still be less attractive than a qualitywise inferior competitor that offers a larger user base.

Network effects imply that the decision of a user to join a network impacts not only herself but also others. In economic parlance, there is an "external effect" that could lead to market failure.[10] Specifically, users can fail to coordinate on the best network good and become stuck in an inferior network configuration. Given that

---

[8] See only Farrell and Klemperer, Coordination and Lock-in, p. 1974.
[9] For network effects of human languages, see J. Church and I. King, Bilingualism and Network Externalities (1993) 26 *Canadian Journal of Economics* 337; Grewal, *Network Power*, pp. 71 et seq.
[10] An "external effect" entails an "externality" only if it is not internalized through pricing or otherwise. For example, while joining a network produces network effects for other members, one also benefits from their membership. If these benefits are equivalent to the additional network effects, no externality occurs. As a result, there would be no risk of market failure. For possible internalization of network effects, see Farrell and Klemperer, Coordination and Lock-in, pp. 2020–2021; S. J. Liebowitz and S. E.

users are interested both in network effects and in quality, one can classify market failure in three categories: An inferior good may succeed in becoming the market standard because existing network effects outweigh the quality differences ("mis-standardization"). Network effects can prevent desirable segmentation of the market according to differing quality preferences ("over-standardization"). Finally, a market can fail to achieve the optimal amount of network effects because too many competing networks coexist ("under-standardization").

As far as mis-standardization is concerned, suppose that one of two network goods is qualitywise superior, while both are capable of equivalent network effects. Still, there is the danger of a pernicious self-fulfilling prophecy: If users expect others to go for the inferior good or to have already done so, they will tend to do the same.[11] The same pattern can thwart useful differentiation. Network segmentation is preferable if quality demand varies and the advantages of a better tailored good outweigh the benefits of uniting in a single network. Nonetheless, the market can end up in over-standardization – not using sufficiently many different networks – if users with differing requirements fail to coordinate on a common alternative network good. Finally, a market can miss the optimal amount of network effects. If users expect sufficiently strong network effects to be maintained with one good (say, their original choice), while others flock to a new network, the market may splinter into more networks than would be desirable from the perspective of all users combined, resulting in under-standardization.[12]

An impediment to coordination on the most valuable network configuration is "switching costs": Acquisition and use of a network good often demands investments, such as the price paid for buying the network good. The investments are often specific to the particular network and irrecoverable if the network is no longer used. If such specialization is needed, any change to another network requires a second investment. The need for a new investment constitutes switching costs: Having made the investment, it causes opportunity costs to no longer make (exclusive) use of it. This applies, for example, to learning a language: Specialization occurs because learning a language requires time and effort. Because these resources cannot be recovered, it is cost-saving to restrict oneself to the languages one already knows.

Margolis, Network Externality: An Uncommon Tragedy (1994) 8 *Journal of Economic Perspectives* 133, 140–144.

[11] For coordination on an inferior network, see Farrell and Saloner, Standardization, Compatibility, and Innovation, 70 (distinguishing "excess inertia" in an inferior standard from "excess momentum" toward an inferior standard); see generally Farrell and Klemperer, Coordination and Lock-in, pp. 2024–2026.

[12] On the danger of network fragmentation, see Katz and Shapiro, Network Externalities, Competition, and Compatibility, 424, 434 et seq. (focusing on the provider's decision to foster network effects by increased product compatibility). See also generally Farrell and Klemperer, Coordination and Lock-in, pp. 2022–2024.

Switching costs explain why the past of the market also shapes its future. If a network already has an "installed base" of specialized users, new entrants will tend to expect strong network effects in that network, which can drive further growth. An already established frontrunner of competing network goods can dominate the market. This is known as path dependence[13] or a "lock in" of the market in an established standard.[14] Information technologies have been claimed to be subject to a "10X" rule: A competing product has to be ten times better to assert itself against an established standard.[15]

6.3 LAW AS A STANDARD

The law serves to form, coordinate, stabilize, and enforce behavioral expectations. To achieve this, all parties involved must share the same set of legal rules. In this basic sense, the law resembles other modes of exchange, as is aptly captured by the characterization of the law as the "language of interaction."[16] Therefore, it is no bold claim that legal terms show network effects just like other means of communication.[17] In the following, the economics of network effects are adopted for laws (Section 6.3.1). The resulting framework is then applied to contract law (Section 6.3.2) and company law (Section 6.3.3) to better understand how laws can be standardized in the marketplace, without the intentional design of a policymaker and governments.

6.3.1 Network Effects of Laws

6.3.1.1 Direct Network Effects: Specific Investment in Laws

Direct network effects arise if parties benefit from using the same or a compatible good as facilitator of exchange. At first blush, one could find this benefit in the plain necessity that any right of an obligee has to match the corresponding duty of the

---

[13] For a representative overview about form of path dependence, see P. A. David, Path Dependence: A Foundational Concept for Historical Social Science, in P. Zumbansen and G.-P. Calliess (eds.), *Law, Economics and Evolutionary Theory* (Cheltenham: Edward Elgar, 2011), p. 88. A classic example is the keyboard layout "QWERTY," which is said to have originally been introduced to reduce writing speed at mechanical typewriters, P. A. David, Clio and the Economics of QWERTY (1985) 75 *American Economic Review* 332.

[14] Path dependence need not be inefficient, cf. Farrell and Saloner, Installed Base and Compatibility ("excess inertia" and "excess momentum").

[15] Shapiro and Varian, *Information Rules*, p. 196 (ascribing the rule to Andrew Grove, CEO of Intel till 1998).

[16] See n. 3 above.

[17] To the point, see Druzin, Buying Commercial Law, 18 et seq.; B. J. Broughman and D. M. Ibrahim, Delaware's Familiarity (2015) 52 *San Diego Law Review* 273, 277–279. Similarly, A. Ogus, The Economic Basis of Legal Culture: Networks and Monopolisation (2002) 22 *Oxford Journal of Legal Studies* 419, 423.

obligor. As a consequence, the parties to a particular transaction have to agree on an identical set of legal rules. Yet merely selecting a single set of rules – such as a contract or company law – to govern an exchange does not affect other transactions or market participants. A "network" beyond the individual transaction arises only if actors commit to a law for more than a single transaction. There is an immediate analogy with a telephone network: The direct network effects from other members depend not on currently held telephone conversations but on the number of connections. Just like telephone users join the network by acquiring a telephone and connecting it, a law starts becoming a network good when market actors make specific investments in using it for transactions. These are primarily learning investments but also the costs of adapting a firm and its business processes to particular legal requirements. Such investments reduce the cost of transacting under the law; they are "specific" in the sense that they cannot be used with another law. And, once made, they also cannot be recovered. Law-specific investments create a commitment to the respective law insofar as the actor would forgo a transaction cost saving if she agreed to have a different law apply to the exchange.

Direct network effects result from the impact of one actor's commitment on other market participants: If A has specialized in law X, her contract partner B, all else equal, will also want to choose law X because A's lower transaction costs translate into a larger surplus that can be shared between the parties. Anticipating an exchange with A, it is also more attractive for B to specialize in law X herself rather than in an alternative law Y. Hence, A's adoption increases the appeal of law X to B as well as to anybody else who expects to be dealing with A at some point in time. This is a direct network effect.

Hence, someone becomes a "user" of a given law only if she has specialized in applying the law on a repeated basis. A party who blindly agrees to applying a law in a transaction counts not as a user in this regard. Insofar as she is indifferent, she incurs no higher transaction costs from letting different laws apply to her dealings. As a consequence, she constrains neither specific investments by others nor their choice of law. Direct network effects tend to be mutual: A prefers to specialize in law X because (and if) her potential contract partner B also specializes in X, and vice versa for B.[18]

To provide a sense of the nature and weight of a user's commitment, two types of specialization investment in laws can be distinguished.

Investment in legal information. To comply with behavioral expectations, one has to become acquainted with the legal rules governing the transaction. Much like learning a language, one has to learn a law. Depending on its complexity, the required learning effort may be substantial. As an indication, lawyers sometimes

---

[18] Using the same set of standard terms – including a uniform choice-of-law clause – in all of a firm's dealings can entail major cost savings from legal "standardization." Yet such standardization takes place only within a firm's organization, not between traders, and, therefore, does not reflect network effects.

spend years of training to obtain command of the laws of a single jurisdiction. Of course, the parties need not (and probably should not) strive to become legal experts. They can delegate the legal aspects of a transaction to legal advisers. In this regard, lawyers may be regarded as the main users of laws as network goods, which they utilize to design and guide the transactions of their employers or clients. For the moment, it is safe to ignore the distinction between lawyers and clients and to blur them into a single hypothetical user.[19]

Often, the parties or their lawyer need not devote extra time and resources to acquiring legal expertise. Experience with a law comes naturally with the recurring use of it, for example through arguments over contract implementation. Yet learning by doing is also not for free. It involves an opportunity cost because any given transaction creates experience with only one particular law. The opportunity cost of recurrent use makes itself felt when one is asked to give up the advantage of the familiar law by submitting to an unknown law.

Investment in compliance. Specializing in compliance with a given law can be another investment besides acquiring knowledge. It often is of a more tangible character than the effort of familiarizing oneself with the respective law. An example from contract law is the drafting of a party's general terms and conditions. Contract forms have to be adjusted to the law applicable if one wishes to avoid unpleasant surprises such as the invalidity of important provisions. In addition, the routines for executing transactions and for monitoring performance have to conform to the applicable law. As a reflection of these specific investments, operating costs grow if one's contractual relationships are governed by different laws. For instance, if a manufacturer purchases supplies under different sales laws, its business processes have to heed the relevant notice requirements for defects of the goods. Disputes fought under different contract laws cause higher management expenses, among others for retaining specialized legal counsel.

Compliance with company law requires even greater and more irreversible commitment: An essential tenet of company law is that an organization can be subject to only a single set of company law rules attaching to its "legal form." If a firm chooses to incorporate as, say, a Singaporean private company limited by shares, it cannot at the same time apply the company law of a Spanish sociedad de responsabilidad limitada. The choice of one particular legal form constitutes a singularly specific investment into compliance with a particular company law. The investment consists not so much of the fees and expenses for incorporation, registration, or drawing up the necessary documents as of the forgone opportunity of organizing in a different company form.

---

[19] See, for example, Sanga, Choice of Law, 923 (arguing that lawyers are the actual "users" of laws as regards their network effects).

6.3.1.2 Indirect Network Effects

Indirect network effects arise when the frequent use of a network entails more and better complements. The immediate users of a network are joined by the suppliers of complementary goods and services as a new class of network members. The latter improve and extend the usefulness and applicability of the network. They are tied to the actual users because investments for them become more lucrative the larger the network; they both enjoy and produce network effects.[20]

With regard to laws, legal services come to mind.[21] The more common a law is, the more qualified are the advisers and litigators that become available as it is worthwhile building up and preserving specialized knowledge, including through developing boilerplate provisions, forms, and databases. Frequent use of a law produces further advantages: The more often a legal rule is applied, the more often litigation occurs. This increases the quality of adjudication. If the interpretation of a body of law typically rests on special courts, their reputation grows with the practical importance of the law. This makes it easier to find able and specialized judges.[22]

Laws themselves also gain from frequent use.[23] Courts have more opportunities to clarify ambiguities and promote future legal certainty.[24] Greater use of a national law in a given field can entice the competent legislator to revise and improve it.[25] The law also receives more attention from practitioners and scholars, who devote

---

[20] Something between a direct and an indirect network effect occurs if a right or claim created under a particular law is traded on a secondary market; see M. Klausner, Corporations, Corporate Law, and Networks of Contracts (1995) 81 Virginia Law Review 757, 785–786 ("marketing network externalities"); R. B. Ahdieh, Between Mandate and Market: Contract Transition in the Shadow of the International Order (2004) 53 Emory Law Journal 691, 714–716 (for bonds). The subsequent acquirer can be regarded as an immediate user of the law (direct network effects) or as provider of a complementary service (indirect network effects).

[21] Klausner, Corporations, 782–784; M. Kahan and M. Klausner, Standardization and Innovation in Corporate Contracting (or 'the Economics of Boilerplate') (1997) 83 Virginia Law Review 713, 719 et seq. (albeit distinguishing "learning externalities" from "network externalities").

[22] An often cited example is the Court of Chancery of the State of Delaware with regard to company law; see M. Kahan and E. Kamar, The Myth of State Competition in Corporate Law (2002) 55 Stanford Law Review 679, 708 et seq.

[23] See C. J. Goetz and R. E. Scott, The Limits of Expanded Choice: An Analysis of the Interactions between Express and Implied Contract Terms (1985) 73 California Law Review 261, 286–288; S. Grundmann and W. Kerber, European System of Contract Laws: A Map for Combining the Advantages of Centralised and Decentralised Rule-Making, in S. Grundmann and J. Stuyck (eds.), An Academic Greenpaper on European Contract Law (The Hague: Kluwer, 2002), pp. 295, 300 ("dynamic economies of scale").

[24] Klausner, Corporations, 775–779. The number of precedents is often cited as a decisive advantage of Delaware's company law; see R. Romano, Law as a Product: Some Pieces of the Incorporation Puzzle (1985) 1 Journal of Law, Economics, and Organization 225, 277–278.

[25] See H. Hansmann, Corporation and Contract (2006) 8 American Law and Economics Review 1, 9–10; J. Dammann, Homogeneity Effects in Corporate Law (2014) 46 Arizona State Law Journal 1103, 1113–1116 (emphasizing the importance of company law changes for adapting the constitution of companies to changing circumstances).

their research to widely used laws rather than obscure ones. In addition, business circles and lawyers develop a shared sense of what the law demands.[26] An example is the fiduciary requirements of company directors in a critical situation, such as in a corporate acquisition or financial distress. This is particularly important for transactions that are rarely adjudicated in courts. In lieu of case law, the consent of the parties has to fulfill the precedents' function to coordinate behavioral expectations. Overall, indirect network effects create a stock of "legal capital" associated with a particular law,[27] and accumulating with the number of transactions and resolved disputes. In parallel to the specific investments by individual users, one can consider this a collective investment of all network members in the law.

6.3.2 Market Standardization in Contract Law

In developing a theory of law standardization without the guidance of a central planner or coordinator, this section begins with the law governing contracts. Freedom of contract enables the parties to tailor the contract to their needs. The applicable law guides the formation of the contract, its interpretation and implied terms; it also defines the limits of party choice by imposing mandatory rules or a judicial review of contract terms. Parties use contract laws to connect in much the same way as they use languages or phone lines. Direct and indirect network effects are bound to matter provided that more than one party to the contract cares for the applicable law. This excludes most business-to-consumer contracts from the following analysis as consumers tend to pay little regard to choice of governing law.

6.3.2.1 Theory – of Local Communities and Bridge Standards

To fix ideas, it helps to start with a simple framework about parties' choice of law. Suppose that the following variables determine how useful a given contract law is for the parties.

The law's quality Q. The available contract laws can differ in their substantive quality. A contract law can increase expected surplus from the transaction by creating proper, value-enhancing incentives. More surplus is always desirable for all parties to the transaction as it can be freely divided through the price term. Indirect network effects also bear on Q as frequent usage tends to enhance the legal certainty and sophistication of a contract law.

The law's proximity P to a party. Laws can be more or less accessible to a trader based on long-term characteristics such as geography, language, or culture. It is also

---

[26] Klausner, Corporations, 780–782, 786–789 (also pointing to the possibility of discovering unexpected consequences of a legal rule); Goetz and Scott, Limits of Expanded Choice, 286 et seq.
[27] See W. A. Landes and R. A. Posner, Legal Precedent: A Theoretical and Empirical Analysis (1976) 19 *Journal of Law and Economics* 249, 262–264 (coining the term "legal capital" to describe the growth in the body of precedents).

often argued that laws respond to varying local needs and preferences,[28] though this seems less compelling for contract laws.[29] In addition, P captures certain indirect network effects insofar as they differ among users: the (geographical) availability of legal advice and legal resources or the familiarity of local courts. Typically, the law of one's own jurisdiction is most proximate, but there are significant differences among foreign laws: For a Hong Kong seller, English law is more proximate – albeit not geographically – than Brasilian law.

The party's specialization S. Any contract party will prefer to deal under a contract law to which her business processes are attuned. Although familiarity or "specialization" to a law comes with repeated use, it is also a matter of individual choice. We think of specialization as an investment with positive but diminishing returns: The more a trader invests in a contract law, the greater her benefit S in each transaction governed by the law. Yet the returns from investment fall: The main features and most severe pitfalls of a particular law are learned quickly. Adding more knowledge and experience improves matters by less.[30] These assumptions ensure that individual investment and specialization S in law X increases with the expected number of transactions governed by law X. But if the trader anticipates a few transactions to be governed by law Y, she also specializes somewhat in this law.

When the parties conclude a contract, they seek to maximize their joint gain. One can expect them to pick the contract law resulting in the greatest sum of Q, P, and S – with the proviso that P and S will differ for the parties; fully written out, they maximize $Q + P_1 + P_2 + S_1 + S_2$, where the subscripts denote the party. This can require both sides to compromise by choosing a law that neither of them favors most. For instance, a seller from China and a buyer from Brazil may well pick English law.

Traders specialize anticipating choice of law in future transactions. This leads to a first theoretical prediction. Suppose a grossly simplified world in which laws differ neither in substantive quality Q nor in proximity P from the various market participants. Contract parties are homogenous and paired at random, with equal probability. Also, everyone knows the specializations of all others. In this artificial world, independently of the initial state of affairs, the market likely converges toward a single contract law as the sole standard. Each trader knows the contract law that

---

[28] R. Van den Bergh, Subsidiary as an Economic Demarcation Principle and the Emergence of European Private Law (1998) 5 *Maastricht Journal of European and Comparative Law* 129, 132–135; F. Gomez, The Harmonization of Contract Law through European Rules: A Law and Economics Perspective (2008) 4 *European Review of Contract Law* 89, 101–103; Grundmann and Kerber, European System of Contract Laws, pp. 300–301.

[29] Cf. A. Ogus, Competition between National Legal Systems: A Contribution of Economic Analysis to Comparative Law (1999) 48 *International and Comparative Law Quarterly* 405, 410–412; Ogus, Economic Basis of Legal Culture, 420–421 (differentiating between laws promoting "mutually desired outcomes," where preferences are likely to be homogenous, and "interventionist" laws with heterogenous preferences).

[30] A little more technically: S is the per-transaction benefit from using the law. It is a continuous, monotonically increasing, concave function of the amount invested by the party in the respective contract law.

happens to command the largest aggregate specialization and, therefore, is expected to be chosen most frequently. Each trader then tilts her own investment toward the frontrunner. As a consequence, the prevalent law becomes the one to attract all specialization investment and the only one to be chosen in contracts.[31]

Comprehensive standardization on a single contract laws is an unrealistic prediction, but it provides an instructive benchmark. If full standardization fails despite obvious benefits from specialization, at least one of the assumptions must be amiss. Allowing differences in substantive quality Q might change the winner of the contest but not the general outcome. We therefore continue to ignore Q. It is more interesting to tinker with the composition and pairing of traders. Suppose that contract parties belong to two distinct groups or "countries." To start from an opposite extreme, let parties deal exclusively with other parties from the same group or country; there is no cross-border trade. Applying the same logic as before, one expects a single standard within each country but not – or only accidentally – across countries. Diverging standards are especially likely if group boundaries reflect underlying differences among traders, which leads to variance in proximity P of laws to traders. Recall that P reflects stable characteristics – such as language – and benefits that derive from long-run usage patterns, including persistent indirect network effects, such as availability of legal advice.

Trader communities in the real world are not fully separated. While more exchange takes place within countries, there is significant international trade. Assuming that the parties specialize primarily in their home laws, the interesting question becomes which law is chosen in cross-border transactions. There are two main options. Perhaps the more natural one is to choose the home law of either of the parties. It has the obvious advantage of exploiting the highest possible S and P of one party, a benefit that increases surplus and can be shared between the parties. The second option is for both parties to go out of their way by choosing a third law. While each party forgoes her most preferred law, the sum of the two parties' S and P with respect to the third law can still be larger. For one thing, the distance to the other party's home law in terms of P could be large but each party can be closer to a third law – as in the example of a sale between China and Brazil with English law as the more proximate alternative because of the English language and the global presence of UK-based law firms. For another thing, traders' specializations in foreign laws will not be random. If their transactions relate to various countries, a second round of standardization specifically for cross-border trade is apt to arise. Rather than

---

[31] This is only an intuitive argument. A rigorous analysis would require more specific assumptions about the timing and depreciation of specialization investments, the discount rate, initial specializations, and the functional form of S. One can imagine a set of assumptions under which more than one contract law survives. For instance, when a minority of traders is strongly specialized in a law that is not prevalent among the majority, an equilibrium could emerge where the minority's preferred law governs all contracts with minority traders, which forces the majority to retain some specialization in that law as well. Nonetheless, it seems safe to predict that in most settings a single standard will emerge when traders are homogenous (apart from initial specialization).

spreading their specialization effort over various foreign laws, focusing on one particular law – or a few laws – as the "bridge standard" for cross-border transactions allows traders collectively to enjoy higher levels of S. The comparison with languages is suggestive: International exchange usually resorts to a common bridge language or "lingua franca."[32] Today this is for most purposes English.[33] A bridge standard emerges in much the same way as a local standard: Gauging existing specializations S and other factors, notably the proximities P of the candidate laws (or languages), market participants shift their specialization investments toward the laws (or languages) that they anticipate to be used in most transactions.

As observed, the choice of either one of the home laws or a third law depends on the parties' proximities P to the laws in question. With respect to the second relevant factor, the parties' specialization S, we can make another specific prediction: A party should be more willing to cede her own law if cross-border contracts constitute a larger share of her total business volume. Although a trader will be more accustomed to her own law, she optimally specializes less in it, compared to others, when her domestic trade volume is lower.[34] Because such a trader has a relatively low S in his home law, choosing it for the contract adds less surplus and, as a result, occurs less frequently, which results in even lower specialization. Conversely, forcing a firm with mostly domestic dealings into a foreign law is more costly for the parties and therefore less likely. Because firms from smaller countries – with smaller domestic markets – tend to do more business internationally, this suggests that the contract laws of larger economies should be more prevalent in the cross-border transactions of their firms.[35]

6.3.2.2 Evidence

Providing conclusive evidence of network effects poses a formidable challenge.[36] With network effects, one expects that many users attract more users. Yet if a

---

[32] "Lingua franca" refers to a common language used for communication among members of different language communities; see C. Meierkord, Lingua Francas as Second Languages, in K. Brown (ed.), *Encyclopedia of Language and Linguistics* (2nd ed., Amsterdam: Elsevier, 2006). Originally, "lingua franca" signified a hybrid language based on Italian and Spanish that was spoken in the Mediterranean from the fifteenth to the nineteenth century; see J. Arends, Lingua Franca, in P. Strazny (ed.), *Encyclopedia of Linguistics*, vol. 1 (New York: Fitzroy Dearborn, 2005), p. 625.

[33] See D. Crystal, *English as a Global Language* (2nd ed., Cambridge: Cambridge University Press, 2003), pp. 59–71.

[34] In fact, the prevalence of the trader's home law in international transactions also matters. If the trader's home law happens to be the international bridge standard, her optimal S likely would be higher even if she conducted most of her business cross-border.

[35] Without much explanation, this is often attributed to greater "bargaining power" of firms from larger economies. See L. Spagnolo, Green Eggs and Ham: The CISG, Path Dependence, and the Behavioural Economics of Lawyers' Choices of Law in International Sales Contracts (2010) 6 *Journal of Private International Law* 417, 426–427.

[36] Birke, Economics of Networks, 783–788; Farrell and Klemperer, Coordination and Lock-in, pp. 2015–2016.

particular good offers advantages other than network effects, demand should increase as well.[37] If contract law X expands its market share, this could reflect a rise of traders' specialization S in law X or simply its superior quality Q.

Various studies show that parties routinely include choice-of-law clauses in their (international) contracts.[38] As regards the laws chosen, a first strand of evidence relates to contract laws within the USA. The largest study to date considers half a million contracts from 1996 to 2012 filed by public corporations with the Securities and Exchange Commission. It finds a large market share of New York law (27.3 percent), followed by Delaware (12.4 percent) and California (10.5 percent). More important is that choice of law reflects more than just geographic proximity but tends to concentrate in two jurisdictions.[39] Delaware's and less so New York's contract laws are used significantly more often than one would expect based on the location of firm headquarters.[40] Market concentration appears to be increasing over time.[41] Given that the USA is a more integrated economic area than East Asia or the EU, the process could reflect market standardization – a narrowing of traders' specialization S in conjunction with a relatively minor advantage of the parties' home laws in terms of proximity P. However, the evidence is also consistent with Delaware and New York offering intrinsically better contract laws (higher Q).[42]

At the international stage, data from contracts in arbitration proceedings in Asia and Europe provide evidence for the emergence of bridge standards. English law and – in Europe – Swiss law are preferred choices when parties from different jurisdictions agree on a third law; US contract laws have surprisingly little appeal.[43]

[37] The problem consists of distinguishing the causal effect of aggregate behavior (network effects) from that of other environmental variables or common group characteristics that also impact individual, and hence aggregate, behavior; see W. R. Hartmann, P. Manchanda, H. Nair, M. Bothner, P. Dodds, D. Godes, K. Hosanagar, and C. Tucker, Modeling Social Interactions: Identification, Empirical Methods and Policy Implications (2008) 19 *Marketing Letters* 287, 293–295.

[38] See Sanga, Choice of Law, 903 (estimating the percentage of contracts with choice-of-law clauses in a large sample of US contracts at 89 percent); G. Cuniberti, The International Market for Contracts: The Most Attractive Contract Laws (2014) 34 *Northwestern Journal of International Law & Business* 455, 468–469 (reporting explicit choice-of-law provisions in more than 80 percent of a sample of contracts in ICC arbitration cases).

[39] For the natural tendency to choose local law, see T. Eisenberg and G. P. Miller, The Flight to New York: An Empirical Study of Choice of Law and Choice of Forum Clauses in Publicly-Held Companies' Contracts (2008) 30 *Cardozo Law Review* 1475, 1492–1500.

[40] Sanga, Choice of Law, 906, 908 (Delaware exceeds this measure forty-sixfold, New York threefold).

[41] Sanga, Choice of Law, 908–917 (extrapolating the present trend toward predicted obsolescence of other states' contract laws by 2050).

[42] For the perceived superior quality of Delaware and New York laws, see Eisenberg and Miller, Flight to New York, 1500.

[43] Cuniberti, International Market for Contracts, 467–475 (calculating percentages of parties choosing a third-country law from aggregate data of the International Chamber or Commerce on more than 4,400 cases for 2007–2012, with an average percentage for English law of 11.2 percent, for Swiss law of 9.9 percent, for US laws of 3.6 percent, and for French law of 3.1 percent); G. Cuniberti, The Laws of Asian International Business Transactions (2016) 25 *Washington International Law Journal* 35, 66–67 (using a similar measure to show the dominance of English contract law in four Asian arbitration centers outside mainland China 2011–2012). See also S. Voigt, Are International Merchants Stupid?

Practitioner surveys likewise point to the prevalence of English law in cross-border transactions.[44] Again, this need not be evidence of standardization but could reflect a higher Q of English law (with P accounting for the prevalence of the parties' home laws in domestic transactions). Survey responses suggest that both factors are in play.[45] An empirical analysis of choice of law in European debt securities shows that English law has long been prevalent for debt securities with an international scope (eurobonds). More importantly, the study demonstrates that the market share of English law increased even for domestic bonds – from less than 10 percent to well over 50 percent – when the respective country introduced the euro. As the European Monetary Union is unrelated to the quality of contract laws, this change likely reflects the increased demand for a bridge standard in the newly created Eurozone market.[46] Finally, the study also speaks to the prediction that parties from larger economies more often use their home law. English law is significantly more prevalent in countries with small domestic debt markets.[47]

6.3.3 Market Standardization in Company Law

It has long been debated whether companies are mere creatures of contract or whether "organizational law" is distinct from contract law.[48] Be this as it may, the

---

Their Choice of Laws Shed Doubt on the Legal Origin Hypothesis (2008) 5 *Journal of Empirical Legal Studies* 1.

[44] See Institute of European and Comparative Law, *Civil Justice Systems in Europe: Implications for Choice of Forum and Choice of Law*, 2008, p. 16, available at https://ogy.de/ww2n (last visited September 27, 2021) (reporting that 59 percent of respondent in-house counsels of European firms name English law as most used "by anyone" in cross-border transactions, followed by 13 percent for Swiss law); White & Case and Queen Mary University of London, 2010 *International Arbitration Survey*, 2010, available at www.arbitration.qmul.ac.uk/research/2010/ (last visited September 27, 2021), p. 14 (reporting 40 percent English law, 17 percent New York law, and 8 percent Swiss law in a worldwide survey among 136 firms).

[45] See The English Law Society, *Firm's Cross-Border Work* (2010), Chart 10 (reporting that 73 percent of respondent practitioners named "legal certainty" as a guiding factor in choice of law, followed by 71 percent for "familiarity with the legal system" and 60 percent for "location of parties"). Note that "legal certainty" could also reflect rule-of-law concerns with certain jurisdictions. For a summary of further findings, see G. Rühl, Regulatory Competition in Contract Law: Empirical Evidence and Normative Implications (2014) 9 *European Review of Contract Law* 61, 70–72 (emphasizing the importance of quality concerns); S. Vogenauer, Regulatory Competition through Choice of Contract Law and Choice of Forum in Europe: Theory and Evidence (2013) 21 *European Review of Private Law* 13, 36–60 (concluding that "substantive quality of contract law rules is at most a marginal consideration in making choices of law").

[46] A. Engert and L. Hornuf, Market Standards in Financial Contracting: The Euro's Effect on Choice of Law in European Debt Securities (2018) 85 *Journal of International Money and Finance* 145 Figure 4.

[47] Engert and Hornuf, Market Standards, Figure 1. See also Cuniberti, Laws of Asian International Transactions, 55–61 (documenting that firms from the USA often succeed in imposing the contract law of a US state).

[48] A standard reference for the nexus-of-contracts view is M. C. Jensen and W. H. Meckling, Theory of the Firm: Managerial Behavior, Agency Costs and Ownership Structure (1976) 3 *Journal of Financial Economics* 305, 310–311. For one – among very many – views of company law as "more than contract,"

founders of a company – like the parties of a contract – can often choose which company law governs their entity.[49] It is therefore worthwhile to ask whether company law could also experience voluntary, market-based standardization. In fact, the notion of network effects in choice of law has first been developed with a view to company law, specifically the market dominance of Delaware in the USA.[50]

6.3.3.1 Theory – of Uniform Choices and Different Clienteles

The same factors that guide standardization in contract law should also affect choice of company law. In selecting an incorporation state, shareholders likely consider differences in the substantive quality Q of company laws, the proximity P to the jurisdiction, and preexisting legal knowledge and other specialization S in the candidate laws.[51] Yet choice of a company law differs in two cardinal ways from stipulating a contract law.

The first point of departure is that for any legal entity only a single company law can be chosen. While the applicable contract law can be varied across contracts, the entity must select one and the same company law for all its relations. The governing company law cannot be negotiated with individual counterparties; shareholders unilaterally select an incorporation state. In making this decision, shareholders have incentives to take the interests of outside parties into account as the firm's profitability depends on the latter's willingness to deal with the company. When outsiders find the company law unfavorable (low Q), alien (low P), or unfamiliar (low S), the firm forgoes valuable opportunities or has to make costly concessions to attract business partners. Their profit interest thus drives shareholders to balance the various demands and to maximize total surplus in terms of Q, P, and S.[52] But even when all parties count in the decision, the choice of company law amounts to a highly rigid specialization investment: At any given point in time, the entity can specialize in no more than one law. The investment also involves a strong

---

see H. Hansmann and R. Kraakman, The Essential Role of Organizational Law (2000) 110 *Yale Law Journal* 387.

[49] How much freedom shareholders enjoy depends on conflict-of-laws rules. For the shift toward more choice of law in the EU since 1999, see J. C. Dammann, Freedom of Choice in European Corporate Law (2004) 29 *Yale Journal of International Law* 477; T. Tröger, Choice of Jurisdiction in European Corporate Law – Perspectives of European Corporate Governance (2005) 6 *European Business Organization Law Review* 3.

[50] Klausner, Networks. On the US market for corporate charters, see n. 52.

[51] Cf. Broughman and Ibrahim, Delaware's Familiarity, 278–290 (distinguishing "network effects" from "familiarity").

[52] This internalization account – with a focus on Q – is a key argument by proponents of regulatory competition in company law; see R. K. Winter, State Law, Shareholder Protection, and the Theory of the Corporation (1977) 6 *Journal of Legal Studies* 251, 256–258 (arguing that firms' incorporation decisions reflect investor preferences). For overviews of the debate, see R. Romano, The Market for Corporate Law Redux, in F. Parisi (ed.), *Oxford Handbook of Law and Economics*, vol. 2 (Oxford: Oxford University Press, 2017), 358 et seq.; R. Romano, *The Genius of American Corporate Law* (Washington: American Enterprise Institute Press, 1993).

commitment: The techniques for reincorporating in another jurisdiction vary depending on the company laws involved. Sometimes, both laws permit a genuine transition of the entity from the original jurisdiction to the destination.[53] Otherwise, the shareholders must establish a new entity in the target jurisdiction, transfer all assets to the new entity, and liquidate the old company. Both techniques can carry significant legal fees, involve other complexities,[54] and often trigger a profit realization with a hefty tax burden. Overall, switching costs tend to be substantial.[55] Combined with the long life span of many firms, one expects path dependence to be much stronger in company law than in contract law.

The second distinctive feature of company law is a direct implication of the first. Because it must commit to a single law, the entity has to contemplate a diverse range of parties with greatly different demands. For market standardization, the type and extent of specialization investments are particularly important. In this regard, one can distinguish three broad categories:

Insiders. Company law directly affects the company's directors, officers, and major shareholders. These active players within the firm need to know the nuts and bolts of the corporate constitution and, therefore, make the largest specialization investment. If a person – for instance, an executive – is active in only one company, she needs to specialize in only one law. By contrast, active investors with several holdings will be eager to limit the number of different company laws in their portfolio.

Outside stakeholders. Many different parties hold a "stake" in the company that depends on the firm's viability and success. Company law arguably influences how well the firm is managed and whether insiders can exploit outsiders. Creditors, outside investors, employees, and other long-term stakeholders have to evaluate the effect of the applicable company law on their position, for instance through bankruptcy risk. Such a general estimate of expected outcomes requires no detailed knowledge of the law. The specialization investment will be lower than that of corporate insiders, although it will depend on the amount at stake. Also, company laws vary in the degree of attention given to certain stakeholders, such as

[53] Since 2008, the EU requires its member states to enable cross-border mergers, thereby effectively permitting such a transition. For a comparison with the reincorporation-friendly law of US states, see F. M. Mucciarelli, The Function of Corporate Law and the Effects of Reincorporations in the U.S. and the EU (2012) 20 *Tulane Journal of International and Comparative Law* 421. The number of cross-border mergers in the EU since then has not exceeded 400 in any given year; see T. Biermeyer and M. Meyer, *Cross-Border Corporate Mobility in the EU, Empirical Findings* 2017, available at https://ssrn.com/abstract=3116042 (last visited September 27, 2021).

[54] When the new company law is less favorable for certain parties, reincorporation engenders disputes over their interests and vested rights; see G. Kurtulan, Minority Shareholder Protection in Cross-Border Mergers: A Must for or an Impediment to the European Single Market? (2017) 18 *European Business Organization Law Review* 101.

[55] Consider as an indication that a mere 1,281 cross-border mergers have been recorded in the entire EU in 2008–2012; see Bech-Bruun and Lexidale, *Study on the Cross-Border Mergers Directive* (2013), available at https://op.europa.eu/s/ssMp (last visited September 27, 2021), p. 968.

creditors;[56] if a given company law has little to offer for a particular group, that group's specialization matters less too.

Contract partners. Anyone dealing with the company should be able to identify the company's name and legal form as well as to verify its existence and the powers of its organs.[57] In these respects, company law complements contract law. While the relevant rules involve legal detail, the specialization investment in company law by a contract partner remains limited. Obviously, this category overlaps with the previous – one usually becomes a stakeholder by contracting with the company.

The broad-brush classification helps to clarify how specializations of various parties affect the firm's choice of company law. Corporate insiders need a high degree of specialization, but their positions are often concentrated so that they achieve a high specialization in whatever law the firm picks. This suggests that the decision often turns on the perspective of the less involved, yet more numerous future stakeholders and contract partners. Because the firm can pick only one law, it is likely to choose the highest specialization in the largest and most relevant group of outsiders. Given that most firms consider their home market to be more important than any single foreign market, it is not surprising that firms tend to adopt their domestic company law.

A similar home bias was hypothesized for contract law – but what of a bridge standard for cross-border transactions? At first blush, the restriction to choose only one law seems to preempt this approach. One can, however, imagine a company law gaining so much currency internationally that the benefit of an *intermediate specialization* in *many markets* eventually trumps the advantage of *high specialization* (and proximity) only in the firm's *home market*. Such a law could become a bridge standard for firms with high levels of cross-border activity. Large firms should be the first to reach this threshold. Yet new ventures rarely anticipate growing past this tipping point and, accordingly, choose to incorporate in their home jurisdictions. Once a firm obtains sufficient international exposure potentially to benefit from using a bridge standard, it faces the considerable cost burden of midstream reincorporation. This suggests that national company laws continue to breed and retain new businesses. Establishing any single law as a bridge standard in international business is exceedingly difficult under these conditions. The large installed base of local laws combined with significant switching costs – including the inability to use more than

---

[56] Many continental European jurisdictions conceive of company law as also serving the interests of creditors and perhaps employees. By contrast, common law jurisdictions tend to view the company more as an affair of only the shareholders; see W. J. Carney, The Political Economy of Competition for Corporate Charters (1997) 26 *Journal of Legal Studies* 303, 319–327 (providing a quantitative comparison of EU law provisions being adopted by US states).

[57] This has been the overriding concern behind the first legislative measure of the EU in company law: The First Company Law Directive 68/151/EEC, OJ L65, March 14, 1968, p. 8, aimed at harmonizing the validity of incorporations, the power of representation, and disclosure requirements for companies. The provisions have been recodified in the consolidated Company Law Directive (EU) 2017/1132, OJ L169, June 30, 2017, p. 46.

one law simultaneously so as to gradually creep into a second law – favors uniformity within jurisdictions and discourages local stakeholders and contract partners from specializing in a second company law. The rigidity of company-law choice weakens the prospect of a bridge standard even for large, more international firms.

Perhaps multinational firms would nonetheless have adopted an international bridge standard if they had had no alternative to using their home law in penetrating foreign markets.[58] Firms can, however, present themselves in a legal form that foreign stakeholders and contract partners find more familiar and trustworthy – by establishing a subsidiary in the target jurisdiction. The economics of network effects thus might contribute to explaining the prevalence of international groups of companies. Dividing a single firm into multiple entities confers the advantage of speaking the local language of company law. The cost lies in intra-firm frictions caused by separate legal entities, governed by different company laws.[59] Also, while the multinational group shows the familiar face of a local company, the subsidiary often has little economic substance. The local company law facilitates contracting but provides little assurance to stakeholders.

6.3.3.2 Evidence

There is strong evidence of home bias in company law. This very predictable pattern was first established statistically in the US debate over charter competition, calling into question the law's substantive quality as the sole driver of company law choice.[60] At the same time, the USA provides an impressive example of market concentration in a single company law, namely – again – the law of Delaware: Of the firms that escape the gravity of their home state, a whopping majority opts for

---

[58] Consider whether a Chinese business customer would be comfortable dealing with a French SAS (société par actions simplifiée).
[59] See F. Chiappetta and U. Tombari, Perspectives on Group Corporate Governance and European Company Law (2012) 9 *European Company and Financial Law Review* 261, 265–271(describing a multinational group's centralized management and the frictions caused by national company laws); Informal Company Law Expert Group, *Report on the Recognition of the Interest of the Group* (2016), available at https://ssrn.com/abstract=2888863 (last visited September 27, 2021), pp. 29–39 (laying out difficulties of cross-border groups that a limited harmonization by the EU could address).
[60] R. Daines, The Incorporation Choices of IPO Firms (2002) 77 *New York University Law Review* 1559, 1571–1574, 1576–1582 (reporting that 56 percent of firms going public between 1978 and 2000 chose Delaware law and virtually all others their home law, and discussing reasons for the home bias); L. A. Bebchuk and A. Cohen, Firms' Decisions Where to Incorporate (2003) 46 *Journal of Law and Economics* 383, 388–402 (likewise for the stock of US listed firms in 1999); J. Dammann and M. Schündeln, The Incorporation Choices of Privately Held Corporations (2011) 27 *Journal of Law, Economics, and Organization* 79, 84–85 (finding around 93 percent of privately held corporations with more than nineteen employees in a large sample dating from 2008 to be incorporated in their home state); J. Dammann and M. Schündeln, Where Are Limited Liability Companies Formed? An Empirical Analysis (2012) 55 *Journal of Law and Economics* 741, 745–746 (likewise for limited liability companies).

Delaware.[61] Traditional defenders of charter competition attribute this success to substantive company law and the superior abilities of Delaware courts,[62] each of which enters our framework as quality Q. A very recent study seeks to dissect the Q and S effects by showing that a major change in the substance of Delaware law only gradually lifted the market share of Delaware to a new level, interpreting this drift as evidence of network effects.[63] Also, the distribution of Delaware firms also aligns with the conjecture that large firms pick a bridge standard with greater specialization S by corporate outsiders: In two studies of private firms, only around 2 percent of firms with 20 to 100 employees chose Delaware as compared to 50 percent or 59 percent with 5,000 or more employees.[64] An alternative explanation is that Delaware's Q advantage grows disproportionately with firm size, for instance because larger firms are more prone to legal disputes. However, a study of venture-capital funded start-ups shows that the likelihood of incorporation in Delaware increases significantly when more financiers are located outside the firm's home state.[65] These venture capitalists benefit from using a company law that they and their legal advisers are more familiar with. The specialization effect receives further support from a survey of lawyers representing issuers and underwriters in initial public offerings; these experts admitted to recommend only the corporate law of either Delaware or their home state because they felt unfamiliar with other company laws.[66] Lastly, Delaware is chosen more frequently if legal advisers maintain a nationwide practice.[67]

Evidence from outside the USA is more scattered. After the European Court of Justice substantially widened choice of company law in the EU in 1999,[68] empirical work focused on substantive differences as drivers of company law choice.[69] Overall, the home bias of European firms continues to rule supreme. Public firms rarely incorporate outside their home jurisdiction. For private companies, the percentage of out-of-state incorporations remains in the low

[61] See n. 60. For the development over time, see S. Sanga, Network Effects in Corporate Governance (2020) Journal of Law and Economics 1, 5.
[62] See n. 52 above and, for the importance of the judiciary, M. Kahan and E. Kamar, The Myth of State Competition in Corporate Law (2002) 55 Stanford Law Review 679, 708–709.
[63] Sanga, Network Effects.
[64] Damann and Schündeln, The Incorporation Choices of Privately Held Corporations, 84; Damann and Schündeln, Where Are Limited Liability Companies Formed?, 746.
[65] B. Broughman, J. M. Fried, and D. Ibrahim, Delaware Law as Lingua Franca: Theory and Evidence (2014) 57 Journal of Law and Economics 865 (also finding a strong size effect); see also Broughman and Ibrahim, Delaware's Familiarity, 290–300.
[66] W. J. Carney, G. B. Shepherd, and J. S. Bailey, Lawyers, Ignorance, and the Dominance of Delaware Corporate Law (2012) 2 Harvard Business Law Review 123, 134, 137, 143 (also reporting lawyers' belief that investors were most familiar with Delaware law).
[67] Daines, Incorporation Choices, 1593–1595.
[68] See n. 49 above.
[69] See C. Gerner-Beuerle, F. M. Mucciarelli, E.-P. Schuster, and M. M. Siems, Study on the Law Applicable to Companies (Brussels: European Commission, 2016), available at https://op.europa.eu/s/sAPU/ (last visited September 27, 2021), pp. 34–37 (providing an overview of empirical research).

single digits,[70] with the United Kingdom capturing slightly more than half of them.[71] In spite of many decades of economic and legal convergence, no bridge standard has emerged in European company law. An offhand evaluation of a sample of listed European firms from the Amadeus database offers a glimpse at the alternative strategy of establishing subsidiaries under local law: On average, each firm had subsidiaries incorporated in nine different jurisdictions.[72]

6.4 OPTIMAL LAW STANDARDIZATION

Interest in legal convergence is motivated by policy concerns: Should governments and international organizations strive to harmonize or unify private law fields, particularly in contract or company law? If so, by which means? The economic theory of network effects has its special merit in highlighting the chances and pitfalls of standardization through market forces – an option that policymakers easily overlook but that may well be the most promising avenue in Asia. The following analysis starts from defining the task of crafting an optimal configuration of contract laws and company laws (Section 6.4.1) and goes on to characterize the efficiency of market standardization (Section 6.4.2) before assessing the merits of jursdictional competition and uniform lawmaking as policy options (Section 6.4.3).

6.4.1 *The Quest for the Optimal Law Configuration*

The taxonomy established in Section 6.2.2 contains three types of of standardization failure, depending on the source of the inefficiency.[73] A "mis-standardization" occurs if the wrong law is selected as standard. A different law would offer greater proximity P or quality Q for a given set of transactions, yet, because of existing specialization S (or government *fiat*), market participants are locked in the inferior law. Furthermore, the inefficiency can consist of too little or too much standardization. "Under-standardization" arises if market participants use several laws even though the specialization benefits S from using fewer laws would outweigh possible shortfalls in P and Q.[74]

---

[70] Gerner-Beuerle, Mucciarelli, Schuster, and Siems, Law Applicable to Companies, pp. 40–43 (estimating the number of private companies located outside the incorporation state in the EU at around 420,000 against a total number of more than 14 million private companies).

[71] Gerner-Beuerle, Mucciarelli, Schuster, and Siems, Law Applicable to Companies, p. 43.

[72] The sample was drawn by the author from Bureau van Dijk's Amadeus database in January 2017 and contains 2,381 listed firms that the database marks as "global ultimate owners." Sample countries are France, Germany, Italy, the Netherlands, Spain, Switzerland, and the United Kingdom. The mean total number of subsidiaries per firm is forty-eight. See also M. Becht, L. Enriques, and V. Korom, Centros and the Cost of Branching (2009) 9 *Journal of Corporate Law Studies* 171 (documenting the costs of and impediments to establishing branch offices in EU member states, which can explain firms' preference for local subsidiaries).

[73] See text following n. 10 above.

[74] In overcoming under-standardization, one would of course choose the law with the highest average Q and P.

Finally, "over-standardization" obtains when more diversity would produce P and Q advantages that exceed the decline in specialization benefits S. One can capture under- and over-standardization under the common denominator of the proper "configuration" of laws: how many laws should be used, and how should their scope of application be delineated? Configuration raises issues specific to network effects, namely which specialization investments are optimal. By contrast, picking the best law (s) for a given configuration merely requires one to compare laws with respect to substantive quality Q and proximity P.

It takes little reflection to realize how daunting a task it would be for policymakers to craft an optimal law configuration. A social planner would have to estimate the specialization benefits S under different possible configurations, and weigh them against the corresponding differences in P and Q. She would have to know the relative volume of trade within and between countries (or other groupings), the returns on specialization investments as well as the relevant Ps and Qs to determine whether a single standard for all traders, separate local standards combined with a single bridge standard for cross-border transactions, or the use of local standards even in cross-border transactions would be optimal. To complicate matters further, trade volumes – a key determinant of optimal law configuration – might not be exogenously given but could reflect the transaction costs from using particular laws. This endogeneity of trade motivates policies toward promoting legal convergence.[75] Indeed, a burgeoning literature studies the trade constraints associated with political borders,[76] albeit without firm conclusions whether and how much legal – as opposed to cultural, economic, or other – differences contribute to this "border effect."[77] A social planner wishing to devise the optimal law configuration would need to know how greater standardization translates into higher equilibrium specialization S, lower transaction costs, and a higher equilibrium level of cross-border trade.

The difficulties do not end there for the daring policymaker. Specialization investments concern only direct network effects. Including indirect network effects

---

[75] See, for instance, O. Lando, Optional or Mandatory Europeanisation of Contract Law (2000) 8 *European Review of Private Law* 59, 61–63; see also G. Wagner, The Economics of Harmonization: The Case of Contract Law (2002) 39 *Common Market Law Review* 995, 1013–1018 (discussing the effects of different contract laws on cross-border trade).

[76] See, seminally, J. McCallum, National Borders Matter: Canada–US Regional Trade Patterns (1995) 85 *American Economic Review* 615. For a recent critique, see F. Borraz, A. Cavallo, R. Rigobon, and L. Zipitria, Distance and Political Boundaries: Estimating Border Effects under Inequality Constraints (2016) 21 *International Journal of Finance and Economics* 3.

[77] Causal factors are hard to disentangle; see S. Kalemli-Ozcan, E. Papioannou, and J. L. Peydró, What Lies beneath the Euro's Effect on Financial Integration? Currency Risk, Legal Harmonization or Trade (2010) 81 *Journal of International Economics* 75; A. Turrini und T. Van Ypersele, Traders, Courts and the Border Effect Puzzle (2010) 40 *Regional Science and Urban Economics* 82; M. Giannetti and Y. Yishay, Do Cultural Differences between Contracting Parties Matter? Evidence from Syndicated Bank Loans (2012) 58 *Management Science* 365 (providing evidence for the effects of cultural differences). From a legal perspective, see G. Rühl, The Problem of International Transactions: Conflict of Laws Revisited (2010) 6 *Journal of Private International Law* 59, 61–65.

in the analysis adds another layer of complexity.[78] The benefits of specialized legal services, judicial experience, and legal certainty rise with the volume of transactions carried out under a given law. Yet the returns to greater use likely diminish. For widely used laws, the marginal increase of indirect network effects should be small. The number of contracts of a given type concluded and performed under the laws of any larger jurisidiction should suffice to produce authoritative court rulings for the most important controversies. But if law communities with fewer users could be optimal in terms of proximity P and direct network effects from S, a lack of indirect network effects may well tip the balance.

6.4.2 Promise and Limitations of Market Standardization

The difficulties of divining the optimal law configuration are disheartening. Even the most sophisticated and resourceful lawmakers or agencies – at the national, international, or supranational level – must fear missing the mark, and by a wide margin. This suggests leaving the market the major role in finding the right configuration of contract and company laws. However, one naturally wonders whether the market is better suited to bringing about the right balance of unification and variety. The answer is related to the general advantage of markets compared to central planning: The market has the virtue of eliciting and aggregating decentralized information from private parties.[79] In contrast to a central legislator, market participants know their own needs and introduce their own individual balancing of Q, P, and S into the aggregate outcome.

To be more specific, allowing the market to choose a law configuration amounts to granting free choice of applicable law. Any market outcome reflects the parties' attempt at minimizing transaction costs by choosing the law with the greatest benefits in terms of Q, P, and S. Ignoring for the moment indirect network effects, the only source of inefficiencies then are the parties' specializations: Their existing specialization might drive them to choose a law with less Q and P even when a different specialization would make them prefer another law (with greater Q and P).[80] The inefficiencies from choosing a particular law can never exceed the benefits from existing specialization in the law; if the losses were greater, the parties would rather forgo the S from using the inferior law than give up the higher Q and P from the superior law. An important implication is that inefficient equilibria are more likely to obtain for laws in which traders are more specialized, typically their home laws. For a foreign law, including one that serves as a bridge standard, specialization benefits are

---

[78] Indirect network effects are expounded in Section 6.3.1.2. For inefficient equilibria due to indirect network effects, see Klausner, Networks, 789–815.

[79] On the ability of markets to use dispersed knowledge, see, famously, F. A. Hayek, The Use of Knowledge in Society (1945) 35 *American Economic Review* 519; F. A. Hayek, Competition as a Discovery Procedure (2002) 5 *Quarterly Journal of Austrian Economics* 9.

[80] Note that this constitutes an inefficiency only if the alternative specialization would increase the sum of P, Q, and S across all transactions and all users.

considerably smaller, and so is the potential for inefficiencies. Overall, there is an inherent limitation to how far the market can go wrong. No such natural barriers would exist for a government's attempt to force a law configuration on traders.

Similar reasoning leads to the conjecture that markets more likely fail at overcoming unwanted diversity (under-standardization) than through overshooting toward excessive unification (over-standardization). There are two reasons for this prediction. The first is that when a contract or company law is presently in use, at least some traders have specialized in it. Relinquishing the law would mean abandoning specialization benefits that one can readily enjoy. Although one acquires specialization in the new law over time, there is a short-run opportunity cost from not using the law with the greater S. Expending these switching costs pays only if sufficiently many other traders move simultaneously. While the coordination problem plagues any change in law configuration, abandoning a law seems more difficult than starting to use a new one. Most national laws have existed for a long time and usually command a sizable user base. Even traders willing to make the switch retain their previous specialization, and thus should be ready to use the previous law if other parties insist on it.

The second reason to expect market failure in the direction of under-standardization is the ability and willingness of jurisdictions to promote their laws. States can force parties to use their law, and sometimes they choose to do this.[81] In addition, default rules secure each law those transactions in which the parties have, for whatever reason, failed to exercise their choice of law. Any national law almost inevitably comes to application in a significant number of cases.

The prediction that under-standardization is the more likely type of market failure is in line with the general policy impulse toward unification rather than toward a conservation of endangered laws or the promotion of legal variety. The fate of the UN Sales Law can serve as an example of under-standardization: The convention was signed in 1980 and came into force for the first contracting states in 1988. It applies to cross-border sales contracts between businesses as long as the parties do not specifically elect national law. A multitude of surveys in the last years indicated that many legal advisers – often considerably more than 40 percent – opt out of UN Sales Law as a matter of principle.[82] The explanations brought forward support the view that switching costs prevent the UN Sales Law from establishing itself as a bridge standard.[83]

---

[81] This happens, for instance, in contract law in relation to consumer protection; see G. Rühl, Consumer Protection in Choice of Law (2011) 44 *Cornell International Law Journal* 569, 586–592 (providing an overview of restrictions to choice of law in contracts with consumers).

[82] See the overview provided in U. G. Schroeter, Empirical Evidence on Courts, Parties' and Counsels' Approach to the CISG (with some Remarks on Professional Liability), in L. DiMatteo (ed.), *International Sales Law: A Global Challenge* (New York: Cambridge University Press, 2014), p. 649. See also White & Case and Queen Mary University of London, 2010 International Arbitration Survey, p. 15 (reporting that 53 percent of respondents had never closed contracts under international uniform law).

[83] See the references in n. 82. But see, for a different interpretation, C. P. Gillette and R. E. Scott, The Political Economy of International Sales Law (2005) 25 *International Review of Law and Economics* 446, 473–478 (pointing to the vagueness of the convention's legal rules and the lack of uniformity due to signatory state reservations).

6.4.3 Policy Options

Governments can force standardization, as witnessed by the many examples of national codifications as well as instances of international and supranational rules replacing national laws. At first sight, forced standardization has some appeal: Markets can be stuck in an unfavorable equilibrium when individual investments and collective legal capital lock traders in a less-than-optimal law configuration. Curing market failures is a quintessential task of the government. Another way to phrase this is that selecting from a variety of possible law configurations is a collective decision on behalf of all traders in the market. Law configuration could be seen as a natural part of the government's domain of collective decision-making.

However, such a far-reaching conclusion would overlook the enormous complexity of evaluating the efficiency of competing law configurations. While we can single out the important choice variables, estimating even their orders of magnitude is plain guesswork. As the preceding section has shown, although markets can miss the optimal law configuration, they are bound to the preferences of the immediate parties; at the very least, they provide a reliable assurance against over-standardization.

The following analysis therefore confines itself to evaluating, in general terms, two approaches at promoting desirable market standardization. The first envisions standardization as an additional role for competition among national jurisdictions (Section 6.4.3.1). The second compares it with optional uniform law as a more conventional method of overcoming fragmentation (Section 6.4.3.2).

6.4.3.1 Jurisdictional Competition

Choice of law permits the parties to select the law most suitable for their transaction – the one that maximizes the sum of Q, P, and S. The idea of jurisdictional competition views the users of laws as the demand side of a market in which states act as the suppliers of laws as their "products."[84] Jurisdictional competition has sparked a voluminous literature in company law and, to a lesser extent, in contract law.[85] Until now, the discussion has focused on the effects of competition on the substance of the laws being offered. While proponents praise jurisdictional competition for incentivizing lawmakers and courts to offer more efficient legal rules, critics warn of a pernicious "race to the bottom" that compromises the law's protective role for those with little or no say in the

---

[84] Consider the title of Romano, Law as a Product. The general debate about regulatory competition goes back a long time; see, seminally, C. M. Tiebout, A Pure Theory of Local Expenditure (1956) 64 *Journal of Political Economy* 416.
[85] Regarding company law, see the references in n. 49 (for the EU) and n. 52 (for the USA); see also, as a starting point for the US debate, W. L. Cary, Federalism and Corporate Law: Reflections upon Delaware (1974) *Yale Law Journal* 83, 663. Regarding contract law, see Vogenauer, Regulatory Competition; G. Rühl, Regulatory Competition in Contract Law; H. Eidenmüller (ed.), *Regulatory Competition in Contract Law and Dispute Resolution* (Munich: C. H. Beck, 2013); L. E. Ribstein and E. O'Hara, *The Law Market* (Oxford: Oxford University Press, 2009).

choice-of-law decision.[86] Network effects open up a new perspective:[87] The competitive success of laws could hinge as much on the magnitude of network effects as on their substantive quality. It may pique the professional self-esteem of lawyers to admit that legal substance could matter little for the success of a given law. And yet, the substantive differences between mature laws could be quite unimportant for the efficiency of the transaction. Again, the analogy with human languages is instructive: Any two languages can lend themselves equally well to expressing a particular idea. The limiting factor is that speakers and listeners need a language they both know.

Even if jurisdictions do not compete on substance, there is still room for rivalry at the level of network effects: What makes the difference between providers of laws is not the quality of their product but – similarly to social networks on the internet – the size and scope of their user base. The examples above demonstrate that national laws can become bridge standards for cross-border transactions or even the standard for purely domestic transactions outside their home market.[88] For a country, elevating one's law to an international standard can be desirable for various reasons. It helps domestic firms to insist on their home law in cross-border transactions, giving them greater specialization benefits S. Exporting a country's national law rises the demand for complementary legal services, often provided by domestic lawyers and law firms.[89] If, for instance, English contract law has come to dominate the European market for debt securities,[90] this gives English law firms an edge over their competitors from the Continent (at least, it did as long as Britain was still a member of the EU). It is also to the advantage of the respective places of jurisdiction and arbitration if one's law is widely used.[91] On some occasions, states even generate immediate revenue from exporting their law.[92]

---

[86] This concern was famously expressed by Justice Brandeis as early as 1933: *Louis K. Liggett Co. v. Lee*, 288 US 517, 557–564 (1933) (Brandeis, J., dissenting).

[87] Indirect network effects had already been introduced to the debate by Klausner, Networks.

[88] See Sections 6.3.2.2 and 6.3.3.2.

[89] See TheCityUK, *Legal Excellence, Internationally Renowned: UK Legal Services 2020* (London, 2020) and TheCityUK, *The Impact of Brexit on the UK-Based Legal Services Sector* (London, 2016), both available at www.thecityuk.com (last visited September 27, 2021) (documenting the relevance of legal services for the UK economy); J. Linarelli, The Economics of Uniform Law and Uniform Lawmaking (2003) 48 *Wayne Law Review* 1387, 1430–1434 (describing the significance of "Legal London").

[90] See text before n. 46 above.

[91] Cf. Cuniberti, International Market for Contracts, 475–481 (considering the link between arbitration venue and choice of contract law); Cuniberti, Laws of Asian International Business Transactions, 59–61 (finding an association between arbitration forum and contract law); E. Lein, R. McCorquodale, L. McNamara, H. Kupelyants, and L. del Rio, *Factors Influencing International Litigants' Decisions to Bring Commercial Claims to the London Based Courts* (London: Ministry of Justice, 2015), p. 10 (reporting that around 80 percent of disputes before the London Commercial Court involved at least one and 50 percent only foreign parties); Eisenberg and Miller, Flight to New York, 1504–1505 (reporting an overwhelmingly strong correlation); White & Case and Queen Mary University of London, 2010 International Arbitration Survey, p. 9 (documenting 68 percent of survey respondents viewing choice of law and seat of arbitration as interdependent).

[92] In 2020, Delaware obtained 1.64 billion US dollars from its franchise tax on capital companies, more than one-third of its total tax revenues (source: *U.S. Census Bureau*, https://census.gov/data/tables/2020/econ/stc/2020-annual.html, last visited September 27, 2021).

Harnessing jurisdictional competition to establish a national law as an international standard also has efficiency advantages. An existing national law has an installed base. Market participants from the exporting country need not specialize in another law, saving them the cost of switching to a new international standard. This constitutes a benefit, even if it is confined to some traders. In addition to individual knowledge and experience, an existing law already commands indirect network effects from precedents, legal literature, and common practice. A new law – such as a uniform international contract law – would have to build such legal capital painstakingly while undergoing a period of legal uncertainty. After the new law had caught up, its use as a bridge standard for cross-border transactions would add one more legal regime to the abundance of existing laws. Recruiting a national law for the role of bridge standard avoids legal fragmentation and the cost of maintaining another set of rules.

As a possible objection, it could be speculated that legislators and courts are less sensitive to the regulatory needs in other states or in cross-border legal transactions. The desire to promote one's own legal terms, however, counteracts that indifference. Actively competing jurisdictions should be sympathetic to foreign needs. Also, the geographical distance to the respective jurisdiction and its courts could be held against the use of national law as a bridge standard. The parties generally are interested in letting those courts decide that are best acquainted with the applicable law.[93] As a consequence, they could end up litigating in a remote forum. Yet the opportunity to invoke a proficient, if distant, court should be seen as an advantage of using a national law. A newly drafted uniform law would lack any forum of special expertise. Compared to uniform international law, parties suffer no disadvantage from using a national law, but they enjoy the additional option of resorting to the knowledgeable courts of the respective state if they are willing to bear the costs.

A final argument in favor of jurisdictional competition is the self-interest of states. Owners of networks have an incentive to market their offerings.[94] In doing so, they seek to orchestrate users' expectations toward their national law as the market standard. In the case of contract and company laws, the main driver behind promotion activities is usually the legal services industry that profits directly when its home law is chosen.[95] This advocacy could help overcome the market's predisposition toward under-standardization. However, the advantage of a self-interested owner also has a flip-side. The struggle to promote one's law can lead to anticompetitive behavior. The corollary of growing business opportunities for lawyers from a successful jurisdiction is the declining demand for legal services from other jurisdictions. States and lawyers may be tempted to thwart standardization on a competing

---

[93] See n. 91 above.
[94] See Farrell and Klemperer, Coordination and Lock-in, p. 2021 (discussing the ability of network owners – like the producer of an operating system for computers – to internalize network effects).
[95] See, for example, the lobbying activities of TheCityUK, as documented by the references in n. 89 above.

law. Economically speaking, this is a case of harmful rent-seeking.[96] Legal advisers could fight for the application of their own domestic law and for that make concessions in bargaining at the expense of their clients. Likewise, competition at the state level can degenerate into harmful law protectionism.[97] For example, the fact that the United Kingdom has never ratified the UN Sales Law might be attributed to the market potential of English law as an international standard.[98]

6.4.3.2 Uniform Law

Different from jurisdictional competition, uniform law needs less introduction as a policy tool; it is the conventional way of pursuing legal unification. At first glance, however, it comes with many disadvantages compared to national law. First of all, uniform law starts without a user base. All parties and lawyers have to learn a legal "Esperanto." The collective capital tied to a law – legal certainty from precedents, discourse, and established practice – has to be built from scratch. If uniform law does not replace national laws, it adds the ongoing costs of operating and updating a distinct set of rules. The way it is drafted and enacted further burdens uniform law. As it is created through international conventions or supranational legislation, it often reflects a compromise between different legal concepts.[99] It is then up to a lengthy process to give the vague and ambiguous rules a practicable and clarified content. The cumbersome process of enacting uniform law also makes amendments exceedingly difficult. Uniform law is more prone to petrifaction.[100]

The special virtue of uniform law arises from what was just declared an advantage of national laws. If a national law succeeds as an international standard, the benefits are distributed unevenly: Lawyers and traders from the prevailing jurisdiction gain much from their unique proximity P to the standard and the opportunity to concentrate their specialization investment in a single law. Other jurisdictions likewise obtain specialization benefits S, but less so if they continue to use their own law for domestic transactions. The asymmetry between the standard-setting jurisdiction and all others weighs less heavily for traders because they will, on average, share transaction cost savings. It is, however, of great concern for lawyers whose proximity and specialization in the applicable law directly affect the cost and

---

[96] Seminally, G. Tullock, The Welfare Costs of Tariffs, Monopolies, and Theft (1967) 5 *Western Economic Journal* 224; the term itself was coined by A. O. Krueger, The Political Economy of the Rent-Seeking Society (1974) 64 *American Economic Review* 291.

[97] On the alliance between lawyers and their home law, see Ogus, The Economic Basis of Legal Culture, 426–427.

[98] See Linarelli, The Economics of Uniform Law, 1426–1435; S. Moss, Why the United Kingdom Has Not Ratified the CISG (2005) 25 *Journal of Law and Commerce* 483 (pointing to lack of interest but also to concern over London's position as arbitration and adjudication venue).

[99] See Gillette and Scott, Political Economy of International Sales Law, 459–462; likewise for restatements und uniform laws in the USA, A. Schwartz and R. E. Scott, The Political Economy of Private Legislatures (1995) 143 *University of Pennsylvania Law Review* 595, 604–607.

[100] Gillette and Scott, Political Economy of International Sales Law, 482.

quality of their service. The prospect of a foreign law becoming the international standard can, therefore, stir resistance in other jurisdictions because their lawyers would find themselves at a competitive disadvantage.

Ironically, the wasteful duplication of specialization investments and legal capital could be the greatest advantage of uniform law in competing against national laws. An indication of this is the observation that lawyers tend to pick a neutral law instead of either party's domestic law.[101] To the same effect, the laws of small jurisdictions seem particularly successful as bridge standards; Switzerland and Singapore are examples. Intuitively, lawyers may develop a special fondness for uniform law precisely because it is not "owned" by a single state and its lawyers. Its neutrality sets uniform law apart from national laws.[102]

6.5 OUTLOOK

The economics of network effects provide a framework for analyzing the international standardization of private laws. An advantage of standardization is cost savings from greater specialization of the parties to a transaction – direct network effects. Next to them are indirect network effects, the benefits from refining laws through extensive use and from reducing maintenance costs across all laws and for society at large. In addition to explaining efficiencies from standardization, economic theory contributes to understanding the reach and potential shortcomings of voluntary standardization in markets. In this regard, the main conclusions are both hopeful and sobering. They are hopeful insofar as the market has an ability to detect and realize gains from standardization. At the same time, network effects can cause the market to remain stuck in an inferior equilibrium, especially one with understandardization and an excess of laws being used. The prospect for optimal standardization is especially dim in company law. The inability to vary the company law of an entity for different stakeholders and contract partners makes it hard to escape the gravity of a firm's home law. Apart from the special case of the USA, there is little chance of a company law bridge standard for large firms with international exposure. The multinational company group with subsidiaries under various local laws is the only imperfect substitute.

In theory, a very valuable role for governments and legislators could lie in helping the market to overcome fragmentation by removing some unneeded laws. Given

---

[101] See White & Case and Queen Mary University of London, 2010 International Arbitration Survey, p. 14. Another likely motivation is to avoid a pronounced asymmetry in legal knowledge to prevent attempts at exploiting legal mistakes by the other, less informed party, which could cause or exacerbate costly disputes.
[102] One reason cited by firms incorporating as a Societas Europaea (SE) – the public company form provided by EU law – is that it is seen not as a national entity but as truly European; see H. Eidenmüller, A. Engert, and L. Hornuf, Incorporating under European Law: The Societas Europaea as a Vehicle for Legal Arbitrage (2009) 10 *European Business Organization Law Review* 1, 27–28.

that this would mean discarding the creatures of their own (national) lawmaking, they are unlikely to embrace this role. It then only remains to promote a more efficient configuration of the existing laws. The immense complexity cautions against much confidence in engineering an optimal configuration. Markets may fail to achieve the optimum but, at the very least, are unlikely to over-standardize. Conflict-of-laws rules can support market standardization by abolishing restrictions on choice of law to avoid artificial fragmentation. National jurisdictions can then compete through promoting familiarity and widespread adoption of their laws as market standards.

7

Is the Harmonisation of Asian Contract Law Possible? The Example of the European Union

Mateja Durovic and Geraint Howells

1 INTRODUCTION

The East and Southeast Asian jurisdictions and that of the European Union have in common the heterogeneity of their contract law traditions. In particular, in the case of both Asia and Europe, there is a high level of divergence when it comes to the contract law regimes reflecting different legal traditions. Among the sixteen contract law jurisdictions of East and Southeast Asia, a majority belongs to the civil law legal tradition. These are Japan, South Korea, PR China, Indonesia, Macau SAR, Taiwan, Laos, Cambodia and Vietnam. However, a significant number of the jurisdictions have developed under the primary impact of common law. These include Hong Kong SAR, Singapore, Malaysia and Brunei. In addition to this, some of the jurisdictions have been influenced both by civil law and by common law, as is the case with the Philippines, Myanmar and Thailand. Some of the cities belonging to these jurisdictions represent major global centres of commerce, as is the case with Singapore, Shanghai, Tokyo and Hong Kong.

In the European Union, among twenty-eight Member States, there exist twenty-nine different contract law regimes. Each of the EU Member States has its own contract law regime, but the United Kingdom has both English and Scottish contract law. Similar to the case of the Asian jurisdictions, in the European Union, there is also a high level of contract law heterogeneity. English and Irish contract laws are part of the common law tradition; Cypriot, Maltese and Scottish contract laws belong to the mixed legal traditions; whereas the contract laws of Austria, Belgium, Bulgaria, Croatia, the Czech Republic, Denmark, Estonia, Finland, France, Germany, Greece, Hungary, Italy, Latvia, Lithuania, Luxembourg, the Netherlands, Poland, Portugal, Romania, Slovakia, Slovenia, Spain and Sweden all represent the examples of the civil law legal traditions. The civil law traditions themselves can be further subdivided into those based on legal families the two most significant of course being the French and German. In Asia, the influence of European traditions is also felt to different degrees. For instance, German law in particular is influential in China, French law was used as the main model in the case of Vietnam, whereas Indonesia relies on Dutch law for colonial historical reasons.[1]

The contract law jurisdictions of the European Union have already a decades-long history of more or less successful attempts at national and regional harmonisation and the more recent attempt to develop a pan-European Civil Code.[2] In that sense, where Asian jurisdictions attempt to harmonise their contract and commercial laws, the European experience may potentially be valuable for better comprehending the process of promoting harmonisation. In particular, the experience gained from the European contract law process is primarily beneficial to understand whether harmonisation among different contract law legal traditions is at all possible and, if so, to what extent and under what conditions.

It is important to note that the European model is not to be taken as 'a perfect model', but only as a valuable practical experience which may help explain the complexity and challenges of the harmonisation process.

2 A BETTER COMPREHENSION OF THE DIVERSITY OF CONTRACT LAWS

In order to better understand similarities and differences among the national contract laws, the comparative detailed examination of the national contract laws is essential. In the European Union, there were several studies of that kind. Among them, probably the most notable one is the 'Trento project' of the Common Core of European Private Law Project, which was launched in 1993 under the leadership of the late Professor Rudolf B. Schlesinger.[3] This project used a case method, where a particular set of facts have been examined under each of the national contract laws of the Member States.

This project resulted in the publication of more than a dozen volumes of studies of diverse fields of private law. Some of them covered the elements of contract law where the differences among the national contract laws are the most notable. These include the principle of good faith,[4] consent defects,[5] recovery of non-pecuniary loss in contract law[6] or the pre-contractual liability.[7] This series of books has certainly

---

[1] See K. Zweigert and H. Kötz, *An Introduction to Comparative Law*, 3rd ed., trans. T. Weir (Oxford University Press 1998).
[2] M. Durovic, *European Law on Unfair Commercial Practices and Contract Law* (Hart Publishing 2016) at 38.
[3] M. Bussani and U. Mattei, *The Common Core of European Private Law, Essays on the Project* (Kluwer Law International, 2002).
[4] R. Zimmermann and S. Whittaker, *Good Faith in European Contract Law* (Cambridge University Press, 2000).
[5] R. Sefton-Green, *Mistake, Fraud and Duties to Inform* (Cambridge University Press, 2005).
[6] Vernon Palmer, *The Recovery of Non-Pecuniary Loss in European Contract Law* (Cambridge University Press 2015).
[7] J. Cartwright and M. Hesselink, *Precontractual liability in European Private Law* (Cambridge University Press, 2011).

materially contributed to a better understanding of national contract laws. Besides this series, some other projects also dealt with the similarities and differences among the national contract law concepts.[8]

A similar concept was adopted by the *Ius commune* casebooks. This project aims to collect the materials regarding

> the similar problems or factual situations under the various legal systems under study. The materials are accompanied by short introductory and explanatory notes to situate them in context. At the end of each section, a comparative overview ties together the materials included under that section, with emphasis, where possible, on existing or emerging general principles in the national and supranational legal systems of Europe.[9]

There have also been more overt moves to bring about political reform. The European Commission initiated and/or supported, directly or indirectly, several projects on European contract law, among which the most important outcomes are the published Principles of European Contract Law led by Ole Lando and Hugh Beale ('PECL')[10] and the Draft Common Framework of Reference ('DCFR') edited by a number of leading European private law scholars.[11] However, they never managed to become a European Contract Code or a European Civil Code, but have only remained outstanding examples of legal scholarship, used as important benchmarks and reference points in debates on the Europeanisation of contract law.[12]

3 WHY IS THE HARMONISATION OF CONTRACT LAW NEEDED?

The starting question relating to harmonisation is why a harmonised contract law is needed at all. In other words, besides academic success, what aims are to be achieved with harmonised contract law? The harmonisation of contract law has traditionally been seen as a necessary instrument to improve and strengthen the cross-border trade among different contract law jurisdictions.[13] Both the businesses and the traders want to have a high level of legal certainly while acting in the market. In practice, this means that market participants need to be familiar with the rules applying to a particular market and the related transactions. Moreover, the presence

---

[8] S. S. Hartkamp et al. (eds.), *Towards a European Civil Code* (4th ed. Kluwer Law International, 2011).
[9] Available at www.casebooks.eu.
[10] O. Lando and H. Beale (eds.), *Principles of European Contract Law*, Part I (1996) and Part II (1999); O. Lando, E. Clive, A. Prum and R. Zimmermann (eds.), *Principles of European Contract Law*, Part III (2003), http://frontpage.cbs.dk/law/commission_on_european_contract_law/pecl_full_text.htm.
[11] C. Von Bar et al., Principles, Definitions and Model Rules of European Private Law. Draft Common Frame of Reference (DCFR) (Sellier, 2008), http://ec.europa.eu/justice/policies/civil/docs/dcfr_outline_edition_en.pdf.
[12] C. Twigg-Flesner, *Europeanisation of Contract Law*, 2nd ed. (Edward Elgar, 2013), 175.
[13] R. Goode, Contract and Commercial Law: The Logic and Limits of Harmonisation (2010) 7 *Electronic Journal of Comparative Law* 4.

of the divergence among the contract law regimes also leads to additional cross-border costs, as it requires compliance with the applicable rules.

Accordingly, harmonisation of contract law should result in market players being keener to perform cross-border transactions, as they reduce the cost required to secure compliance and the market participants are aware of what kind of rules will regulate these transactions. Eventually, harmonisation should lead to the establishment of a higher level of trust among the market participants, which is something that the entire society and the economic system profits from.[14] However, it must be noted that it is unlikely that any harmonised law will cover the entire field of private law, or even the entire area of contract law.

This was the main argument to push forward for the harmonisation of contract laws in the European Union, where harmonisation of contract laws has been considered as one of the means which would contribute to the establishment and functioning of the internal market.[15] The differences among the contract law regimes of the EU Member States have been seen as the obstacle to developing cross-border trade, so harmonisation has an aim to overcome these barriers.

The European Commission constantly points out the existence of divergences among the contract law regimes of the different Member States as a material obstacle for the further development of the internal market. It has thus used this as the main argument in favour of the unification projects of contract law in the European Union.[16] Under the veil of explanation that the unification of contract law throughout the European Union is a necessary prerequisite for overcoming these obstacles and for strengthening the internal market, the European Commission has, as of the beginning of the twenty-first century, invested significant efforts directed towards the unification of contract law.[17] A significant debating point is, however, what degree of harmonisation is needed to promote successful trading conditions. While a few favour the adoption of a uniform private law in the form of a European Civil Code, others believe that targeted harmonisation of only certain areas of contract law such as consumer contract law or even just a better mutual understanding or use of common terminology can assist.

---

[14] H. Collins, Transaction Costs and Subsidiarity in European Contract Law in S. Grundmann and J. Stuyck (eds.), *An Academic Green Paper on European Contract Law* (Kluwer Law International, 2002), 270.

[15] S. Weatherill, Constitutional Issues – How Much Is Best Left Unsaid? in S. Vogenauer and S. Weatherill (eds.), *The Harmonisation of European Contract Law – Implications for European Private Laws, Business and Legal Practice* (Hart, 2006), 28.

[16] As the first initiative of the European Parliament for the unification of private law, this has been used as the main argument to promote the unification of contract law in Europe. See Resolution of 26 May 1989 on action to bring into line the private law of the Member States [1989] OJ C158/400 and Resolution of 6 May 1994 on the harmonization of certain sectors of the private law of the Member States [1994] OJ C205/518.

[17] Communication from the Commission on European Contract Law, COM (2001) 398 final; Commission, A More Coherent European Contract Law – An Action Plan, COM (2003) 68 final; Commission, European Contract Law and the revision of acquis: the way forward, COM (2004) 651.

7 Is the Harmonisation of Asian Contract Law Possible?

Prominent jurists in Asia, such as the Chief Justice of Singapore Sundaresh Menon, have urged for the harmonisation of contract law in order to facilitate greater regional economic integration.[18] As in the case of the European Union, the harmonisation of contract law is also seen as an instrument for the facilitation of cross-border trade among different Asian jurisdictions.[19] In that context, the establishment of an ASEAN Contract Law regime among its ten Member States has been the subject of the discussions as a part of the harmonisation process of the trade laws aimed at enhancing cross-border trade among Member States.[20]

Besides argumentation based on economics, the harmonisation of contract law is also seen as a political project. The achievement of harmonisation among different contract laws is seen as also strengthening the mutual ties among the different jurisdictions. Harmonisation of contract laws is underpinned by politics – as the European model shows.[21] That was also one of the ideas behind the failed project on the European Civil Code.[22] It was to a large extent inspired by the contract law history of a number of its Member States, where strengthening of the national states was also followed by the adoption of a unitary Civil Code. In that sense, it has been seen that the strengthening of the European Union as the union of different countries also presumed the unification of its different national contract laws. In Asia, the political connections between states may be weaker, but legal harmonisation can still send an important political message about the desire to cooperate on a common basis to promote trade.

Asian contract law scholars, as initiators of regional contract law harmonisation, have emphasised the necessity for the establishment of the common principles of the Asian contract law.[23] If in the case of Asia, the goal of harmonisation is to make Asian contract laws closer to each other, the question which remains is what can be achieved in practice.[24] As viewed from the perspective of East and Southeast Asian jurisdictions, the differences among contract law regimes may be seen as obstacles for further growth of the cross-border trade among diverse jurisdictions. Moreover, the harmonisation of contract laws in the region may shape legal, economic and social development of that region. Essentially, it is important to note that any harmonised contract

---

[18] ASEAN Integration through Law Concluding Plenary, 25 August 2013, Keynote Address by Chief Justice Sundaresh Menon at [13].
[19] Roland Amoussou-Guenou, Perspective of ASEAN (Asian) Principles of Contract Law (Conference Drafting of International Commercial Contracts Hanoi December 2004), 14.
[20] Joint Communique of the 6th ASEAN Law Ministers Meeting (ALAWMM), 19–20 September 2005.
[21] M. W. Hesselink, *The Politics of a European Civil Code* (Kluwer Law International, 2006).
[22] H. W. Micklitz, Failure or Ideological Preconceptions – Thoughts on Two Grand Projects: The European Constitution and the European Civil Code, in K. Tuori and S. Sankari (eds.), *The Many Constitutions of Europe* (Ashgate, 2010).
[23] Y. J. Lee, Basic Guideline for the Principles of Asian Contract Law (2009) 3 *Asia Private Law Review* 325–341.
[24] K. M. Sun, Scope of Damages (2010) 4 *Asia Private Law*, 396.

law instrument would need to address the particularities of the Asian culture and its different legal traditions.[25]

However, a high degree of caution is always required. Legal certainty requires that the harmonisation of contract law should be performed in such a manner that it resolves the existing legal complexity. The outcome should not increase it further.[26] This is why a particularly important question that needs to be examined in detail is the potential value that would be added by any Asian harmonised contract law instrument. In the case of European Contract Law, it is possible to observe that harmonisation has resulted in increasingly complex contract law regimes. The relationship between the European Contract Law and the national contract laws is sometimes problematic and rather ambiguous.

An example is the fact that the standard of the average consumer may be interpreted differently depending on the particular piece of legislation. In the context of unfair commercial practices law (which is related to contract law) within the European Union, the average consumer is considered as a rather high standard when it comes to the expected behaviour of the consumer at the market, so as to support the traders to promote their products.[27] However, under unfair contract terms law, the Court of Justice of the European Union has imposed high transparency requirements so that the average consumer can understand the implication of terms.[28] The unclear European concept of the average consumer then conflicts with the national approaches towards understanding the average consumer, which are sometimes quite different.[29]

All in all, the need for and legal design of a harmonised commercial contract law instrument ought to be carefully considered. In particular, the harmonised commercial contract law instrument needs to be checked among businesses, as they would use this law instrument. On the other hand, as consumer contract law is an area of law that is still developing in Asia, it may be argued that there is a greater need for the development of a harmonised consumer contract law instrument than a commercial contract law instrument. This instrument would not only facilitate the performance of cross-border consumer transactions but also improve the overall wellbeing of consumers in Asia. In that sense, it might be useful to observe the existing efforts of the ASEAN Committee on Consumer Protection. However, this Committee seems to be more focused on product safety and liability issues than on

---

[25] G. F. Bell, New Challenges for the Uniformisation of Laws: How the CISG Is Challenged by 'Asian Values' and Islamic Law, in I. Schwenzer and L. Spagnolo (eds.), *Towards Uniformity: The 2nd Annual MAA Schlechtriem CISG Conference* (Eleven International Publishing, 2015).

[26] Qi Zhou, Harmonisation of European Contract Law: Default and Mandatory Rules, in Larry A. Dimatteo, Qi Zhou, Séverine Saintier and Keith Rowley, *Commercial Contract Law Transatlantic Perspective* (Cambridge University Press, 2013), 526.

[27] Recital 18 of Directive 2005/29/EC on unfair commercial practices.

[28] Case C-26/13, *Árpád Kásler and Hajnalka Káslerné Rábai v. OTP Jelzálogbank Zrt* [2014] ECR I-282, para 74.

[29] See: B. Duivenvoorde, *The Consumer Benchmarks in the Unfair Commercial Practices Directive* (Springer, 2015).

consumer contract law. Further work in the area of consumer protection is envisaged among the ASEAN Member States until the year 2025, but directions of the cooperation among the ten ASEAN countries are defined rather vaguely, so it is not clear how much, and whether at all, they will affect the national consumer contract laws.[30]

The development of supranational contract law also requires a policy decision regarding the legal nature of the contract law instrument. When developing a supranational contract law instrument, there is always a policy dilemma of whether to opt for binding legislation or to rather go for a soft law instrument.[31] Both options have their advantages and disadvantages. The choice is tightly linked with the question of competence and possibility. In other words, the promoters of harmonisation always need to check what in reality can be passed.

The main advantage of opting for a soft law instrument is that it is an easier option, as it does not preclude any of the existing contract law rules but establishes a parallel one. However, this may have indirect effects on the national legal order. As it interferes significantly less with the national legal order, it is much easier to reach the necessary consensus and to pass it. For the same reason, a soft law instrument will be more complete, as it is easier to include provisions that adopt different approaches of the national contract laws for the very reason that they need not be applied.

However, a major problem with soft law instruments is the difficulty of securing their usage in practice. The promotion of a contract law instrument is a very difficult task, especially in the commercial relations where the parties have at their disposal contract laws that they are used to and familiar with, as is the case with the Vienna Convention for the International Sales of Goods (CISG) or English contract law, both of which are extensively used in Asia. For this reason, to promote the success of the harmonisation process, it is certainly much more desirable to opt for a binding legal instrument. The success herein is not to be only understood as the achievement of a high level of harmonisation, but should also refer to the application of the harmonised rules in practice as the set of rules which actually regulate a contractual relationship.

The body of European contract law consists of a number of binding pieces of legislation, adopted through a complex system in which participate a number of the European institutions and the Member States. The complex process for adoption of pieces of legislation also means that it is not easy to secure political support and reach a compromise. The binding pieces of legislation are, typically, the directives that regulate contract law in a fragmented manner.[32] The directives deal with specific types of consumer contracts (package travel, timeshare, consumer credit),

---

[30] ASEAN Strategic Plan for Consumer Protection 2016–2025 (ASAPCP), available at www.aseanconsumer.org/acep/index.php?r=portal/article&id=53.

[31] F. Ferrari, International Uniform Law Conventions, Lex Mercatoria and Unidroit Principles (2000) 5 *Uniform Law Review*, 3.

[32] J. Smits, Coherence and Fragmentation in the Law of Contract, in P. Letto-Vanamo, *Coherence and Fragmentation in European Private Law* (Sellier, 2012), 18 et seq.

consumer contracts which are concluded in a particular manner (distance contracts, doorstep selling contracts) or specific elements of consumer contracts (fairness of contract terms). All these European directives represent hard law, i.e. the EU Member States have to implement their provisions into their national legal systems, properly, timely and to apply them in practice. Otherwise, in case of failure to do so, the European Commission is entitled to take legal actions against that EU Member State before the Court of Justice of the European Union.[33] In the area of contract law, a number of such cases have already been recorded.[34]

The European example also demonstrates well how the question of legal nature is tightly linked with the question of which legal instrument may be adopted at all and the competence involved. In the case of the European Union, the constitutional basis and competence for the development of the European contract law is set out in the Treaties.[35] The Court of Justice of the European Union, as the highest judicial instance in the EU, has also emphasised that the EU competence for the adoption of the common legislation is not absolute but limited.[36] The lack of clear competence and limited political support from the relevant stakeholders were the main reasons why different legislative proposals and academic projects in the area of contract law projects on the European level have failed.[37] These include the idea of a European Civil Code and some other related projects, such as the Principles of European Contract Law (PECL)[38], the Draft Common Frame of Reference (DCFR)[39] and the Common European Sales Law (CESL).[40]

However, despite their failure to become binding law, these projects and practices have had an impact on the Europeanisation of contract law.[41] In reality, they have become some kind of soft law. Accordingly, the provisions of the DCFR have been applied in the case law of the Court of Justice of the European Union; however, not

[33] Article 258 of the Treaty of the Functioning of the European Union.
[34] Case C-144/99 *Commission v. Netherlands* [2 001] E CR I-3541, para 17; Case C-478/99 *Commission v. Sweden* [2002] ECR I-4147; Case C-70/03 *Commission v. Spain* [2004] ECR I-07999.
[35] Stephan Vogenauer and Steven Weatherill, The European Community's Competence to Pursue the Harmonisation of Contract Law – An Empirical Contribution to the Debate, in Stephan Vogenauer and Steven Weatherill (eds.), *The Harmonisation of European Contract Law – Implications for European Private Laws, Business and Legal Practice* (Hart Publishing, 2006), 125–26.
[36] Case C-376/98 *Federal Republic of Germany v. European Parliament and Council of the European Union (Tobacco Advertising I)* [2000] ECR I-08419.
[37] M. W. Hesselink, The Politics of European Civil Code (2004) 10 *European Law Journal* 675.
[38] O. Lando and H. Beale (eds.), *Principles of European Contract Law, Part I* (1996) and *Part II* (1999); O. Lando, E. Clive, A. Prum and R. Zimmermann (eds.), *Principles of European Contract Law, Part III* (2003), http://frontpage.cbs.dk/law/commission_on_european_contract_law/pecl_full_text.htm.
[39] C. Von Bar et al., *Principles, Definitions and Model Rules of European Private Law. Draft Common Frame of Reference (DCFR)* (Sellier, 2008), http://ec.europa.eu/justice/policies/civil/docs/dcfr_outli ne_edition_en.pdf.
[40] Commission, Proposal of the Optional Instrument on a Common European Sales Law ('The Optional Instrument') COM (2011) 635 final.
[41] S. Vogenauer, The DCFR and the CESL as Models for Law Reform in G. Dannemann and S. Vogenauer (eds.), *The Common European Sales Law in Context* (Oxford University Press, 2013), 732 cf.

so much in the judgements, as in the Opinions of the Advocate Generals.[42] The national courts of some EU Member States, in particular their supreme courts, have also referred to the DCFR in their decisions. This has been the case in Spain, Estonia and Sweden.[43] Also, the DCFR and the CESL have been widely used as a model law for the redevelopment of the national contract laws of the EU Member States.[44] Surprisingly, they seem to have had only a limited impact on the drafting of EU Law, as was the case with Directive 2011/83/EU on consumer rights. In Asia, the lack of any legal basis for a binding instrument might suggest a soft law instrument is the most practical way forward.

4 WHAT PART OF CONTRACT LAW SHOULD BE HARMONISED?

The issue of the harmonisation of contract laws gives rise to another important question – namely, whether the entire corpus of contract law needs to be harmonised or only some parts of it. In that context, a distinction between commercial contract law and consumer contract law can be made. Commercial contract law includes the set of rules that regulate the contractual relations between businesses, where consumer contract law covers contractual relations between businesses on the one side and consumers on the other side. Due to the presence of an unequal relationship between the trader and the consumer, consumer contract law has a significantly more regulatory character than commercial contract law. Much of consumer contract law is mandatory, whereas commercial contract law relies on default rules. It seems that the harmonisation of consumer contract laws is more desirable and more feasible than the harmonisation of commercial contract laws. The fact that consumer contract law is easier to harmonise politically is also well proven by the example of the European Contract Law, which has almost exclusively consisted of consumer contract law rules. It is less connected to core national legal traditions. However, it has been emphasised that the harmonisation of the rules in the area of consumer contract law may result in a spillover effect on the provisions of the commercial contract law.[45] In that sense, European consumer contract law might be a very useful model, as it represents the most advanced example of harmonised consumer contract law, which is aimed to secure a high level of consumer protection.[46]

[42] Opinion of Advocate General in Case C-180/06 *Renate Ilsinger v. Martin Dreschers* [2009] ECR I-03961; Opinion of Advocate General in Case C-540/08 *Mediaprint Zeitungs- und Zeitschriftenverlag v. Österreich-Zeitungsverlag GmbH* [2010] ECR I-10909.
[43] G. Kalouta, The DCFR in the Courts, in M. Andenas and D. Fairgrieve, *Courts and Comparative Law* (Oxford University Press, 2015), 717.
[44] S. Vogenauer, The DCFR and the CESL as Models for Law Reform, in G. Dannemann and S. Vogenauer (eds.), *The Common European Sales Law in Context* (Oxford University Press, 2013).
[45] A. Johnston, Spillovers from EU Law into National Law: (Un)intended Consequences for Private Law Relationship, in D. Leczykiewicz and S. Weatherill, *The Involvement of EU Law in Private Law Relationships* (Hart, 2013).
[46] J. Stuyck, 1993 – Twenty Years Later. The Evolution of Consumer Law in the European Union (Intersentia, 2013).

In the case of commercial contract law, the question is whether in the twenty-first century businesses need a harmonised contract law instrument. Freedom to contract, including freedom to choose the applicable contract law rules, is much more present in the case of commercial contract law than in the case of consumer contract law. In Asia, the Singapore Academy of Law has recently published the results of its study on the applicable contract law on commercial transactions in the case of Singaporean businesses. The study was made based on data collected from around five hundred lawyers involved in diverse forms of cross-border transactions. The results of the study have shown that in the case of cross-border transactions, in 48 per cent of examples, English law has been stipulated as applicable. English law is followed by Singapore law, which is opted for as the applicable law in 25 per cent of commercial transactions; then by New York law, in 7 per cent; and, eventually, Hong Kong law, applied in 3 per cent of transactions.[47] Accordingly, it is possible to observe that English law regulates almost half of the transactions and that the common law by far represents the most desired applicable law.

This shows well that promoters of a harmonised contract law instrument in Asia should first check among the relevant stakeholders whether there is a need for the existence of a harmonised commercial contract law instrument and what the features of this new set of rules should be. The question of whether businesses would use a harmonised contract law instrument in practice would, of course, be conditional upon the contract law instrument being drafted in such a manner to suit the businesses. Businesses need to have some incentive to use the new set of rules; otherwise, it will stay just a black letter law. In that sense, the experience with the UNIDROIT Principles of International Contracts should be always borne in mind, as that contract law instrument is hardly ever used in practice as the applicable law, though in certain cases it has been used by arbitrators. The Vienna Convention on the International Sale of Goods (CISG) has already promoted a partial international regime that states (and, by implication, parties) can choose to opt into.

Contrary to the example of commercial contract law, in the area of consumer contract law, the situation seems to be a bit different. Harmonisation of consumer contract law needs also to be concerned with the fact that the contractual relationship between a trader and a consumer is a relationship where an inequality of bargaining power between the parties is present. This is something that the harmonised contract law instrument should certainly adequately address, and for this reason, consumer contract law has a much more regulatory character than commercial contract law.[48] In these kinds of contractual relationships, the freedom of contract should be more restricted. Consumers have much less choice when it comes to choosing the applicable law in the case of cross-border transactions. This

---

[47] Singapore Academy of Law, Study on Governing Law and Jurisdictional Choices in Cross-Border Transactions, 2016. Available at www.sal.org.sg/Documents/SAL_Singapore_Law_Survey.pdf.
[48] H. W. Micklitz, The Regulatory Character of EU Consumer and Contract Law, in C. Twigg Flesner, *Research Handbook on EU Consumer and Contract Law* (Edward Elgar, 2016).

is something that is traditionally decided by businesses through their standard terms and conditions. As a result of the fact that they are not sure which contract law will regulate their transaction and what the content of that law is, consumers may be less willing to perform cross-border consumer transactions.

The example of European consumer contract law has demonstrated that the harmonisation of the consumer contract law among the Member States has led to the increase of cross-border trade among the Member States as consumers become more confident to perform cross-border transactions.[49] European consumer contract law is constantly evolving in an attempt to provide an adequate regulatory response to the development of society and changes in techniques in the market (e.g. the digital age).[50] The development of European consumer contract law has also increased the general level of consumer protection in the European Union. In the case of Asia, the sixteen contract law jurisdictions of East and Southeast Asia have, as a general observation, very limited rules on consumer contract law. Some Asian jurisdictions have started developing consumer contract laws, inspired in part by European consumer law.[51]

5 THE ACHIEVEMENT OF FULL HARMONISATION IN PRACTICE

If the harmonisation of contract law is desirable, then the follow-up question is whether harmonisation among the different contract law regimes is at all possible and, if so, how to achieve it. The beginnings of the harmonisation processes in Europe were followed by strong criticism that harmonisation is simply not possible.[52] However, decades of work on European contract law have demonstrated that harmonisation is possible to some extent.

However, the adoption of a harmonised contract law instrument is just the first step towards reaching the substantial harmonisation of contract law. For that purpose, a second step is also essential to put in place measures to ensure uniformity in the application of the supranational contract law in practice.[53] In accordance with that, it may be observed that deep, full and meaningful harmonisation cannot probably be fully achieved without the existence of a common judicial body in charge of interpreting the harmonised legal instrument.[54] The court and its judges need to be independent of the influence of those national legal traditions.

---

[49] H. W. Micklitz, N. Reich, P. Rott and K. Tonner, *European Consumer Law*, 2nd ed. (Intersentia, 2014).
[50] A. de Franceschi, *European Contract Law and Digital Service Market* (Intersentia, 2016).
[51] J. Stuyck and M. Durovic, The External Dimension of EU Consumer Law, in M. Cremona and H. W. Micklitz (eds.), *The External Dimension of EU Private Law* (Oxford University Press, 2016), 240.
[52] P. Legrand, European Legal Systems Are Not Converging (1996) 45 *International and Comparative Law Quarterly* 52.
[53] I. Schwenzer (ed.), *Commentary on the CISG* (Oxford University Press, 2016), 6–7.
[54] M. Heidemann, *Methodology of Uniform Contract Law* (Springer, 2010), 54.

European contract law may provide a useful example, as the Court of Justice of the European Union has, in the last three decades, provided a number of important decisions providing unified, autonomous explanations of a number of contract law notions. For instance, this was the case with the notion of the invitation to purchase.[55] Within Asia, it is hard to see any desire for such a supra-national court.[56] Other innovative means to ensure uniformity may need to be considered.

It seems that harmonisation of consumer contract law is an easier task in cases when the national rules are still, to a large extent, nascent. This is well demonstrated by European consumer contract law, as it is possible to observe that it is easier to harmonise consumer contract law than commercial contract law, especially in areas where the rules are still not being fully developed within national legal orders. The insufficiently developed consumer contract law seems to exist in the majority of the sixteen jurisdictions of Eastern and Southeast Asia, which also gives more leverage for the harmonisation process in the area of consumer contracts than in the case of commercial contracts.

Moreover, what can be learnt from the European experience is that sometimes in order to avoid political obstacles to the harmonisation of national contract laws, a non-contract law instrument may be used.[57] This was the case with Directive 2005/29/EC on unfair commercial practices, which clearly stated that it is without influence on contract law.[58] However, this Directive eventually has had a material impact on the development of the European Contract Law, in particular due to the broadening of its scope of application by the European Court of Justice in its case law.[59]

For the harmonisation of contract law, the presence of material differences among national contract laws, particularly if they belong to different legal families (e.g. common law versus common law), represents a major challenge. For that reason, it was even argued that harmonisation among contract laws belonging to diverse legal families is actually not possible at all. The European Union is often singled out as a concrete example of such an impossibility, with the explanation that the basics of contract laws are so different that no harmonisation is possible.[60] Another good example is the United Nations Convention on Contracts for the International Sale of Goods ('CISG'), where some choices between the common, civil and socialist legal systems were made, with some blending of the rules and, in other instances, preservation of differences. This turned out to be a good approach,

---

[55] Case C-122/10 *Konsumentombudsmannen (Ko) Ving Sverige AB* [2011] ECR I-03903.
[56] See contribution of Sir Francis Jacobs in this volume.
[57] M. Durovic, *European Law on Unfair Commercial Practices and Contract Law* (Hart Publishing, 2016).
[58] Article 3(2) Directive 2005/29/EC on unfair commercial practices.
[59] M. Durovic, *The Impact of Directive 2005/29/EC on Unfair Commercial Practices in Contract Law* (European Review of Private Law, 2015).
[60] P. Legrand, European Legal Systems Are Not Converging (1996) 45 *International and Comparative Law Quarterly* 52.

as the CISG today represents the most successful example of an international contract law instrument.[61] However, a more detailed examination of the CISG is beyond the scope of this chapter.

The development of European contract law in the last three decades, and its acceptance and incorporation into national contract laws by such a large number of countries, have shown that this argument can be hardly taken as a valid one and that harmonisation is, in reality, possible. Of course, the work on harmonisation is not an easy task. In the case of European contract law, the process of drafting a pan-regional set of rules was plagued by the presence of sometimes fundamental differences among the national contract law regimes belonging to civil law, common law and mixed legal systems.

Indeed, the experiences gained from European contract law show that not a full but only a partial harmonisation seems to be possible. The more the reforms connect to fundamental principles of general contract law, the harder it has been to reach an agreement on harmonisation. Even within the distinct segment of European consumer contract law, the legal instruments often do not form complete regimes but need to be supplemented by the provisions of the national contract laws, as in certain areas where differences are so radical that compromises could not be reached.

Regarding general contract law, areas such as pre-contractual liability good faith or consent defects have been particularly difficult to find common approaches for. These are the areas where the approaches among common law and civil law are radically different.[62] Likewise, the CISG also does not regulate the parts of contract laws where the differences are the most noticeable. Accordingly, there are no rules on pre-contractual liability or consent defects, whereas the application of the principle of good faith is reserved only for the interpretation of the contract.[63]

European contract law has had some success in overcoming some but not all areas of national irreconcilability managed to be overcome, albeit only in the context of consumer law. This is the case, for instance, with the imposition of a general pre-contractual duty of information, which is a completely new approach for English contract law. The introduction of the pre-contractual duty of information as a general pre-contractual duty has occurred only in the case of consumer contract law. A universal pre-contractual obligation of information in business-to-consumer relations was first brought by the Directive 2005/29/EC on unfair commercial practice.[64] Subsequently, the general character of this duty in the case of consumer contracts was confirmed by Directive 2011/83/EU on consumer

---

[61] See I. Schwenzer and L. Spagnolo (eds.), *Towards Uniformity: The 2nd Annual MAA Schlechtriem CISG Conference* (Eleven International Publishing, 2011).

[62] J. Cartwright and M. W. Hesselink, *Precontractual Liability in European Private Law* (Cambridge University Press, 2011); R. Zimmermann and S. Whittaker, *Good Faith in European Contract Law* (Cambridge University Press, 2000); R. Sefton-Green, *Mistake, Fraud and Duties to Inform* (Cambridge University Press, 2005).

[63] Article 7(1) CISG.

[64] Article 7 of Directive 2005/29/EC on unfair commercial practices.

rights.[65] Similarly, good faith has been introduced as a common legal principle but only for consumer contracting.

6 THE CURRENT SITUATION WITH HARMONISATION OF CONTRACT LAW IN EAST AND SOUTHEAST ASIA

East and Southeast Asia are a part of the world with an increasing number of commercial and consumer transactions among different jurisdictions.[66] It is therefore not surprising that the development of cross-border commercial activities has also been followed by a closer cooperation of contract law scholars interested in providing a regulatory response to the development of cross-border trade. One of the products of the legal scholars' cooperation is the launching of an initiative for the harmonisation of contract law in Eastern and Southeastern Asia. This initiative has been a purely academic project, without organised political support of the jurisdictions involved. Some interstate support for the establishment of common supranational contract law exists only in the case of the ten countries of the ASEAN, but it does not involve the remaining six jurisdictions of Eastern Asia.

Some Asian contract law scholars have been trying to develop the Principles of Asian Contract Law (PACL). As can be observed from its name, the development of PACL was inspired by and modelled after the Principles of European Contract Law (PECL). The PACL project is important, as it represents the first comparative contract law cooperative work in Asia, something that previously was missing.[67]

PACL is drafted in such a manner to address and incorporate the particularities of the national contract laws of the regional jurisdictions. It is also designed in such a way as to provide a legal response to globalisation through the establishment of rules which would fit into global laws and transactional commercial practices. PACL's drafters have identified four principal aims. The first one is to serve as a model law for reform of the national contract laws of the East and Southeast Asian jurisdictions. The second aim is to provide help the national courts and arbitrations when they need make decisions regarding the applicable law for cross-border commercial transactions. The third purpose is to be 'a soft law' and, as such, to be used as the applicable law for contractual transactions by the parties themselves. The fourth goal of PACL is to be a widely developed academic project which would

---

[65] Article 5 of Directive 2011/83/EU on consumer rights.
[66] B. Zeller, Facilitating Regional Economic Integration: ASEAN, ATIGA and the CISG, in I. Schwenzer and L. Spagnolo (eds.), *Towards Uniformity: The 2nd Annual MAA Schlechtriem CISG Conference* (Eleven International Publishing, 2011), 255–267.
[67] M. Chen-Wishart, A. Loke and S. Vogenauer, Introduction, in M. Chen-Wishart, A. Loke and S. Vogenauer (eds.), *Studies in the Contract Laws of Asia: The Formation and Third Party Beneficiaries* (Oxford University Press 2018), 1.

7 Is the Harmonisation of Asian Contract Law Possible?

touch upon and compare similarities and differences which exist among contract laws of the jurisdictions of East and Southeast Asia.[68]

PACL is a private, academic initiative of a number of contract law scholars coming from Southeast and East Asian jurisdictions. It has been imagined as an instrument for providing a set of supranational rules which are designed in such a manner to secure a convenient and functional application by the Asian parties and courts.[69] The development of the PACL project started in 2009.[70] The first outcome of the project was visible already in 2010. These were the Draft Articles of PACL on Non-Performance of a Contract.[71] Importantly, what needs to be emphasised is that contrary to the example of the European Union, in the case of the sixteen jurisdictions of East and Southeast Asia, there is no supranational entity which has the authority to impose any kind of contract law legislation, such as the PACL, on these jurisdictions.

Another contemporary Asian academic project is 'Studies in the Contract Laws of Asia'. This project has gathered together a number of leading contract law scholars not only from East and Southeast Asia but also from South Asia, each exploring and explaining a particular contract law concept in the national contract law context. This is preceded by a common introduction and common conclusive remarks. The conclusions eventually identify the existing mutual similarities and differences among the national contract laws in Asia.

The main goal of 'Studies in the Contract Laws of Asia' project is twofold. First, the studies aim to contribute to the dialogue among the different national contract laws of different jurisdictions in Asia, as this is something that needs to be improved further. Second, the outcomes of the project will enable the interaction not only among the Asian contract laws but also with the contract laws of the Western Hemisphere.[72] Such a comparative study has been missing thus far, and this will be the first study ever of its kind in the English language. The results of the research project are to be published in six books as six volumes. The comparison is performed primarily through the application of a functional method and comparing diverse national contract law notions of the same or similar purpose.[73]

Accordingly, each of the six books of the series deals with one of six specific contract law notions. The examined areas include remedies, formation

---

[68] Y. J. Lee et al., *A Study on Draft Articles Principles of Asian Contract Law Performance and Non-performance*, Research Institute for Asia Private Law (Research Institute for Asia Private Law, 2016), 3.

[69] Ibid., 1–2.

[70] S. Y. Han, Principles of Asian Contract Law: An Endeavour or Regional Harmonisation of Contract Law in East Asia (2013) 58 *Villanova Law Review* 4, 589–599, 590.

[71] Y. J. Lee et al., *A Study on Draft Articles Principles of Asian Contract Law Performance and Non-Performance*, Research Institute for Asia Private Law (Research Institute for Asia Private Law, 2016).

[72] M. Chen-Wishart, A. Loke and B. Ong, Introduction, in M. Chen-Wishart, A. Loke and B. Ong (eds.), *Studies in the Contract Laws of Asia, Remedies for Breach of Contract* (Oxford University Press 2016), p. 1.

[73] R. Michaels, Functional Method, in M. Reimann and R. Zimmermann (eds.), *The Oxford Handbook of Comparative Law* (Oxford University Press, 2006).

and third-party beneficiaries, the contract contents, the invalidity of contracts, the contract ending and public policy and illegality. The first book from the series, on contract law remedies, was published in 2016. The second one, on formation and third-party beneficiaries, was published in 2018.[74] This volume covers two very important areas of contract law: the formation of contracts and contracts for the benefits of third parties. It demonstrates that despite the differences among the national contract laws, functional convergence happens in a number of cases.[75] What is interesting to observe is that one of the editors of the second book is Professor Stefan Vogenauer, who has been very active in the last decades on the project of the European Contract Law.

The remaining four volumes are expected to be published in the following years.[76] The results of this study will certainly represent an unavoidable material for any future discussion on the harmonisation of contract law in East and Southeast Asia. Hopefully, once all six volumes get published, this will foster a better understanding of the similarities and differences of different contract law regimes in Asia and will also enhance not only their mutual communication but also their conversation with the contract law regimes worldwide.[77]

7 CONCLUSIONS

In summation, this chapter examined the phenomenon of harmonisation of the Asian diverse contract law traditions from the perspective of the European Contract Law. Accordingly, it may be concluded that there are two principal questions related to the harmonisation of contract laws which need to be answered by the promoters of a harmonised Asian contract law. The first one determines the goals of harmonisation, and the second one determines what can be realistically achieved in practice. These two questions are tightly connected. To answer these two questions, it is very beneficial to have a look at the experience gained from the European model of the harmonisation of contract law.

For the first question, it is important to decide which area of contract law is to be harmonised and also in what manner, and whether through binding legislation or through a soft law instrument. This is linked with the second question regarding what can be achieved in reality. Due to its long history and very rich experience,

---

[74] M. Chen-Wishart, A. Loke and S. Vogenauer (eds.), *Studies in the Contract Laws of Asia: The Formation and Third Party Beneficiaries* (Oxford University Press, 2018).

[75] See A. Loke, Conclusion, in M. Chen-Wishart, A. Loke and S. Vogenauer (eds.), *Studies in the Contract Laws of Asia: The Formation and Third Party Beneficiaries* (Oxford University Press, 2018), chapter 23.

[76] M. Chen-Wishart, A. Loke and C. Ong (eds.), *Studies in the Contract Laws of Asia: Remedies for Breach of Contract* (Oxford University Press, 2016).

[77] M. Chen-Wishart, A. Loke and S. Vogenauer, Introduction, in M. Chen-Wishart, A. Loke and S. Vogenauer (eds.), *Studies in the Contract Laws of Asia: The Formation and Third Party Beneficiaries* (Oxford University Press, 2018), 23.

European contract law may be used as a model to provide the answers to these questions. The examination of European contract law enables a better understanding of the process of harmonisation of diverse contract law traditions present both in the case of the jurisdictions of Eastern and Southeastern Asia and in the case of the European jurisdictions.

European contract law demonstrates that harmonisation among different contract law traditions is possible. However, what can be learnt from the European model is that full harmonisation seems to be an impossible task; only a partial harmonisation can be achieved. The harmonisation of contract law rules was rather successful in the area of consumer contract law, whereas in the area of commercial contract law, the effects of harmonisation are minimal. Full harmonisation thus has been achieved in fields such as consumer information and right of withdrawal in the Directive 2011/83/EU on consumer rights, but the original proposal to also extend this with unfair terms and sales law met national resistance and had to be dropped.[78]

Still, despite its marginal effects in the area of commercial contract law, the development of European contract law has contributed to a greater mutual understanding and interchange in all areas of contract law. This may be considered as the greatest achievement of the work on European contract law. However, all of the ambitious European projects that have as their goal a broad harmonisation of contract law (e.g. the European Civil Code or a more complete Consumer Contract instrument) have failed. In the case of Europe, harmonisation was successful in two directions: first, through piecemeal harmonisation of consumer contract law, as an innovative area of contract law, and second, through the development of different model contract laws (e.g. PECL or DCFR) which do not represent binding laws, but only soft law. Therefore, care should be taken so that the Asian projects on harmonisation of contract laws are not overambitious. Moreover, harmonisation also requires strong political support from stakeholders; without this element, harmonisation is not possible.

Interestingly, from a substantive law perspective, the European model shows that harmonisation is possible in some of the areas of contract law where the differences of contract laws have been traditionally the most notable. This is particularly the case with the pre-contractual duty of information, which has become a general duty in all the European contract laws regarding consumers, but which previously the national contract laws regulated in a radically different manner.

For the achievement of a higher level of harmonisation of contract laws, what also seems to be very important from the European example is to have a supranational court. The Court of Justice of the European Union, through its case law, has not only contributed to a more uniform interpretation of the European Contract Law

---

[78] European Commission, Proposal for a Directive of the European Parliament and of the Council on Consumer Rights, COM (2008) 614 final.

but has also itself materially helped the harmonisation of diverse contract law traditions. In that sense, for the achievement of a higher level of harmonisation of Asian contract laws, the establishment of some kind of the Asian Court of Justice, modelled after the Court of Justice of the European Union, would certainly be needed as a binding law was adopted.

However, this seems unlikely and is another reason favouring soft law solutions. In this process, the development of academic research and its impact on teaching cannot be underestimated as important factors in bringing the legal culture of Asia closer together. In a global trading world, the work in Europe and Asia should also feed off one another. One beneficial aspect of the United Kingdom leaving the European Union may be that it will participate more in these global discussions and be an important bridge between the two continents of Asia and Europe. One can always dream!

8

The Presumption of Regularity in Chinese Corporate Contracting: Evidence and the Prospect of Regional Convergence

Charles Zhen Qu

1 INTRODUCTION

When entering into transactions, whether directly as a principal or through an agent, a company acts through individuals. A transaction is a corporate act if the individuals through whom the company has acted are duly authorised. A transaction purportedly made in the name or on behalf of the company, however, may not have been duly authorised, either because the transaction was not authorised at all or because the internally prescribed conditions or limitations for the exercise of the power conferred on the relevant corporate organ or agents have not been satisfied or observed.

An issue that courts often confront is therefore the enforceability of corporate contracts not duly authorised. A decision on this issue allocates the risks for corporate transactions to either the company or the person seeking to deal with it. The difficult task for the courts is to locate the point of balance in the need for protecting both parties in the transaction in allocating the risks.

Within Anglo-Commonwealth jurisdictions, a tool kit has been developed for resolving disputes arising from corporate contracts. The instruments that this tool kit contains include the common law, as well as statutory, 'indoor management rule' (IMR), which is a 'presumption of regularity', supplemented by the doctrines of actual and apparent authority.[1] The common law or statutory IMR protects the contractor by, broadly, giving the latter the right to make presumptions on the regularity of internal machinery for effecting the transaction. These apparatuses come with rules that delineate the scope of operations of the presumption of

---

I am grateful to the helpful comments of Professor Michael Tilbury of Melbourne Law School on the earlier drafts of this chapter. The work described in this chapter was fully supported by a grant of the Research Council of the Hong Kong Special Administrative Region, China [Project No. CityU11604217].

[1] *Northside Developments Pty Ltd v. Registrar-General* (1990) 170 CLR 146 per Brennan J at 176 (common law presumption of regularity); Companies Ordinance (HK) ss. 117–119. Other tools in the kit include principles of actual authority and apparent authority.

regularity, which rules shield the company from liability where the contractor should not be entitled to the presumption.[2]

In the People's Republic of China (PRC), the courts are less equipped. Neither the PRC general civil law system nor the PRC company law framework provide for a presumption of regularity. PRC Company Law art. 16, which has been enacted to regulate corporate transactions that give a security, is silent on third-party rights.[3] Also, as will be seen shortly, the provision put in place to regulate corporate contracts that give a security arguably precludes the operation of the rules on apparent authority. This raises a question on the ways in which the party seeking to deal with the company, as well as the company itself, is protected.

This chapter explores the possibility of completing a nascent presumption of regularity evidenced in the PRC courts adjudication of art. 16 cases, using the common law IMR as a model.

The paper will achieve its purposes through the accomplishment of three tasks. These are (i) an examination of the ways in which the common law presumption of regularity[4] operates, or should operate, where the transaction in question is entered into *without* (as distinguished from beyond) authority; (ii) a discovery of the patterns of practice of the higher people's courts (the Supreme People's Court (SPC) and the High People's Courts (HPC)) in resolving the type of dispute under consideration; and (iii) a consideration of the desirability and possibility, on the basis of the existing judicial practice, of developing the emerging presumption of regularity in China into an IMR-like dispute resolution device under the PRC legal framework.

The patterns of judicial practice in the higher people's courts[5] will be discovered by way of a review of the decisions of these courts on art. 16 disputes listed in *pkulaw*, a respected case database.[6] The case review will discover, among other things, an

---

[2] Text to n. (45). Where the transaction in question is made through a professed corporate agent, the presumption of regularity apparatuses are assisted, where necessary, by rules on actual or apparent authority: *Freeman and Lockyer v. Buckhurst Park Properties (Mangal) Ltd* [1964] 2 QB 480 CA; *Crabtree-Vickers Pty Ltd v. Australian Direct Mail Advertising and Addressing Co Pty Ltd* (1975) 133 CLR 72.

[3] This provision is supplemented by art. 121, which provides, inter alia, that a contract committing a public company as a security provider, where the value of the liability under a security agreement is to exceed 30 per cent of the total assets of the company, must be approved by the general meeting.

[4] The issues raised for this paper will be debated by reference to the common law, rather than the statutory, presumption of regularity. It is more realistic to address the inadequacy of the emerging presumption of regularity approach by reference to the IMR through a Judicial Interpretation by the Supreme People's Court. The statutory presumption of regularity (adopted in Anglo-Commonwealth jurisdictions) will be more relevant when considering the enactment of a formal statutory presumption of regularity regime.

[5] For the purposes of this paper, 'Higher people's courts' refer to the Supreme People's Court and the High People's Court.

[6] The data set consists of all of the decisions by the higher people's courts on art. 16 decisions listed in the *pkulaw* database as of 9 December 2016. These include six SPC decisions and twenty-six cases decided by the HPCs of Anhui, Guangdong, Guizhou, Henan, Hunan, Jiangxi, Jiangsu, Liaoning, Shandong, Xinjiang, Xizang, and Zhejiang provinces/autonomous regions. For a list of the cases collected, after discarding the irrelevant cases, see the Appendix.

emerging court-made presumption of regularity that protects creditors at the expense of the company (the reason to believe or RTB approach). This paper will argue that this approach can be amended into a fair and efficient tool for resolving art. 16 disputes by, inter alia, adopting rules similar to those that have applied to delineate the scope of the common law IMR.

The remainder of the chapter will start with a consideration of the effect of art. 16 and the main issue arising therefrom. The paper then proceeds to an examination of the three main approaches that the courts have developed to fill the gap on presumption of regularity. After an evaluation of RTB, the emerging presumption of regularity, the paper will debate the preferability, as a matter of policy, of changing the risk-allocation proclivity of RTB and, if so, how this may be done. This part of the discussion will be followed by an assessment as to the prospect of completing the convergence of RTB and IMR, which is necessary for the accomplishment of the previously mentioned task.

2 ARTICLE 16 AND THE MAIN ISSUE

Article 16 regulates corporate security transactions by providing mandatory rules on three aspects of the corporate decision-making process. These are (i) the location of decision-making power, (ii) voting by members who stand to benefit from the transactions, and (iii) the amount of security prescribed in the constitution.

Article 16 provides, inter alia, that (i) a decision to act as a security provider in favour of a company outsider is to be made by the directors or the general meeting, as is provided in the company's constitution;[7] (ii) where the company's constitution limits the liability of the company under a security contract in favour of an outsider to a given amount, that amount must not be exceeded where the company decides to act as a security provider;[8] (iii) where the borrower is a shareholder or 'actual controller',[9] the decision must be made by the general meeting;[10] and (iv) where the security is to be provided in favour of a shareholder, that shareholder is prohibited from participating in the voting process.[11] Article 16 does not stipulate a default position where the alleged surety's constitution is silent on the location of the decision-making power where the surety is to be provided in favour of a company outsider.

---

[7] PRC Company Law art. 16.1.
[8] PRC Company Law art. 16.1.
[9] An 'actual controller', for the purposes of the Company Law, means a person, while not a shareholder, who is able to control the 'behaviour' of the company pursuant to an investment relationship, an agreement, or other arrangements: PRC Company Law art. 217 (3); 吴灿朴, 田笛《中华人民共和国公司法实用解读版》(法律出版社, 北京, 2016) 50 (Canpu Wu and Di Tian, *Annotated Company Law of the People's Republic of China* (Law Press, 2016), p. 50).
[10] PRC Company Law art. 16.2.
[11] PRC Company Law art. 16.3.

TABLE 8.1 *Patterns of cases: percentage of authorised transactions*

Total number of cases reviewed	Transaction authorised – meeting held	Transaction authorised by unanimous consent or the only member of the company	Transaction not authorised – no meeting held
32	2 (6%)	3 (9%)	27 (85%)

Corporate contracting disputes can arise where the corporate organ or agent on which/whom authority is conferred has acted where the conditions or limitations to which the authority is subject have not been fulfilled or observed.[12] They can also arise where the individual(s) who purportedly acted in the name or on behalf of the company did so without authority.[13] As the decision to enter into an art. 16 contract must be made by either the board or the general meeting, which are corporate organs, a corporate security contract is one that is made by the company directly, rather than one entered into through an agent.

On whether the transaction has been authorised, issues may arise as to, inter alia, the effect of procedural regularity of the meeting at which the company's decision has been made.[14] Where the transaction is found to have been authorised, there can be a further dispute on whether the corporate organ wherein the decision-making power is vested has, in making the decision, exceeded its power as stipulated in the company's constitution (e.g. as to the limit as to value).[15] The case review conducted demonstrates, however, that the first issue mentioned above was raised in only one case,[16] and easily resolved, and that the second issue mentioned has not been raised. As Table 8.1 shows, in 85 per cent of the cases reviewed, the transaction in question was not authorised at all. The issue for the courts is therefore largely the company's liability where the transaction in dispute has been entered into *without authority*.

3 GAP FILLING: JUDICIAL APPROACHES

That 85 per cent of the art. 16 disputes have arisen in situations where the transaction was entered into without authority leaves one to wonder how the PRC courts, in

---

[12] *Royal British Bank* v. *Turquand* (1856) 6 El. & Bl. 327; (1856) 119 ER 886.
[13] *Northside Developments Pty Ltd* v. *Registrar-General* (1990) 170 CLR 146; *Ruben* v. *Great Fingall Consolidated* [1906] AC 439; *Hua Rong Finance Ltd* v. *Mega Capital Enterprises Ltd* [2001] 3 HKLRD 623; *National Commercial Bank* v. *Albert Hwang* (2002) 2 HKLRD 408; *Thanakharn Kasicorn Thai Chamkat* v. *Akai Holdings Ltd* (2010) 13 HKCFAR 479.
[14] *Ford* v. *Polymer Vision Ltd* [2009] 2 BCLC.
[15] *Re Hampshire Land Co* [1896] 2 Ch. 743.
[16] Case no. 6.

TABLE 8.2 *Pattern of court decisions: Contract enforceability and company liability*

Number of cases	Contract held enforceable	Contract held unenforceable	Company held wholly liable	Company held partially liable	Company held not liable
32	26 (81%)	6 (19%)	28 (88%)	3 (9%)	1 (3%)

settling these disputes, have made their decisions based on the company's liability. A common law court's decision on a party's liability for a contract hinges on, inter alia, the courts' ruling on the validity of the contract. Is this the case in art. 16 decisions?

Table 8.2 provides the answer.

One would be surprised by a couple of facts presented in Tables 8.1 and 8.2. The first is that, whereas in 85 per cent of cases the transaction in dispute was unauthorised,[17] in 81 per cent of the cases the contract has been held enforceable. The second is that although in 19 per cent of the cases the contract was held unenforceable (*wu xiao*), 97 per cent of the cases the company was held either wholly or partially liable for the portion of the debt that the debtor failed to discharge. The questions that the previously mentioned facts prompt are, naturally, how these results have been reached, and whether the outcomes are justifiable. These questions are best answered through a comparison with the common law presumption of regularity.

3.1 *The Common Law Approach: Presumption of Regularity*

In Commonwealth jurisdictions, the issue presented in the previously described situations is resolved by the application of, inter alia,[18] the court-made, as well as statutory, presumption of regularity apparatuses. These apparatuses, which are called 'indoor management rule (IMR)' and 'statutory indoor management rule' (statutory IMR),[19] protect a person seeking to contract with the company (the contractor) by giving the former the right to presume that the company's internal machinery for effecting the contract is in order.

Under the IMR, 'persons dealing with a company in good faith may assume that acts within its constitution and powers have been properly and duly performed and are not bound to inquire whether acts of internal management have been regular'.[20] The statutory IMR protects the person dealing with the company in good faith by either removing any limitation on the directors' power to bind the company as set

---

[17] As is indicated in Table 8.1.
[18] Rules on actual or apparent authority may also be relevant. Especially where the transaction in dispute was allegedly entered into through an agent of the company.
[19] P. R. Austin and I. M. Ramsay, *Ford's Principles of Corporations Law*, 16th ed. (LexisNexis, 2015) [13.150]; [13.280],ff.
[20] *Halsbury's Laws of England*, 4th ed., re-issue, vol. 7 at para. 980, quoted in Austin and Ramsay n. 20.

forth under the company's constitution (the UK approach),[21] or entitling the outsider to a set of presumptions in relation to that person's dealing with the company, notwithstanding any fraud or forgery committed by the company's officer or agent (the Australian approach).[22]

The utility of these presumption-of-regularity apparatuses lies in the difficulty for contractors to satisfy themselves 'as to the authority of the corporate organ or agent who professes to contract in the name or on behalf of company'.[23] Requiring a third party to investigate internal proceedings to satisfy itself about the authority of individuals acting in the name or on behalf of the company and about the validity of the instrument would make transactions with companies inconvenient and costly.[24]

3.2 PRC Courts' Solutions

The absence of a presumption of regularity structure under the PRC legal framework raises a question on the ways in which art. 16 disputes have been resolved. The PRC courts have developed three approaches to filling this gap in their adjudication of art. 16 cases. As pointed out above, the issue in typical art. 16 cases is the company's liability for an unauthorised contract. The law on the liability of the alleged principal for an unauthorised contract is clear. Under PRC Contract Law art. 48, the contract entered into by a person without or beyond authority, or where the authority has lapsed, unless ratified, is ineffective vis-à-vis the alleged principal. The liability under the contract shall be borne by the professed agent. The third party has the right to request ratification within a month of the contract. The failure of the alleged principal to respond (within this period of time) to the request is deemed to be a refusal to ratify. If follows that, absent a ratification by the company ex post, the company is not privy to the unauthorised contract.

The PRC courts, however, appear to have conceptualised the issue differently. In developing the various approaches to the issue raised, the courts appeared to have based their decisions on a view that sees a security contract made without authority as, instead of an unauthorised transaction, a contract that the company has made with the creditor in contravention of art. 16. The inquiries that a court makes, with this view of art. 16 disputes, therefore include (i) the enforceability of the contract,

---

[21] Companies Act 2006 (UK) s. 40; Companies Act (Sing) ss. 25B-25C; Companies Ordinance (HK) ss. 117-119.
[22] Corporations Act 2001 (Aust.) ss.128-129. The 'good faith' element under s. 128 is that the person will lose the entitlement to make an assumption if that person knows or suspects that the assumption is incorrect: s. 128(4).
[23] Paul Redmond AM, *Corporations and Financial Market Law*, 16th ed. (Law Book, 2013) [5.130].
[24] Text to n. (62). The common law tool set for resolving issues arising out of corporate contract also includes the rules on actual authority and apparent authority.

and (ii) the respective liabilities of the company, the alleged security provider, and the creditor.[25] The PRC courts have developed the aforementioned approaches in making decisions on the enforceability of the contracts in dispute.

3.2.1 The First Approach: The Validity Approach

The first approach that the PRC courts have developed looks at whether a security contract made in contravention of art. 16 amounts to an illegal contract and, if so, whether that contravention renders the contract unenforceable.[26] This approach has been developed through an interpretation of the PRC Contract Law art. 52.5. That provision states that a contract made in contravention of a mandatory statutory or administrative rule is unenforceable. The SPC's Judicial Interpretation of the PRC Contract Law (the Contract Law Interpretation) (II) art. 14 narrows the scope of art. 52.5 by stating that the mandatory rules under art. 52.5 refer to those the breach of which renders the contract unenforceable.

The SPC appears to hold the view that (i) mandatory rules the breach of which goes to the enforceability of the contract are those that contain an express provision that a contravention renders the contract unenforceable and those, although containing no such express provision, the violation of which will harm the state and public interest, and (ii) the mandatory rules that are made to facilitate 'administrative or disciplinary management' (行政管理或纪律管理), as a general rule, do not render a contravening contract unenforceable.[27] A decision made under the validity approach would hold that art. 16 is a mandatory rule the breach of which does not affect the enforceability of the contract, and that a contravening surety agreement is therefore enforceable.[28]

Whereas there is much to be said about the workability of arts. 52.5 and 14 as rules on the effect of illegal contracts,[29] these rules are arguably irrelevant for resolving art. 16 disputes. Arts. 52.5 and 14 would be relevant only where disputants are parties to a contract entered into in contravention of mandatory rules. Prima facie, a surety

---

[25] Under art. 5 of the PRC Guaranty Law, parties (including the alleged security provider) may be held liable even if the security contract in dispute is found to be ineffective.

[26] 高圣平，《公司担保相关法律研究》，载《中国法学》2013 年第 2 期第 104 页 (Shengping Gao, 'A study on the law relating to corporate security transactions' (2013) 2 *Chinese Legal Science* 104 at 104); 吴飞飞，《公司担保案件司法裁判路径的偏失与矫正》，载《当代法学》2015 年第 2 期第 56 页 (Feifei Wu, 'The incorrect paths in the adjudication of corporate security cases and the correction' (2015) 2 *Modern Legal Science* 56); Table 8.4 below.

[27] 最高人民法院研究室编著，沈德咏，奚晓明主编《最高人民法院关于合同法司法解释（二）理解与适用》(人民法院出版社，北京，2009) 106 (Deyong Shen and Xiaoming Xi, *The Understanding and Application of the Supreme People's Court's Judicial Interpretation on PRC Contract Law (II)* (Beijing: People's Courts Press, 2009), p. 106).

[28] Gao, Wu n. (27).

[29] Gao, Wu n. (27); 周伦军《公司对外担保的合同效力判断规则》，载《山东大学法学评论》2015 年第 166 页。(Lunjun Zhou, 'The rules on deciding the effect of corporate security contracts' (2015) *Shandong University Law Review* 166).

contract made in the name of the company without authority is not one to which the company is a party until the company ratifies it.[30] It is besides the point to consider the effect of the contract on a company if it is not a party to that agreement.

3.2.2 The Second Approach: The Externality Approach

This approach is based on the view that art. 16 aims to protect shareholders and other creditors from company controllers' abusive activities. In other words, art. 16, according to this view, regulates internal relations and does not affect a party external to the company. A contract made in contravention of art. 16 therefore should not affect the binding effect of the contract as far as the contractor is concerned. It follows that a contract between the company and the creditor made in contravention of art. 16 does not render the contract unenforceable as far as the latter is concerned.[31] The problem with this view is, again, that it is based on the false premise that the alleged principal, who has not authorised the transaction, is a party to a contract (made in contravention of art. 16). As mentioned, under PRC Contract Law art. 48, the contract in this situation, if any, would be between the contractor and the unauthorised agent/corporate representative.

In any event, the view that rules regulating a company's internal decisions do not have an effect on a party seeking to deal with that company is an unsubstantiated assertion that contradicts some of the mandatory rules within the PRC legal framework. One of the mandatory rules that refutes the previously mentioned assertion is PRC Contract Law art. 50. This provision states that a contract entered into by the Legal Representative (LR)[32] of a company beyond the LR's authority is valid unless the counterparty knew or ought to have known about that fact. The LR's authority is surely delineated by way of, inter alia, an internal rule of the company. That rule will have an effect on the contractor if the state of his knowledge about the scope of the LR's authority warrants it.

Although the two approaches considered so far are doctrinally unsustainable, a third approach that appears to be emerging from the art. 16 decisions is more encouraging. This is what can be termed the 'reasons to believe' approach (the RTB approach), which can be seen as a crude equivalent of the common law IMR[33] that the PRC courts have developed. This approach will be examined in the section below.

---

[30] See Section 3.2.2 in this chapter.
[31] See Wu n. (27).
[32] Under the PRC General Principle of Civil Law (GPCL), the legal representative of the company is the responsible individual who represents the company in exercising the latter's powers and rights: GPCL art. 38, only the company's board chairperson, executive directors, or general manager can be appointed as the company's legal representative.
[33] *Royal British Bank v. Turquand* (1856) 6 El. & Bl. 327; (1856) 119 E.R. 886.

3.2.3 The RTB Approach

THE APPROACH. Under this approach, the alleged security contract is held to be valid on the basis that, inter alia, the imprint of what appears to be the alleged surety's company seal and/or the signature of the company's LR affixed on the security instrument gives the creditor reasons to believe that the internal machinery for effecting the transaction is in order.[34] This version of presumption of regularity entitles the creditor to assume regularity on the basis of the apparent formal validity of the security instrument. The courts, however, have not articulated a formula for the application of this approach. What the creditor is entitled to presume under the approach, however, can be gauged from the various states of affairs, which, in the views of the courts, should entitle the contractor to presume regularity. These, as Table 8.3 illustrates, include (i) that the company had formed an intention to act as the security provider, (ii) that all statutorily or internally prescribed conditions on the authorisation of the transaction were fulfilled, or (iii) that the professed representative of the company executed the guarantee contract within power. What all of these states of affairs indicate is, in essence, the same – namely, that the company has authorised the transaction.

THE WAYS IN WHICH THE RTB APPROACH HAS BEEN APPLIED. The first case where the RTB approach was adopted, among those reviewed for the purposes of this project, is case no. 5. In this case, The Zhejiang High People's Court held that the company seal affixed on the guarantee section of the loan contract by the LR of the alleged surety company gave the creditor reason to believe that the company had the intention to act as the guarantor. The decision that has played a greater role in the emergence of the RTB approach is perhaps case number 8, an SPC case decided three years later. In

TABLE 8.3 *The RTB approach: what the contractor is entitled to assume*

Total number of cases where approach adopted	The company has formed an intention to act as surety	Conditions for exercising power conferred fulfilled	The corporate representative has acted within power
11	5 (46%)	3 (27%)	3 (27%)

[34] In ten out of the eleven cases where the RTB approach was adopted, the presumption given was based on the imprint of what appears to be the company's seal on the security instrument. In six out of these ten cases, the presumption given was also based on the signature of the professed company LR or agent. In the only case where no reference to the affixing of the company seal or LR signature on the instrument was made, that the lender had no reason to believe that the company has passed a resolution to provide a guarantee was evidenced in the fact that the general meeting resolution only approved the offering of some of the company's assets as security, rather than the company as a guarantor.

this case, the SPC upheld the validity of the guarantee agreement in dispute on the ground that, inter alia, the company seal affixed in the loan instrument, together with the LR's signature, gave the lender reasons to believe that the LR was acting within authority. This was notwithstanding the fact that the seals affixed by four out of five corporate members on the resolution of the general meeting (which never took place) were forged, two of which visibly so.[35] The fifth one was that of the borrowing member, which was not, according to art. 16.3, qualified to vote.

The patterns of courts' decisions on the validity of unauthorised corporate security contracts, in terms of the avenues through which the decisions on the validity of contract were reached, are summarised in Table 8.4.

As can be seen from Table 8.4, decisions on the enforceability of the contract in close to 20 per cent of the cases where the security contract was entered into without authority were made through the RTB approach alone, and in more than 20 per cent of cases, the decisions were made through the RTB approach in conjunction with either the externality or the validity approaches, or both. The fact that the RBT approach has been relied on in more than 40 per cent of cases where the enforceability of contract was at issue evidences the emergence of RTB as the most frequently relied upon approach to art. 16 disputes.

RTB AS A PRESUMPTION OF REGULARITY – EVALUATION. As a tool to resolve art. 16 disputes, the RTB approach has some advantages as compared with the externality and the validity approaches. Doctrinally the former is less problematic. The other two approaches, it will be remembered, rest on the fallacious premise that the company is involved in a contract formed in contravention of art. 16.[36] The RTB approach, in contrast, can operate on the basis that the contract in dispute was executed without authority. The function of a presumption of regularity is to enable the creditor to enforce a contract against the alleged corporate surety when the latter's internal machinery for effecting the transaction was in fact not in order.

That the RTB approach operates without having to treat the company as a party to a subsisting contract is potentially consequential. Treating the company as a party to the contract triggers the operation of the PRC Guaranty Law art. 5 and art. 7 of the Supreme People's Court's Judicial Interpretation of the PRC Guaranty Law (The Guaranty Law Interpretation). The effect of these provisions is that the alleged security provider can be held liable, no matter whether the contract in dispute is found to be enforceable. Under the PRC Guaranty Law art. 5, provided that the main (loan) contract is enforceable, if the surety contract is declared to be unenforceable, the debtor, the security provider, and the creditor 'ought to' bear the civil liability for their faults, provided that they were at fault.

---

[35] The shareholder who is the borrower is not qualified to vote: PRC Company Law art. 16.3.
[36] Text to nn. (27–32).

TABLE 8.4 *Approaches to the determination of the validity of unauthorised corporate security contracts*

No. of cases where the contract in dispute was made without authority	Externality approach	Validity approach	RTB approach	Externality + validity	Externality + RTB	Validity + RTB	Externality + validity + RTB	Other approaches
26	6 (23%)	5 (19%)	5 (19%)	2 (8%)	4 (15%)	1 (4%)	1 (4%)	2 (8%)

Article 7 of the Guaranty Law Interpretation makes matters worse. This provision stipulates that in case the primary loan contract is enforceable but the surety contract is unenforceable, where the creditor was not at fault, the surety is jointly liable for the debtor's debt. Where both the surety and the creditor were at fault, the civil liability of the surety should not exceed 50 per cent of the part of the debt that the primary debtor is unable to discharge.

Article 7 is biased against an alleged security provider, as it holds the latter liable even where the surety is faultless. Moreover, under that provision, the alleged security provider is held liable to a greater extent where it is faultless than where it is at fault.[37] An approach that activates the operation of arts. 5 and 7 would therefore be likely to allocate all the risks for unauthorised security contracts to the alleged security provider.

The RTB approach, which does not activate the previously mentioned provisions, makes it possible to allocate the risks to the contractor where the latter should not be entitled to the right to the presumption to regularity. It is, for example, possible for courts to do that on the basis that, inter alia, the company has not authorised the transaction. In fact, all of the cases, out of the thirty-two cases reviewed for the purposes of this paper, where the court held the contract in dispute to be unenforceable could be rationalised under the RTB approach. In six of the thirty-two reviewed cases, it will be remembered, the court held the contract in dispute to be unenforceable.[38] One of these cases was based on the RTB approach.[39] In the remaining five cases, the court's decision was reached on the basis of a breach of art. 16.1 or 16.2. The decisions in all of these five cases may be rationalised on the basis that, given the professed agent's failure to provide the requisite company resolution, the creditor did not have reason to believe that the internal machinery for effecting the transaction was in order.

Notwithstanding its potential, RTB has been applied to allocate the risks for art. 16 transactions to the alleged security provider on most occasions. This is demonstrated in the courts' decision outcomes where the RTB approach was applied. As can be seen from Table 8.5, in close to 85 per cent of the cases where the RTB approach was applied, the company was held to be liable for the un-authorized transaction; and of the only two cases where the company was held not liable, the decisions were made on the basis that that lenders had *actual knowledge* of the lack of company authorization, or (even though the security agreement was held valid) that the guarantee had lapsed when enforcement action was taken.

---

[37] Art. 7 is silent on the parties' liability where the creditor is at fault, but the alleged surety is not.
[38] See Table 8.2.
[39] This is case no. 17, where the court held that that the resolution passed by the general meeting has authorised the offering of company's assets as security (but has not committed the company as a guarantor) suggested that the lender had *actual knowledge* that the company has authorised the charge transaction but not the guarantee transaction. In other words, the lender had no reason to believe that the company has passed a resolution to act as the guarantor. As a consequence, the company was held not liable as a guarantor.

8 *The Presumption of Regularity in Chinese Corporate Contracting*

TABLE 8.5 *Decisions based on (inter alia) the RTB approach: outcomes*

Number of cases where the approach was applied	Contract valid and company liable	Contract valid but company not liable (guarantee lapsed)	No contract formed and company not liable
11	9 (82%)	1 (9%)	1 (9%)

RTB has functioned as a tool to allocate all the risks to the company because of the lack of a delineation of the contours within it operates. This can be seen through an examination of the ways in which the IMR operates.

3.3 IMR: The Presumption of Regularity

Under the rule in the *Turquand* case (which is the *locus classicus* of IMR), all parties seeking to deal with a company are taken to be aware of the provisions of the company's constitution on the authority of a corporate organ to enter into the transactions in question.[40] If, however, that corporate organ's authority as stipulated in the company constitution is subject to internally prescribed conditions, the contractor may infer that those conditions have been fulfilled.[41] IMR, however, does not protect the third parties at the expense of the company's interest. It is equipped with a number of company protection mechanisms.

Company Protection Mechanisms

Under the IMR, the company is protected by mechanisms that delineate the contour of the presumption of regularity. These are (i) the notice and insider exceptions and (ii) the rules on the effect of unauthorised transactions.

The Notice and the Insider Exceptions

There is no dispute that the operation of IMR is subject to a couple of exceptions, namely, the actual or constructive notice exception and the insider exception. IMR is a presumption of regularity designed to save a contractor the trouble and expense of inquiring into the regularity of internal management. It does not operate where the third party has actual or constructive notice of that which IMR entitles it to make inference about.[42] The third party is treated as having constructive notice if it

---

[40] This constructive notice rule, however, has been abolished by way of a statutory provision in jurisdictions where the statutory IMR is introduced. For an example, see Companies Ordinance (HK) s. 120.
[41] *Royal British Bank v. Turquand* (1856) 6 E.l. & Bl. 327; (1856) 119 E.R. 886 at 888 per Jervis CJ.
[42] *Morris v. Kanssen* [1946] AC 459.

proceeds with the contract without making an inquiry when it is put on inquiry.[43] The notice exception protects the company by shielding the latter from liability under the contract not properly authorised where the contractor had at least constructive notice that the company's internal management machinery for authorising the contract was not in order. The insider exception denies a company officer who has allegedly dealt with the company the right to make presumptions on the regularity of the company's internal management. The reason for this is that it is a director's duty to comply with the company's constitution.[44]

Unauthorised Transactions

There is arguably a further company protection mechanism under IMR – namely, the body of rules on the scope of IMR. Apart from the previously mentioned exceptions, IMR does not operate where the professed corporate representative acted without authority. In *Turquand*, where the board was *authorised* to borrow, which authority was subject to a condition, namely the approval of the shareholders, the lender was held to have the right to assume that that condition was fulfilled, and that the authority was *'made complete* by a resolution'[45] (emphasis added). However, IMR arguably does not protect the third party where no power for entering into the type of transaction in question had been granted to the individual(s) purporting to represent the company. As Dawson J said in *Northside Developments Pty Ltd v. Registrar-General*,[46]

> The correct view is that the indoor management rule cannot be used to create authority where none otherwise exists, it merely entitles an outsider, in the absence of anything putting him upon inquiry, to presume regularity in the internal affairs of a company *when confronted by a person apparently acting with the authority of the company*. (emphasis added)

An incidence of a purported corporate representative acting without authority is where the unauthorised agent procures the contract through forgery, either in the sense that a counterfeit of a seal or signature is affixed on the instrument, or where the document is false, although the seal affixed or signature put on that false document are genuine.[47]

Dawson J's view on the scope of the application of IMR maintains an even hand between the company and the contractor. Where the purported corporate representative has acted *without authority*, actual or apparent, Dawson J's approach would

---

[43] B Liggett (Liverpool) Ltd v. Barclays Bank Ltd [1928] 1 KB 48; Thanakharn Kasikorn Thai Chamkat v. Akai Holdings Ltd (2010) 13 HKCFAR479 at [61].
[44] Morris v. Kanssen [1946] AC 459.
[45] Royal British Bank v. Turquand (1856) 6 El. & Bl. 327; (1856) 119 E.R. 886 at [332].
[46] (1990) 170 CLR 146 at 198.
[47] See Dawson J's discussion on the distinction on the two types of forgery in *Northside Developments Pty Ltd v. Registrar-General* (1990) 170 CLR 146 at 194.

allocate the risks to the contractor, who is better placed to discover whether the transaction is authorised. Where the 'middleman' acted with actual authority, the company is liable because the outsider has entered into a transaction with the company through the agent. Where the professed agent acted with apparent authority, Dawson J's approach will hold the company liable, as the latter has, by holding the purported agent out as having authority, induced reliance by the contractor and is therefore stopped from setting up the true facts.

There is, however, also a view that a contractor may rely on the apparent authorised affixing of the company seal on the instrument. Mason CJ expressed his support of this view in *Northside Development*, where he opined that 'if the person dealing with the company receives a document to which the common seal has been affixed in the presence of individuals designated in the articles of association, he is entitled to rely on its formal validity'.[48]

In his Honour's view, 'it is the presence of the seal on the document that gives rise to the presumption that the seal has been affixed with the authority of the directors'.[49] The justification of this view appears to be that '[t]he affixation of the seal to an instrument makes the instrument that of the company itself; the affixing of the seal is in that sense a corporate act'.[50] Having said this, his Honour added that the contractor's entitlement to the formal validity in the previously mentioned situation is qualified by the 'put on inquiry' exception, referred to above.[51] The High Court of Australia was unanimous on the outcome of the *Northside Development* case, as the lender was, in the circumstance, put on inquiry. So even on Mason CJ's test, the lender must lose its case.

The balance of decisions made by the Hong Kong courts is consistent with Dawson J's view.[52] Dawson J's view on the scope of IMR, for example, was cited with approval by both Deputy Judge Lam in the Hong Kong case of *National Commercial Bank* Ltd v. *Albert Hwang*[53] and Lord Neuberger NPJ in the Hong Kong Court of Final Appeal's decision in *Thanakharn Kasikorn Thai Chamkat v. Akai Holdings Ltd*.[54]

4 RTB VERSUS IMR: DIVERGENCE ON POLICY POSITIONING

The difference between the RTB approach and IMR, especially with regard to the company protection properties of the two respective presumptions of regularity

[48] (1990) 170 CLR 146 at 160.
[49] (1990) 170 CLR 146 at 160 per Mason CJ.
[50] Ibid.
[51] Ibid.
[52] *Rua Rong Finance Ltd v. Mega Capital Enterprises Ltd* [1998] 4 HKC 532; *National Commercial Bank Ltd v. Albert Hwang* [2002] 2 HKLRD 408; *Thanakharn Kasikorn Thai Chamkat v. Akai Holdings Ltd* (2010) 13 HKCFAR 479. Stefan HC Lo and Charles Z Qu, *Law of Companies in Hong Kong*, 2nd edn (HK: Sweet & Maxwell, 2015), p. 551.
[53] *National Commercial Bank Ltd v. Albert Hwang* [2002] 2 HKLRD 408 at [40] (although Dawson J's words cited were on the effect of forgery, which was an instance where the unauthorised corporate represented acted without authority).
[54] (2010) 13 HKCFAR 479.

apparatuses, reflects a prima facie difference in terms of policy positioning. The decision to equip IMR with company protection mechanisms, as will be seen shortly, was based on a consideration of the need for providing balanced protection to both the third party and the company itself. The lack of company protection mechanisms under RTB is perhaps due both to the policy positioning of the courts and to the fact that the RTB approach is still in its formative stage. That under the RTB approach the PRC courts have allocated largely all the risks for unauthorised corporate security transactions to the company raises the question of the need for equipping the RTB approach with company protection mechanisms. This question cannot be answered properly without a consideration of the policy objectives of a presumption of regularity apparatus.

In the context of corporate contracting, the need for a presumption of regularity is obvious. As mentioned, requiring the contractor to investigate internal proceedings to satisfy herself about the authority of officers and validity of instrument would make transactions with companies inconvenient and costly.[55] Rules based on a policy that protects parties dealing with companies therefore help promote commercial transactions, thereby maximising the number of exchanges. Encouraging maximisation of wealth through exchanges is necessary for any exchange-driven society.[56]

On the other hand, there is also a public interest in the protection of property rights. The long-standing common law judicial policy of property protection,[57] as well as the guarantee for the protection of private property under China's Constitution,[58] reflects the importance lawmakers attach to property protection. In the context of corporate contracting, the needs for achieving the two policy objectives may collide. The challenge for courts is how to strike a balance between safeguarding a company's assets and protecting persons seeking to deal with said company. As Mason CJ pointed out, in considering the application of IMR:

> What is important is that the principle and the criterion which the rule in *Turquand's* case presents for application give sufficient protection to innocent lenders and other persons dealing with companies, thereby promoting business convenience and leading to just outcomes. The precise formulation and application of that rule call for a fine balance between competing interests. On the one hand, the rule has been developed to protect and promote business convenience which would be at hazard if persons dealing with companies were under the necessity of investigating their internal proceedings in order to satisfy themselves about the actual authority of officers and the validity of instruments. On the other hand, an overextensive application of the rule may facilitate the commission of fraud and unjustly favour those who deal with companies at the expense of innocent

---

[55] Text to n. (25).
[56] Michael Bridge, *Personal Property Law*, 3rd ed. (Oxford University Press, 2002), p. 116.
[57] *Bishopsgate Motor Finance Corpn v. Transport Brakes Ltd* [1949] 1 KB 322 at 336 per Lord Denning.
[58] The People's Republic of China Constitution art. 13.

8 *The Presumption of Regularity in Chinese Corporate Contracting*

creditors and shareholders who are the victims of unscrupulous persons acting or purporting to act on behalf of companies.[59]

The situation referred to in the above-quoted words of Mason CJ is exemplified in most of the art. 16 cases. The typical situation in those cases is, it will be remembered, one where an unscrupulous person purporting to act on behalf of the alleged surety committed the latter to a security contract *without authority*.[60] The RTB approach, unequipped with any company-protecting mechanisms, has arguably functioned to facilitate fraud by the unscrupulous person, and has unjustly favoured the creditor at the expense of innocent shareholders and creditors. By the false pretense of acting on behalf of the company while unauthorised, the professed company representative defrauds both the company and the creditor. The RTB approach unjustly favours the creditor at the expense of the shareholders and creditors because it holds the company liable to the creditor under a surety contract, which is beneficial to the creditor, to which the company has never been a party. The transaction has occurred at the expense of shareholders and creditors because it results in a loss of the company's assets, in which the shareholders and creditors have an interest.

In case no. 8, referred to previously, the SPC refused to impose a duty to inquire, and held the unauthorised security contract valid where the general meeting resolution tendered to the lender was visibly false. The SPC based its decision on, inter alia, a policy consideration – namely, the need to ensure the transactional security and the efficiency. The SPC held, it will be remembered,[61] that the lender had reasons to believe that the LR was acting with authority on the strength of the imprint of the company seal and the LR signature on the surety instrument, adding that the detection of internal irregularity was beyond the ability of an outsider.

The SPC's policy discussion, however, is one-sided. The SPC made no reference to the competing public policy of protecting the property of the shareholders and creditors against the fraud of unscrupulous persons who falsely represent themselves as the authorised representative of the company. The failure of the SPC to consider the policy of property protection is bewildering, as art. 16 was in fact enacted out of this same policy consideration.[62]

The SPC court's view on the policy to protect third parties in case no. 8 was couched in the language of law and economics ('transactional efficiency', etc.) However, even in law and economics terms, the SPC's view on that point does not

---

[59] *Northside Developments Pty Ltd v. Registrar General* (1990) 170 CLR 146 at 164.
[60] Text to n. (13).
[61] See n. (34) above.
[62] 全国人大法律委员会副主任委员洪虎，《全国人大法律委员会关于《中华人民共和国公司法 (修订草案)》修改情况的汇报 (Hu Hong, Deputy Director, the Law Committee of the National People's Congress, Report of the Law Committee of the National People's Congress on the revision of the PRC Company Law (Amendment Bill), at www.npc.gov.cn/wxzl/gongbao/2005-10/27/content_5343119.htm, accessed 12 June 2017).

stand up. One-sided outsider protection is likely to result in the allocation of all risks arising from corporate contracting to the company. The company, knowing that it would bear the costs for acting as a surety provider through unauthorised transactions, would undoubtedly externalise the costs incurred to other parties it deals with, including lenders, thereby increasing costs for dealing with it.

Moreover, law and economics scholars would say that contractual risks should always be allocated to the party, who is the better risk bearer[63] and better informed.[64] In the context of art. 16 cases, vis-à-vis the company, the creditor is definitely the better risk bearer. The company is likely to be completely ignorant of unauthorised transactions entered into in its name. The creditor, in contrast, has an opportunity to confirm with the company whether the transaction was indeed authorised, at least where its suspicion is excited. In case no. 8, the creditor's suspicion should definitely be excited on sighting the corporate shareholders' signatures on the general meeting resolution, which are visibly fake.[65]

There should be an even stronger reason for the suspicion of the company to be excited where the professed company representative fails to provide the creditor with a copy of the board or general meeting resolution, as the case may be. That an art. 16 contract must be made by the company itself (through one of its power organs) is an announced legal rule, which everybody is taken to have knowledge of. Where it is necessary to sight the company's constitution (e.g. for art. 16.1 cases), it would not be costly for a lender to request the supply of a copy of that document.

The SPC's policy positioning on the resolution of the issue raised was apparently based on an efficiency consideration. The above discussion, however, suggests that the policy considerations underlying the common law IMR make better economic sense. If efficiency is the true underlying policy objective, then the divergence between the PRC courts and the common law courts on the policy dimension should be closed in favour of the latter's position.

4.1 Achieving the Policy Objective: Completing the Convergence

A convergence in terms of policy objective cannot be achieved by mere rhetoric. A balanced protection of both sides of an art. 16 dispute calls for the completion of the convergence between RTB and IMR. The problem is how this is to be done. As mentioned,[66] the common law IMR is qualified by rules on the scope within which the presumption operates. The convergence, it is submitted, can be completed if the application of RTB is similarly delineated.

---

[63] Andrew Griffiths, *Contracting with Companies* (Hart, 2005), p. 35.
[64] I. Ayres and R. Gertner, 'Filling gaps in incomplete contracts: An economic theory of default rules' (1989) 99 *Yale Law Journal* 97; Robert Cotter and Thomas Ulen, *Law and Economics*, 5th ed. (Boston: Pearson, 2007), p. 208.
[65] Text to n. (34).
[66] Text to nn. (42–54).

4.1.1 Unauthorised Transactions

Since the typical issue arising from art. 16 cases is the allocation of risks for unauthorised transactions, an issue that courts will face, one would have thought, is whether unauthorised transactions are within RTB. The superior courts' answer appears to be, bar cases where evidence on the creditor's actual knowledge is available, in the affirmative. This position can be assessed through a comparison of the answers by Dawson J and Mason CJ to the same question in the context of the IMR.

4.1.2 Dawson J's View

According to Dawson J, it will be remembered, cases where the corporate organ in question or the professed agent had not been granted any authority are not within IMR. This view is superior to the view of Mason CJ in terms of its company protecting properties. Dawson J's approach protects the company more because it holds that IMR, as a contractor-protecting tool, is not activated where the person(s) whom the contractor dealt with had not been authorised to act on behalf of the company.

Dawson J's view is also superior in terms of doctrinal purity. The 'put on inquiry' exception is one for the IMR, which was developed in the *Turquand* case. In *Turquand*, it will be remembered, the board had been *granted authority* to borrow. That authority was subject to a condition, which was the approval of the general meeting. Strictly speaking, *Turquand* stands for the proposition that where a corporate organ or an agent has been granted a conditional authority, the outsider may assume that the condition has been satisfied when dealing with the company. In other words, the same case does not stand for the proposition that an outsider may assume that the internal machinery for effecting the transaction is in order where *no (conditional) authority* had been conferred on a corporate organ or the professed agent.

An implementation of Dawson J's position in relation to the RTB approach would help reduce companies' transaction costs, as it will help reduce incidences where the company is made to pay as a surety where the company has never acted as such. Doing the same would provide an incentive to the creditor to satisfy itself, before executing a loan agreement, that the alleged surety has indeed made a decision to act as such. This due diligence step will help shield innocent companies from possible suits brought by the creditor. The due diligence step should not impose significant costs on creditors. Requesting a copy of the company's resolution, as mentioned, does not increase the so-called transaction costs for obtaining loan security by a significant margin. Dawson J's view, therefore, when applied in the context of art. 16 disputes, helps strike a fair balance between the competing policy objectives discussed previously.

4.1.3 Mason CJ's Opinion

Mason CJ, it will be remembered, seemingly approved of the view that 'if the person dealing with the company receives a document to which the common seal has been affixed in the presence of individuals designated in the articles of association, he is entitled to rely on its formal validity'.[67] If the phrase 'the person dealing with the company' means that the professed agent was authorised (for, technically, that person could only be dealing with the company where the 'middleman' was authorised), Mason CJ's words quoted above would be consistent with the position of Dawson J, as the situation would still be within the scope of IMR.

If the previously mentioned phrase means 'a person seeking to deal with the company', what Mason CJ would be saying is that even if the 'individuals designated in the articles of association', in affixing the company's common seal, acted without authority, the IMR still protects the outsider, subject to the 'put on inquiry' exception. The individuals designated as having the power to affix the common seal may act without authority, as 'authority to affix the seal is not the same as authority to determine those documents to which the seal should be affixed'.[68]

It is only possible to implement Mason CJ's words quoted above, when understood in the latter sense, in the Chinese context if there is (i) a uniform understanding, under the PRC legal framework, of the role of the company's common seal, and (ii) a rule or established practice on the mode in which the company's 'signature' is affixed. Since no rules on the execution of corporate documents are provided under the PRC legal framework, the problem is whether a norm has been established in practice. A review that the author has conducted on the modes in which corporate documents have been executed in China answers the question in the negative.

4.1.4 Existing Modes of Executing Corporate Documents

AFFIXING THE COMMON SEAL. Whereas the affixing of the common seal of a company incorporated in Commonwealth jurisdictions can be treated as the company's signature, there does not appear to be a similar rule or understanding in the Chinese context. The facts on the ways in which instruments were executed summarised in Table 8.6 illustrate the point. In none of the thirty-two cases were the instruments held to be invalid because of the modes in which they were executed.[69]

As can be seen in Table 8.6, the court has upheld the validity of an instrument where (i) the instrument was executed by way of, instead of the company seal, the finance seal of the company, (ii) the authenticity of the seal affixed on the

---

[67] *Northside Developments Pty Ltd v. Registrar-General* (1990) 170 CLR 146 at 160.
[68] *Northside Developments Pty Ltd v. Registrar-General* (1990) 170 CLR 146 at 202 per Dawson J.
[69] There are six cases out of the thirty-two cases where the security contract was declared to be invalid. In five of these cases, the decision was made on the basis that the company had not passed the requisite resolution. In the sixth case, the court's decision was reached by deeming PRC Company Law 2013 art. 148 equivalent to PRC Company Law 2005 art. 60, which prohibited the directors from committing the company as a security provider.

8 The Presumption of Regularity in Chinese Corporate Contracting

TABLE 8.6 *Evidence on modes of executing security instrument: seal*

Number of cases	Company seal (公章) affixed	Finance chop (财务 用章) affixed	Authenticity of company seal affixed in dispute	Seal affixed proven false	No reference to the affixation of seal in case report
32	25 (78%)	1 (3%)	1 (3%)	1 (3%)	4 (13%)

instrument was in dispute, and (iii) where the seal affixed has been proven not to be the right company seal. Moreover, in 13 per cent of the cases reviewed, the case reports made no reference at all to whether the security instrument bore the imprint of the company seal. Also, in none of the cases reviewed did the courts articulate, or made reference to authorities on, the ways in which an instrument was validly executed.

The previously mentioned facts indicate the lack of a uniform standard in China on the type of seal the affixation of which is to be regarded as attaching the company's signature. The same facts also seem to suggest that the affixing of the correct corporate seal is not even essential for executing corporate documents. The view that the role of the corporate seal is trivial seems to command some judicial support. Case no. 20 is an example. Here, where the authenticity of the company seal was in dispute, the trial court held, *obiter dictum*, that the LR's signature, even if the instrument had not been affixed with the company's seal, would have been sufficient to make the instrument that of the company. This was because, the court remarked, there was 'uniqueness' in the LR's signature, not in corporate chops. The SPC upheld the decision of the trial court on the validity of the contract.

According to the trial court's view in case no. 20, it would seem that the LR's signature, rather than the affixing of the corporate seal, is to be treated as the company's signature. The comment of the court below on the lack of uniqueness of the company seal can perhaps be taken as a tacit admission that a PRC company may have a number of seals, and that it is not sure which one, when properly affixed, can be treated as the company's signature.

The trial court's view on the role of the LR's signature, however, conflicts with the view of the court in case nos. 25 and 27, where the judge held that the company seal indicated the true intention of the company, and that whether the LR has signed the contract or whether the signature affixed on the instrument was genuine had no bearing on the validity of the contract. The conflicting judicial views on the role of the company seal and signature indicate the lack of a uniform rule of judicial view on this matter.

COMPANY OFFICERS' SIGNATURES. In Commonwealth jurisdictions, under the traditional rules/practice, to execute a corporate document, the common seal

TABLE 8.7 *Evidence on modes of executing security instrument: signature*

Number of cases reviewed	LR's signature affixed	Signature of other officer or agent affixed	Authenticity of LR signature in dispute	LR signature affixed proven false	No reference to the affixation of LR/agent signature in case report
32	13 (41%)	2 (6%)	2 (6%)	1 (3%)	14 (44%)

must be affixed in accordance with the company's articles.[70] A typical provision in the articles would require the common seal to be affixed before a director, who is to attest to the affixation by signing the corporate document. The instrument must also be countersigned by a second corporate officer (e.g. a director or company secretary) or by another person appointed by the directors.[71] Under the statutory framework, a company is not required to have a common seal. The documents of a company that does not have a common seal must be executed in accordance with the manner prescribed in the relevant provisions, which is similar to the manner in which the affixing of the common seal is to be attested to in the traditional way.[72]

No rules on the execution of corporate documents are provided under the PRC legal framework and practice.[73] Is it, however, possible to discern established practices or views on the necessity of the LR/agent's signature for executing corporate documents from the decisions reviewed? The facts summarised in Table 8.7 answer the question in the negative.

As can be seen, that the instrument bore the signature of the company's LR was confirmed in only 41 per cent of the cases reviewed. In contrast, in 44 per cent of the cases, no reference was made in the case reports as to whether the instrument bore the signature of the LR or agent. That in most cases the instrument was still held to be validly executed suggests that on the whole, the PRC courts did not consider the LR/agent's signature as being essential for establishing the validity of the instrument or the transaction. Moreover, judging from the situations in the remaining 15 per cent of the cases (on whether the instrument bore the genuine signature of the LR), there is no hard and fast rule stipulating that the person who signs on the instrument must be the company's LR, or that the signature must be genuine. Nor is

[70] Companies Ordinance (HK) ss. 127 (1), (2).
[71] For an example, see *Northside Developments Pty Ltd* v. *Registrar-General* (1990) 170 CLR 146. The director in whose presence the common seal is affixed attests to the sealing as part of the operation of sealing, not as witness: Robert F. Norton, Robert J. A. Morrison, and Hugh J. Goolden, *Norton on Deeds*, 2nd ed. (Sweet & Maxwell, 1928), p. 24. The purpose of requiring a countersignature is to authenticate the signature of the director: *Equity Nominees Ltd* v. *Tucker* (1967) 116 CLR 518 at 523.
[72] For an example, see Companies Ordinance (HK) s. 127(3).
[73] Although there is a view that the company's intention to enter into the transaction can be inferred from the affixation of the company's seal: 赵旭东《公司法学》(第四版, 高等教育出版社, 北京, 2015)150–151 (Xudong Zhao, *Corporation Law*, 4th ed. (Higher Education Press, 2015), pp. 150–151).

8 The Presumption of Regularity in Chinese Corporate Contracting

it possible to find or infer a rule or practice from any sources of law or from the facts summarised in Table 8.7 stipulating that the sealing of the company chop must be attested to by the signature of a company officer.

SUMMATION. An analysis of the facts on the relationship between the outcome of the decisions and the modes in which the instrument was executed has not revealed any consistently applied norms on the proper execution of corporate documents. The PRC courts do not appear to have treated either the affixation of the correct corporate seal or the attachment of the LR/agent's signature as essential for executing an instrument. The conflicting views that courts have expressed on the relevance of affixing the correct corporate seal and the LR/agent's signature under different circumstances fortify this conclusion.

That the law and practice on the modes of executing corporate documents are in a state of flux makes it impossible to give the creditor the right to presume regularity on the basis of the so-called formal validity that Mason CJ referred to in *Northside Development*.[74] It is impossible for a creditor to rely on the formal validity of the instrument unless it knows what constitutes formal validity. It follows that Dawson J's approach to unauthorised transactions should be used as a guide for defining the scope of operation of RTB.

4.2 Notice and Duty to Review

There appears to be a convergence between the common law courts and their PRC counterparts in the treatment of actual notice on the part of the creditor. The common law and PRC courts, however, diverge on their willingness to uphold the creditor's duty to make an inquiry. As mentioned, failing to make an inquiry when having been put on inquiry constitutes a constructive notice in common law. In contrast, in only two of the thirty-three cases under review did the court held that the creditor failed to fulfil its 'duty to review' on the basis that the creditor executed the security contract without sighting or requesting a copy of the company's resolution.[75] Also, in common law, an imputation of constructive notice to the creditor concludes the matter in favour of the company. In contrast, a failure to fulfil the 'duty to view', in the context of art. 16 cases, due to the way in which an unauthorised transaction is conceptualised,[76] tends to lead to a finding that the creditor was at fault in forming the security contract,[77] which, given the effect of Guaranty Law Interpretation art. 7, may still result in a partial liability for the putative surety, irrespective of whether it was at fault.

If Dawson J's approach to IMR is to be followed, the RTB approach operates only where the alleged security agreement has been authorised. That which the creditor is

---

[74] Text to n. (48).
[75] Case nos. 2, 13.
[76] Text to nn. (30–31).
[77] As evidenced in case nos. 2, 13.

entitled to presume under the RTB approach should be that all conditions prescribed for the exercise of authority have been fulfilled. Where the presumption of regularity under RTB is operative, the creditor should still be subject to a duty to inquiry (or in a term used in the PRC legal system, 'the duty to review'). The creditor should lose its entitlement to the presumption of regularity where it knew or ought to have known that the internal machinery for effecting the transaction was not in order, or where it fails to make an inquiry when its suspicion on whether the transaction has been authorised is excited. Further, a finding that the creditor has failed to fulfil its duty to review should lead to a finding that the contract is *void ab initio*, as there is no legal basis for conceptualising a transaction made without authority as a subsisting contract entered into in contravention of a mandatory rule. Such a finding, which does not activate the Guaranty Law Interpretation art. 7, should help shield the company from unworthy claims.

The previously discussed conditions for triggering the operation of RTB would not be too onerous to creditors. Since art. 16 is an announced rule, the creditor should be aware of the need to sight the relevant corporate documentation to establish a prima facie case of the surety company's approval. It should not be costly for a surety company to produce a copy of the company resolution authorising the transaction and, where necessary, a copy of the company's constitution evidencing the corporate organ designated as the decision maker and the limit, if any, as to the company's commitment as a security provider. It should not be inconvenient for the creditor to make a request on the supply of the previously mentioned documentary evidence to satisfy itself as to the company's approval to act as the security provider.

It may, however, be difficult, in the absence of recognised norm or legal rules on the execution of corporate documents, to uphold the creditor's duty to inquire on the basis of the latter's suspicion as to the formal validity of the instrument. It is, however, possible to do so in the future by stipulating a set of rules on the modes of executing corporate documents. This could also be done by way of an SPC statutory interpretation or a guiding case.

4.3 *RTB and IMR: Is a Convergence Possible?*

The emergence of RTB evidences a convergence of the presumption of regularity devices under the PRC and Commonwealth jurisdictions. The driver of this divergence appears to be the common need for protecting a person seeking to deal with the company in a legal environment in which courts were/are not equipped with workable rules on apparent authority. IMR had been developed a hundred and eight years before the development of the doctrine of apparent authority was finally completed in the UK when *Freeman and Lokyer* v. *Buckhurst Park Propoerties (Mangal) Ltd* was decided.[78] RTB is being developed, as pointed out, partly because of the lack of utility of the rules on apparent authority under the PRC civil law framework.

---

[78] [1964] 2 QB 480.

The main difference between IMR and RTB is that the former is equipped with a relatively well-developed set of company protection mechanisms, whereas the latter is not. Hence the difference in the risk-allocation propensities between the two devices. Convergence with the IMR will transform RTB into a more sophisticated conceptual tool that affords a balanced protection to both parties to the dispute, which helps facilitate economic development.

Such a convergence is possible. This is because the company protection mechanisms under IMR, such as a delineation of the contours within which the presumption operations and the 'put on inquiry' rule, as well as the notion of constructive notice, are not based on uniquely common law doctrines. Put differently, an implementation of these mechanisms does not involve judicial discretions that could only be exercised by reference to common law rules. That the creditors in a couple of cases under review had been found to have failed to fulfil their duty to review is telling.

5 CONCLUSION

The crux for the resolution of disputes arising from art. 16 is the allocation of risks for security contracts entered into in the name of the alleged principal without authority. The potential of the RTB approach lies in an important feature of this approach. This is that a decision under that approach is made by treating the situation not as one where a contract between the alleged surety and the creditor actually *exists* (which is the case under the externality and the validity approaches), but as one where a contract may be *deemed to exist*, between the putative security provider and the creditor. This feature of RTB makes it potentially possible to activate the rules on unauthorised agency, the activation of which is doctrinally unproblematic. In so far as both RTB and IMR entitle a contractor to presume regularity, the emergence of the RTB approach can be seen as a sign that the 'living' law on corporate contracting under the PRC legal framework is moving towards a point where the RTB approach and IMR will converge. The need to strike a fine balance between the competing policy objectives in settling the type of dispute under consideration calls for a completion of the convergence. The convergence will be completed when rules are put in place to delineate the scope within which the RTB approach operates.

APPENDIX
CITATIONS OF CASES SUMMARISED

1. Hangzhou Zhongrui Properties Co Ltd *v.* Zhu Liming and Another (2009) Zhe Shang Zhong Zi No. 269
2. Zhou Guofang and Another *v.* Jin Wenquan and Another (2009) Zhe Shang Zhong Zi No. 270

3. Sichuan Yuanjing Industrial Group Co Ltd v. Meishan Branch of Agricultural Bank of China Limited (2009) Min Er Zhong Zi No. 124
4. Jin Yinguo v. Fenglong Properties (Huzhou) Co Ltd and Li Weizhen (2011) Zhe Shang Wai Zhong Zi No. 63
5. Yang Ronghua v. Fan Chunlei and Another (2011) Zhe Shang Ti Zi No. 31
6. Shenzhen Office of China Cinda Asset Management Co Ltd v. Shenzhen Saichen Software Technology Co Ltd and Jiangxi Cuilin Shanzhuang Co Ltd (2012) Yue Gao Fa Min Er Zhong Zi No. 19
7. Zhejiang Jingfa Industrial Group Co Ltd v. Hangzhou Hongyue Industrial Group Co Ltd (2011) Min Ti Zi No. 351
8. Dalian Donggang Sub-Branch of China Merchants Bank Co Ltd v. Dalian Zebon Fluorocarbon Paint Joint Stock Co and Dalian Zebon Goup Co Ltd (2012) Min Ti Zi No. 156
9. Xu Erbing v. Jinshuo Properties Co Ltd, Wang Lujun and Another (2014) Su Shang Zhong Zi No. 00472
10. Xinxiang Zhongxin Chemical Engineering Co Ltd and Another v. Wang Aihua (2015) Min Shen Zi No. 1058
11. Qinghai Chuangxin Mining Co Ltd and Another v. Hong Ying and Another (2014) Yue Gao Fa Min Er Po Zhong Zi No. 110
12. Hunan Sansure Biotech Co Ltd v. Hunan Office of China Cinda Asset Management Co Ltd and Another (2015) Xiang Gao Fa Min Er Zhong Zi No. 14
13. Zhou Ye v. Xie Maihua and Another (2015) Xiang Gao Fa Min Yi Zhong Zi No. 40
14. Anhui Haicheng Railway Equipment Technology Co Ltd v. Hefei Branch of Dongguan Bank (2015) Wan Min Er Zhong Zi No. 00061
15. Anfu Mingjun Concrete Co Ltd v. Liu Aiqing and Another (2015) Gan Min Yi Zhong Zi No. 120
16. Xinxiang Zhongxin Chemical Engineering Co Ltd v. Ma Yine and Another (2015) Yu Fa Min Yi Zhong Zi No. 78
17. Yang Huali and Another v. Zhao Longmei (2015) Wan Min Er Zhong Zi No. 00234
18. Tian Chuanxiang and Another v. Zhang Shuo (2015) Lu Min Zai Zhong Zi No. 7
19. Shenzhen Hongguangyang Vacuum Craft Co Ltd and Another v. Zhuang Ming (2015) Yue Gao Fa Min Er Shen Zi No. 544
20. Shanxi Huajin Dyeing and Printing Co Ltd and Another v. Dai Jun (2015) Min Yi Zhong Zi No. 72
21. Jiaxian Huatai Ceramics Co Ltd and Another v. Jiaxian Rural Credit Cooperatives and Another (2015) Yu Fa Min San Zhong Zi No. 16
22. Qinxi Shunfeng Driving School Co Ltd v. Qi Heng and Another (2015) Qian Gao Min Shen Zi No. 227

23. Su Wei and Another v. Kong Shunwei (2015) Yun Gao Min Yi Zhong Zi No. 172
24. Zhejiang Chicheng Construction Co Ltd v. Zhou Zhongyun (2015) Zhe Shang Ti Zi No. 52
25. Anhui Yanshi Industrial Co Ltd v. Li Ting and Wuhu Oumeide Sheet Material Co Ltd (2015) Wan Min Er Zhong Zi No. 00383
26. Green Energy Hi-tech Group Co Ltd and Another v. Sui Sike and Another (2015) Yu Fa Min Yi Zhong Zi No. 00120
27. Xinjiang Shixin Pawning Co Ltd v. Ruoqiang Ronghui Small Loan Co Ltd and Another (2015) Xin Min Er Zhong Zi No. 171
28. Qinghai Xiancheng Mining Joint Stock Co and Another v. Zhou Yamin (2015) Min Shen Zi No. 2086
29. Xinyang Wuyue Properties Co Ltd v. Jia Jianqiang and Another (2015) Yu Fa Min Er Zhong Zi No. 96
30. Zhang Bo and Another v. Hunan Dingwang Investment Joint Stock Co and Another (2015) Xiang Gao Fa Min Yi Zhong Zi No. 269
31. Anhui Dongfang Jinhe Real Estate Co Ltd, Qu Yong and Bengbu Leye Land Co Ltd v. Liu Hui and Lu Guobin (2015) Wan Min Er Zhong Zi No. 00563
32. Liang Yin v. Xing Qian and Another (2014) Zang Fa Min Yi Chu Zi No. 4

9

Mind the Gap: Studying the Implementation Discrepancy for the ASEAN Economic Community

Sanchita Basu Das

1 INTRODUCTION

The announcement of the establishment of the ASEAN Economic Community (AEC) at the end of 2015 marked a major milestone for its member states. The Chairman's statement of the November 2015 Summit highlighted that 'we were pleased with the achievements of the regional economic integration efforts as demonstrated by the near completion of implementation of the AEC Blueprint 2015, and were also pleased to formally announce the establishment of the AEC. We also note that outstanding measures will be implemented as a priority under the AEC post-2015 agenda'.[1] However, following another report, describing the progress made under the AEC, it was evident that while the ASEAN countries were able to implement quite a number of the regional measures by 2015, many of them remained incomplete.[2] Moreover, scores of measures, even after being officially reported as 'implemented', were not very effective for the business community in easing the conduct of their cross-border activities.[3]

One reason for this observed gap in implementation comes in the form of conflicts of interest. These conflicts of interest could be between countries or firms or even between government agencies responsible for implementation. This chapter looks at this aspect of policy implementation in the context of AEC and provides suggestions for ASEAN and the national governments to address some of the conflicts that are slowing down the process of implementation. It seeks to answer why the ten ASEAN members, despite committing themselves to AEC measures, have so far fallen short of their final deliverable of an integrated market. The chapter takes a qualitative approach and uses several secondary sources to observe the progress in AEC implementation. The underlying causes for discrepancies in policy

---

[1] ASEAN Secretariat, Chairman's Statement of the 27th ASEAN Summit, Kuala Lumpur, 21 November 2015 (www.asean.org/wp-content/uploads/2015/12/Final-Chairmans-Statement-of-27th-ASEAN-Summit-25-November-2015.pdf).

[2] ASEAN Secretariat, ASEAN Integration Report 2015 (http://asean.org/storage/2015/12/ASEAN-Integration-Report-2015.pdf).

[3] Based on the author's discussions with individuals in the private sector.

implementation are derived from existing literature and several discussions that the author had with different AEC stakeholders during the 2015–2016 period. It should be noted that although the AEC is a regional polity, implementation responsibility resides with the national governments.[4] Hence the empirical discussion in the paper adopts the perspective of the member countries, rather than that of ASEAN itself as a regional organisation.

Section 2 discusses the theoretical literature on policy implementation and conflicts of interest affecting the same. The gaps in AEC implementation are highlighted in Section 3. The underlying reasons and conflicts resulting in the disconnect between countries' commitments and eventual implementation are examined in Section 4. Section 5 provides policy suggestions to improve the implementation record in ASEAN with a view to actually realising the envisaged convergence in national laws and regulations. Section 6 provides some concluding thoughts.

2 UNDERSTANDING POLICY IMPLEMENTATION AND CONFLICTS OF INTEREST

There are many conceptual definitions of policy implementation available in the literature. As pioneers in implementation studies, Pressman and Wildavsky define implementation as 'means ... to carry out, accomplish, fulfil, produce, complete'.[5] Van Meter and Van Horn view policy implementation as actions by public and private individuals or groups to attain objectives set in a prior policy decision.[6] This covers both one-time efforts to translate decisions into operational action and ongoing efforts to realise the changes authorised by policy decisions. O'Toole describes implementation as a phase between the establishment of an intent to do something (or to stop doing something) by the government and the final impact on the world, thereby conceptually differentiating the policy implementation process and policy outcomes.[7]

According to Mazmanian and Sabatier, 'policy implementation is the carrying out of a basic policy decision, usually incorporated in a statute, but which can also take the form of important executive orders or court decisions. Ideally, that decision identifies the problem(s) to be addressed, stipulates the objective(s) to be pursued, and, in a variety of ways, "structures" the implementation process'.[8] Hence one can

---

[4] R. Severino, *Southeast Asia in Search of an ASEAN Community: Insights from the former ASEAN Secretary-General* (Singapore: Institute of Southeast Asian Studies, 2006).
[5] J. Pressman and A. Wildavsky, *Implementation* (Berkeley: University of California Press, 1984) xxi.
[6] D. Van Meter and C. Van Horn, The Policy Implementation Process: A. conceptual Framework (1975) 6(4) *Administration & Society* 445–487.
[7] L. J. O'Toole Jr, Research on Policy Implementation: Assessment and Prospects (2000) 10(2) *Journal of Public Administration Research and Theory* 263–288.
[8] D. Mazmanian and P. Sabatier, *Implementation and Public Policy* (Lanham: University Press of America, 1989) 20–21.

infer that in the course of policy implementation, the policy itself carries immense importance. It is the policy that defines the ultimate goals and the means to achieve these. The policy goal itself functions as a barometer against which to measure the extent of achievement.

Pressman and Wildavsky, however, contend that 'implementation, under the best of circumstances, is exceedingly difficult'.[9] There are many obstacles for effective implementation in developing countries, including lack of political support for implementing agencies, lack of qualified personnel, insufficient funds to meet the cost of implementing projects, illegal fees and unfavourable socio-economic conditions.[10] Most of these challenges arise due to conflicts of interest in the economic and organisational arenas of a country. Parties operating in such arenas behave as rational agents, trying to maximise their private welfare either through the policy itself or by slowing down the course of implementation.

2.1 Economic Conflict

Under regional economic cooperation, economic conflict comes about as a result of the interaction of international and domestic levels.[11] At the international level, it is generally assumed that states have a good understanding of their interests and the outcome they desire from a foreign economic policy like regional economic cooperation, given their interaction through trade and investment and their understanding of the global strategic context. However, when the international policy decisions need to be operationalised at the domestic level, the interests of economic and political actors will come to the fore. Economic conflict arises as economic cooperation, which largely involves trade liberalisation, adversely affects the owners of relatively scarce factors of production and benefits the owners of abundant factors of production.[12] It is also suggested that factors that are generally tied to export-oriented industries tend to gain from trade liberalisation, whereas the factors tied to import-competing industries tend to lose.[13] These kinds of economic conflicts at the domestic level determine whether a participating country favours more liberal economic cooperation or prefers a relatively protectionist approach. It is assumed that the electorate in a country is able to measure the economic consequences of

---

[9] J. Pressman and A. Wildavsky, *Implementation* (Berkeley: University of California Press, 1984) xxi.
[10] J. Quah, The Public Policy-Making Process in Singapore (1984) 6(2) *Asian Journal of Public Administration* 108–126.
[11] J. Frieden and L. Martin, International Political Economy: Global and Domestic Interactions, in I. Katznelson and H. Milner eds., *Political Science: the State of the Discipline* (New York: W. W. Norton, 2003) 118–146.
[12] This is derived from international trade theories – the Hecksher-Ohlin (HO) model and its related Stolper Samuelson (SS) theorem.
[13] This is from the Ricardo-Viner (RV) model, which assumes immobility of at least one factors of production to an industry.

policies under regional economic cooperation and vote according to the impact of these policies on their individual economic well-being.[14]

As national policymakers often have to balance competing objectives in seeking to maximising a country's economic welfare, given the international developments, and considering domestic interests which are key for future sustainability of the project, this leads to regional policies that are broad in nature or offer in-built flexibilities, thereby accommodating the interests of all participating members. As a result, however, it can be difficult to implement broad regional policies, especially when it is left to national government agencies to understand and interpret these policy measures.[15]

2.2 *Organisational Conflict*

Organisational conflicts derive from the nature of public administration. In the past, public administration was seen as a comprehensive, functionally uniform and hierarchical organisation. Public administration was envisaged as comprising a strong executive, who was politically appointed, and assisted by a number of capable civil servants carrying out their tasks. Also termed as 'lonely organisation syndrome', this brought all related functions under one public agency.[16] In reality, however, public administration of a single policy measure is not the responsibility of one, but of multiple agencies – public, non-governmental bodies and sometimes, private sector – and in that case the lessons learnt from managing a single 'lonely' organisation are no longer useful.[17]

This environment with multiple government agencies makes public policy implementation very difficult. While it is important for the multiple organisations to understand their mutual dependence to achieve a common goal through a policy commitment, there often is a lack of trust that impedes the exchanging of resources and the development of a shared interest.[18]

Moreover, the involvement of several participants distorts and delays implementation.[19] This happens because the officers of government agencies who are responsible for implementation may have personal goals and other political

---

[14] R. Hicks, H. Milner, and D. Tingley, Trade Policy, Economic Interests and Party Politics in a Developing Country: The Political Economy of CAFTA (2014) 58 *International Studies Quarterly* 106 at 108.

[15] K. Flanagan, E. Uyarra, and M. Laranja, Reconceptualising the 'Policy Mix' for Innovation (2011) 40 *Research Policy* 702–713.

[16] B. Hjern and D. Porter, Implementation Structures: A New Unit of Administrative Analysis (1981) 2(3) *Organization Studies* 211–227.

[17] T. E. Hall and L. J. Toole, Structures of Policy Implementation: An Analysis of National Legislation 1965–66 and 1993–94 (2000) 31(6) *Administration & Society* 667–686.

[18] L. J. O'Toole, Interorganizational Relations in Implementation, in J. Pierre and B. G. Peters ed., *Handbook of Public Administration* (London: Sage, 2003) 234–244.

[19] D. F. Kettl, The Perils – and Prospects – of Public Administration (1990) 50(4) *Public Administration Review* 411–419.

pressures that cause them to alter their actions from the stated goal, thus distorting implementation. Difficulties continue as bureaucrats and civil servants may delay or hesitate to comply with policy instructions as they have concerns over their own gains and losses once certain reforms would be effected.[20] There is a general lack of enthusiasm to learn from past mistakes or adapt to new trends in and across government agencies. Bureaucracy becomes 'a preference for procedure over purpose'.[21] Often, civil servants become blindsided as they are (too) caught up in their daily routines and existing conventions.

In addition, public administration suffers from the persistence of a traditional bureaucratic culture in most developing countries. This refers to an adherence to rules and procedures that involve paperwork, hierarchical control and a strict division of responsibility. Such traditional attitudes among government bodies that are, for instance, responsible for licences and permits are often accompanied by bureaucrats' obstinate behaviour to pursue their own policies, irrespective of new executive orders or legislations.[22] All these imply that despite political leaders' good intentions vis-à-vis policies like regional economic cooperation, implementation falters due to organisational conflicts among government agencies and other related actors.

3 THE ASEAN ECONOMIC COMMUNITY 2015: PROGRESS AND GAPS

ASEAN, or more particularly the ASEAN Economic Community (AEC), is presently at a crossroads, with policy implementation becoming a matter of critical importance. In 2003, ASEAN developed the AEC so as 'to create a stable, prosperous and highly competitive ASEAN economic region in which there is a free flow of goods, services, investment and a freer flow of capital, equitable economic development and reduced poverty and socio-economic disparities in year 2020'. In January 2007, the deadline to realise the AEC was brought forward by five years to 2015.[23]

Subsequently, ASEAN achieved a major milestone at the November 2007 ASEAN Summit in Singapore as the heads of State and government endorsed the AEC Blueprint that laid out a roadmap to strengthen economic integration and realise the AEC by 2015. The AEC Blueprint is a legally binding declaration and stipulated that 'each ASEAN Member Country shall abide by and implement the

---

[20] M. Painter, The Politics of Administrative Reform in East and Southeast Asia: From Gridlock to Continuous Self-Improvement? (2004) 17(3) *Governance: An International Journal of Policy, Administration, and Institutions* 361–386.

[21] J. Pressman and A. Wildavsky, *Implementation* (Berkeley: University of California Press, 1984) at 133.

[22] D. S. Jones, Regulatory Reform and Bureaucracy in Southeast Asia: Variations and Consequences (2007) 8(2) *International Public Management Review*.

[23] ASEAN Secretariat, Declaration of ASEAN Concord II (Bali Concord II), Bali, 7 October 2003; ASEAN Secretariat, Cebu Declaration on the Acceleration of the Establishment of an ASEAN Community by 2015, Cebu, Philippines, 13 January 2007.

AEC by 2015'.[24] It was organised along the AEC's four objectives of establishing: (i) a single market and production base; (ii) a highly competitive economic region; (iii) a region of equitable economic development; and (iv) a region that is fully integrated to the global economy, with 17 'core elements' and 316 'measures' to be undertaken within a Strategic Schedule of four implementation periods (2008–2009, 2010–2011, 2012–2013 and 2014–2015).[25]

As the ASEAN countries approached the year of forming a community, the ASEAN Integration Monitoring Office (AIMO) at the ASEAN Secretariat, Jakarta, published two reports – the ASEAN Integration Monitoring Report 2015 and the ASEAN Economic Community: Progress and Key Achievements – that outlined the progress in implementing AEC measures from 2008–2015.[26] The original set of 316 ASEAN-wide measures had expanded to 611, as the measures were updated in line with changing circumstances in global and regional economies.[27] Following a prioritisation approach, a focused list of 506 AEC measures was also created.[28] According to the reports, as of 31 October 2015, the ten ASEAN countries had realised 469 out of 506 measures, or more than 90 per cent. It was reported that the implementation rate of AEC measures stood at 79.5 per cent, or 486 out of 611 measures over the same time period.

Although these were substantial figures in terms of ASEAN countries' progress towards meeting regional commitments, there was criticism that ASEAN is still far away from its headline commitment of an integrated market, described as a single market and production base. Extensive academic studies concluded that ASEAN countries fell short of delivering such an integrated market.[29] It was found that, despite some noticeable progress, the ASEAN region still comprises ten disparate markets, thereby reflecting member countries' differences in socio-economic development, policy formulation and

[24] ASEAN Secretariat, ASEAN Economic Community Blueprint, Jakarta 2008.
[25] Ibid.
[26] ASEAN Integration Report 2015 (http://asean.org/storage/2015/12/ASEAN-Integration-Report-2015.pdf); ASEAN Secretariat, ASEAN Economic Community 2015: Progress and Key Achievements, Jakarta.
[27] Author's discussion with policymakers.
[28] The focused list was a result of discussion in 2012, when ASEAN decided to come up with prioritised high-impact AEC measures to realise a community by 2015. Two lists were drawn up for this Prioritised Key Deliverables (PKDs): (a) first, for implementation by 2013 and (b) second, for implementation by 2015. The two lists were adopted by the ASEAN Economic Ministers in 2013. Since then, monitoring activities for AEC Scorecard mainly focused on the PKDs. However, in the first quarter of 2015, ASEAN countries reviewed the unimplemented PKDs and decided on 54 measures that have the greatest impact on trade and can be achieved by end-2015. These were termed as high-priority measures (HPMs). The 54 HPMs, along with the measures that were fully implemented since 2008, formed a focused base of 506 measures for the final monitoring exercise.
[29] S. Y. Chia and M. Plummer, ASEAN Economic Cooperation and Integration: Progress, Challenges and Future Directions (Cambridge University Press, 2015); P. Intal, et al., ASEAN Rising: ASEAN and AEC Beyond 2015 (Jakarta: Economic Research Institute for ASEAN and East Asia (ERIA)); S. Basu Das et al. (eds.), The ASEAN Economic Community: A Work in Progress (Singapore: ISEAS, 2013).

institutional capacities.[30] Furthermore, the business community remained ambivalent towards regional integration. Despite the pronouncement of a 92.7 per cent achievement rate, business leaders expressed concerns over the usefulness about many of the measures. Companies complained about a lack of information, increases in the amount of documentation required for preferential tariff use, and the prevalence of non-tariff barriers due to different rules across participating member countries.[31]

Annex 1 shows selected areas where ASEAN has managed to deliver on its commitments as well as those that remain very much a work-in-progress for the future. For instance, regarding trade in goods, the ASEAN-6 members have eliminated intra-regional trade tariffs, with 99.2 per cent of tariff lines at 0 per cent. The corresponding figure for the CLMV countries stands at 90.86 per cent.[32] To lower trade cost, the ASEAN countries have furthermore simplified the Rules of Origin (ROO); enacted a self-certification scheme; established a national single window (NSW) and national trade repository (NTR) for a subset of ASEAN countries; and signed the legal framework for implementing the ASEAN Single Window.[33] However, non-tariff barriers (NTBs) continue to prevail in the region. These can be in the form of national standards, the imposition of the local content requirement rules at the national level, export or import taxes, non-automatic licenses to name but the most common ones. Hence, whatever positive effect had been achieved by tariff elimination or measures like the self-certification scheme has largely been negated by the enduring prevalence of the NTBs.

Also, some of the implemented measures targeted only a subset of ASEAN countries, thereby compromising a region-wide benefit for final users. The ASW, a network of NSW of every ASEAN member state, targeted to operationalise the NSWs of the ASEAN-6 by 2008 and of the CLMV by 2012. By the end of 2015, although there was notable progress in the development of NSWs in Indonesia, the

---

[30] Intal et al. (ibid.); D. Carpenter et al., Narrowing the Development Gap in ASEAN: Context and Approach, in Mark McGillivray and David Carpenter (ed.), Narrowing the Development Gap in ASEAN: Drivers and Policy Options (London and New York: Routledge, 2013) 1–20.

[31] M. Kawai and G. Wignaraja, Main Findings and Policy Recommendations in Masahiro Kawai and Ganesh Wignaraja (ed.), Asia's Free Trade Agreements: How Is Business Responding? (ADB, ADBI and Edward Elgar, 2013) 33–75; A. G. Hu, ASEAN Economic Community Business Survey, in S. Basu Das, et al. (eds.), The ASEAN Economic Community: A Work in Progress (Singapore: ISEAS, 2013) 442–481.

[32] ASEAN-6 countries refer to Brunei, Indonesia, Malaysia, the Philippines, Singapore and Thailand. CLMV countries refer to Cambodia, Laos, Myanmar and Vietnam. CLMV countries have a longer timeline till 2018 to fully eliminate their intra-regional trade tariffs.

[33] Under the Self-certification scheme, traders and manufacturers are given the primary responsibility for origin certification. This was devised to encourage traders to avail themselves of the trade preferences provided under the ASEAN Trade in Goods Agreement (ATIGA). The ASEAN Single Window (ASW) creates a single point of entry for all trade-related documents to speed up customs clearance, thereby reducing transaction time and costs. The trade repository is meant to keep all trade-related information in one place. This includes MFN tariff rates, ATIGA preferential tariff, other ASEAN FTAs, ROO, non-tariff measures, national trade and customs laws and rules.

Philippines, Singapore, Malaysia, Thailand and Vietnam, there remained a serious lack of coordination between agencies, data standardisation issues or lack of appropriate human resources. The NSWs of Cambodia, Laos and Myanmar were at a very early stage of development. There was also a lack of compatibility of the NSWs across countries. Although ASEAN planned to launch a pilot project to test the exchange of Form D among seven ASEAN countries on 1 January 2016, this was eventually delayed due to eleventh-hour technical issues.[34]

A number of ASEAN regional legal initiatives, like fashioning a single competition regime, intellectual property rights protection framework and narrowing development divide, were designed to help the countries, especially the less developed ones, to understand the usefulness of these policies and encourage them to gradually introduce the relevant legal measures to increase their competitiveness over time and thereby benefit from economic integration. There were, however, no tangible plans to develop these measures across the ten ASEAN economies with a view to prospective harmonisation. For example, with regard to the competition policy, several ASEAN-wide activities were initiated: an ASEAN Expert Group on Competition was set up and ASEAN Regional Guidelines on Competition Policy and the Handbook on Competition Policy and Laws in ASEAN for Businesses were drawn up. The Guidelines provide a reference point for countries' current approaches and international best practices, while the Handbook provides a basic idea of competition law as applicable to some ASEAN countries.[35] However, none of these mentioned a region-wide standardised competition policy and left the issue pretty much to the national level for regulation. Similarly, harmonising standards, technical regulations and conformity assessment were trade facilitation initiatives that were listed as important measures for ASEAN integration. But the measures were for selected ASEAN industries[36] only and implementation has depended heavily on the availability of financial and technical resources and manpower in the individual countries.

Hence, although the ten ASEAN countries have committed themselves to several regional integration measures under AEC 2015, implementation is quite clearly a different matter. For some areas, such as the NSWs, there is no coherence in implementation across the member states, thereby defeating the purpose of an ASEAN-wide initiative. Also, many of the initiatives were not formulated with

---

[34] Just before the 1 January 2016, three ASEAN countries – Singapore, Malaysia and Thailand – decided to do a parallel test (i.e. exchange of documents both electronically and physically) to check for any data discrepancies. The test came up with some errors in data between Singapore and Thailand and hence the pilot project on 1 January 2016 was stopped. The countries are now working on compatibility of systems across ASEAN.

[35] ASEAN Secretariat, Chairman's Statement of the 27th ASEAN Summit, Kuala Lumpur, 21 November 2015 (www.asean.org/wp-content/uploads/2015/12/Final-Chairmans-Statement-of-27th-ASEAN-Summit-25-November-2015.pdf), ASEAN Secretariat, ASEAN Integration Report 2015 (http://asean.org/storage/2015/12/ASEAN-Integration-Report-2015.pdf).

[36] These measures are currently targeted towards priority integration sectors in ASEAN, including automotive products, textiles, healthcare products, cosmetics and electrical and electronic products.

a view to deliver concrete outputs, but merely sought to raise countries' awareness of the desirability to adopt new policies and carry out reforms with a view to raise the region's competitiveness in the future. Overall, the ASEAN region remains far away from realising its headline commitment of 'single market and production base' that has, understandably, disappointed a section of the private sector and attracted the attention of critics.

The following section examines some of the most pertinent reasons that may account for the gap in member countries' implementation of AEC measures.

4 EXPLAINING THE DISCREPANCY IN IMPLEMENTATION

The ASEAN countries committed themselves to the establishment of AEC in 2003 as they perceived a need to align their economies to cope with the forces of globalisation. They realised in the late 1990s that globalisation was prompting structural change in the pace and quality of Foreign Direct Investment (FDI) flows, which could result in investment diversion to the bigger economies of the Asian region, most particularly to China.[37] While this became a primary catalyst for the ASEAN countries to offer economies of scale and work towards an AEC, other factors too played a part.

In the early 1990s, multinationals (MNCs) began to change how they conducted manufacturing activities in the region. Manufacturing tasks were increasingly diffused across multiple countries, thereby creating international production networks.[38] As the production networks were spread not only among the ASEAN countries but also in the larger geography of East Asia, ASEAN's economic cooperation with China, South Korea, Japan, India, Australia and New Zealand became important. The automotive and the electronic industries were the leading examples of production networks in the East Asian region. Both of these were assembly industries, where parts and components (P&C) were produced by independent industries typically located across different jurisdictions.

4.1 *Misaligned National Interests and the Development Divide*

Although the concern about the impact of globalisation was shared among all ASEAN members, their willingness to liberalise sectors and pursue domestic reform remained uneven. Countries like Singapore, Thailand and Malaysia were more willing to agree to liberalisation and facilitation measures, while countries like Cambodia, Laos and Myanmar were keen on developing their soft and hard

---

[37] D. Hew, Introduction: Brick by Brick – The Building of an ASEAN Economic Community, in D. Hew (eds.), *Brick by Brick: The Building of an ASEAN Economic Community* (Singapore: Institute of Southeast Asian Studies, 2007).
[38] K. Cheewatrakoolpong et al., Impact of the ASEAN Economic Community on ASEAN Production Networks, *ADBI Working Paper 409* (Tokyo: Asian Development Bank Institute, 2013).

infrastructure. The difference in interests was mainly derived from their varied economic structures and orientation. The countries were, and still are, also different in terms of social indicators (shown by the HDI ranking), competitiveness and infrastructure (Table 9.1).

The mix of interests for liberalisation and domestic reform was observed in the broad and accommodative nature of the foundational AEC policy document, i.e. the AEC Blueprint. There was a mismatch between the headline commitments like establishing 'single market and production base' and the actual policy actions through which such objectives were to be achieved. The use of words and phrases like 'freer', 'promote', 'minimal', 'where appropriate and possible' and 'possibly' in the blueprint document provided ample opportunities for different interpretation among the member countries. The AEC blueprint also offered flexibility in meeting targets and timelines for complying with the various AEC measures. In addition, the implementation mechanism set out in the Blueprint was kept generic.

All these unavoidably led to challenges during the actual implementation phase. It became difficult for countries to comply with policies that were broad in nature and were not given a single, clear and consistent interpretation. Attention was instead often placed on realising narrowly defined outputs that were easily quantifiable rather than on achieving the overall general policy objectives. For example, in the case of the NSW, which requires the establishment of links between a country's customs agency and all government bodies involved in export-import processes, reporting of compliance was done at an early stage of output delivery for some ASEAN countries, when, in reality, the NSW was not yet functioning as the way described in policy documents.[39] Indeed, the emphasis on notifying the achievement of some form of output, no matter how insignificant, played an important political role in ASEAN context as it is seen as a public display of individual government's willingness and implementation progress on AEC matters.[40] However, this may not be sufficient to actually achieve the general commitments listed in the AEC policy documents.

As processing the information contained in the complex documents pertaining to the AEC involved financial and cognitive resources, many of the ASEAN governments struggled with earmarking sufficient domestic resources to be dedicated to their commitments towards regional integration. They focused on selected deliverables that were generally easy to achieve, ignoring the measures that were more complex and politically sensitive in nature. The excuse of not implementing measures in time became easier whenever the relevant policy document spelt out broad policy actions. This was observed in the case of the 'elimination of non-tariff barriers', which, though an important policy directive to develop a single market, offered broad policy actions (such as the voluntary declaration of non-tariff measures

---

[39] Based on the author's discussion with policymakers and businesspeople.
[40] Based on the author's discussion with policymakers.

TABLE 9.1 *State of development divide in ASEAN*

	GDP per capita, PPP (current $) 2015	Trade (% of GDP) 2015	Share of Intra-ASEAN trade (%) 2015	HDI ranking (2015)	Ease of doing business rank (2017)	Global Competitiveness Index 2016–2017 ranking	Logistics Performance Index ranking (2016)
Brunei	78,369	85	27.6	30	72	58	70
Cambodia	3,490	128	22.7	143	131	89	73
Indonesia	11,058	42	21.7	113	91	41	63
Laos	5,691	87	64.4	138	139	93	152
Malaysia	26,950	134	27.4	59	23	25	32
Myanmar	5,250	47	39.4	145	170	N.A.	113
Philippines	7,387	63	19.9	116	99	57	71
Singapore	85,382	326	27.5	5	2	2	5
Thailand	16,340	127	25.1	87	46	34	45
Vietnam	6,034	179	12.8	115	82	60	64

Sources: World Development Indicators, the World Bank; The ASEAN Secretariat; Human Development Report 2016, UNDP; Global Competitiveness Index 2016–2017 rank out of 138 economies, The World Economic Forum; Doing Business 2017, The World Bank (out of 190 economies); Logistics Performance Index Ranking (out of 160 economies), The World Bank.

with no system for verification) from the member countries and eventually was not delivered on time. However, ASEAN has a 100 per cent implementation record for Equitable Economic Development that merely requires the delivery of documents or facilitating the exchange of general information. This bias towards the implementation of certain policies, while simultaneously ignoring others, was made possible due to the accommodative nature of the AEC blueprint, which thus is in part to blame for the resultant implementation gap.

The ASEAN countries also faced several internal conflicts (discussed as follows) that negatively affected implementation.

4.2 Economic Conflicts

The economic conflicts come about as a result of socio-economic differences among the ASEAN countries. There are four key characteristics that explain the underlying reason for ASEAN countries' preference for flexible and accommodative policy measures.

First, the ASEAN countries generally lack indigenous big firms that support economic liberalisation. The countries are dominated by small-and medium-scale enterprises (SMEs), who operate in parallel with a handful of big multinationals. These SMEs constitute around 95 per cent of all business enterprises in the member states and are said to have little interest to expand overseas.[41] This lack of interest stems from limited knowledge on the part of SMEs about overseas customers, their language and culture as well as the regulatory and bureaucratic issues involved in cross-border transactions. They fear competition from large firms.[42] Moreover, most of the SMEs are not clear about what to expect from regional integration initiatives like the AEC.

Second, the larger businesses in the ASEAN region have emerged with significant state assistance. These constitute state-owned enterprises (SOEs) or government-linked companies (GLCs) and other firms that have close links to bureaucrats and politicians. While politicians or bureaucratic figures receive material wealth in return for providing state facilities, such as export and import license, forestry concessions or state bank loans, state enterprises are used to provide business opportunities to well-connected firms in order to generate extra-budgetary revenues for organisations like the military.[43]

This has changed somewhat as a result of domestic reforms in the wake of the 1997–98 Asian Financial Crisis (AFC). While some of the state-owned or sponsored firms have matured and no longer require government assistance in the more

---

[41] CIMB ASEAN Research Institute, *The ASEAN Economic Community: The Status of Implementation, Challenges and Bottlenecks* (Kuala Lumpur: CIMB ASEAN Research Institute, June 2013).

[42] ERIA and OECD, *ASEAN SME Policy Index 2014: Towards Competitive and Innovative ASEAN SMEs* (Jakarta: Economic Research Institute for ASEAN and East Asia, June 2013).

[43] K. Jayasuriya and A. Rosser, Pathways from the Crisis: Politics and Reform in South-East Asia since 1997, in G. Rodan et al. (ed.), *The Political Economy of South-East Asia: Markets, Power and Contestation* (Oxford: Oxford University Press, 2006).

advanced ASEAN economies, others continue to request protection in the face of increasing competition in order to maintain their profit margins. These latter firms can be divided into two categories: tradeable ones largely owned by foreign capital and domestic ones that include firms and enterprises with strong connections to the political establishment. It is the second group of firms that by and large remains apprehensive about any form of regional cooperation that may lead to structural change in domestic economies.[44] They often request the State to adopt domestic laws and regulations to circumvent the reform necessary due to membership of regional integration initiatives.

Third, the importance of economic growth is an imperative for all ASEAN economies to help ensure political stability and avert any social unrest.[45] This economic growth is mainly delivered by FDI and exports, as many of the ASEAN countries have long embraced an export-oriented growth strategy. But some ASEAN countries are not very deeply integrated into the global economy. For example, for Myanmar and Indonesia, trade only accounts for around 40 per cent of total GDP (Table 9.1). Moreover, intra-ASEAN trade is mostly dominated by firms operating in Laos and Myanmar (around 65 per cent and 40 per cent, respectively), and to some extent by firms in Brunei, Malaysia and Singapore (around 27 per cent). This suggests that while there are a few economies that calculate the benefits associated with liberalisation and reform under the AEC, the prospects of regional integration remain uncertain at best for the rest. For this group, participating effectively in AEC will expose their relatively closed economies to global competition. This state of affairs has resulted in the need for an institutional framework that serves the interests of both competitive firms in open economies and uncompetitive enterprises in relatively closed ones.

Fourth, market-driven economic integration covers a wider geographic area than East Asia, which is where ASEAN plays a significant role. This market force is primarily led by Japanese firms, followed by European and American firms and more recently by Chinese capital. Much of the intra-ASEAN trade originated from the intra-firm trade of these foreign multinationals.[46] Moreover, it has been observed that the regional production networks formed by these multinationals are both sectorally and geographically focused, i.e. the intra-regional flows are not across all ASEAN countries, but rather across selected ones, depending on the technical and market requirements of different industries. For example, the Japanese automakers in ASEAN, since its early days in the 1970s, were operating in four ASEAN economies – Thailand, Indonesia, the Philippines and Malaysia – mostly in joint

---

[44] L. Jones, Explaining the failure of the ASEAN economic community: The primacy of domestic political economy (2015), *The Pacific Review*, 26 March.

[45] H. Nesadurai, *Globalisation, Domestic Politics and Regionalism: The ASEAN Free Trade Area* (London and New York, Routledge, 2003).

[46] H. Lim, Regional Economic Cooperation and Production Networks in Southeast Asia, in I. Kuroiwa and T. M. Heng (eds.), *Production Networks and Industrial Clusters: Integrating Economies in Southeast Asia* (Singapore: ISEAS, 2009), 301–334.

ventures with local firms. However, the idea was not to set up a regional production base but instead to circumvent national import restrictions in each ASEAN economy.[47] With the progressive elimination of intra-ASEAN tariff since the advent of AFTA in 1992, the Japanese firms have exploited economies of scale and predominantly concentrated production in Thailand, from where automobiles are exported overseas.[48] While the Thai automobile industry surged, the Malaysian and the Philippines ones suffered damages and incurred large trade deficits in the automobile sector.[49] This uneven importance of ASEAN economies to serve as production base for certain industries creates intra-ASEAN friction and acts as a hindrance to intra-regional liberalisation.

These underlying dynamics in ASEAN countries explain the struggle between liberal reformers and their opponents, who advocated for protectionism, thereby leading to broad AEC measures and patchy implementation.

4.3 Organisational Conflicts

In the ASEAN countries, organisational conflicts are often observed among government bodies or within a single government agency, among its civil servants.

By way of example, for a complex policy measure like the NSW system, the most significant challenge is inter-agency cooperation in ASEAN countries. As the NSW system does not come within the purview of a single public authority, mutual resource dependence and shared interest are important pre-requisites for cooperative behaviour across the relevant government bodies. For many ASEAN countries, though there are harmonised goals at the highest level of the political establishment, this does not automatically translate into cooperation among the national ministries. In fact, the ministries regularly have different priorities, which in turn results in a lack of trust to exchange manpower and financial resources. Furthermore, the understanding of the AEC and associated policy documents varies across ministries and is diluted among the lower level of bureaucrats, creating a lack of common interest and a sense of urgency to ensure timely compliance with AEC measures.[50]

Another form of organisational conflict arises from the attitude of bureaucrats in national government agencies. In case of implementation of a multi-agency measure like the NSW that envisages cross-ministerial interdependence and an exchange of resources, the bureaucrats in question may be hesitant to take action as they may be affected by a resultant redistribution of power and wealth. For ASEAN, the development of production networks adds to further complexity as the higher

[47] P. Dickens, Tangled Webs: Transnational Production Networks and Regional Integration (2005), SPACES Working Paper 2005-04.
[48] H. Lim, Regional Economic Cooperation and Production Networks in Southeast Asia.
[49] P. Wad, The Automobile Industry of Southeast Asia: Malaysia and Thailand (2009) 14(2) Journal of the Asia Pacific Economy 172–193.
[50] The observation is derived from author's interaction with government officials in trade ministries and several of the line ministries working on NSW.

intensity of import and export implies not only more wealth for the private sector but also more power for bureaucrats in their decision-making capacities. Hence, any negative change in bureaucrats' authority and power, derived from new AEC initiatives, is likely to adversely affect implementation.[51]

A related point concerns bureaucrats' opportunity to secure unethical income. In border administration processes, this comes from private businesses willing to pay illegal fees in order to expedite otherwise protracted procedures, obtain licence and permits or get clearance for goods inspection. This is typically reflected in the Doing Business and Enabling Trade Indices.[52] Except for Singapore and to a certain extent Malaysia, illegal fees are a major issue for trading goods across national borders for all ASEAN countries. The issue of unethical fees or corruption in ASEAN countries is also repeatedly highlighted by the businesses operating in the region.[53] According to the 2015 Transparency International report on ASEAN, 'public sector corruption remains a major problem for many ASEAN countries. Only Malaysia and Singapore score above 50 out of 100 (where 100 is very clean and 0 highly corrupt) in Transparency International's Corruption Perceptions.'[54] For an AEC measure like the NSW, the issue of unethical income is likely to go down significantly as permits and licences will be issued online in the future, almost eliminating personal contact and hence opportunities to extract such illegal fees. This is not viewed favourably by the bureaucrats of ASEAN countries, as they are likely to lose income from the border administrative reform, incentivising them to delay the implementation process.

It can be said that a country's institutional efficiency is directly correlated to its level of socio-economic development, implying that better socio-economic development is either a cause or a result of better institutional efficiency. To appreciate these relations, consider Table 9.1 again (supra), where a country's institutional inefficiency can be derived from columns 6–8 and its level of socio-economic development is illustrated by the per capita GDP in terms of purchasing power parity (PPP) and Human Development Index.

From Table 9.1, it is apparent that the ASEAN membership can be divided into three broad categories. One group encompasses the developed economies in terms of human development indicators and per capita income (Brunei, Malaysia, Thailand and Singapore), showcasing per capita income of above $12,000, while on the other end are Cambodia, Laos and Myanmar, as significantly less developed countries with a low HDI ranking and an average per capita income of $4,800. Indonesia, the Philippines and Vietnam fall in the middle. A similar categorisation

---

[51] Ibid.
[52] The Doing Business Index is published by the World Bank; the Enabling Trade Index is published by the World Economic Forum.
[53] AmCham and US Chamber of Commerce, ASEAN Business Outlook Survey 2015 (p. 30).
[54] Transparency International, ASEAN Integrity Community: A Vision for Transparent and Accountable Integration (Transparency International, 2015), at 4.

can be observed in the last three columns of Table 9.1. For example, under the *Doing Business* indicators, Malaysia, Singapore and Thailand rank among the top 50 countries (out of a total of 190); Brunei, Indonesia, the Philippines and Vietnam fall in the 70 to 90 range, while Cambodia, Laos and Myanmar are the worst performers, with a ranking outside of the top 100.

This correlation between the level of development and efficiency in institutional systems implies that countries with low ranks in the HDI index have heavily regulated bureaucratic procedures and face challenges in domestic reform. Both of these can be either the cause or the effect of each other. While improved border procedures imply lower institutional impediments and better business prospects, logically leading to better quality human resources and income; low-quality human resources imply a lack of competent manpower to undertake domestic reforms, resulting in cumbersome border procedures. For the ASEAN NSW ASEAN initiative, then, the less-developed members, in addition to lack of financial resources, face a serious challenge regarding the quality of human resources, more particularly technical know-how, that slows down the process of implementation.

5 GOING FORWARD: THE ROLE OF ASEAN AND NATIONAL GOVERNMENTS

In the wake of the official launch of the AEC 2015, ASEAN has moved to the new phase of attaining the AEC 2025. The new phase retains the key vision of the earlier blueprint and emphasises the importance of creating a deeply integrated and cohesive ASEAN that can deliver inclusive economic growth. Alongside the earlier focus on trade and investment initiatives for businesses, the new blueprint mentions the use of science and technology and the need for the development of human resources, good governance and connectivity.[55]

There are three main differences between AEC 2025 and AEC 2015 (see Annex 2). First, the new blueprint comprises five pillars instead of four. 'Enhanced Connectivity and Sectoral Cooperation' is added, which largely includes elements listed under pillars 1 and 2 in the old blueprint. For example, transport and ICT of the second pillar of AEC 2015 now appear under the new pillar of connectivity. Moreover, the priority integration sector of AEC 2015 in pillar 1 is recast as sectoral cooperation (involving tourism, healthcare and minerals) and now allocated to pillar 3. Second, headings and subheadings in the AEC 2025 Vision are formulated as necessary implementation targets rather than as aspirational phrases. For example, the aspirational goal of a 'Single market and production base' in AEC 2015 is now rephrased as a 'Highly integrated and cohesive economy'. The earlier subheading of 'Free flow of goods' has been changed to 'Trade in goods', minimising the risks of misunderstanding among civil servants and the ultimate beneficiaries.

[55] ASEAN Secretariat, ASEAN 2025: Forging Ahead Together, Jakarta.

Third, the fourth pillar of the new blueprint mentions 'people' exclusively, responding to the longstanding complaint that AEC had developed in top-down style and with minimal involvement from below. The pillar also mentions the business community and civil society organisations as key stakeholders in ASEAN's integration, thereby demonstrating the inclusive nature of the 2025 policy.

Looking at these differences, one may infer that ASEAN policymakers have learnt from past experiences. With the AEC 2025, the policymakers have tried to clear most of the misunderstandings created by the aspirational phrases in the AEC 2015. They have specified new elements of economic growth for member countries over the next ten years. These include a new emphasis on innovation and productivity, the use of digital technology to enhance trade and investment, strengthening the role of small enterprises and promoting good governance. AEC 2025 also recognises more clearly that regional economic integration is a dynamic process and that the member countries and the global environment are constantly evolving. It is in this context that the AEC is conceived as a work-in-progress. The question of implementation, however, continues to loom large: what can ASEAN do to improve its current, rather dismal record and meet the social expectations of an integrated market?

5.1 ASEAN Level

At the ASEAN level, the top-level decision makers (i.e. the national cabinet members) of the individual countries need to be clearly briefed on the need for regional integration and the necessary reforms such a regional exercise entails. They need to be advised that regional economic integration is one of the many policies that a country can pursue to raise its competitiveness vis-à-vis the rest of the world. This should help them appreciate that regional and domestic policies are not, and should not be seen as, conflicting in nature. In the case of the AEC 2015, while all countries agreed on the usefulness of regional integration in terms of attracting FDI and participation in the production networks, the majority did not appear to realise that such benefits were dependent on domestic reforms, especially in terms of ease of doing business, soft and hard infrastructure, human resources and governance. Hence, towards the end of the period, as FDI inflows to ASEAN increased and reached almost the same level as China ($125 billion in 2015), the principal beneficiary was Singapore. The city-state attracted a disproportionate amount of almost 50 per cent of the total FDI in the region as it offered the most conducive investment climate and supplemented regional policies with domestic ones.

There is a related need to systematically match the overarching AEC goals, headline targets and action lines. The AEC 2015 did not only articulate goals such as 'free flow of goods, services, investment and a freer flow of capital, equitable economic development and reduced poverty and socio-economic disparities', but also highlighted headline commitments as 'single market and production base' or 'competitive economic region'. This raised people's expectations that seamless movement of goods, services and investment across the ten ASEAN members would be a reality from the date of the AEC's establishment in 2015. Little attention was paid to the 'technical' action lines – which were also not clearly mentioned on the part of ASEAN – to obtain a fuller understanding of how far the countries promised to match the headline commitments to actual actions. This created disappointments and frustrations with the AEC process in the post-2015 phase. Alternatively, if goals, targets and policy actions were matched, expectations would have been more realistic as individuals and businesses would have appreciated ASEAN's gradual approach to economic integration. AEC 2025 tries to address the issue to some extent.

ASEAN needs to be more methodical in formulating its policies, identifying the steps to be taken to implement its policies in the national economies, clearly presenting the number of main measures needed to comply with a regional policy and providing guidelines as to what must be achieved before full implementation can be reported. For AEC 2015, the announcement of an achievement rate of 93 per cent created considerable misunderstanding among political leaders and ultimate beneficiaries, who considered that this belied actual progress achieved. To develop a narrative of substantial achievement, ASEAN has created a number of lists like Prioritised Key Deliverables (PKDs) and High-Priority Measures (HPMs) that defy understanding of common people and the private sector. For example, in the case of the NSW, the AEC 2015 Blueprint only provided a deadline. However, the establishment of NSW is a mammoth task for a country that requires appropriate legal, regulatory and technical set-up. It involves discussions among the public and the private sectors and coordination across several government ministries and agencies. A better understanding of key intermediary steps to achieve the final output would have been useful to give an extensive list of measures that a member country has to comply with. It also helps in robust reporting of implementation progress later. To reiterate a point made earlier, ASEAN should provide guidelines to member countries on when the 'implementation box' can be ticked: at an initial step when legal barriers are addressed and dismantled, when the relevant institutional adjustments to link government agencies and customs authorities have been carried out or when the NSW is full working. If the reporting on implementation is done at an early level, final users of the NSW service will discount the achievement. Hence, to improve on the issue, while it is important to set a deadline, it is also useful to mention the key policy actions needed to achieve the final outcome. It is equally important to set a common guideline when a country should report for complete implementation of a measure. A matrix indicating 'not achieved', 'work-in-progress' and 'fully achieved' is a convenient and transparent way to communicate to people and minimise misunderstanding going forward.

For some of the ASEAN-wide measures, it could be more efficient to outsource implementation to private sector and work with Public-Private-Partnerships (PPP). The private sector may already have the necessary technical skills and knowledge to translate the visions to actual actions. It also possesses the actual business knowledge to address the issues in the policies and the subsequent implementation. Moreover, being an outside agent, it is typically easier to work with multiple agencies and the bureaucrats who are responsible for the change in the system. This is happening to some extent for some of the less developed ASEAN countries, which receive assistance under different foreign government programs such as USAID, AUSAID and ARISE. These programs bring together experienced people from the public and private sector and for instance help these countries set up their NSW in order to improve on their customs facilities.

5.2 National Level

The ASEAN countries should be (more) mindful that the AEC Blueprint only lists the measures needed to help create an integrated market. It creates an awareness among the countries, especially among the less developed ones, that competition law or rules on intellectual property right should be put in place to move up the manufacturing value chain. It helps generate discussion and adduces ideas to address infrastructure gaps in countries and ways to include SMEs in the process of economic integration. However, it leaves it to the individual member states to take charge of implementation. Instead of looking for flexibilities or loopholes, member countries should change their mindset and aim for robust and timely implementation of AEC policies. This is useful not only to compete for FDI with other ASEAN countries in the region, but also to make the most of opportunities from the wider process of globalisation. ASEAN should be appreciated as a building block for the member countries to participate more effectively in the global economy.

In each country, background discussions of all ASEAN meetings should be documented and archived for future reference of the public servants. This is especially in an era of democracy when political leaders are appointed for relatively short periods of time, whereas economic integration and legal convergence are long-term processes. As ASEAN policies are formulated at the political level by ministers or by the Cabinet as a whole, it is important to have systematic documentation of both confidential and public information. When public officials in ministries are responsible for providing information, advice and share past experiences, they may lack the institutional memory. This may hinder not only the advancement of ASEAN economic integration, but also may affect the pace of policy implementation. Being less equipped with ASEAN's history and detailed (technical) knowledge may tempt political leaders to put ASEAN regional issues on the backburner and may even compel them to replace ASEAN matters with short-term domestic issues or the pursuit of economic cooperation on a bilateral basis.

Although national trade ministries are generally responsible for the AEC as a whole, implementation of each of the AEC measures also involves government officials in other ministries. For instance, the customs agency under the Ministry of

Finance is responsible for the execution of the NSW. Similarly, for standards and conformance, responsibility may lie with the Ministry of Industry or affiliated entities. However, it was noted earlier that knowledge regarding the AEC and its objectives is diluted as one moves away from the AEC coordinating ministry, i.e. the trade ministry. When implementing officials lack an understanding of their work purpose and do not properly realise the necessity for timely delivery, the overall implementation of AEC is negatively affected. To overcome the issue, ASEAN member countries should develop proper internal communication of policy standards and objectives to the implementers. Policy objectives should be accurately and consistently explained to and shared with all affected civil servants so that they know what is expected of them. To this end, member countries should think seriously about introducing short courses on ASEAN or more particularly on AEC and its policies to a common understanding of this regional organisation among all officials of the government ministries. In an era of digital economy, these courses can be offered online and could even be a pre-requisite to undertake ASEAN-related activities.

Finally, once an AEC policy is ratified, member countries need to clearly demarcate resources intended to facilitate effective policy implementation. As part of such an exercise, countries should train and assign personnel for ASEAN activities. They may develop a reward system to appreciate implementing agencies and implementers for delivering desired outcomes and doing so in a timely fashion. It is also important to make sure that the requisite national legal measures are adopted or amended to avoid any domestic legal barriers to the realisation of the AEC. Moreover, ministries of finance, which are responsible for the financial resources and allocation of budget, have been known to assign politically sensitive or technical ASEAN issues (like standards and conformance) a relatively low priority or look for external funding to aid for implementation, thereby prolonging the execution process. Regarding human resources, the great majority of ASEAN countries can do with an increase in both from quantity and quality of personnel, with a strong case for anti-corruption instruction in a number of jurisdictions. Prioritising ASEAN issues and developing an appropriate incentive system in national systems may resolve some of the challenges in member countries. It should hopefully also result in better coordination among national government agencies.

6 CONCLUSION

ASEAN, or more particularly the ASEAN Economic Community (AEC), is at a point where policy implementation is a matter of the utmost importance. While political leaders have proclaimed a significant rate of implementation, the private sector and citizens have yet to experience the reality of an integrated market. There is increasing concern, or even criticism, that ASEAN has fallen short of its aspiration of a 'single market and production base'. The discussion in this chapter confirms that while there has been some significant progress in terms of tariff cuts, politically sensitive issues like the non-tariff barriers or standardisation of products remain a laggard. For these issues, implementation remains patchy across member countries, thereby limiting the practical usefulness of ASEAN-wide initiatives. There is also a subset of AEC measures that are framed so as to only generate discussion or deliver broad frameworks, negating any hope for tangible implementation.

Turning to the underlying causes for the observed implementation gap, it has been shown that although ASEAN members were united in their desire to respond to and capitalise on the opportunities offered by globalisation, particularly the flow of FDI to bigger economies and development of production network, they were hesitant to undertake domestic legal and other reforms. This led to an AEC blueprint document that offered flexibilities and contained loopholes, in turn inevitably producing problems during the implementation phase.

As implementation is the responsibility of the ASEAN member states, those in charge – mainly civil servants – have found it difficult to comply with broad policies or have used the flexibilities as an excuse not to comply in a timely manner. Moreover, countries struggle with their financial and manpower constraints in processing complex information regarding AEC measures. This chapter has highlighted the existence of economic and organisational conflicts as a significant obstacle to implementation, with some stakeholders in ASEAN states supporting liberalisation, whereas others insist on protection from increased competition. At the country-level, the ASEAN states do not always see eye to eye about the desired extent of liberalisation and the range of supporting domestic reforms due to their different economic structure and heterogeneous allocation of integration benefits across countries.

With ASEAN moving to the next phase of economic integration, remedial action must be taken if the AEC is to be realised and yield benefits for end-users and businesses alike. Communication must be improved both between government agencies and between governments and the end-users. AEC goals, headline commitments and concrete measures should be carefully delineated and matched so as to manage expectations. Finally, within each ASEAN state, there is a need for a better understanding of ASEAN affairs in the State bureaucracy, which should go hand-in-hand with the allocation of dedicated resources to enhance coordination among government agencies and the inculcation of pro-integration and pro-ASEAN thinking. This will surely be no easy feat, but failure to commit to the operationalisation of the lofty market-making objective could place the whole enterprise in jeopardy.

ANNEX 1 *Progress made under selected AEC measures*

Completed tasks	Remaining tasks
Trade in goods	
Tariff has been eliminated/ reduced; ROO has been simplified; started with a self-certification scheme.	Non-tariff barriers prevail.
A subset of ASEAN Countries have set up their NSW and have established their NTR.	NSW suffers from a lack of coordination mechanism between agencies, lack of human resource and technical capabilities; NTR is also not fully effective.
Harmonisation of technical standards for three sectors have been signed: electronics and electrical equip, cosmetics and pharma products (auto discussion is in advanced stage).	Implementation in national economies is incomplete and uneven. (Foodstuff and building and construction materials are a work in progress.)
Trade in services	
Mode 1 (cross-border supply, where neither the provider nor the consumer moves) and Mode 2 (implies consumption abroad, like tourism) have been met.	Mode 3 (commercial presence, i.e. FDI liberalisation) has not been met.
Mode 4 (movement of people) has been signed for eight professionals: engineering, nursing, architect, surveying, accountancy, medical, dental and tourism professionals.	Different ways of cooperation across the professionals; national rules governing the professional remain.
Free flow of investment	
ASEAN Comprehensive Investment Agreement (ACIA), describing liberalisation, protection, promotion and facilitation, has been put in place.	Liberalisation is difficult to achieve.
Promotion is done – linked investment agencies' website, developed and disseminated investment publications and conducted roadshows and public seminars.	Investment facilitation (transparency, regulations, infrastructure, institutions) has to be carried out in national economies.
Competition policy and IPR	
ASEAN Expert Group on competition has been set up, ASEAN Regional Guidelines on Competition Policy and the Handbook on Competition Policy and Laws in ASEAN for Businesses were written.	None of these talk of a region-wide standardised competition policy and leaves it as a national subject.
ASEAN IPR Action Plan 2011–2015 has been adopted.	There is no mention of a region-wide IPR regime. It is a national subject.
Infrastructure development	
ASEAN Highway Network, Singapore-Kunming Railway Line, ASEAN Open	All these are multi-year projects and none of them are completed yet. Many challenges

(continued)

ANNEX 1 *(continued)*

Completed tasks	Remaining tasks
Skies Policy, ICT Development have been identified.	remain, including securing financial resources.
Narrowing development gap	
Initiative of ASEAN Integration (IAI) finished two phases: 2002–2008 & 2009–2015.	Lack of coordination efforts among donor agencies did not completely fit into CLMV needs; new issues of climate change etc. not addressed.
SME development	
Strategic Action Plan for the ASEAN SME Development (2010–15) – ASEAN Benchmark for SME Credit Rating Methodology, web-based SME Service Centre, ASEAN Common Curriculum for Entrepreneurship, an ASEAN SME Policy Index.	Earlier issues remain: limited access to finance and technology, severe competition from MNCs and SMEs of other countries, weak human resources, lack of awareness of AEC initiatives.
Integration into the global economy	
ASEAN has signed five FTAs with Australia-New Zealand, China, India, Japan and South Korea.	All the five FTAs are different from each other and there is a need to put them under a common framework. Negotiation of the Regional Comprehensive Economic Partnership (RCEP) agreement is ongoing since 2013, with many challenges unresolved.

Source: Author's compilation

ANNEX 2 *Characteristics and elements of the AEC 2025 and AEC 2015 blueprints*

AEC 2025	AEC 2015
I. A highly integrated and cohesive economy	**I. Single market and production base**
Trade in goods	Free flow of goods
Trade in services	Free flow of services
Investment environment	Free flow of investment
Financial integration, financial inclusion and financial stability	Free flow of capital
Facilitating movement of skilled labour and business visitors	Free flow of skilled labour
Enhancing participation in global value chains	Priority integration sectors
	Food, agriculture and forestry
II. A competitive, innovative and dynamic ASEAN	**II. Competitive economic region**
Effective competition policy	Competition policy

(continued)

ANNEX 2 *(continued)*

AEC 2025	AEC 2015
Consumer protection	Consumer protection
Strengthening intellectual property rights cooperation	Intellectual property rights (IPR)
Productivity-driven growth, innovation, research and development and technology commercialisation	Infrastructure development (includes transportation and ICT)
Taxation cooperation	Taxation
Sustainable economic development	E-commerce
III. Enhanced connectivity and sectoral cooperation	
Transport	
Information and communication technology	
E-commerce	
Energy	
Food, agriculture, forestry	
Tourism, healthcare, minerals and science and technology	
IV. A resilient, inclusive, people-oriented and people-centred ASEAN	**III. Equitable economic development**
Strengthening the role of micro, small and medium enterprises (MSME)	SME development
Narrowing the development gap (includes IAI)	Initiative for ASEAN integration (IAI)
Strengthening the role of the private sector	
Public-private-partnership	
Contribution of stakeholders on REI	
V. A global ASEAN	**IV. Integration into the global economy**
(Covering ASEAN+1 FTAs and RCEP)	Coherent approach towards external economic relations
	Enhanced participation in global supply networks

Source: ASEAN Secretariat (2015d) and ASEAN Secretariat (2008).

10

The Rule of Law as Key to the ASEAN Legal Order: How Can It Be Ensured?

Francis Jacobs

1 INTRODUCTION

This chapter seeks to provide an introduction to three main questions: (1) What is the rule of law and how far is it a universal concept? (2) How is the rule of law key to the ASEAN legal order? (3) How is the rule of law to be ensured in ASEAN?

While building on some considerations which may be valid for other Asian legal orders, this chapter addresses more specifically the role of the rule of law in ASEAN (Association of Southeast Asian Nations), the intergovernmental association which today includes Brunei, Cambodia, Indonesia, Laos, Malaysia, Myanmar, the Philippines, Singapore, Thailand and Vietnam.

In view of their common nature as regional associations, the meaning and development of the rule of law in ASEAN will be compared with the European Union's experience, analysing and highlighting some of the main differences and commonalities among the two entities.

2 WHAT IS THE RULE OF LAW, AND HOW FAR IS IT A UNIVERSAL CONCEPT?

There is no univocal definition of the rule of law. Generally speaking, the rule of law means government of the law as opposed to arbitrary use of power. In terms of its content, the rule of law has been regarded as encompassing some formal attributes that laws should have to be capable of guiding one's conduct in order that one can plan one's life (e.g. openness, generality and clarity)[1] According to others, the rule of law must be complemented by more 'procedural' principles,[2] such as the control of the courts over the exercise of power. A more extensive understanding of rule of law also includes in the

---

With thanks for helpful comments from the reviewer of the first draft of this chapter. I am also very grateful to Giorgia Sangiuolo, PhD candidate, Centre of European Law, King's College London, for her valuable assistance in revising the paper for publication.

[1] J. Raz, 'The Rule of Law and Its Virtue' (1977) 93 *Law Quarterly Review* 198, at 198–202.
[2] A.W. Tashima, 'The War on Terror and the Rule of Law' (2008) 15 *Asian American Law Journal* 245, at 245–265.

rule of law some substantive qualities of the law (e.g. proportionality), or even fundamental rights.[3] In this myriad of different reconstructions, it has rightly been noted that the rule of law remains 'a complex and, in some respects, uncertain concept'.[4]

In an attempt to shed some light on this uncertainty, this contribution will focus more closely on the role of the judiciary as a key for the affirmation of the 'rule of law' in ASEAN. This, on the consideration that international organizations like ASEAN and the EU greatly rely on the creation of an effective system of dispute settlement as both an integrationist and legitimizing tool *vis-à-vis* the international community.[5]

2.1 Is the Rule of Law a Universal Concept?

Although the modern conception of 'rule of law' has mainly been developed in western democracies, and is thus strongly influenced by their values, it has some important universal traits. To begin with, I suggest, the rule of law requires that the exercise of power – thus including all acts of public authorities affecting individuals or companies – should be subject to review by the courts. This is necessary so as to ensure that the exercise of power was authorised by law, and that the power has been correctly exercised.

That raises the further questions of what is to be understood by acts of public authorities and whether those should include, at least to some extent, review of acts of the legislature in terms of protection of fundamental rights, or of other basic principles of the constitutional order. Parliamentary sovereignty, as established in the United Kingdom, is certainly not the only model. Many States in Europe[6] and beyond[7] have in place: constitutional courts, supreme courts with some powers of constitutional review or even decentralised systems of constitutional control, as in Sweden where ordinary and administrative judges may occasionally challenge the constitutionality of the acts of the Riksdag.

The rule of law lifts law above politics by limiting the exercise of arbitrary powers. Thus it is supported by a clear division among governmental functions (separation of powers) where courts oversee the exercise of power by legislature and executive alike. In some modern systems which uphold the rule of law, on many (if not all) issues, it is the courts which have the last word, so that one could even talk nowadays of the sovereignty of *Law*, the title of a little book for the general reader which I wrote some years ago.[8]

[3] T.H. Bingham, *The Rule of Law* (Penguin, 2011) at 68.
[4] House of Lords Select Committee on the Constitution, Relations between the executive, the judiciary and Parliament (2007 HL 151).
[5] G. Dimitropoulos, A common GAL: The legitimating role of the global rule of law, paper presented at the 4th Viterbo Global Administrative Law Seminar, 13–14 June 2008 at www.iilj.org/GAL/documents/Dimitropoulos.pdf.
[6] For instance, the *Conseil Constitutionnel* in France, the *Bundesverfassungsgericht* in Germany, the *Corte Costituzionale* in Italy and, since the 1989 events, several constitutional courts in central and eastern Europe.
[7] South Africa has a constitutional court in place since 1994.
[8] F.G. Jacobs, *The Sovereignty of Law: The European Way* (The Hamlyn Lectures, 2006) (Cambridge University Press, 2007).

Moreover, the rule of law should apply not only to public authorities, but also to other 'powerful' bodies, which sometimes seem able to act above the law, taking advantage of their status and mobility to avoid the law, or to evade taxation. These bodies include large corporations and multi-nationals, even banks and financial institutions. It thus seems appropriate that courts can review the systemic effects of their actions. Along this line, in the *Google Spain* case,[9] the European Court of Justice (ECJ) broadly interpreted Directive 95/46/EC – on the protection of individuals with regard to the processing of personal data and on the free movement of such data[10] – attributing to the search engine the responsibility of such processing. The judgment is notable in so that the ECJ innovatively attributed an obligation to a private company (Google) on the basis of its 'decisive role' in the effective protection of individuals' fundamental rights to privacy and to the protection of personal data.

Let us take a little further the requirement of review by the courts. This must include review by established and fully independent courts, with appropriate procedures for appointment of judges (e.g. rules on conflict of interest), conditions of employment (e.g. remuneration commensurate with the importance of the functions), and with a special responsibility of governments to protect their independence (e.g. protection against external interventions or pressure), to comply with their decisions, and to ensure respect for their judgments.[11] Independence, impartiality of judges and effectiveness of the courts' decisions are not only needed to guarantee just decision making and preserve the system of checks and balances among the different branches of the government, but also to ensure the (real and perceived) legitimacy of the judiciary vis-à-vis other national and international actors.

In the European Union, further procedural requirements of the rule of law include that standing before the courts is adequate to ensure that those affected by potentially unlawful measures can challenge them[12] and can do so without incurring excessive costs;[13] that the courts' procedures are effective; that the courts are adequately staffed and financed; and so on.

Many attempts have been made to develop a full list of the attributes of the rule of law. Among others, in Europe, the Council of Europe's Venice Commission for Democracy through Law has set out its own catalogue.[14] This is of particular

---

[9] Case C-131/12 *Google Spain SL and Google Inc.* v. *Agencia Española de Protección de Datos (AEPD) and Mario Costeja González* [2014] ECLI:EU:C:2014:317.

[10] Directive 95/46/EC of the European Parliament and of the Council of 24 October 1995 on the protection of individuals with regard to the processing of personal data and on the free movement of such data, OJ L 281, 23 November 1995, at 31–50.

[11] On the conditions of independence of courts and tribunals, see recently Case C-64/16 *Associação Sindical dos Juízes Portugueses* v. *Tribunal de Contas* [2018] ECLI:EU:C:2018:117.

[12] Art. 19(1)(2) Treaty on European Union.

[13] Case C-268/06 *Impact* v. *Minister for Agriculture and Food and Others* [2008] ECR I-2483.

[14] Rule of Law Checklist, European Commission for Democracy through Law, 106th Plenary Session in Venice, 11–12 March 2016, at www.venice.coe.int/webforms/documents/default.aspx?pdffile=CDL-AD(2016)007-e.

importance in terms of 'universalization' of the rule of law. Not only the Council of Europe is a broadly based organisation (even more extended than the European Union) counting today forty-seven members, which include all European States except Belarus, but also the Venice Commission's membership is open to non-European States as well. Among others, South Korea has joined and is an active member of its council on constitutional justice. The Venice Commission has worked together with the Korean Constitutional Court in setting up the Asian Association of Constitutional Courts and Equivalent Institutions, which inter alia seeks to promote the implementation of the rule of law. The work of the Venice Commission highlights the importance of adherence to the rule of law and suggests that there can be fundamental values shared across an entire region and beyond, although not necessarily of universal validity.[15]

An analogous conclusion is reached by the great English judge Lord Bingham of Cornhill in his classic book *The Rule of Law*.[16] Setting out his own account of the requirements of the rule of law, the author suggests that the fundamental requirements can be of universal validity.

2.2 *Rule of Law and Fundamental Rights*

It was noted above that the rule of law is sometimes understood as encompassing fundamental rights.[17] However, it is important, I suggest, not to go too far, by including within the rule of law other values which may be of equal or almost equal importance and value, but which inevitably risk diluting the concept. While the rule of law can have universal aspirations, systems of values of different countries upholding the rule of law may differ. Thus any aspirations to reach a universal definition of rule of law may be frustrated by the inclusion of fundamental rights in its definition.

There is some overlap, of course. Some rights are essential to the rule of law: so the right of access to the courts to obtain judicial review is a fundamental right, as well as being a fundamental requirement of the rule of law. In contrast, other rights, such as the right to family life, the right to freedom of religion, the right to education, may be fundamental rights without, as it seems to me, being part of the rule of law.

I note that this distinction is reflected in the ASEAN Charter: the rule of law, and respect for fundamental rights, are covered separately in Article 2(2)(h) and (i) respectively. The same is true in Article 2 of the Treaty on European Union, considered below, which mentions separately, though within the same provision, the rule of law and respect for human rights.

---

[15] Ibid. 'The Rule of Law is a concept of universal validity. The "need for universal adherence to and implementation of the Rule of Law at both the national and international levels" was endorsed by all Member States of the United Nations in the 2005 Outcome Document of the World Summit.'

[16] T.H. Bingham, *The Rule of Law* (Penguin, 2011) at 172.

[17] Ibid.

Nevertheless, there is an important link between the rule of law and fundamental rights. A breach of the rule of law will be particularly serious when the executive defies a judgment upholding fundamental rights. Conversely, protection of fundamental rights in a rule of law–based system further supports its legitimacy. This is particularly relevant in international and transnational organisations, which, not being able to rely on the traditional democratic tools (like elections), most commonly assert their legitimacy by upholding both of them. This is true for ASEAN as well as for the European Union.

In this context, it is interesting to compare how fundamental rights are protected in ASEAN and in Europe.

The basic system of protection of human rights in Europe is the European Convention on Human Rights (ECHR),[18] an international treaty drawn up in 1950 by the Council of Europe. In some respects the Council of Europe's Convention and the European Community can be seen as complementary: while the ECHR was meant to uphold fundamental rights in Europe, the EC was a more restricted organisation with a strong economic connotation, aiming at uniting the peoples of Europe by setting up a common market among its Member States.[19]

The European Convention on Human Rights, initially ratified by a few western European States (the United Kingdom being the first), was gradually accepted by all forty-seven members of the Council of Europe. The jurisdiction of the European Court of Human Rights, originally optional, was subsequently made compulsory and automatic.

The Convention is both the oldest and the most advanced regional system for the protection of fundamental rights worldwide, and the European Court of Human Rights, whose jurisdiction is now compulsory for all forty-seven member-states of the Council of Europe, has developed an impressive body of case-law. Overall, the Court has promoted an effective system of protection while respecting genuine differences in the value systems of the States. This was achieved by ensuring an effective individual access to justice while leaving to the contracting states a certain 'margin of appreciation', as it is termed, both in the assessment of the alleged violations and in the implementation of the Court's final decisions.

However, experience with the European Convention on Human Rights has been mixed, particularly in recent years. Regrettably, the United Kingdom has set a bad example on the rule of law in its poor response to a series of judgments of the European Court of Human Rights on prisoners' voting rights,[20] refusing for many years to give effect to them and making the Court a political football. Even if the judgments may on some counts seem questionable and open to criticism, the late

---

[18] Council of Europe, Convention for the Protection of Human Rights and Fundamental Freedoms, 4 November 1950, in force 3 September 1953, ETS 5 (ECHR).

[19] This divergence has been partially bridged in the years, with the EU now having its own Charter of Fundamental Rights.

[20] E.g. ECHR, *Hirst v. United Kingdom* (No 2), no. 74025/01 [2005] ECHR 681.

and unsatisfactory response of the UK has been regrettable: in a rule of law–based system, it cannot be open to a State to choose whether and when to comply with a judgment given against it.[21] Far more seriously, the United Kingdom government has recently threatened to withdraw its acceptance of the Court's jurisdiction altogether, which must entail denouncing the Convention. That would set a most unfortunate example to other States.[22] Should it do so, the United Kingdom would then be in the company only of Belarus, the only dictatorship in Europe, the only European State which is not in the Council of Europe, nor party to the Convention.

In comparative terms, it may be interesting to note that no similar individual-based independent structure of judicial protection – seen as an essential trait of the rule of law in Europe – exists in ASEAN.

Protection of human rights in ASEAN is based on the rules laid down in the ASEAN Charter and the ASEAN Human Rights Declaration. The ASEAN Intergovernmental Commission on Human Rights (AICHR) occupies a central place among the human rights bodies operating in the organisation.[23] However, these instruments have political more than legal significance. Focusing specifically on the existing procedural mechanism of protection of fundamental rights, the AICHR, provided for in the ASEAN Charter,[24] is a relatively new[25] consultative body whose aim is to uphold human rights and promote regional cooperation on human rights in the region.

Over the years, many have supported the creation of a human rights judicial body in ASEAN to replace or integrate the AICHR.[26] On this view, one may be tempted to look at the experience of the European Commission of Human Rights in the ECHR as a precedent for a path towards judicialization of human rights bodies. It will be remembered that, until 1998, when Protocol 11 entered into force, the European Convention on Human Rights had a two-tier system formed of the European

---

[21] This especially in light of the fact that, in its judgment on prisoners' rights, the Court was objecting only to a blanket, comprehensive and unconsidered ban: the Court made it clear that a limited grant of voting rights – for example, to those serving short sentences – would be sufficient to comply with its judgments. That would reflect the practice of nearly all the forty-seven members of the Council of Europe, which extends, as I have mentioned, far beyond the European Union.

[22] Notably to Russia and other States which still take action to comply with at least some of the Court's judgments.

[23] Association of Southeast Asian Nations (ASEAN), Terms of Reference of ASEAN Intergovernmental Commission on Human Rights (AICHR Terms of Reference), adopted by the ASEAN Foreign Ministers Meeting in July 2009, Article 6(8), 'The AICHR is the overarching human rights institution in ASEAN with overall responsibility for the promotion and protection of human rights in ASEAN.' Other regional sectorial bodies working in the field of human rights exist in the Region, such as the ASEAN Commission for Promotion and Protection of the Rights of Women and Children (ACWC) and the ASEAN Committee on the Implementation of the ASEAN Declaration on the Protection and Promotion of the Rights of Migrant Workers (ACMW).

[24] AICHR Terms of Reference, Articles 1.7, 2.2.i and 14.

[25] The AICHR Terms of Reference were signed in 2009.

[26] See the proposal of H.D. Phan, *A Selective Approach to Establishing a Human Rights Mechanism in Southeast Asia: The Case for a Southeast Asian Court of Human Rights* (Martinus Nijhoff Publishers, 2012) at 185–233.

Commission of Human Rights, receiving and acting on individual complaints at first instance, and the European Court of Human Rights, serving in effect as a second instance body. The European Commission, just like the AICHR, was not a judicial organ but performed a number of important functions: it decided on the admissibility of applications against governments; adopted reports on the merits; provided its services for 'friendly settlements'; and could refer cases to the Court, before which it served as an adviser. Only States and the Commission could refer a case to the Court, and that indeed proved to be very rare. As an important step towards both the liberalisation of individuals' access to judicial protection and the full judicialization of the ECtHR, from 1998 Protocol 11, replaced the two-tier system with a full-time European Court of Humans Rights, and gave 'any person, non-governmental organisation or group of individuals claiming to be the victim of a violation by one of the High Contracting Parties of the rights set forth in the Convention or the Protocols thereto' the right of direct access to the Court.[27]

Parallels between the ASEAN and the European experiences of human rights protection should however be made with caution. In addition to the structural differences between the AICHR and the Council of Europe's dispute settlement body from its inception,[28] one should remember that the historical and political background underlying the creation and development of the ECtHR is very different from ASEAN. The Council of Europe was set up by an organisation of like-minded States, to some extent sharing a common history, in which the already strongly rooted value of the individual as the basis for democracy was complemented, in much of continental Europe after World War II, by some distrust among Europeans towards the State.

ASEAN countries are in contrast community-based societies, characterised by a strong sense of respect for national and regional particularities. The ASEAN Charter makes it clear that the regional group is based on the principles of sovereignty, non-interference[29] and consensus.[30] This approach seems thus incompatible with a universal, individual-based system of protection of fundamental rights on the model of the ECHR or other Western human rights organisations and bodies.[31]

---

[27] Article 34, ECHR.
[28] E.g. Provision of an organ to supervise enforcement: The Committee of Ministers of the Council of Europe.
[29] Article 2, Charter of the Association of Southeast Asian Nations (ASEAN Charter), 20 November 2007, in force 15 December 2008.
[30] Article 20, ASEAN Charter.
[31] On this view, the reference to the Vienna Declaration and Programme of Action of the World Conference on Human Rights (adopted in Vienna by the World Conference on Human Rights under the auspices of the United Nations High Commissioner for Human Rights on 25 June 1993) included in the AICHR Terms of Reference (Preamble no. 1.6) is thus a clear restatement of these ASEAN (and Asian) specificities rather than the expression of a willingness to participate in an overarching global system of protection of human rights. While the bloc undertakes to safeguard civil, political, economic, social and cultural rights, it recalls its right under the Vienna Declaration to

This does not mean that the AICHR does not fulfil important functions in ASEAN[32] or that a fully fledged ASEAN Court of Human Rights is unachievable; rather that its future development may be based on different considerations: while the principles of sovereignty, unanimity and non-interference which govern the relations among ASEAN States seem bound to remain the basis of its structure of protection of fundamental rights, the organisation may reconcile them with individuals' protection by safeguarding their rights not in themselves, but as part of the community.[33]

3 HOW IS THE RULE OF LAW KEY TO THE ASEAN LEGAL ORDER?

Here I would start from how the rule of law has been understood in various international initiatives as compared with the 'regional experience' of the European Union. In the subsequent paragraphs, I will draw some parallels with ASEAN.

3.1 International Organisations

The idea is to compare how the concept of 'rule of law' has been understood and implemented in various multilateral experiences. I will consider three very different examples, from three very different types of international entities.

First, the World Bank has developed a considerable interest in this subject. It has published books, working papers and reports on the rule of law, contributing through these means to the development of a universal conception of the rule of law.[34] The World Bank supports the creation of objective standards of a universal rule of law, which include the substantive values of democracy and human rights, to

---

require that such protection should not impair 'national sovereignty, territorial integrity and non-interference in the internal affairs of states': see the Joint Communique of the Twenty-Sixth ASEAN Ministerial Meeting Singapore, 23–24 July 1993, at www.asean.org/?static_post=joint-communique-of-the-twenty-sixth-asean-ministerial-meeting-singapore-23-24-july-1993.

[32] Notably, it has been said that the AICHR equips ASEAN with the tools for autonomously assessing the state of universal rights in the area vis-à-vis international human rights standards and norms; aims at setting its own benchmarks of protection based on the nationals' specificities (see in this sense M. Darusman, Opening remarks to the Sixth Workshop held in Manila, Philippines on 16–17 July 2007, at www.aseanhrmech.org/downloads/6th%20WS%20Summary%20of%20Proceedings.Session.pdf); and, most of all, forms a catalytic, complementary, and coordinative tool for the national human rights bodies of ASEAN countries.

[33] This indeed seems to be the way forward envisaged by the ASEAN member States, see 1997 ASEAN Vision 2020, Kuala Lumpur, 15 December 1997, at https://cil.nus.edu.sg/wp-content/uploads/formidable/18/1997-ASEAN-Vision-2020–1.pdf.

[34] The World Bank has supported a large number of 'rule of law' projects dealing with legal and judicial reform in over 100 countries. L. Alexander et al., Literature Review of Impact Evaluations on Rule of Law and Governance Programming Report prepared for USAID's Center of Excellence on Democracy, Human Rights, and Governance (DRG), June 2013, at www.3ieimpact.org/media/filer_public/2016/03/22/alexander_et_al_2013_-_rule_of_law.pdf.

promote economic development. The organisation has implemented the rule of law *inter alia* through 'economic' sectors[35] as a tool to bridge global inequalities,[36] for instance, by encouraging access to legal technical assistance and institutional reforms.

Second, non-governmental organisations have also embraced the subject. For example, the World Justice Project has adopted its own explication of the rule of law, based on full accountability of the executive, transparency in the creation and enactment of legislation, protection of fundamental rights, and an independent, effective and diverse judiciary reflecting the makeup of the communities it serves. These universal principles are supplemented by nine further factors which are taken into account in the World Justice Project 'Rule of Law Index'. Specifically, the index measures rule of law adherence in 113 countries and jurisdictions worldwide based on households and expert surveys seeking, admirably in my view, to measure how the rule of law is experienced and perceived by ordinary people around the globe.[37] The World Justice Project also lists countries in a league table of compliance with the rule of law. It is noteworthy that the United Kingdom came tenth in the table in 2016, next after Singapore.[38]

A third organisation applying a broadly accepted concept of the rule of law is the World Trade Organisation (WTO). The WTO has developed, together with a uniform body of trade rules with quasi-global application,[39] a remarkable system for adjudication of international trade disputes to interpret and apply them (the 'Dispute Settlement Understanding' or 'DSU').[40] As is well known, such disputes are heard first by a panel and then may be taken on appeal to the Appellate Body, a standing tribunal which has in effect the status of an international supreme court. The DSU can, however, only issue recommendations and suggestions and lacks tools of enforcement as effective as those available in the EU. The rationale of the functioning of the WTO's structure lies in the concept of sovereignty: a dispute settlement mechanism provided with effective tools of enforcement constitutes a very intrusive governance tool that not all States are prepared to accept. This does not mean however that the WTO DSU's decisions have not been complied with. In its first ten years of existence, the WTO dispute settlement achieved a remarkable 83 per cent

---

[35] See Convention on the Settlement of Investment Disputes between States and Nationals of Other States, opened for signature 18 March 1965, in force 14 October 1966 (ICSID Convention).
[36] United Nations, The Secretary General's Report: The rule of law and transitional justice in conflict and post-conflict societies, no. S/2004/616, 23 August 2004, par. III(6), at www.ipu.org/splze/unga07/law.pdf.
[37] World Justice Project, at www.worldjusticeproject.org.
[38] World Justice Project, Rule of Law Index 2016 Report, at https://worldjusticeproject.org/sites/default/files/documents/RoLI_Final-Digital_0.pdf.
[39] In July 2016, the World Trade Organization counted 164 members.
[40] Understanding on Rules and Procedures Governing the Settlement of Disputes, Marrakesh Agreement Establishing the World Trade Organization, Annex 2, 15 April 1994, in force 1 January 1995, 1869 U.N.T.S. 401.

compliance rate.[41] Among various factors to explain this phenomenon are the largely accepted legitimacy (actual and perceived) of the body and its rules of procedure, as well as considerations in terms of economic 'reputation' of States.

Interestingly, the World Bank[42] and the WTO,[43] as will be noted for both the European Union and ASEAN,[44] have endorsed the rule of law primarily in 'economic' sectors. Thus, it may be argued that international organisations tend to obtain broader consensus among States on the application of the rule of law, leading in some cases to stronger dispute resolution mechanisms, when they set up economic frameworks. The way the rule of law is understood among these entities changes on the basis of their history and social and economic environment: the EU was set up by like-minded States who shared a common enough idea of the rule of law to accept limitations on their 'sovereign rights'[45] for the benefit of common institutions and grant effective tools for its enforcement to the Court of Justice. The very broad membership of the WTO narrows down the values and principles shared among its participants. Thus, if the organisation as a whole and its DSU are still based on a sufficiently defined rule of law, an area of discretion is required in the enforcement of these rules for the system to work and be regarded as legitimate.[46] In terms of the rule of law, ASEAN can perhaps be placed somewhere between the EU and the WTO. Like the WTO, it aims at facilitating economic exchanges among its member States. Like the EU, it is a regional organisation based on a more closely shared set of values than the WTO. However, such values are very different from the European ones: ASEAN is based on strongly community-based systems of law. Its member States greatly value sovereignty and non-interference in their internal matters, so that the bloc favours the non-judicial settlement of disputes, allowing States a very broad area of discretion in the implementation of the rule of law.

The respective characteristics of ASEAN and the EU will be more fully highlighted in the following sections of this chapter.

---

[41] W.J. Davey, The WTO Dispute Settlement System: The First Ten Years (2005) 8 *Journal of International Economic Law* 17, at 17–23.
[42] See Article 1 of the Agreement setting up the International Bank for Reconstruction and Development, 22 July 1944, in force 27 December 1945.
[43] See preamble to the General Agreement on Tariffs and Trade, 30 October 1947, 61 Stat. A-11, 55 U.N. T.S. 194.
[44] See Article 14 ASEAN Charter: 'In conformity with the purposes and principles of the ASEAN Charter relating to the promotion and protection of human rights and fundamental freedoms, ASEAN shall establish an ASEAN human rights body.'
[45] Case C-26/62 NV Algemene Transport- en Expeditie Onderneming van Gend & Loos v. Netherlands Inland Revenue Administration [1963] ECR 3.
[46] And this may not even be sufficient: on the basis of an alleged bias against the US, recently the US administration is blocking the appointment of new judges to sit on the WTO's appellate body, substantially paralysing its functioning.

3.2 The Rule of Law in the European Union

The experience of regional convergence of the EU seems of especial interest for the development of the rule of law in ASEAN.

One difference needs however to be highlighted from the outset. The role of the rule of law has a very particular function in the European Union, probably due to its very different legal nature of a 'legal order', as it was memorably described by the Court of Justice more than fifty years ago in *van Gend en Loos*.[47] In the system of multilevel governance aimed at the creation of an 'ever closer Union among the peoples of Europe' the rule of law is an instrument of integration, a politico-legal benchmark for Institutions, Member States, non-state actors and acceding States.[48] By depoliticising national law, it ensures that a higher system of common norms, common values and common principles applies equally to all existing and prospective actors in the EU. By ensuring access to justice for Institutions, States and non-State entities, the rule of law guarantees them the equal effective exercise of the rights conferred upon them by EU law.[49]

Interestingly enough, if the rule of law was thus de facto present from the outset in EU law and upheld by the ECJ, it is striking that the notion does not appear, in those words, in the founding Treaties. In fact, it made its first formal appearance in the amendments to the Treaty on European Union introduced by the Lisbon Treaty, which entered into force on 1 December 2009. Previously the rule of law is only to be found in the case-law of the Court: an example of the constitutional principles being fashioned in the first place by the Court, and then being given Treaty status.

The founding case for the rule of law in the EU was brought by the French Green Party ('*Les Verts*') against the European Parliament[50] and decided more than thirty years ago. In that case, the applicant was confronted with the difficulty that the Treaty made no provision for actions to be brought against measures adopted by the Parliament. The Court, according to the Treaty, could review legally binding acts of the Council and the Commission but not of the Parliament. That was no doubt because, when the Treaty was drawn up, the European Parliament (then 'the Assembly') was not directly elected and had no law-making powers. Moreover, the measure challenged by *Les Verts* was an administrative measure, concerning the allocation among political parties of funds for elections to the Parliament.

---

[47] *van Gend & Loos*, above, n. 45.
[48] L. Pech, Rule of Law as a Guiding Principle of the European Union's External Action, CLEER Working Papers 2012/3.
[49] In view of the importance of the rule of law as a unifying factor of the EU legal order, Article 7 of the Treaty, as amended by the Lisbon Treaty, makes provision for sanctions in the event of serious breaches by a Member State. The supervision of these guarantees is a matter for the political institutions of the EU, the Parliament, Council and Commission. Each of the institutions has been seeking to develop an agenda for dealing with these sensitive issues, confronted with apparently serious threats to the rule of law in some Member States.
[50] Case C-294/83 *Parti écologiste 'Les Verts'* v. *European Parliament* [1986] ECR 1339.

Nonetheless, the Court accepted the admissibility of the challenge to the Parliament's measure. Relying on the notion of the rule of law (although that notion was not yet expressly recognised by the Treaty), the Court held that 'the European Community "is a Community based on the rule of law, inasmuch as neither its Member States nor its institutions can avoid a review of the question whether the measures adopted by them are in conformity with the basic constitutional charter, the Treaty"'. Very recently the Court has asserted that 'the European Union is a union based on the rule of law in which individual parties have the right to challenge before the courts the legality of any decision or other national measure relating to the application to them of an EU act', and that 'the very existence of effective judicial review designed to ensure compliance with EU law is of the essence of the rule of law'. [51]

More generally, it can be said that the rule of law, or the closely related principle of legality, has been a lode-star inspiring the Court's case-law on the obligations of both the EU Institutions and the EU Member States. Indeed, in the decision the Court put the accent on the fact that the Treaty was to be understood as 'the basic constitutional charter' of the Union's legal system.[52]

In the constitutional rule of law–based system of the EU, courts have a crucial unifying role: if the European Court of Justice is attributed a 'monopoly' to ensure the uniform application of EU law by means of interpretation and decision on the validity of Union measures, national courts are the first points of contact with EU law for non-state actors.

In view of the key role of the system, it is worth setting out the respective roles of the courts in the EU more fully as they have evolved. The implications can hardly have been self-evident to the authors of the Treaty when they crafted its provisions, but it has proved remarkably effective.

It is worth recalling that the function of the Court of Justice was from the outset, and still is today, described in the Treaties as follows: The Court 'shall ensure that in the interpretation and application of the Treaties the law is observed' (now Article 19 of the Treaty on European Union). The provision is neutral and open to interpretation. However, the jurisdiction conferred to the Court (below) offers some guidance.

If we go back to the original European Community, the European Coal and Steel Community established in 1952, we find that the main functions of the Court then established, the predecessor of today's Court of Justice of the European Union, were essentially what might be described as 'rule of law functions', and were in effect neatly balanced: on the one hand, to ensure that the powerful new 'High Authority' of the ECSC, established by the Treaty, would act within the limits of its powers and

---

[51] Ibid. Case C-64/16, judgment of 27 February 2018, cited in footnote 12.
[52] Ibid. This follows a similar statement in a previous decision of the Court in Opinion 1/76, 'On the Draft Agreement establishing a European laying-up fund for inland waterway vessels' [1977] ECR I-741, at para. 12 ('internal constitution of the Community').

would not exceed those powers; on the other hand, to ensure that the Member States (then only six in number) would comply fully with their Treaty obligations.

The foundational principles governing the exercise by the Court of its powers of review were developed under the ECSC Treaty. But it was, as might be expected, when the Court became the Court of Justice of the European Communities, including the European Economic Community, with its far more extensive powers, that the rule of law became a fundamental principle underlying the Court's role across the legal system of the Community. The 'new' Court of Justice became a unitary judiciary for the three communities (ECSC, EEC, EURATOM), thus ensuring a unitary system of interpretation among the three Treaties. The Court's jurisdiction was also strengthened, and in addition to the interpreting the meaning and validity of EU law, it acquired some of its most important features, such as a somewhat wider (yet still very limited) access for individuals[53] and the far broader preliminary reference system,[54] which set the basis for the European Court system as we know it today.

To illustrate the respective role of the courts, it may be useful to outline the relationship between the State court and the EU Court on a preliminary reference. If for example a State measure which restricts imports is challenged by an importer in that State's court by way of judicial review, the State may seek to justify the measure on grounds of, say, public health or safety under the Treaty. The State court may then refer to the EU Court a question on the interpretation of the Treaty. As already mentioned, the EU Court's jurisdiction in these cases is only to interpret EU law, not to apply it. That is the function of the national court when it receives the ruling, and it is the national court which must decide the facts. But the EU Court's ruling on the interpretation of EU law, which is binding on the national court, may lead the State court to hold that the restriction on inter-State trade is not justified on the grounds advanced by the State. So the measure will be held to be unlawful, and therefore inapplicable. The EU provision is likely to have direct effect, and the effect will then be immediate: the State court will 'disapply' the State measure, without the need for it to be revoked by the government or repealed by the State legislature. (But the State measure should of course be repealed or amended by the State authorities in due course to the extent that it has been held to be contrary to the Treaty.)

The combination of transnational court and national court is particularly effective in this context. The transnational court may be able to take a broader view of the case: effectively, in the EU context, a European view. A national court may be more influenced by national practices, or tastes, or traditions, and it may have a greater degree of deference to the national legislature and executive. But it may be prepared to overcome those factors in response to a ruling which it has requested from a transnational court – a transnational court which will bear the responsibility for

---

[53] Article 173 Treaty Establishing the European Economic Community.
[54] Article 177 Treaty Establishing the European Economic Community.

the ruling. At the same time, since the resultant decision, applying the ruling and where appropriate holding the national measure unlawful, is taken by the national court, it may carry more weight within the jurisdiction than a decision of the transnational court would carry.

A further consideration, perhaps at first sight paradoxical, is that the European courts were the tool to oversee the application of an impartial and independent system of law, which, especially in the case of a dispute between two conflicting national systems of law, may be a significant advantage.

It should also be stressed that the avoidance of conflicting legal systems is of great importance for the rule of law: such conflicts make the law inherently unpredictable.

It is perhaps particularly relevant to ASEAN that a large part of the development of the EU's internal market has been due to the EU Court. The 'common market' set up in the Treaty of Rome was meant to be in effect a domestic market, one in which it is as easy to trade in goods as in your home market. Such an ambitious aspiration, largely achieved in regard to goods, but not yet comprehensively for services, was greatly facilitated by Court decisions like that in *Cassis de Dijon*.[55] On that occasion, the ECJ established as a basic principle that, subject to overriding considerations of public health, etc., goods lawfully produced in a Member State must be admitted by other Member States. That principle, in effect a principle of mutual recognition, greatly reduced the need for harmonisation and the development of common standards, and greatly facilitated the free flow of goods. Cases such as this may have a particular resonance for the ASEAN legal order, illustrating the point that harmonisation of national legislation and other regional or national measures may not always be necessary to ensure the free movement of goods.

In order to draw some parallels with the dispute resolution mechanisms in ASEAN, it may be useful to mention the other principal heads of jurisdiction of the EU Court which are also relevant for the observance of the rule of law: (1) actions brought by the European Commission against Member States, challenging any infringement of EU law – infringements which often include restrictions on the supply of goods or services;[56] (2) actions brought by Member States against the EU institutions;[57] (3) opinions on whether a treaty which the EU intends to conclude is consistent with EU law and whether such a treaty is within the competence of the EU or of its Member States.[58]

A topical illustration of this last head of jurisdiction is provided by the EU Court's opinion on the EU-Singapore Free Trade Agreement, the far-reaching commercial treaty concluded in September 2014 between the EU and Singapore. The European Commission asked the Court of Justice for an opinion primarily on the issue of the

---

[55] Case C-120/78 *Rewe-Zentral AG v. Bundesmonopolverwaltung für Branntwein* [1979] ECR 649.
[56] Article 258 Treaty on the Functioning of the European Union (TFEU).
[57] Article 263 TFEU.
[58] Article 218(11) TFEU.

division of competence between the EU and the Member States – essentially a federal question which may also be relevant to future EU agreements, including perhaps future agreements between the EU and the UK. In its opinion of 16 May 2017, the ECJ held that the competence to conclude the EU-Singapore FTA partially[59] falls within the shared competences of the EU and its Member States and can therefore only be concluded as a mixed agreement, so that the Agreement has to be ratified by both the EU and each of the Member States.[60]

4 HOW IS THE RULE OF LAW TO BE ENSURED IN ASEAN?

References to the rule of law as the basis of ASEAN similar to Article 2 or 7 TEU are at present missing from the ASEAN Charter, and, notably, ASEAN does not presently require compliance with the rule of law (or other substantive values) as a precondition for membership as the EU does.[61] However, such references came relatively late in the development of the EU, although the principle has been present in the case-law of the ECJ for much longer.[62]

4.1 Towards an ASEAN Court of Justice?

Having delineated the structure and functioning of the ECJ, the question follows immediately whether ASEAN should have its own 'Court of Justice' to foster unity of the block and, in that case, whether this should be structured on the model of the Court of Justice of the EU.

Many attempts have been made to set up regional courts in different parts of the world on the EU model. There are numerous[63] such courts, including several regional courts in different parts of Africa; the Caribbean Court of Justice; the

---

[59] Specifically the chapter on (i) non-direct foreign investment (portfolio investments), (ii) investor-state dispute settlement (ISDS), and (iii) state-to-state dispute settlement relating to provisions regarding portfolio investment and ISDS.

[60] The decision seemed to have ground-breaking consequences for the role of the EU as an international player. Indeed, the decision equating 'shared competences' to 'mandatory mixity' would have subjected the Union to the choice of either reducing the scope of its international agreements in order to proceed to a speedy ratification, or maintaining the broad scope which characterised the 'new generation' of Union FTAs but with the risk of their not being ratified by any of the national parliaments of the Member States. The Court 'corrected' its decision in Opinion 2/15 in its later decision in Case C-600/14 *Federal Republic of Germany v. Council of the European Union* [2017] ECLI:EU:C:2017:296, specifying that shared competence does not equate to mandatory mixity. This latter *revirement* might be seen as a welcome development also in the light of a future EU-UK agreement, as it may simplify its ratification procedure.

[61] European Commission, Rule of Law, European Neighbourhood Policy and Enlargement Negotiations, at https://ec.europa.eu/neighbourhood-enlargement/policy/policy-highlights/rule-of-law_en.

[62] *Parti écologiste 'Les Verts' v. European Parliament*, above n. 50.

[63] K.J. Alter, 'The Global Spread of European Style International Courts' (2012) 35 *West European Politics* 135, at 135–154.

Court of the Andean Pact; and the EFTA Court for the EEA in Europe. There was even, in the time of Mikhail Gorbachev, a visionary proposal from Moscow to replace the Soviet Union with a Community of Independent States with its own Court of Justice modelled on the EU Court – as is reported briefly in my book *The Sovereignty of Law*.[64] That last idea did not succeed. The same could be said for the Tribunal of the Southern Africa Development Community (SADC), which also adopted the EU process of regional adjudication and preliminary reference procedure. Indeed, after several judgments ruling against the Zimbabwean government, in 2010 the Tribunal was de facto suspended. As for the others, undoubtedly successful has been the EFTA Court which oversees the European Economic Area although it is limited in its jurisdiction to three States: Norway, Iceland and Liechtenstein. Its success is no doubt partly based on its close partnership with the Court of Justice of the European Union and the fact that the EFTA countries substantially share a common history with their EU counterparties.

The feasibility and desirability of a 'Court of Justice' for ASEAN need to take into account the specificities of the legal framework of both the organisation and its member States, including the importance of the principles of sovereignty, equality and non-interference in member States' internal affairs, summarised in the expression 'the ASEAN way'.[65] Chapter VIII of the ASEAN Charter on dispute settlement – together with the Protocol to the ASEAN Charter on Dispute Settlement Mechanisms – not only attributes great importance to consultations and alternative dispute resolution mechanisms, such as mediation and conciliation,[66] but also confers flexibility on member States in the choice of the tools to resolve their differences.[67] In a similar fashion, the last resort where no peaceful agreement is reached between member States on how to resolve a dispute, or for complaints about inadequate enforcement of decisions reached among them, is the non-judicial forum of the ASEAN Summit.[68]

Despite some advances in recent years in the effectiveness of ASEAN dispute settlement mechanisms,[69] the system in its current form has provoked a number of criticisms, all connected to ASEAN's characteristic trait of the predominant role of consensus and protection of State sovereignty. Among other things, the ASEAN's dispute resolution mechanisms are said to lack the following attributes: a preventive

---

[64] F.G. Jacobs, *The Sovereignty of Law: the European Way* (The Hamlyn Lectures) (Cambridge University Press, 2007).

[65] M. Ewing-Chow and L. Bernard, 'The ASEAN Charter: The Legalization of ASEAN?', in S. Cassese et al. (eds.), *Global Administrative Law: The Casebook* (Institute for International Law and Justice, 2012) at 115.

[66] Article 23 ASEAN Charter, Articles 3 and 6 of the Protocol to the ASEAN Charter on Dispute Settlement Mechanisms.

[67] Article 25 ASEAN Charter, Articles 8 and 9 of the Protocol to the ASEAN Charter on Dispute Settlement Mechanisms.

[68] Articles 26–27 ASEAN Charter.

[69] Such as the adoption of the Rules for Reference of Non-Compliance to the ASEAN Summit, April 2012.

and proactive approach to dispute settlement; an institutional framework for the peaceful prevention of disputes and conflicts;[70] and effective enforcement tools.[71]

These criticisms can be partially shared in view of the important functions of convergence and coordination performed by regional courts: the European experience suggests that important regional achievements, such as an internal market effectively free of barriers to trade, would not have been possible without an effective Court system.

This is, however, not to say that an ASEAN dispute settlement organ should necessarily be modelled on the European Court of Justice. The very different aims and political background of the EU and ASEAN may call for a different, and probably more flexible, ASEAN dispute settlement mechanism. Indeed, the elements of the 'ASEAN way' make clear that, despite the constitution-like inception 'We, the peoples' in the ASEAN Charter, the organisation does not have any supranational element like the EU, but remains an inter-State system.

And yet regionalism, as a tool to develop interdependence, may still seem intrinsically incompatible with full protection from interference in the internal affairs of States. After all, the favourite tool of dispute settlement of ASEAN, namely arbitration, could also be considered as a constraint on sovereignty.

It may therefore be suggested that what is needed for regional organizations such as the EU and ASEAN is a permanent dispute settlement mechanism which complies with all the requirements of the rule of law and is able to adopt enforceable decisions. An ASEAN Court of Justice could however be structured in such a fashion as to take account of the 'ASEAN way'. For instance, not all of the CJEU's heads of jurisdiction described above are found in other transnational courts which have followed the EU model. If providing an analysis of which of them should be conferred on a future ASEAN Court may be over-ambitious, perhaps consideration should be given to a jurisdiction which does not feature significantly in the EU system: namely to hear disputes between Member States. (In the EU system, the grievance of the complainant Member States can be taken over by the European Commission, and there are virtually no inter-State cases before the ECJ.) Considerations of respect for State sovereignty and non-interference in States' internal affairs might also suggest that an ASEAN Court of Justice might hear only disputes between States, and possibly some categories of preliminary references from national courts. Further, it could be open to ASEAN member States to amend by agreement (for the future) legal provisions where they disagreed with the court's interpretation of those provisions.

---

[70] G.J. Naldi, The ASEAN Protocol on Dispute Settlement Mechanisms: An Appraisal (2014) 5(1) *Journal of International Dispute Settlement* 105, at 105–138.

[71] H.D. Phan, Promoting Compliance: An Assessment of ASEAN Instruments since the ASEAN Charter (2014) 41(2) *Syracuse Journal of International Law & Commerce* 379, at 379–411.

4.2 Courts and Arbitration in ASEAN

In the European Union, national courts are an essential point of connection and unity between the national and European level. If the same unifying function does not apply to courts in ASEAN, national tribunals and arbitration will still play a key role in the application of the rule of law, especially in the commercial sector. Comparisons can be drawn between leading judicial centres in Europe and ASEAN.

There are indeed some important parallels and some significant differences between Singapore and London. Singapore is of course one of the leading centres of arbitration in Asia, and many international law firms have established themselves in Singapore. An interesting recent development is the establishment of the Singapore International Commercial Court, which is a division of the High Court of Singapore, and was specifically designed to develop the legal services sector and to expand the scope for the internationalisation and export of Singapore law. The Court was launched on 5 January 2015, after a remarkably rapid planning process. It provides a panel of experienced judges comprising specialist commercial judges from Singapore and, on a part-time basis, international judges from both civil law and common law traditions.

It is of interest to note that, as well as international law firms, leading sets of English barristers' Chambers have established themselves in Singapore.

Conversely, in London, there seem increasing threats to the key role that English courts and English law have traditionally had in commercial disputes. Senior judges have expressed in public their concerns with the low morale of the judiciary, and even with unprecedented difficulties of recruitment to the Bench. It is said that there is little recognition by the government of the importance of legal services both for the rule of law and for the economy, and of the special place which English law has occupied in international trade. Brexit threatens the straightforward recognition and enforcement of English judgments across the European Union which have been available under EU law, and it may even have an adverse impact on the use of English law in commercial contracts.

5 CONCLUSIONS FROM ASEAN AND CONCLUSIONS FOR ASEAN

I will start with conclusions which might be drawn from ASEAN, which may be of interest for the EU or the UK; then I will turn to possible conclusions for ASEAN from the European experience.

5.1 Conclusions from ASEAN

In recent years, Asian governments have increasingly given high priority to promoting free trade and economic integration. ASEAN has recently negotiated its own

Free Trade Area,[72] and has also negotiated FTAs with China, India, South Korea, Japan, Australia and New Zealand. The next step is to group all those sixteen nations together as a single bloc with one FTA, to be known as the Regional Comprehensive Economic Partnership, or RCEP. Those negotiations have been going on since 2012 and now concluded. An RCEP trade bloc will comprise almost half the population of the world and would account for approximately 40 per cent of world trade. In relation to scope and rule of law, unlike the CPTPP, the RCEP deal lacks protection for labour, human rights and the environment.

Also, in 2016, the Trans-Pacific Partnership (TPP) was signed. The TPP, as originally conceived, was to be a regional FTA among twelve Asia-Pacific countries: Australia, Brunei, Canada, Chile, Japan, Malaysia, Mexico, New Zealand, Peru, Singapore, the United States and Vietnam. As an effect of the Presidential Memorandum to withdraw the United States from the TPP, signed by President Trump in January 2017, the remaining eleven countries (TPP11) reviewed the original agreement and signed a year later (January 2018) what is now called the 'Comprehensive and Progressive Agreement for Trans-Pacific Partnership' (CPTPP).

There appears to be a link between trade agreements in the region: ASEAN and CPTPP have seven members in common,[73] and Japan is leading both negotiations. The recent consensus on CPTPP has also increased momentum for RCEP countries to reach a deal as well.

These developments are particularly important for the EU and the UK for a number of reasons. To begin with, it is interesting for both the UK and the EU, which are looking to expand their trade relationships towards the East, that the CPTPP will be open to other States to sign. The CPTPP, including some countries of the Commonwealth, may represent a fast-track option for the UK after its withdrawal from the EU. The main unresolved issue for the UK, and also to an extent for the EU, in many of those negotiations is that of services, and in particular financial services, as these are generally not covered by the agreements.

The flurry of dynamic activity in the signing of economic agreements in Asia, including that on the ASEAN Economic Community, may represent another valuable lesson for the EU and the UK. ASEAN, RCEP, CPTPP are all successful examples of regionalism and economic agreements to create wealth and growth, stabilise political relations and attract foreign investments. More generally, in a globalised world countries cannot afford to adopt an inward-looking policy. Rather, strong tools of economic cooperation and regionalism are of the essence to allow them to play an active role in international relations and effectively further their interests abroad.

---

[72] The ASEAN Free Trade Area was agreed at the 2012 ASEAN Summit in Singapore and provides for the progressive reduction and elimination of tariff and non-tariff barriers among the Member States through various instruments of liberalisation on a preferential basis.

[73] Australia, Brunei, Japan, Malaysia, Singapore, New Zealand and Vietnam.

One can hardly discuss the advantages of free trade today without taking some account of current threats. And the main threat very recently has been populism and mass protest. Obviously, these may not be quite on target, but they can prove extremely effective. It is interesting here to note that populism often rides the idea of State sovereignty, one of the main pillars of ASEAN. However, the strong affirmation of State sovereignty in Western countries and Asia is giving rise to very different trends in ASEAN (and Asia), compared to the US and Europe. In these latter countries, populist forces are pushing towards the disintegration of economic and regional structures, creating isolationism. The US, historically the 'free trade champion' of the Western world, is a stark example of this process with the US president, for instance, recently reintroducing customs tariffs on aluminium and steel and stalling the WTO's DSU. In Asia, the idea of sovereignty is instead being increasingly reconciled with a concentration of economic power: the ASEAN and CPTPP experiences show the awareness of these countries that economic regionalism is the only way to achieve the position of rule-makers on the international plane.

Referendums are a good example of the difficulties and dangers which have recently arisen from populism. Experience shows that in a referendum campaign it is hard to have a proper debate; that there is a great risk, on complex issues, of misinformation; that a simple binary choice as is usually given may not include the appropriate choice; and that the outcome may be influenced by unrelated concerns. So, it may be difficult to read the real message.[74] One of the more obvious risks with a system of popular votes is not only that, as experience suggests, the public can easily be misled, especially when the issues are complex; but also that to some extent the votes may not be directed to the issues but reflect other concerns. The long-established system of representative democracy seems preferable, on important and complex issues, to the currently fashionable device of the referendum. And

---

[74] There have been some unfortunate examples of referendums very recently, of which I will mention four. They are on very different issues, but perhaps to some extent carry a similar negative signal. To some extent, they can all be interpreted as an anti-establishment, anti-elitist message, to some extent expressing discontent with the current regime and/or with how the voters perceive their own situation.

In *Colombia*: the initial rejection, by referendum, of the peace deal which had been agreed between the government and the warring faction, to put an end to the fifty-year war which had led to a quarter of a million deaths and millions of homeless people; fortunately, the result of the referendum was subsequently reversed.

In the *Netherlands*: rejection of the Agreement between the European Union and Ukraine, of great importance for the future of Ukraine. Fortunately, the rejection was again overcome.

In *Italy*: on 4 December 2016, the vote on constitutional reform, which led to the fall of the government and a period of great political and economic uncertainty, with continuing repercussions in recent elections.

In the *United Kingdom*: on 23 June 2016, the vote to leave the European Union. This again seems to me an unfortunate example. Especially if it is recalled that in Parliament there was a very large majority in favour of remaining, yet Parliament paradoxically decided, also in apparent contradiction with the fundamental doctrine of Parliamentary sovereignty, that the outcome of the referendum should be treated as definitive.

the use of the referendum seems unlikely to promote the rule of law in international relations.[75]

Returning to the issue of the United Kingdom's vote to leave the European Union, I will say no more than that it seems to me damaging both to the European Union and to the UK. From the point of view of trade, it has left the United Kingdom the difficult task of negotiating new arrangements with the European Union and with the rest of the world, striving to maintain the best available access both to the European Union's internal market, which currently takes nearly half of the UK's output, and to the rest of the world – to much of which the UK currently enjoys favourable terms precisely through its membership of the European Union. And it is not only a matter of trade. Scientific and medical research, culture, education, environmental protection, employment rights, etc. have all been dependent to a substantial degree on EU membership for more than 40 years. And that is without taking account of the impact on defence and security, or indeed on relations among the peoples of Europe in the broadest sense.

5.2 Conclusions for ASEAN

I will list a few points very briefly. To begin with, the European experience may constitute an interesting precedent for ASEAN as a case-study of the benefits of effective regional economic integration. Specifically, two elements seem of the utmost importance as a conclusion for ASEAN.

The rapid developments in all sectors of international law, from fundamental rights to regulatory standards in trade, represent an invitation to strong regionalism: in an increasingly integrated 'global economy', small, isolated economic actors seem destined to become rule-takers rather than rule-makers. It may be reasonably assumed that, without the European Union, Europe would hardly be today one of the world's leaders in trade, environment and human rights.

However, effective regional integration requires strong institutions and binding supranational compliance mechanisms. In recent years there has been a remarkable consensus among economists, with confirmation from experience, that, broadly speaking, free trade is key to economic prosperity; and, it may be added, that strong institutions are of fundamental importance in this context. Here I would mention just one authority: the work of Douglass North, a Nobel Prize winner who died in 2016, has proved extremely influential on the connections between institutions and economic performance. He defined institutions as 'the humanly devised constraints that structure political, economic and social interaction'.[76] These constraints

---

[75] As a flippant postscript, I would add that there was outrage in some highly placed quarters in the UK when a public poll which was organised, perhaps misguidedly, to vote on the name to be given to a highly valued new Polar research ship, voted overwhelmingly to give the new ship what appeared to some the ridiculous name *Boaty McBoatface*.

[76] D.C. North, Institutions(1991) 5(1) *Journal of Economic Perspectives* 97–112.

include the rule of law and property rights, so that contracts are legally enforceable, and politicians cannot expropriate the assets of private companies. Strong institutions encourage competition, enterprise, investment and entrepreneurial risk-taking. And nowadays institutions are increasingly international, indeed supranational. Leaving aside any considerations about political integration, which probably do not apply to ASEAN in the same way as to the EU, economic integration is an on-going process, requiring constant effort and vigilance by all members of the organisation. To achieve this aim, only effective supranational entities can truly ensure respect for the rule of law, understood as 'rule under the law', by the members of the regional organisation to guarantee a real opening of national markets. International judiciaries play an especially crucial role to overcome political dissent among members of a transnational organisation, to set aside particularist divergences and to achieve real integration. This was demonstrated in the EU by the essential guidance provided by the ECJ in cases like *Cassis de Dijon*, which paved the way for mutual recognition of standards in different EU countries.[77]

There is no optimal structure for international judiciaries: the varying level of success of the numerous efforts around the world to follow the model of the European Court of Justice shows that regional courts do not exist in a vacuum, but instead need to adapt to the local context. Thus, it is not only possible, but also necessary, that they differ from one another in terms of their structure and approach to understanding and implementing regionalism: specifically, such differences will depend both on the value systems they are based upon and the aims for which they are established. As happened both with the European Union and with the European Convention on Human Rights, transnational courts' structure and functioning may vary over time according to the evolution of such value systems and aims. After all, law is purely a social construct.

It is indeed striking to observe how both the European systems have evolved gradually and progressively over a period of many years: that may suggest that such courts should start from a rather limited base, but with the potential to develop.

A replica of the European Court of Justice may thus not be suited for ASEAN. What seems however of the utmost importance is that any dispute mechanism in ASEAN should be provided with binding jurisdiction and with effective enforcement powers in order for the bloc to achieve sufficient economic integration among its member States.

From another standpoint, too broad an understanding of the rule of law as encompassing also a certain set of fundamental rights may impair any attempt to 'universalize' the concept. However, the experiences of the ECtHR and the AICHR may suggest that a rule of law–based system upholding a certain set of fundamental rights can constitute a powerful legitimising tool for non-State entities. One may thus argue that the protection of fundamental rights, independently of its substantive

---

[77] *Rewe-Zentral AG v. Bundesmonopolverwaltung für Branntwein* above n. 55.

content, is nowadays an essential complement of the rule of law and is inextricably intertwined with the existence and good functioning of transnational organisations aimed at influencing the development of transnational law. Thus, it may be important that ASEAN progressively strengthens its system of protection of fundamental rights with a view to a fuller judicialisation of the AICHR.

Finally, the existence of different languages, and different legal systems, is not an obstacle to the application of common rules, but again the responses are easier within a regional context. In practical terms, it would be most appropriate for the free trade provisions themselves to be accompanied by common rules on competition (including subsidies) and rules on public procurement (providing for a transparent system and excluding discretionary awards of public contracts).

6 CONCLUSIONS ON THE RULE OF LAW

In conclusion, at the end of his book *The Rule of Law*, Tom Bingham has a remarkable passage, where he asks the question, What makes the difference between good and bad government? His answer: the rule of law. And on the issue we are addressing of whether the rule of law is universal, he is very clear. He says, 'In a world divided by differences of nationality, race, colour, religion and wealth it is one of the greatest unifying factors, perhaps the greatest', even adding, 'the nearest we are likely to approach to a universal secular religion'.

He concludes: 'It remains an ideal, but an ideal worth striving for, in the interests of good government and peace, at home and in the world at large.'

To which I would venture to add that, even if this ideal cannot be fully obtained, it can also be suggested that the rule of law is a value which is simply necessary in the modern world. We cannot, without great difficulty, turn the page back from globalisation and openness, which have proved their value and which, despite current setbacks, can be expected to continue to do so. So long as the world's economies embody these trends, the political systems seem bound, however haltingly, to reflect them. The rule of law can be seen as more than a virtue, even as a necessity. And regional systems with effective courts can contribute to developing it.

11

How Asian Should Asian Law Be?

Ralf Michaels

1 INTRODUCTION

In 2016, Singapore saw a conference with the ambitious title 'Doing Business Across Asia: Legal Convergence in an Asian Century'.[1] Among other things, the conference celebrated the inauguration of the Asian Business Law Institute (ABLI).[2] The keynote address was given by Sundaresh Menon, Chief Justice of the Republic of Singapore and chair of ABLI's board of governors.[3] Menon CJ invoked the demands of globalization and lamented the fragmentation of laws in Asia as appearing 'somewhat out of kilter'. Legal convergence, he suggested, was necessary because 'a fragmented Asia is holding business back,' inconsistent regulations and regimes across the Asia-Pacific were the single biggest barrier to trade. Menon juxtaposed this situation in Asia with that in Africa, where the Organization for the Harmonization of Business Laws (OHADA) had made significant progress towards unification. That success could not be copied, however: 'A world with an identical legal framework that applies in every space would neither be realistic nor even desirable. Laws reflect political, social and economic realities and these realities are not evenly flat even in an otherwise flattening world.[4] 'The conditions in Asia are different and we must find what best suits our needs.'[5]

On its face, such a plea for convergence sounds familiar to European observers. The dual invocation of matters of trade and business on the one hand, political and social commonalities on the other, seems familiar from discussions about legal unification in Europe. The European Union has always invoked both aspects, as have proponents of a European Civil Code. On the one hand, legal unification is

---

Thanks for extremely valuable advice on earlier drafts to Naoki Kanayama, Annelise Riles, Teemu Ruskola and Maartje de Visser, as well as workshop participants at Kyoto University, where Nakata Kumihiro provided insightful comments. Any shortcomings are all mine.

[1] For information on the conference, see www.ijc.bc/img/user/files/pdf-cn/doingbusinessacrossasia.pdf
[2] http://abli.asia/.
[3] S. Menon, Doing Business Across Asia: Legal Convergence in an Asian Century (Opening Address, launch of the Asian Business Law Institute, 21 January 2016).
[4] Ibid. at p. 12.
[5] Ibid. at p. 7.

often said to be necessary for trans-border commerce. Such commercial justification underlies much of EU law; it has also repeatedly been brought up in favour of a European civil code. On the other hand, legal unification in Europe is regularly linked to an idea of a European cultural identity.[6] Behind these two justifications are two ideas about what Europe is. For the commercial justification, Europe is an optimal market, facilitated through the institution of the European Union. Nothing much hinges on a more precise definition of Europe that goes beyond such economic considerations. Or, put differently, the definition of Europe is institutional: it hinges on membership in the European Union. For the cultural justification, by contrast, Europe is a natural unity, bound together by a common culture, a common history, a common background in religion and subsequent secularization. Here, therefore, the idea of Europe is substantive.

Can the same be said about Asia? Is there an Asian identity comparable to European identity and therefore similarly useful as a justification for unification projects? If so, what does it look like? And if so, does this make Asia more like Europe, or less so? Or is this question itself already a mere European projection? When Menon speaks of different conditions in Asia, what are these? When he speaks of Asia's needs, and what exactly suits them best, is he talking only economics or also culture? In short, what is meant by 'Asia?' And when we speak of Asian law, what makes law Asian?

This chapter tries to address such questions. In particular, I look at a concrete project of Asian law unification – the Principles of Asian Comparative Law – and connect discussions about its Asian identity with four concepts of Asia. The first such concept is a European idea of Asia and Asian law, which defines a presumably homogeneous Asia on the basis of its level of difference from Europe. The next three concepts are concepts that emerged from local debates. Two of them explicitly invoke the leadership of one country. A sinocentric concept of Asian law attempts to reinvigorate concepts from the time of Chinese dominance of East Asia prior to colonization. A Japanese concept of Pan-Asian law by contrast is built on Japanese modernization, which in turn was influenced by Europe. Finally, the idea of Asian values attempts to avoid leadership by any one country in favour of a truly Asian identity. None of these three concepts can fully avoid the central problems of the European projection: they are all defined by their relation to the West, and all of them invoke a relative degree of homogeneity as a basis for identity. I close, therefore, with an alternative concept of Asia 'as method' that attempts to overcome these two shortcomings and may offer a more promising path towards an idea of Asian law.

---

[6] N. Jansen, Binnenmarkt, Privatrecht und europäische Identität – Eine historische und methodische Bestandsaufnahme (Mohr/Siebeck, 2003); S. Law, From Multiple Legal Cultures to One Legal Culture? Thinking About Culture, Tradition and Identity in European Private Law Development, (2015) 31 *Utrecht Journal of International and European Law* 68.

2 ASIAN LAW? THE EXAMPLE PRINCIPLES OF ASIAN CONTRACT LAW

If the ABLI discussion largely avoids discussions on an Asian identity, another project has generated such a debate: the Principles of Asian Contract Law (PACL).[7] Their origin lies in a proposal made by Naoki Kanayama, Professor for French law at Keio University in Japan, during a conference at Tsinghua University 2009 for an Asian project after the model of the PECL. The project was inaugurated on the spot with what Shinyuan Han, professor of civil law at Tsinghua University in China, calls the 'Beijing declaration'.[8] It involves a good number of East and Southeast Asian countries and has since led to a number of conferences, country reports and draft chapters towards a final product.

The PACL are being conceived in view of existing non–Asian Restatements like PECL and UPICC; in addition, the Convention on the International Sale of Goods has served as an inspiration.[9] The form of the project is very similar to that of its Western predecessors: to present, in the form of rules, a Restatement of Asian contract law, based on research into existing laws. Its proposed functions also resemble those of PECL and UPICC: to serve as a model law for modernization and to offer themselves as an applicable law in transnational contracts.[10] Even the language of the product (and of the preparatory work) is the same as for the PECL and UPICC, namely English – not a language native to Asia.

Beyond that, however, there are important differences with the work on the PECL. While authors of the PECL and the UPICC strongly emphasize their desire to transcend national law, this seems less prominent with the PACL, which focuses more on the representation of national systems and on national reports. No centralized national background exists, so the projects rest on the shoulders of the national groups, which are in charge of most of the work. Even the drafting of sections of the PACL were left first to representatives of national groups, before the results were

---

[7] S. Han, Principles of Asian Contract Law: An Endeavor of Regional Harmonization of Contract Law in East Asia, (2013) 58 *Villanova Law Review* 589; M. F. Hiscock, The Universality of Good Faith and Moral Behaviour: A Challenge for the Principles of Asian Contract Law, in Chang-fa Lo, Nigel Li, LinTsai-yu (Lin), eds., *Legal Thoughts between the East and the West in the Multilevel Legal Order: A Liber Amicorum in Honour of Professor Herbert Han-Pao Ma* (2016) 355–367; Jung-Joon Ka, Introduction to PACL, in T. Angelo et al. (eds.), *Contributions to the Study of International Trade Law and Alternative Dispute Resolution in the South Pacific* (2014) 55–65; N. Kanayama, PACL (Principles of Asian Civil/Commercial Law) (in French), [2010] *Revue des contrats* 995, revised and updated as N. Kanayama, PACL (Principles of Asian Civil Law) (in French), in *Mélanges Jean-Louis Baudouin* 393–419 (Benoît Moore ed., Éditions Yvon Blais, 2012) (hereinafter Kanayama, Mélanges Badouin), further revised and updated as Kanayama, PACL (Principles of Asian Contract Law) (in French), in *Droit japonais, droit français, Quel dialogue ?* (Béatrice Jaluzot ed., Schulthess, 2014) 185–196 (hereinafter Kanayama, Quel dialogue?); Young-June Lee, The Basic Direction of the Principles of Asian Contract Law (in Korean, with Chinese and Japanese translations), 3 *Asia Private Law Review* Arts. 23–25; Lee, Introduction to the Draft Articles, (2014) 4 *Asia Private Law Review* 3–11. (The Asia Private Law Review is available at www.kcjlaw.co.kr.)
[8] Kanayama, Mélanges Boudouin (n. 7) 398; Han (n. 7) 590–591.
[9] Han (n. 7) 591–592.
[10] Kanayama, Mélanges Boudouin (n. 7) 396–397.

discussed and voted upon. A number of such draft sections have been drafted: the sections on performance and non-performance, prepared by the Korean delegation, are available.[11] Moreover, two participants from Singapore have published the first two of an intended six volumes of essays in a series entitled 'Studies in the Contract Laws of Asia', based on work towards the PACL, though they are no longer involved in the project.[12]

The PACL are not the first project aimed at restating Asian contract law. Earlier proposals exist for an ASEAN project based on the UPICC and PECL.[13] A predecessor project under the guidance of the then-new Law Association for Asia and the Western Pacific led to a book edited by three scholars from the University of Tasmania, but relying on reports from scholars from a number of other Asian countries.[14] The editors of that book decided in favour of a comprehensive presentation of contract law in Asia rather than on a country report, in view of the fact that a country report would be very repetitive, given that most laws in Asia are based on either civil or common law.[15] An unfortunate consequence of this focus was that the editors saw themselves unable to include a detailed comparison with legal systems outside of this dichotomy, for example Islamic or Chinese law.[16] They were mindful, throughout the book, of the practical problems that emerge from imposing Western law on countries with very different traditions, including the inadequacy of both Western concepts and Western solutions for local problems. Nonetheless, the discussion of concrete problems could not avoid going along Western trajectories, and it does not, in the end, become clear what makes the project particularly Asian, other than that it is not European.[17]

[11] Draft articles non-performance of contract for principles of Asian contract law, (2010) *Asia Private Law Review* No. 4 special; Young Jun Lee (ed.), A Study on Draft Articles, Principles of Asian Contract Law: Performance & Non-performance, (2016) *Asia Private Law Review* No. 7 special.

[12] M. Chen-Wishart, A. Loke, and B. Ong (eds.), *Remedies for Breach of Contract* (Oxford University Press, 2016); M. Chen-Wishart, A. Loke, and S. Vogenauer (eds.), *Formation and Third Party Beneficiaries* (Oxford University Press, 2018). The other intended volumes deal with contents of contracts and unfair terms, invalidity of contract, ending and changing contracts, and public policy and illegality.

[13] Y. N. Lim, UNIDROIT Principles – A Model for the Harmonization of ASEAN Contract Law (1997) *Singapore L. Rev* 355; R. Amoussou-Guenou, Perspectives des Principes Asean (ou Asiatiques) du droit des contrats (2005) *Int'l Bus LJ* 573; B. Hardjowahono, The UNIDROIT Principles and the Law Governing Commercial Contracts in Southeast Asia (2002) *ULR* 1005, especially 1010–1011 and 1013–1014; B. Hardjowahono, *The Unification of Private International Law on International Commercial Contracts within the Regional Legal System of ASEAN* (2005) 167–176; S. M. P. Hutabarat, Remodelling ASEAN Contract Law: By Creating ASEAN'S Own Contract Law or by Adoption [of] the Unidroit Principles (2012) 12 *Law Review (Universitas Pelita Harapan)* 215, 236 (http://dspace.library.uph.edu:8080/handle/123456789/1092).

[14] D. E. Allan et al. (eds. 1969), *Asian Contract Law: A Survey of Current Problems*; see also Hiscock (n. 7) 358–360.

[15] D. E. Allan et al. (eds. 1969), Preface in *Asian Contract Law* (ibid.) ix, x. The book does contain, in addition to overview chapters for civil and common law respectively, a brief chapter on Adat contract law; ibid. at 72–78.

[16] Ibid.

[17] See also D. Heydon, Review, (1971) 34 *Modern Law Review* 118–120.

In the PACL project, this question of how Asian a project of Asian contract law should be has been discussed, generating different answers. On the one side stands Shiyuan Han from Tsinghua University in Beijing, head of the Chinese delegation. He supports a specifically Asian nature for the PACL, suggesting that 'the PACL as a model law should not be a simple copy of the PICC or the PECL',[18] because 'the CISG was designed by European and American scholars and specialists. It reflects mainly the experiences of the Western world. For East Asian people, it is still necessary for Asian scholars to produce an Asian voice'.[19] '[T]o "uphold the ideal of a restatement" means to draft a set of rules and principles appropriate for Asian people'.[20] As a consequence, 'if the PACL's position is consistent with the custom of Asia and different from the position of the CISG, we should rethink whether the CISG sufficiently addresses Asian customs'.[21] Indeed, Han finds such Asian specificities, for example in the creditor's right of subrogation and right of revocation, and in unilateral, as opposed to bilateral, release from a contract.[22] His consequence for the working method is that the project would necessarily be thorough and take a long time.[23] In particular, it is necessary, in his view, to base the PACL on thorough comparative law of existing Asian laws, in order to make them compatible with what merchants are already aware of. Rules that are 'appropriate for Asian people' should not, in his view, be too simple and abstract, or they will be of no use to judges.

On the other side stands Naoki Kanayama from Keio University in Japan, head of the Japanese delegation. He does not disagree that the PACL should sometimes diverge from existing European models like PICC or PECL. However, his explanation is not a specific Asian character of the law, but a specific stage of modernity. Kanayama suggests that contemporary Asian law, and by implication the PACL, are by their nature European, and the difference between Japanese law and German or French law is not greater than the difference between French Law and German law. Law in Asia is an import from Europe, he suggests, but that does not imply inferiority: frequently copies can be better than originals. Kanayama calls any specifically Asian character of the PACL a 'pure illusion'[24] and suggests that not a single properly Asian element can be found in them,[25] just as he suggests that the Japanese Civil Code has no particularly Asian quality.[26] As a consequence, Kanayama proposes that the PACL could be written relatively quickly, given that European and international methods already existed. The result and that the

---

[18] Han (n. 7) 593.
[19] Han (n. 7) 591.
[20] Han (n. 7) 593.
[21] Han (n. 7) 592; similarly Ka (n. 7) 65.
[22] Han (n. 7) 598.
[23] Ibid.
[24] N. Kanayama, Quel dialogue? (n. 7) 192–193.
[25] Ibid. at 194. For a largely similar view from the head of the Korea delegation, see Lee, Introduction (n. 7).
[26] N. Kanayama, Le caractère non-occidental du Minpo, mythe ou réalité ?, in P. Brunet et al. (eds.), Recontre franco-japonaise autour des transferts de concepts juridiqyes (2014) 31–38.

emphasis should be on the formulation of simple and clear rules without extensive notes, more like the French Civil Code than the US Restatement.[27] This became indeed the method followed by the Japanese working group under his leadership.

What to make of this debate between Han and Kanayama? Is it idiosyncratic? Or does it reflect a deeper debate about the Asian nature of Asian law, a debate that would be instructive also to the Western observer? It seems to me that through the debate we can see remnants of a fundamental disagreement. It does not merely go to policy questions, a balancing between local culture and global commonality. Rather, it addresses the very question of what would even make a project like the PACL Asian, what it would mean for the project to be Asian. And it reflects very different ideas of what that might mean.

3 A EUROPEAN ASIA: ORIENTALISM AND MODERNIZATION

What makes Asian law Asian? The first answer: the West does. As Chinese historian Wang Hui puts it: 'Historically speaking, the idea of Asia is not Asian but, rather, European'.[28] Asia, was a name given by outsiders, Europeans – first to depict a miniscule part of today's Asia, later extended to the entire continent. Term and concept did not arrive in East Asia before the Jesuits; they did not gain wide currency before the nineteenth century.[29] Today, Asia describes, technically, the part of the Eurasian land mass that is on the other side than Europe from the Ural, an enormous territory with a multitude of cultures and countries and laws. In common parlance, however, Asia is often used in a narrower sense to describe East Asia, possibly in connection with South East Asia. In each case, Asia is a construct, and a primarily Western construct at that. And it is, at the same time, a geographical entity and a cultural concept.[30]

As Asia is a Western concept, so is the idea of 'Asian' law (as opposed to Chinese, or Buddhist, etc.). Courses in 'Asian' or 'East Asian' law have long been taught primarily in Europe and the United States, not in Asia.[31] Chairs and Centres for 'Asian law' exist in Europe and the United States, not in Asia, at least traditionally. At the National University of Singapore (which calls itself 'Asia's Global Law School'),[32] the Asian Law Institute, which brings together law schools all across Asia, the Centre for Asian Legal

---

[27] Kanayama, Mélanges Baudouin (n. 7) 406.

[28] Wang Hui, The Politics of Imagining Asia: A Genealogical Analysis (transl. Matthew A. Hale), (2007) 8 *Intra-Asia Cultural Studies* 1–33, 2; Ralph Weber, On Wang Hui's Re-imagination of Asia and Europe, (2009) 17 *Europa Regional* 221–228.

[29] C. W. A. Szpilman and S. Saaler, Pan-Asianism as an Ideal of Asian Identity and Solidarity, 1850–Present, *Asia-Pacific Journal* 9.17.1 (25 April 2011).

[30] See T. Ruskola, Where Is Asia? When Is Asia? Theorizing Comparative Law and International Law, (2011) 44 *U.C. Davis L. Rev.* 879.

[31] See, e.g., Chin Kim, Asian Law and Comparative Legal Studies: A Proposed Curriculum Design, (1982) 5 *B.C. Int'l & Comp. L. Rev.* 91; Whitmore Gray, The Challenge of Asian Law, (1995) 19 *Fordham Int'l L.J.* 1–8.

[32] Simon Chesterman, The Fall and Rise of Legal Education in Singapore (2017) *Singapore Journal of Legal Studies* 201, 208–210.

Studies, and the Asian Journal of Comparative law, which it publishes, represent recent developments. The study of Asian law is also promoted elsewhere.[33]

If Asian law is primarily a Western concept, what is its content? Essentially, there are two variants of such concepts. One is the idea of an essential difference: Asia is the opposite of Europe; it is everything that Europe is not.[34] The strongest version of this view is the one that suggests that Asia has no law at all. We do indeed find such suggestions in scholarship. René David explained that in the Far East, especially in China, law is only for barbarians, an opposition against law that is explained both with Confucian and with Maoist thought.[35] Zweigert and Kötz posit, somewhat more cautiously, that law matters, but not too much: informal means of dispute resolution are much more important. (They concede, in the third edition, that things are changing.[36]) Patrick Glenn sees Asian law as characterized especially by a relative absence of law, an emphasis on social harmony and a high importance of informal dispute resolution mechanisms.[37] Ugo Mattei defines Asian law as traditional law, apparently in opposition to Western 'professional' law.[38]

This view is now rightly viewed as problematic for a variety of reasons: it overestimates (ancient) history and underestimates modern law in Asia, it reads even that ancient history only partially, and it uses as universal a notion of law that is intrinsically Western.[39] The claim that formal law is irrelevant is certainly overrated for modern Asian legal systems. The frequent claim that Asians prefer informal dispute resolution mechanisms, for example, highlights cultural constraints at the cost of institutional conditions. The view is also problematic in its disproportionate focus on ancient history over contemporary developments. The focus on Confucianism tends to prioritize the past over the present and continuity over disruption; it also ignores the many other ideas and values that have shaped Asia.[40]

---

[33] E.g. S. Y. Kim, The Necessity and the Methodology of Studies on Asian Law (2004) 1 *Asia Law Review* 1–19.
[34] See Ruskola, Where Is Asia? (n. 30).
[35] René David, John E. C. Brierley, *Major Legal Systems in the World Today* (3rd ed., 1985) 30; see René David, Existe-t-il un Droit Occidental?, in *Twentieth Century Comparative and Conflicts Law: Legal Essays in Honor of Hessel E. Yntem* (1961) 56, 60. Similarly, e.g. Michael Bogdan, *Concise Introduction to Comparative Law* Ch. 13; Peter de Cruz, *Comparative Law in a Changing World* (3rd ed., 2007) 209–210.
[36] Konrad Zweigert and Hein Kötz, *Introduction to Comparative Law* (3rd ed. 1998, Tony Weir transl.) 287–288.
[37] H. Patrick Glenn, *Legal Traditions of the World* (5th ed., 2014) ch. 9, pp. 319ff.
[38] U. Mattei, Three Patterns of Law: Taxonomy and Change in the World's Legal Systems, Am. J. Comp. L. 45 (1997) 5, 35ff.
[39] See, especially, T. Ruskola, Legal Orientalism (2013); see also N. P. Ho, Internationalizing and Historicizing Hart's Theory of Law, (2017) 10 *Wash. U. Jurisprudence Rev.* 183. For differentiated conceptions in the introductory comparative law literature, see Dong Jiang, An Introduction to Chinese Legal Culture, in S. Koch et al. (eds.), *Comparing Legal Cultures* (2017) 317, 327ff; M. Siems, *Comparative Law* (2nd ed., 2018) 94–96.
[40] See C. Antons, What Is 'Asian Law'? Asia in Law, the Humanities and Social Sciences, in *Routledge Handbook of Asian Law* (2017) 3–27.

A different Western concept of Asian law responds and goes to the other extreme, viewing contemporary Asian law as essentially similar to Western law. From this perspective, laws in Asia can safely be understood as either civil law or common law; after the effective decline of communism, this is thought true even for Vietnam and China. The widely influential 'Legal Origins' project sees only civil law and common law (and communist law) as legal families across the globe.[41] From this perspective, the biggest conflict among Asian laws is, ironically, a quintessentially European conflict, namely that between civil and common law.[42]

That approach is quite obviously also problematic: it underestimates the other legal cultures that shape law in Asia, and it underestimates the fact that Western law, born against the specific cultural, political and economic background of the West, operates very differently in Asian circumstances. The suggestion that laws in Asia are, essentially, no different from Western laws, makes sense only for a focus on formal law that ignores the interplay between formal law and society. Below the surface of formal rules, laws in Asian countries differ significantly from those in the West.[43]

A third type of view suggests a middle way. Both other views, in this view, err in opposite directions, and the truth is in the middle: Asian law is a little bit like European law and a little bit not. Or, a variant of this, Asian law is formally, on the surface, very much like European law, but substantively (as 'living law') is different. This view seems more accurate. But it is also imprecise and unsatisfactory to find that Asian law is somewhat like and somewhat unlike European law. And the distinction between form and substance is actually problematic as well. Does such a distance not exist in Europe?

There is no need, here, to decide this. What matters more is to see how all three concepts, although in some ways diametrically opposed, actually suffer from common shortcomings. Both views, that of difference and that of similarity, define Asian law primarily by its relation to Western law. They take European law as the universal standard against which Asian law as the particular is measured. Moreover, both exist against an assumed universal historical trajectory from informal to formal law; they only differ on how far along Asian law is on this trajectory. The main problem of such visions is, put simply, that it cannot take Asian law seriously on its own terms: it becomes a mere projection of Western ideas.

[41] Rafael La Porta et al., The Economic Consequences of Legal Origins, *Journal of Economic Literature* 2008, 46:2, 285–332.

[42] See, e.g., Mary Hiscock, *Remodelling Asian Laws*, in *Indonesia: Bankruptcy, Law Reform & the Commercial Court* (Tim Lindsey ed., 2000) 28–42; Margaret Fordham, Comparative Legal Traditions – Introducing the Common Law to Civil Lawyers in Asia, (2006) 1 *Asian Journal of Comparative Law* 1:11; Alexander Loke, Insights from Comparing the Contract Laws of Asia on Formation and Third Party Beneficiaries, in Chen-Wishart, Loke, Vogenauer (n. 12) 516–545; see also K. H. Ng and B. Jacobson, How Global is the Common Law? A Comparative Study of Asian Common Law Systems – Hong Kong, Malaysia, and Singapore, (2017) 12 *Asian Journal of Comparative Law* 209.

[43] M. Chiba (ed.), *Asian Indigenous Law in Interaction with Received Law* (1986).

A related problem is equally important: By defining Asian law purely in juxtaposition to Western law, it is given a unity that it does not have on its own. Patrick Glenn, in earlier editions of his book on comparative legal traditions, conceded that 'Asia may exist more in Western thinking than in Asian' and nonetheless posited the existence of 'a kind of Asian default position, which must necessarily address all the particular traditions which the people of Asia have known'.[44] After it was suggested to him that the concept is far too broad and what he means is, essentially, Chinese law,[45] Glenn replaced in later editions the 'Asian legal tradition' with a 'Confucian legal tradition' where the focus explicitly narrows to China.[46] And yet even a narrower East Asian legal tradition may today be a questionable entity, at least when compared to a Western legal tradition: even East Asia is more diverse in ideological, cultural and religious terms than Europe.[47] Nonetheless, in such presentations, Japan's place is unsure and Korean law is mostly absent altogether.[48]

In the end, then, both the idea of Asian law as essentially different from and that of Asian law as essentially similar to Western law, suffer from the same shortcomings: they define Asian law only in relation to Western law, and they therefore ascribe to it a level of internal homogeneity and identity that are more projections than actual empirical truths. Asia is not Europe, but Asia is also not simply the opposite of Europe. These are not promising avenues.

But is this already the whole story? Is a cultural identity of Asian law really merely a European projection?[49] Can we not find traces also within Asia? The European projections are not fully without an object, even though they define the object in problematic ways. They are constructs, but constructs have their own reality in the world. And although they were originally imposed on Asia from the outside, they spurred inner-Asian alternative concepts.[50] When we comparative lawyers attempt, to the extent we can, to understand debates from the inside rather than from the outside, we find inner-Asian projects of Asian identity of law, too.

---

[44] H. Patrick Glenn, *Legal Traditions of the World: Sustainable Diversity in Law* (2nd ed., 2004) 301ff.
[45] Andrew Huxley, Buddhist Law, Asian Law, Eurasian Law, (2006) *Journal of Comparative Law* 158, 160f; see also Uwe Kischel, *Rechtsvergleichung* (2015) § 9 no. 3.
[46] See H. Patrick Glenn, *Legal Traditions of the World: Sustainable Diversity in Law* (5th ed., 2014) 319ff.
[47] See Teemu Ruskola, The East Asian Legal Tradition, in Mauro Bussani, Ugo Mattei (eds.), *The Cambridge Companion to Comparative Law* 257, 275f; see also Konrad Zweigert and Hein Kötz, *An Introduction to Comparative Law* (3rd ed., 1998) 287–288.
[48] C. K. Choi, Western Jurists on Korean Law: A Historical Survey, (2002) 2 *Journal of Korean Law* 167–193; also in Choi, *Law and Justice in Korea* (2005) 15ff.
[49] This is the tendency, e.g., in Gayatri Chakravrty Spivak, Our Asias – 2001: How to Be a Continentalist, in *Other Asias* (Wiley-Blackwell, 2007) 209ff.
[50] See P. Korhonen, Common Culture: Asia Rhetoric in the Beginning of the 20th century, (2008) 9 *Inter-Asia Cultural Studies* 395; P. Duara, Asia Redux: Conceptualizing a Region for Our Times (2010) 69(4) *Journal of Asian Studies* 963.

4 A CHINESE ASIA: SINOCENTRIC LAW

A first candidate for an Asian identity parallels the idea of difference. Such ideas of difference have often focused on China as stand-in for China, and indeed China is important for such concepts. Recall how Professor Han, in his presentation of the PACL, emphasizes China's leadership (he refers to the founding document as the Beijing declaration[51]) and requests that it be sensitive to the multiculturalism to be found in Asia. These are contemporary suggestions, but they implicitly relate to older ideas about Asia.

The first of these ideas is the old idea of China as the Middle Kingdom, the centre of a potentially universal political order. It established a view of China as a universal kingdom, which covered the entire (known) world (*tianxia*). The historical expression of that idea was the tributary system of the Ming and Qing dynasties.[52] Boundaries were social rather than geographical; the main distinction was that between civilization and barbarity, and the latter was defined by a refusal to accept the values of Chinese culture. Chinese hierarchy rested on power, but that power was mainly perceived to be cultural: China ruled (allegedly) not because it was powerful but because it had the superior culture.[53] Those nations that accepted this superiority engaged in tributary relations with the Chinese emperor, but these were, at least rhetorically, conceived less in terms of colonialism and subjugation and more on the basis of values: an autonomous acceptance of Chinese superiority on the one side, a government based on values on the other.[54] The result, again somewhat idealistically, was a multicultural universalism: joined by the focus on China and the commitment to certain (Confucian) ideas, but otherwise internally plural. A 'Beijing declaration' for the PACL can be viewed as a continuity of such ideas.

The tributary system, of course, largely disappeared, at least for some time. The inherent multiculturalism, by contrast, was revived in connection with the influence of communism, the second important background idea. After World War I, Asian intellectuals became disenchanted when they realized that Wilsonian principles of self-determination were largely confined to European nations. Western nationalism was abhorred by many, both as representing everything that was bad about a Western fascination with rationality at the cost of culture, spirituality, and community, and as underlying the colonialist project. Leninism provided an alternative. Lenin had

---

[51] Han (n. 7) 590.
[52] For scholarship linking the concept to the present, see, e.g., Li Zhaojie, Traditional Chinese World Order (2020) 20 *Chinese JIL* 1 at 24ff; Fei-Ling Wang, From Tianxia to Westphalia: The Evolving Chinese Conception of Sovereignty and World Order, in G.J. Ikenberry, W. Jisi, Z. Feng (eds.), *America, China, and the Struggle for World Order: Asia Today* (2015) 43–68; see also C. W. Phil Chan, China, State Sovereignty and International Legal Order (2015).
[53] See John K. Fairbank, Tributary Trade and China's Relation with the West (1942) 1 *Far Eastern Quarterly* 129.
[54] Whether this is more a self-serving mythization than a historical fact is a different matter; see Peter C. Perdue, The Tenacious Tributary System, (2015) 24 *Journal of Contemporary China* 1002.

celebrated a revolutionary awakening of Asia as early as 1913.[55] His interest in Asia came from the hope of building alliances against Western capitalist nations, and of spurring revolutions in Asia rather than, as classical theory had predicted, in Europe. Asian attraction to Leninism on the other hand came not just from the opposition to the West as such. It also promised an alternative to the Western type of state and law, and an embrace of a multicultural idea of Empire, in accordance with similar such suggestions from Asia, most prominently perhaps by Sun-Yat Sen.[56] Unlike *tianxia*, this now was an explicit idea of an Asian identity, one opposed to European concepts.[57]

The consequence was, for some time, that law in several Asian countries bore some similarities to Chinese and, by extension, Soviet law. Soviet laws were transplanted early, in the short-lived Chinese Soviet Republic (1931–1934)[58] Socialist law became influential again after revolutions in China, Vietnam, and other countries.[59] Much of this borrowing occurred from the Soviet Union, not from China per se, given that Maoist law was more informal than the (civil-law based) law in the Soviet Union.[60] Yet, when China began to formalize its law after 1978 in a way different from both Europe and the Soviet Union, the new 'socialist law with Chinese characteristics'[61] became influential. Such Chinese ideas of law have competed, among socialist countries, with more Soviet Union–oriented laws. In North Korea, Soviet and Chinese legal influence coexisted.[62] Vietnam's legal development, especially in the rule of law context, followed more along China's model than a presumed universal Western model, searching for Confucian values for a move forward.[63]

[55] V. I. Lenin, The Awakening of Asia, Pravda No. 103, May 7, 1913, translation at www.marxists.org/archive/lenin/works/1913/may/07b.htm; Lenin, Backward Europe and Advanced Asia, Pravda No. 113, May 18, 1913, translation at www.marxists.org/archive/lenin/works/1913/may/18.htm; see Shinkichi Etō, China's International Relations 1911–1931, in John K Fairbank and Albert Feuerwerker (eds.), *The Cambridge History of China Vol. 13 – Republican China 1912–1949, Part 2* (1986) 74 at 107ff.
[56] See Wang Hui, The Politics of Imagining Asia: A Genealogical Analysis, (2007) 8 *Inter-Asia Cultural Studies* 1, 12–13.
[57] Ibid., 11; see also Fei-Ling Wang, *The China Order – Centralia, World Empire, and the Nature of Chinese Power* (2017) 209ff.
[58] W. E. Butler (ed.), *The Legal System of the Chinese Soviet Republic 1931–1934* (1983).
[59] B. N. Son, The Law of China and Vietnam in Comparative Perspective, (2017) 41 *Fordham International Law Journal* 135, 153ff.
[60] S. C. Leng, The Role of Law in the People's Republic of China as Reflecting Mao Tse-Tung's Influence, (1977) 68 *Journal of Criminal Law and Criminology* 356–373.
[61] M. Zhang, The Socialist Legal System with Chinese Characteristics: China's Discourse for the Rule of Law and a Bitter Experience, (2010) 24 *Temple Int'l & Comp. L.J.* 1–64; Zhu Jingwen, The Socialist Legal System with Chinese Characteristics: Its Structure, Features and Trends, (2011) 32 *Social Sciences in China* 87–103; English translation at http://en.theorychina.org/xsqy_2477/201306/t20130611_270446.shtml.
[62] See D. C. Zook, Reforming North Korea: Law, Politics, and the Market Economy (2012) 48 *Stan. J. Int'l L.* 131.
[63] D. N. Pham, Confucianism and the Conception of the Law in Vietnam, in J. Gillespie and P. Nicholson (eds.), *Asian Socialism and Legal Change: The Dynamics of Vietnamese and Chinese*

Although both the tribute system and communism have withered, this idea of a plural Asian law under Chinese leadership is arguably still present, most prominently in the current Belt and Road project.[64] The project focuses on transnational trade and infrastructure, linking up to seventy countries in Asia, Europe and Africa. A project like this also requires law, and it is in this law that we can see a revival of a traditional sinocentric concept of Asian law. To some extent, it may look as though China merely attempts to impose its own law on the initiative. The Chinese government has announced the establishment of three special courts: one for the silk road in Xi'an, one for the maritime road in Shenzhen and a headquarters based in Beijing.[65] In addition, a Belt and Road International Dispute Management Centre will assist existing arbitration centres.[66] A push is being made to establish Chinese, rather than English, law as the regularly applied law in arbitration.[67] The Chinese Supreme Court has issued no less than sixteen 'guiding opinions' as information on how to handle legal issues concerning the Belt and Road Initiative.[68]

But the idea does not appear to be merely to expand the application of Chinese law. The concept endorsed by the Chinese government is not Chinese domination but rather 'bringing the outside in' (*youwai zhinei*). In this sense, the project is a sinocentric network – respecting difference, but under the leadership of China, and thus ideally enhancing China's power without limiting that of its neighbours.[69] Xi Jinping explicitly advocated the project as one for a 'community of shared destiny' – an Asian dream, within which each country and region is entitled to its own particular dreams.[70] The International Academy of the Belt and Road published a book titled *The Dispute Resolution Mechanism for the Belt and Road*, which proposes a new system to 'make up for the existing system and formulate a mechanism that can better reflect the culture, customs, traditions, legal systems and values of the countries along

Reform (2005) 76ff; see also J. Gillespie, Changing Concepts of Socialist Law in Vietnam, ibid. 45, 61ff.

[64] T. Miller, *China's Asian Dream – Empire Building along the New Silk Road* (2017).
[65] www.merics.org/en/blog/dispute-settlement-chinas-terms-beijings-new-belt-and-road-courts.
[66] Ibid.
[67] See also more generally on the role for arbitration T. Yu, China's 'One Belt, One Road Initiative': What's in It for Law Firms and Lawyers? (2017) 5(1) *Chinese Journal of Comparative Law* 1; P. M. Norton, China's Belt and Road Initiative: Challenges for Arbitration in Asia, (2018) 13 *U. Pa. Asian L. Rev.* 72; J. Z. Tao and M. Zhong, The Changing Rules of International Dispute Resolution in China's Belt and Road Initiative, in W. Zhang, I. Alon, and C. Lattemann (eds.), *China's Belt and Road Initiative* (2018) 305–320.
[68] See https://cgc.law.stanford.edu/belt-and-road/. More generally on the concept of guiding cases, see X. L. Chen, China's Guiding Case System – A Study on the Mechanisms of Rule Formation, (2014) 1 *Peking University Law Journal* 215–258; J. T. Deng, Functional Analysis of China's Guiding Cases, (2016) 14 *China: An International Journal* 44–70.
[69] W. A. Callahan, China's 'Asia Dream' – The Belt Road Initiative and the New Regional Order, (2016) 1 *Asia Journal of Comparative Politics* 226–243.
[70] Ibid. at 235.

the Belt and Road'.[71] Such calls for mutual coordination, under the leadership of China, are more reminiscent of the tributary system than of a mere imposition of Chinese law.[72] This looks like a sinocentric, not merely Chinese, model of Asian law – one that rests on cooperation rather than legal unification and on attention to cultural differences rather than homogenization.

The project is not confined to Asia; it includes African and European countries, as well as countries in the Pacific. Further, although it is not explicitly directed against the West at large (though it does suggest an alternative to US domination). What makes it Asian is the fact that it is presented as an alternative to a particular Western conception of both economics and of international relations; the initiative is explicitly advertised as an alternative to Western neoliberalism.[73]

5 A JAPANESE ASIA: PAN-ASIAN LAW

If the sinocentric idea of Asian law is one of difference, then a another idea of Asian law emphasizes similarity. Arguably, Prof. Kanayama's quite different ideas of an Asian nature of the PACL, or rather the lack thereof, also have a broader background, though one to be found, originally, in Europe. His preference for a brief and abstract style of codification reflects experience with a European model, namely the French Civil Code, and reflects his own specialization: Prof. Kanayama holds a chair in French law at his University. His idea of a restatement that is detached from local culture, potentially universal, reflects similar ideas of the French civil code.[74] And altogether, the suggestion that an Asian Restatement can be modelled closely after European models, only to improve on them where they appear deficient, reflects the old Japanese idea of emulating Europe in order to surpass it.

This idea of Asia is reminiscent of earlier Japanese ideas of Pan-Asianism.[75] Indeed, although the idea of Asia emerged in Europe, it spurred a counterconcept

---

[71] https://beltandroad.blog/2017/11/26/how-will-china-shape-the-legal-future-of-belt-and-road/; see also G. G. Wang, The Belt and Road Initiative in Quest for a Dispute Resolution Mechanism, (2017) 25 *Asia-Pacific Law Review* 1–16.

[72] See also S. Y. Pan and J. T. Y. Lo, Re-conceptualizing China's Rise as a Global Power: A Neo-tributary Perspective, (2017) 30 *The Pacific Review* 1. Tianxia has been proposed as a general model for global governance, especially in Zhao Tingyang, Rethinking Empire from a Chinese Concept 'All-under-Heaven' (Tian-xia), January 2006 *Social Identities* Vol. 12, No. 1, pp. 29–41; see also W. A. Callahan, Chinese Visions of World Order: Post-hegemonic or a New Hegemony?, (2008) 10 *International Studies Review* 749–761; Zhang Feng, The Tianxia System: World Order in a Chinese Utopia, (2010) 4 *Global Asia*: 108–112; Prasenjit Duara, The Chinese World Order and Planetary Sustainability, in Ban Wenq (ed.), *Chinese Visions of World Order: Tianxia, Culture, and World Politics* (2017).

[73] He Yafei, 'Belt & Road' v. Liberal Order (2017) 34 *New Perspectives Quarterly* 31.

[74] See Ralf Michaels, Code vs Code: Nationalist and Internationalist Images of the Code Civil in the French Resistance to a European Codification, (2012) 8 *European Review of Contract Law* 277.

[75] For an excellent collection of translated primary texts, see Sven Saaler and Christopher W.A. Szpilman (eds.), *Pan-Asianism – A Documentary History* (2 vols., Rowman & Littlefield, 2011). Useful summaries are Sun Ge (transl. Hui Shiu-Lun and Lau Kinchi), How Does Asia Mean? 1 *Inter-Asia Cultural Studies* 13–47 (Part I), 319–341 (Part II).

in Asia, as a concept not to extend European influence but to resist it, as a promise of an identity that could be opposed to, withstand, that of Europe (and, slightly later, America). Japan had, in the nineteenth century, viewed the subjugation of once-mighty China with a sense of horror, fearing a similar fate for itself. Not long after Commodore Perry forced Japan to open its ports for trade and the Tokugawa regime crumbled, the country, under the new Meiji regime, responded with a radical response of modernization – and that meant Westernization. This modernization included all aspects of public life, including, of course, the law. Japanese lawyers travelled to Europe and the United States in order to learn about Western laws. Professorships were established for various Western law: French law, common law, German law.[76] And, of course, Japan adopted a whole series of new codes in civil and criminal law, strongly influenced Western, especially French and German law.[77]

This well-known story has led comparative layers, not only from abroad, to proclaim that Japanese law would be, simply, civil law; it is still often described as such, also by Japanese scholars themselves.[78] This suggests why we can think of Asian law as Western. But that, as we know, is misleading. First, the adoption of European law required a significant translation.[79] Necessarily, even at the level of official law, Japanese law became a careful combination of foreign and domestic elements. Translations of civil codes were difficult because the concepts used were unfamiliar, down to basic issues like the concept of rights.[80] The civil code may be mostly an amalgam of French and German law,[81] but the family system was based on traditional Japanese customs. Similarly, the Constitution was largely Prussian, but state Shintoism as the underlying constitutional identity, codified in the Rescript of Education, was intrinsically local.[82]

---

[76] Kenzo Takanyagi, Contact of the Common Law with the Civil Law in Japan, (1955) 4 *Am. J. Comp. L.* 60–69, 60.

[77] Harald Baum, Comparison of Law, Transfer of Legal Concepts, and Creation of a Legal Design: The Case of Japan, in John O. Haley and Toshiko Takenaka (eds.), *Legal Innovations in Asia: Judicial Lawmaking and the Influence of Comparative Law* (2014) 67ff; comprehensively, *A History of Law in Japan since 1868* (Wilhelm Röhl ed., 2005).

[78] See N. Hozumi, *Lectures on the New Japanese Civil Code as Materials for the Study of Comparative Jurisprudence* (Tokyo, 1904) 19.

[79] Ko Hasegawa, Normative Translation in the Heterogeneity of Law, (2015) 6 *Transnational Legal Theory* 501–517.

[80] See Ken Mukai and Nobuyoshi Toshitani, The Progress and Problems of Compiling the Civil Code in the Early Meiji Era, in *Law in Japan* Vol. 1 (1967) 25, 49–50; Yu-Cheol Shin, Übersetzungsprobleme bei der Rezeption europäischer Rechte in Ostasien, in Martin Josef Schermaier/Werner Gephart (eds.), *Rezeption und Rechtskulturwandel. Europäische Rechtstraditionen in Ostasien und Russland* (2016) 35–55.

[81] Béatrice Jaluzot, Les origines du Code civil japonais, (2015) 40 Journal of Japanese Law 121–146.

[82] On the Rescript's return to national debate, see recently Shaun O'Dwyer, What's So Bad about Imperial Rescript on Education Anyway?, *Japan Times*, 19 March 2017, www.japantimes.co.jp/opinion/2017/03/19/commentary/japan-commentary/whats-bad-imperial-rescript-education-anyway.

Second, the Westernization of Japan and the Westernization of Japanese law must be understood within the broader context of politics, including geopolitics, of the time. Japan did not simply join the West, and Japanese law did not simply join the civil law tradition. Western observers easily overlook that Westernization was not meant to enable Japan to join the West; it was meant to strengthen Japan so it could withstand Western colonization. The Western secularized and centralized state with its bureaucracy served as a forceful model of state success, and as a reason for the military success of European countries in colonizing much of the world. Whatever (cultural) superiority the Japanese saw for themselves, that superiority did not translate into competitiveness. The Meiji regime adopted elements of the Western state in view of its superior effectivity, but the goal was not so far to emulate the West as to keep it at bay. Adopting this model meant, for Japan, to step up to a similar level of development, and to achieve a similar level of strength.

This interest clearly underlays law reform. One important goal of codification of civil law was to move beyond the unequal treaties that Japan, like China, had entered into with Western powers.[83] Under these treaties, foreigners were exempt from the jurisdiction of Japanese courts and the application of Japanese law because these courts and laws were considered inferior and therefore not acceptable for Westerners. The ensuing system of extraterritoriality, under which Western countries had their own courts for their citizens in Japan, created a situation considered unbearable for a Japanese sense of pride and sovereignty. That created an important reason for the Westernization of Japanese laws.[84]

This means that the Westernization of Japanese law did not lead to a submission to the West but rather the opposite: it was an anticolonialist move in that it justified the application of (albeit Westernized) Japanese law to Westerners. What looks like Western law imposed on Japan is actually appropriated law that becomes, through the process of Japanization, Japanese law.[85]

Early-twentieth-century Japanese attitudes can be grouped, with some simplification, into two seemingly opposite positions: 'leaving Asia' and 'leading Asia'.[86] The first idea, that of leaving Asia, is most famously linked to Yukichi Fukuzawa's famous plea, in an editorial, for 'Shedding Asia'.[87] Fukuzawa – whose now-famous essay was

[83] See Michael R. Auslin, *Negotiating with Imperialism – The Unequal Treaties and the Culture of Japanese Diplomacy* (2004).
[84] Tokichi Masao, The New Civil Code of Japan, (1897) 18 *Arena* 64–69, 64; Kazuo Hatoyama, The Civil Code of Japan Compared with the French Civil Code, (1902) 11 *Yale LJ* 296–303, 298.
[85] H. Coing (ed.), *Die Japanisierung des westlichen Rechts* (The Japanisierung of Western Law) (1990); Jean-Louis Halpérin. Transplants of European Normativity in India and in Japan: A Historical Comparison, (2014) 22 *Rechtsgeschichte* 150–157.
[86] Miwa Kimitada, Pan-Asianism in Modern Japan – Nationalism, Regionalism and Universalism, in Sven Saaler and J. Victor Koschmann (eds.), *Pan Asianism in Modern Japanese History – Colonialism, Regionalism and Borders* (Routledge, 2007) 21–33.
[87] Dwight Tat Wai Kwok, *A Translation of Datsu-Aron: Decoding a Prewar Japanese Nationalistic Theory* (MA thesis, University of Toronto, 2009) 25ff. See Urs Matthias Zachmann, Blowing Up

hardly discussed before it was revived after the Second World War[88] – did not call for joining Europe, however, and the Asia he wanted to leave behind was only the old Asia which had been unable to withstand Europe. The idea of leading Asia, on the other hand, draws on Japan's modernization and new confidence, leading to claims for a united Asia – with Japan as its leader. 'Asia is one' proclaimed Okakura in 1903,[89] and this Asia was formulated as an alternative to Europe: Okakura juxtaposed the Western racist concept of a 'yellow peril' with the countercomplaint over a 'white disaster'. From a closer perspective, therefore, both positions are closer to each other than one might think: for each of them, the old Asia has to be left behind and Japan has to endorse modernization. In this sense, the seeming opposition against Asia formulated by Fukuzawa does not stand in complete opposition to the voices of others who argued for an Asian identity.[90]

Underlying this new Pan-Asianism was a (largely counterfactual) suggestion that Asia was racially and culturally uniform – and that its racial and cultural features were, largely, those of Japan. It was such ideas that were used for the subsequent Japanese colonization of large parts of East Asia and its role in World War II. Pan-Asianism and the subsequent colonization project represented a remarkable intellectual step, described by one scholar as 'Japan's orient'.[91] Orientalist ideas about Asia, expressed at first by Europeans and imposed on Asia, were adopted and appropriated by intellectuals and politicians in Japan and elsewhere in Asia themselves. They thereby expanded on the European construct of a largely uniform Asia, in need of development through colonization.[92] What differed was that now Japan, rather than Western powers, had the role of bringing about this development. What did not differ was that this idea of an Asian homogenous identity was a construct, built more on ideology than on empirical facts. The result was a curious, arguably internally incoherent, concept: Japanese Pan-Asianism rejected the West and at the same time adopted its tools and mechanism; it criticized the Western sense of racial and cultural superiority of Westerners over Asians, and at the same time endorsed a sense of superiority of Japanese over other nations in Asia. In this way, it also created mixed reactions among those other Asian nations: they admired the Japanese resistance to the West and its endorsement of a Pan-Asian civilization that could

---

a Double Portrait in Black and White: The Concept of Asia in the Writings of Fukuzawa Yukichi and Okakura Tenshin, (Fall 2007) 15 *Positions: East Asia Cultures Critique* 2:345–368.

[88] Hirayama Yō, *Fukuzawa Yukichi no shinjitsu* (2004), as discussed in Akiko Uchiyama, Translation as Representation – Fukuzawa Yukichi's Representation of the 'Others', in John Milton and Paul Fadio Bandia (eds.), *Agents of Translation* (2009) 63ff.

[89] Okakura Kakuzō, *The Ideals of the East, with Special Reference to the Art of Japan* (1903) 1.

[90] This point is made by Pekka Korhonen, Leaving Asia? The Meaning of Datsu-A and Japan's Modern History, (2013) 11 *Asia-Pacific Journal* 50:1ff. (2013). On Fukuzawa and Okakura and the convergence of their thoughts, see, e.g., Sun Ge, How Does Asia Mean? (Part 1), (2000) 1 *Inter-Asia Cultural Studies* 13–47.

[91] Stefan Tanake, *Japan's Orient: Rendering Pasts into History* (1993).

[92] E.g. Chao-Ju Chen, Producing 'Lack as Tradition': A Feminist Critique of Legal Orientalism in Colonial Taiwan, (2013) 1 *Comparative Legal History* 186–210.

overcome the West, and they opposed a Japanese imperialism that continued the work of Western imperialists.

Pan-Asianism spurred ideas for what can well be called Pan-Asian law: a project of law convergence in Asia, modelled on Japanese law. Japanese imperialism is often, for obvious reasons, compared to the German Nazis. Yet at least insofar as law is concerned law, the more apt comparison may be with Napoleonic France. The Nazis had no great interest in exporting their laws; they were generally suspicious of law. Napoleon, by contrast, not only saw the Civil Code as one of his main achievements; he also actively advocated for its adoption as a European code – an odd amalgamation of a nationalist and transnationalist ideal.[93] And indeed, the French civil Code was adopted elsewhere through different means – sometimes through conquest, sometimes through persuasion, sometimes through inspiration.[94]

We can find similar developments with regards to Western law as adopted by Japan. In the same way in which Japanese expansion in Asia represented an internal colonization, its export of Japanese laws created a secondary wave of transplant of civil law. To some extent, it was exported through conquest as a consequence of Japanese imperialism. After colonizing Taiwan in 1895, the Japanese reformed Taiwanese law, first through a mixture of civil-law-based ideas of customary law and colonial laws; later through a direct expansion of Japanese law – and thus, indirectly, on a civil law model.[95] The situation in Korea was somewhat similar, even though Korea was at first considered, at least nominally, sovereign: Western law (including the idea of customary law) was imposed through its Japanese version.[96] Finally, Manchukuo, the Japanese puppet state in China, was justified in large part on legal grounds: Manchuria, it was said, needed modern law, and this could come only from Japan, not from China.[97] As a consequence, its new law codes resembled closely those in Japan.[98] (Remarkably, the Japanese did not terminate the unequal treaties granting Western nationals special extraterritorial rights, but rather extended this principle of extraterritoriality to themselves.[99])

---

[93] See Ralf Michaels, Code vs Code: Nationalist and Internationalist Images of the Code Civil in the French Resistance to a European Codification, (2012) 8 *Eur. Rev. Contract L.* 277–295.

[94] Jean Limpens, Territorial Expansion of the Code, in Schwartz (ed.), *Code Napoleon and the Common-Law World* (1956) 92–109; Michel Grimaldi, L'exportation du code civil, in *Pouvoirs Do. 107 Le code civil* (2003) 80, 81ff.

[95] Tay-sheng Wang, *Legal Reform in Taiwan under Japanese Colonial Rule, 1895–1945 – The Reception of Western Law* (2000) 36ff; for a briefer version, see Tay-sheng Wang, *The Modernization of Civil Justice in Colonial Taiwan, 1895–1945*.

[96] Marie Seong-Hak Kim, *Law and Custom in Korea: Comparative Legal History* (2015); see also Chongko Choi, On the Reception of Western Law in Korea (1981) 9 *Korean J. Comp. L.* 141, 146–7; Choi, *Law and Justice in Korea* (2005) 161–162.

[97] Thomas David Dubois, Inauthentic Sovereignty: Law and Legal Institutions in Manchukuo, (2010) 69 *J Asian Studies* 749–770, 751.

[98] Ibid. at 756.

[99] Thomas David Dubois, Rule of Law in a Brave New Empire: Legal Rhetoric and Practice in Manchukuo, (Summer 2008) 26 *Law and History Review* 2: 285–317, 296–297.

In all these cases, Western-Japanese law came about as a matter of imposition, but it was not confined to that. Often, this law was also viewed as superior and as necessary for economic modelling. Thus, in Manchukuo, many locals supported the idea of sovereign (Japanese) stewardship in order to bring about modernization – and establish stronger opposition to the West.[100] Koreans were fascinated with German legal thought after the triumph in the French-German War and thus eager themselves to modernize their laws in face of this model – which happened to resemble the Meiji model.[101] And, indeed, just like the French Civil Code, Japanese-Western law was exported not just through conquest but also through inspiration. Japan, at the end of the nineteenth century, was a country that had been able to modernize in record time, had managed to avoid the fate of China, a country whose navy was able to defeat a European nation (Russia) in the battle of Tsushima.[102] The fascination with the success of Japanese modernization had impacts, including in law. Chinese law reformers of the Qing dynasty began to look to Japanese law (and thus indirectly to European law) for inspiration.[103] In this sense, if European law became influential in much of Europe, this happened to a large extent in its Japanese form.

The result was a partial unification of law in East Asia on civil law models. Given the background, it would therefore not appear fully accurate to understand the adoption of civil law in East Asian countries as a mere adoption of Western law, as joining a European legal tradition. Western law indeed influenced East Asian countries significantly, but it did so at least in part by way of what can be called a secondary reception: a reception of Japanese law, which itself had been received from the West.[104] The result, in this regard, is less a mere adoption of civil law and more an establishment of a Pan-Asian law – civilian in form but Asian in its attitude.

Pan-Asianism of course led to Japanese imperialism and then into the catastrophe of the Second World War. That war, and Japan's complete moral and military defeat, shattered any sense of Japanese superiority. After the defeat, any Japanese aspiration for an Asia-wide Empire became as implausible in Japan, as would be the readiness of other Asian countries to accept this. This may also be why, at least to an

[100] Ibid.
[101] Marie Seong-Hak Kim, Can There Be Good Colonial Law? Korean Law and Jurisprudence under Japanese Rule Revisited, in Marie Seong-Hak Kim (ed.), *The Spirit of Korean Law – Korean Legal History in Context* (2015) 129.
[102] For reactions all over Asia and beyond, see Rotem Kowner, Between a Colonial Clash and World War Zero – The Impact of the Russo-Japanese War in a Global Perspective, in *The Impact of the Russo-Japanese War* (2007) 1–25, 15–20; Cemil Ayden, A Global Anti-Western Moment? The Russo-Japanese War, Decolonization, and Asian Modernity, in Sebastian Conrad and Dominic Sachsenmaier (eds.), *Competing Visions of World Order – Global Moments and Movements, 1880s–1930s* (Springer, 2007) 213–236.
[103] Dan Fenno Henderson, Japanese Influences on Communist Chinese Legal Language, in Jerome Cohen (ed.), *Contemporary Chinese Law* (1973) 158–187.
[104] Kun Yang, Law and Society Studies in Korea: Beyond the Hahm Theses, *L. & Soc. Rev.* 23 (1989) 891, 897.

outside observer, it appears that both Japanese and non-Japanese scholars alike often tend to downplay the role that Japan had in the introduction of civilian systems in Korea and elsewhere – even though their subsequent development was independent.[105]

To the extent that ideas of Japanese Pan-Asianism still exist (or are rediscovered), they tend to come without the imperial ambition of earlier times.[106] Today, the Japanese approach to law reform in other Asian countries is unusual for the degree to which the Japanese are willing to defer to local interests: The starting point for Japanese legal aid is not so much the model of their own law (as is the case for much law reform elsewhere) but instead the local needs and traditions of the respective country.[107] The idea that law in Asia should be unified under Japanese leadership and after the Japanese model would appear highly implausible. However, this leaves the idea of Pan-Asian law not without any influence. On the one hand, much law in East Asia remains indeed somewhat similar at least superficially, insofar as it is civilian. This represents a remnant of Japan-led Pan-Asianism. On the other hand, this civilian character of law comes without a deeper aspiration towards a political entity led by Japan.

In this sense, civil law in Asian countries now seems to hold a curious existence: it is linked neither to European civilization (which it never embodied), nor to Japanese projects of Pan-Asianism (which have failed). It remains, in that sense, a formal remnant. Kanayama's perspective that this law does not represent Asia in any meaningful sense becomes plausible against this specific historical background.

6 AN ESSENTIALIST ASIA: ASIAN VALUES

It seems appropriate, thirdly, to discuss at least briefly what is arguably the most well-known recent concept of an Asian identity of Asian law, namely the idea of Asian values. Asian values were promoted in the 1980s and 1990s, under the leadership of Lee Kuan Yew and Mahathir Mohamad, then Prime Ministers of Singapore and Malaysia respectively, as well as other leaders in the region. The main argument was

---

[105] Takao Tanase, The Empty Space of the Modern in Japanese Legal Discourse, in J Feest and D Nelken (eds.), *Adapting Legal Cultures* (Hart, 2001) 187. For a Northeast Asian legal complex, see, e.g., Tom Ginsburg, Japanese Law and Asian Development, in Gerald-Paul McAllinn and Caslav Pejovic (eds.), *Law and Development in Asia* (Routledge, 2012) 68–88; for criticism, see Lee-Eun Young, A Criticism of the Northeastern Legal System Theory, (2003) 24 *Civil Law Study* (Korea Civil Law Study Association) 173–196.

[106] See also Simon Avenell, What Is Asia for Us and Can We Be Asians? The New Asianism in Contemporary Japan, (2014) 48 *Modern Asian Studies* 6:1594–1636.

[107] On this, see Isabelle Giraudou, L'assistance juridique japonaise aux pays dits 'émergents' d'Asie, (2009) 7 *Transcontinentales* 47–67; Hiroshi Matsuo, Let the Rule of Law Be Flexible to Attain Good Governance, in Per Bergling, Jenny Ederlöf, and Veronica L. Taylor (eds.), *Rule of Law Promotion: Global Perspectives, Local Applications* (Iustus, Uppsala, 2009) 41–56; also (briefly) Akio Morishima, Japanese Approach toward Legal Development Assistance (Law and Development), in Yoshiharu Matsuura (ed.), *The Role of Law in Development – Past, Present and Future* (2005) 19–20.

that Asian society is governed by values drawn from Confucianism, and that political and legal systems in Asia would function best when in accordance with these values. Underlying this suggestion is an identity claim: Asian identity brought together different cultures in Asia and at the same time distinguished them from the West.

The idea was, in some ways, a continuation of the earlier two. It took up the Japanese idea of a Pan-Asianism and combined it both with Confucianism as a sinocentric idea and the idea of pluralism that could account for Buddhism, Hinduism and Islam as well. Indeed, although Pan-Asianism started off with an adoption of European over Asian models of governance, the idea of Asian values had (and still has) supporters among Japanese conservatives.[108] At the same time, however, the idea of Asian values represented a powerful new idea. It was voiced after the end of colonization in Asia, and in response to the quick rise of Asian economies that were now becoming competitors to Western countries. It is, in this sense, the most explicit formulation of an Asian identity of law.

Situated in this competition, it becomes clear that the idea of Asian values, even more so than its two predecessors, was directed, at least nominally, against the West and against what was perceived as colonial ideas. The economic success of Asia seemed like a powerful refutation of European ideas about Asian intrinsic backwardness. If Max Weber had suggested that Asian values were anathema to development, did not the existing development suggest that they were actually conducive? And, further, that they therefore provide a valid alternative to Western values?

Western countries had criticized Asian countries for neglecting human rights and democracy, often also for strategic purposes. Asian values were a response to both criticisms. As concerns human rights, the relation is complicated. The Bangkok Declaration of 1993, a leading document of the Asian Values debate, did not reject the idea of human rights or their universal character at least at an abstract level.[109] Instead, the carefully crafted document suggested 'that the promotion of human rights should be encouraged by cooperation and consensus, and not through confrontation and the imposition of incompatible values'. What this meant was that the particular conception of human rights espoused by the West was not universal in nature and should therefore not be imposed on Asian countries.[110] As concerns democracy, Asian values were invoked in favour of a governance structure that is strong on development but relatively weak on individual rights, a structure that Bui Ngoc Son calls Confucian Constitutionalism and Mark Tushnet has recently called authoritarian

---

[108] See Avenell (n. 106) 1604ff; see also Shigenori Matsui, Fundamental Human Rights and 'Traditional Japanese Values': Constitutional Amendment and Vision of the Japanese Society, (2018) 13 *Asian Journal of Comparative Law* 59–86.

[109] www.hurights.or.jp/archives/other_documents/section1/1993/04/final-declaration-of-the-regional-meeting-for-asia-of-the-world-conference-on-human-rights.html.

[110] See, e.g., Randall Peerenboom, Beyond Universalism and Relativism: The Evolving Debates about Values in Asia, 14 *Ind. Int'l & Comp. L. Rev.* 1 (2003).

constitutionalism.[111] Such systems rest on powerful executive branches to deliver stability and internal security and invoke a strong rule of law as concerns commercial interests, in particular the protection of property rights, the enforcement of contracts. They are weak, by contrast, on democratic participation, which is, like individual human rights, viewed as being in the way of both economic development and an Asian sense of harmony.

The idea of Asian values has not, to my knowledge, been linked to the project of contract harmonization, or indeed commercial law more generally. Menon CJ, speaking about legal unification, invokes the diversity of national laws as a potential impediment; a cultural unity of Asia is not mentioned.[112] Even Han, when he promotes an Asian character for the PACL, names only specific doctrinal peculiarities of Asian laws, without invoking deeper underlying Asian values.

One reason for the absence of a reference to Asian values may be that they play no role in this area.[113] But another reason is the decline of the idea of Asian values in general. The international appeal of the idea of Asian values lost force in view of the Asian financial crisis in the late 1990s. Domestically, it retained strength for some time in supporting autocratic regimes' defences against the democracy movement.[114] Today, however, it is mostly rejected as another artificial construct. Worse, the idea of Asian values essentializes an idea that is at the same time incompatible with the internal diversity of Asia and retains, through its opposition, the focus on Europe. Indeed, forceful arguments have been made that the discourse on Asian values was also used strategically: that it was primarily used not against the West, but instead against local opposition. Amartya Sen argued that the idea of democracy is universal, even if the particular way in which it is incorporated is not.[115] Similar arguments have been made with regard to human rights; the ASEAN Human Rights Declaration of 2012, despite its shortcomings, no longer invokes

---

[111] Bui Ngoc Son, *Confucian Constitutionalism in East Asia* (2016); Mark Tushnet, Authoritarian Constitutionalism, (2015) *Cornell Law Review* 391–461.

[112] Sundaresh Menon, Transnational Commercial Law: Realities, Challenges and a Call for Meaningful Convergence, (2013) *Singapore Journal of Legal Studies* 231, at 246: 'Furthermore, even where harmonisation is desirable and practicable, the exercise must be approached with sensitivity towards the national legal systems which will have to implement these laws. Harmonisation without due regard to the idiosyncrasies of national legal systems will produce superficially uniform laws, which leave fundamentally unchanged the undulating legal terrain that results from differences in the national legal systems underpinning these laws'.

[113] But see Gary F. Bell, New Challenges for the Uniformisation of Laws: How the CISG Is Challenged by 'Asian Values' and Islamic Law, in Ingeborg Schwenzer & Lisa Spagnolo (eds.), *Towards Uniformity: The 2nd Annual MAA Schlechtriem CISG Conference* 11 (2011), 1, 15–20; more generally, see Ulrich Schroeter, Does the 1980 Vienna Sales Convention Reflect Universal Values? The Use of the CISG as a Model for Law Reform and Regional Specificities, (2018) 41 *Loy. L.A. Int'l & Comp. L. Rev.* 1–50; Bruno Zeller, Regional Harmonisation of Contract Law: Is It Feasible?, (2016) 3 *Journal of Law, Society and Development*.

[114] Mark R. Thompson, Pacific Asia after 'Asian Values': Authoritarianism, Democracy, and 'Good Governance', (2004) 25 *Third World Quarterly* 6:1079–1095.

[115] Amartya K. Sen, Democracy as a Universal Value, (1999) 10 *Journal of Democracy* 3–17.

Asian values.[116] Seen like this, Asian values represent less a fight of East versus West, and more one of authoritarianism versus democracy.[117] Thus, it may be the case that many people in Asia reject Western-style democracy based on the values they hold,[118] but this would not be different from discussions in the West.

7 BEYOND ESSENCE: ASIA AS METHOD?

What follows from this overview? My conclusions are tentative, as they must be.

First, even if Asia and Asian law are constructs, the question for an Asian identity of Asian law does not appear entirely useless. Granted, a cultural Asian law that would be structurally comparable to European law does not exist. It is not possible to speak of Asian law in the same way in which it is possible to speak of European law. Such ideas are European projections. But that does not mean that the search for an Asian identity is fruitless, and the fact that scholars within Asia invoke some kind of Asian identity suggests as much. I have suggested three models of such an Asian identity: Pan-Asian law, sinocentric law, Asian values. None of these models resembles the European model of cultural identity. Asian values were adopted in explicit rejection of European ideas of universalism. The sinocentric model is more one of a specific type of Empire than of the nation-state. Even Japanese Pan-Asianism, in the way in which it appropriated Western ideas of statehood, cannot be explained fully in those terms. Moreover, all of these concepts are inherently problematic. But this does not make them unworthy of study, quite to the contrary.

Second, all these concepts stand in a certain relation to Western expansion and must be understood, at least in part, as responses to the West. To cite Wang Hui again, 'the idea [of Asia] is at once colonialist and anticolonialist, conservative and revolutionary, nationalist and internationalist, originating in Europe and, alternatively, shaping Europe's image of itself.'[119] On the one hand, Japanese Pan-Asianism is a transplant from the West at the macro level, in the same way in which specific legal doctrines in Japanese law are such transplants at the micro level. What we have learned at the micro level should also help us at the macro level: the transplant does not leave the nature of the transplanted object intact; it changes it and adapts it to local circumstances. Therefore, the similarity of Japanese and Japanese-influenced law with European law is only superficial, as is the similarity of an Asian identity of law with a European identity of law. On the other hand, not only the idea of Asian values is formulated as an explicit rejection of Western law and Western values. The same is true for sinocentric law, which invokes ancient (precolonial ideas) today in

---

[116] Tommaso Visone, The 'ASEAN Way': A Decolonial Path beyond 'Asian Values'?, (2017) 9 *Perspectives on Federalism* 1.

[117] Mark R. Thompson, Whatever Happened to 'Asian Values'?, (2001) 12 *Journal of Democracy* 154–165, 158ff.

[118] See Doh Chull Shin, *Confucianism and Democratization in East Asia* (2012) and the review by Albert Y. Chen in (2013) 75 *Review of Politics* 673–676.

[119] Wang Hui, The Idea of Asia and Its Ambiguities, (2010) 69 *Journal of Asian Studies* 985–989, 987.

explicit rejection of Western concepts. Their origins may be ancient, but their use is modern.

Third, however, despite this importance of relations to the West, to analyse the concepts only in this relation or, worse, to essentialize them, would recapture the mistake of European orientalism. All these concepts are problematic insofar as they remain, like the European projection, focused on Europe as the yardstick and the perspective. If anything characterizes Asia as a region, it is its plurality – of views, of traditions, of governance structures, of cultures and of laws. There are many Asian legal traditions, not one; there are many Asian laws, not one. Any homogeneous concept of Asia, and thus of Asian law, seems inadequate in view of this plurality. All three concepts discussed here have, in the past, been used for either hegemonic or antidemocratic purposes. And all of these concepts are contested internally – in fact, although I attributed the different concepts of law loosely to specific countries, such different concepts can be found within each country. In short, concepts of an Asian legal identity must be seen as positions within internal political struggles and must also be understood with regard to those. European comparative lawyers are aware of this from the European context; we should not be surprised to find this elsewhere.

There is, in fact, a concept of Asia that may help such a perspective. It was first formulated by Yoshimi Takeuchi, a Japanese literary scholar who edited the first collection of writings on Asianism in 1960 and provided an influential analysis of the concept.[120] Takeuchi called his concept 'Asia as method',[121] and although he modestly suggested that 'it is impossible to definitively state what this might mean',[122] some elements become clear. Takeuchi differentiated two kinds of modernization in Asia – the Japanese one, which superficially imposed foreign (Western) achievements on a deeper societal structure left largely intact, and the Chinese one, begun later (1919), but deeper, because it emerged from society itself. This perspective enabled an inner-Asian comparison that went beyond the focus on Europe. The West remained an element of such an idea of Asia, but not more than that, and it lost its logical and epistemological priority:

The concept of Asia as method was later taken up by Taiwanese scholar Kuan-hsing Chen.[123] Following Stuart Hall,[124] Chen strongly opposed a perspective in which the West provided the universal standard and Asia was viewed as a particular, and he opposes ideas of Asia that, in one way or another, Europe as a reference

---

[120] Christian Uhl, Takeuchi Yoshimi: 'Japan's Asianism', 1963, in Saaler, Szpilman (n. 86), vol. 2, 317 ff. (introduction and excerpt); full German translation in German in Toshimi Takeuchi, *Japan in Asien: Geschichtsdenken und Kulturkritik nach 1945* (2005).
[121] Yoshimi Takeuchi, Asia as Method, in Richard F. Calichman (ed.), *What Is Modernity?: Writings of Takeuchi Yoshimi* (Columbia University Press, 2005) 149 (the text dates from 1960).
[122] Ibid. at 165.
[123] Kuan-Hsing Chen, *Asia as Method - Toward Deimperialization*. Chen himself relies strongly on Yūzō Mizoguchi, *China as Method* (in Japanese, 1989). See ibid. 245–255.
[124] Stuart Hall, The West and the Rest: Discourse and Power, in Stuart Hall and Bram Gieben, *Formations of Modernity* (Polity, 1992) 275–332.

point.[125] This means also, for him, to view Asia as a locus of the local and the global alike: analyses of Asia are also analyses of the world, and vice versa. The West is neither dominant over nor absent from Asia. Instead, Chen 'posits the West as bits and fragments that intervene in local social formations in a systematic, but never totalizing, way'.[126] The consequence is a possibility to move beyond a focus on the West, and at the same time to overcome ideas of Asian homogeneity:

> Using the idea of Asia as an imaginary anchoring point, societies in Asia can become each other's points of reference, so that the understanding of the self may be transformed, and subjectively rebuilt. On this basis, the diverse historical experiences and rich social practices of Asia may be mobilized to provide alternative horizons and perspectives.[127]

I am not aware of the applications of this idea in legal unification.[128] This chapter is not the one to develop the idea in full. If anything, the analysis has demonstrated how easily the Western comparative lawyer can go astray by assuming that questions have the same meaning in foreign areas as they do at home. Even the use of the term *convergence*, as opposed to *harmonization* or *unification*, may represent a non-European twist that the comparatist is bound to miss.[129] There is, in fact, a debate about the question of how Asian law should be, inherent in convergence discussion though not always in these terms. But it is a debate that looks very different from the debate of how European law is.

Asia as method would suggest less focus on comparison with the West and more comparison within Asia.[130] The focus would no longer be on the clash between Western and local law as such, it would not merely measure the mere difference between Asian and European law, and instead decentre both East and West[131]. It would undermine the tacit assumption, found not only in Western comparatists, that Western law is universal and Asian law is particular.[132] Developments in Asian law would no longer be reduced to degrees of Westernization and instead be seen on their own terms.[133] The debate between Han and Kanayama referenced above would not be reduced to a debate about the European versus Asian character of the PACL and instead would enable an intra-Asian comparison of different concepts of Asian

---

[125] Ibid. at 216–224.
[126] Ibid. at 223.
[127] Ibid. at 212.
[128] But see the reference to Chen in Ruskola, n. 47 at 896 n. 66.
[129] Simon Chesterman, Asia's Ambivalence about International Law and Institutions: Past, Present and Futures, (2016) 27 *EJIL* 945, 977–978.
[130] See, besides authors cited before, also Sang Yong Kim, The Necessity and the Methodology of Studies on Asian Law, (2004) 1 *Asia Law Review* 1–19.
[131] Ruskola, Where Is Asia? (n. 30) 893ff; see also Dipesh Chakrabarty, *Provincializing Europe: Postcolonial Thought and Historical Difference* (Princeton, 2008).
[132] Ruskola, Where Is Asia? (n. 30).
[133] Holning Lau, The Language of Westernization in Legal Commentary, (2013) 61 *Am. J. Comp. L.* 507–537 (finding the concept of Westernization descriptively and analytically inadequate, and normatively unattractive).

law, in which the West is one of multiple elements. And an emerging Asian law would in turn be fruitful for the Western observer, not merely as an object, but as a perspective on the West itself, and on modernity. As Takeuchi formulates,

> Rather the Orient must re-embrace the West, it must change the West itself in order to realize the latter's outstanding cultural values on a greater scale. Such a rollback of culture or values would create universality. The Orient must change the West in order to further elevate those universal values that the West itself produced. This is the main problem facing East-West relations today, and it is at once a political and cultural issue[134]

At this stage, the question asked at the beginning of this chapter – how Asian should Asian law be – has led in perhaps unexpected directions. It has generated a fruitful discussion and thus is not a useless question. But the question has, through the analysis, changed its character: Asia is no longer object or subject but method, no longer one but many parts that are in dialogue with each other, no longer recipient or opponent of Western law and instead co-producer of modernity and of modern law. In this, the West has at least as much to learn from Asia as Asia did from the West.

[134] Ibid. at 165.

Index

accountability approach, 86
adoption gap, 18
adoption rates, 19, 24
Africa, 19, 29, 219, 227
agreements/MOUs, 7, 16, 63, 89, 90, 93
Amadeus database, 124
Anglo-Commonwealth jurisdictions, 153
approaches
   accountability, 86
   comparative, 10, 11, 26, 30, 83
   comprehensive, 22
   determination table, 163
   externality, 160, 163
   presumption of regularity, 157
   RTB (reason to believe), 161, 162, 163, 165, 167, 169
   validity, 159, 163
arbitration
   acts/rules, 64, 70, 72, 75, 76
   arbitrator immunity, 75
   ASEAN conclusions, 221
   award enforcement, 65, 79
   background, 62
   confidentiality, 74
   decisions, 79
   home laws, 130
   international awards, 64, 76
   New York Convention, 66
Argentina, 28
Asia
   Asia Pacific Loan Market Association (APLMA), 59
   Asian Association of Constitutional Courts and Equivalent Institutions, 207
   Asian Business Law Institute (ABLI), 227
   Asianism, 249
   Bangkok Declaration of 1993, 246
   Confucian Constitutionalism, 246
   convergence and divergence, 135, 227, 231
   cultural identity, 233, 239, 246
   Europe's opposite, 233
   financial crisis, 191, 247
   jurisdictions, 135, 148
   law and values, 245, 247
   law history, 6
   law models, 42, 44, 59, 79, 248
   law, contract, 148, 149, 229, 231, 239
   law, pan-Asian, 239, 242, 246, 248
   law, soft, 141
   law, uniform, 244
   modernisation, 249
   Orientalism, 242, 249
   South Asian Association for Regional Cooperation (SAARC), 59
   Zhejiang High People's Court, 161
Association of Southeast Asian Nations (ASEAN)
   arbitration, 221
   ASEAN Economic Community (AEC)
      2015 vs. 2025, 195, 202
      blueprint, 184, 195, 202
      founding, 180
      objectives, 184
      organisational conflict, 194
      policy ratification and resources, 199
      progress table, 201
   ASEAN Handbook on Competition Policy and Law, 187
   ASEAN Integration Monitoring Office (AIMO), 185
   ASEAN Intergovernmental Commission on Human Rights (AIC), 209
   charter, 207, 218
   competition, 187
   convergence, 59
   corruption, 194
   development divide, 190

Index

harmonisation, 139
human rights, 209
membership divisions, 194
national single window (NSW), 186
outsourcing implementation, 197
priority lists, 197
rule of law, 210, 213, 217
socio-economic differences, 191
UPICC and PECL-based project, 230
Australia, 72, 167
authoritarian constitutionalism, 247
Azerbaijan, 29

Bangkok, 246
bankruptcy law, 37, 43
Beijing declaration, 229, 236
Belt and Road project, 238
best evidence rule, 31
border effect, 126
Brazil, 28
bridge standards, 116, 128, 131, 133
British Retail Consortium (BRC), 95
Brunei, 135
bureaucracy, 184, 193, 194

Cambodia, 135
Cape Town Convention, 19
Caribbean Court of Justice, 218
Case Law on UNCITRAL Texts (CLOUT), 25
case studies/decisions
   Bloomberry Resorts, arbitral award, 79
   Cassis de Dijon, member state-produced goods, 217
   CISG national law reform model, 26
   Draft Common Framework of Reference (DCFR), 143
   Google Spain, personal data protection, 206
   Government of the Lao People's Democratic Republic, international arbitration, 79
   Northside Development, IMR and executing documents, 166
   PRC Company Law art. 16 enforceability, 157
   RTB approach outcomes, 165
   Singapore commercial contract law, 144, 149
   Sun Tian Gang, international arbitration, 80
   Trento project, contract laws, 136
   Turquand, indoor management rule, 165
   UNCITRAL Model Law on Electronic Commerce, 30
   Zhejiang High People's Court, reason to believe approach, 161
centre of main interest (COMI), 51
certification program owners (CPOs), 95
Chile, 219

China (People's Republic of China, PRC)
   Asian legal tradition, 235
   Beijing declaration, 229, 236
   constitution, 168
   government "bringing outside in," 238
   jurisdiction, 135
   law for "barbarians," 233
   law reform and CISG, 27
   law, civil/commercial/contract, 28, 154
   law, PRC Company Law art. 16 discussion, 158
   law, PRC Guaranty Law art. 5, art. 7, 162, 176
   property protection policies, 168
   Zhejiang High People's Court, 161
choice-of-law clauses, 118, 130
civil law
   Asia, 46, 154, 231, 234, 240
   best evidence rule, 31
   contract law, 135, 147
   Europe, 136
   jurisdiction influence, 135
   legislation and code clarity, 54
   model codes, 29
   reform, 28
   unification, 244
CLOUT (Case Law on UNCITRAL Texts), 25
commercial law. *see also* contract law
   adoption rates, 24
   arbitration, 18, 221
   China, 27
   commercial codes, 12, 26, 28
   contract law, 7, 140
   drafting, 14, 17
   economics, 22
   electronic commerce, 16, 21, 30, 31
   harmonisation, 1, 14
   jurisdictions, 20
   leadership, 23
   pluralism, 8
   reform, 15, 17, 19, 20, 21, 22
Common Core of European Private Law Project, 136
common law
   arbitration, 62
   Asia vs. West, 234
   Common European Sales Law, 29
   contract law, 135, 147
   indoor management rule (IMR), 153, 157
   jurisdiction influence, 135
   presumption of regularity, 153, 157
   uniform law, 240
company law. *see also* contract law
   China, PRC courts' solutions, 158, 159
   competition, 187, 192
   duty to review, 175

company law (cont.)
  enforceability, 120, 157
  Europe, 3, 105, 124
  executing security instruments, 172
  externality approach, 160
  guarantors, 161
  home law bias, 122, 131
  indoor management rule (IMR), 156, 161, 166, 168
  markets, 119, 123
  protections, 154, 176, 206
  single set, 112
  transaction disputes, 156, 161, 163, 170, 172
comparative approach, 10, 11, 13, 30
competition, 129, 187, 192
Comprehensive and Progressive Agreement for Trans-Pacific Partnership (CPTPP), 222
comprehensive approach, 22
confidentiality, 74, 206
conflicts
  ASEAN countries socio-economic differences, 191
  company law, 156
  Dispute Settlement Understanding (DSU), 212
  international policy decisions, 182
  mitigating, 90, 93
  organisational, 183
  private sphere, 87
Confucianism, 235, 237, 246
constitutionalism, authoritarian, 247
contract law. *see also* company law
  agreements, 7
  Asia, 139, 148, 229, 239
  case study, 144
  common law tradition, 135
  competition, jurisdictional, 129
  consumer contract law, 143, 144
  contractor protections, 153, 157, 161, 176
  convergence, 11
  Directive 2005/29/EC, 146
  Draft Common Framework of Reference (DCFR), 142
  enforceability, 153, 157, 162
  Europe, 105, 135, 148, 229
  flexibility, 31
  harmonisation, 138, 145
  home law benefits, 131
  instruments of, 141, 144, 146
  International Commercial Terms (INCOTERMS), 12
  market standardisation, 114
  quality of, 114
  risks, contractual, 170
  sale of goods regulations, 141, 147
conventions
  Cape Town Convention on International Interests in Mobile Equipment, 19
  Convention for the Unification of Certain Rules of Law relating to Bills of Lading, 9
  Convention on Contracts for the International Sale of Goods (CISG), 19, 26, 28, 231
  Convention on International Interests in Mobile Equipment, 19
  Convention on the Limitation Period in Contracts for the International Sale of Goods, 25
  Convention on the Recognition and Enforcement of Foreign Arbitral Awards, 18, 62
  Convention Providing a Uniform Law for Bills of Exchange and Promissory Notes, 9
  Convention Providing a Uniform Law for Cheques, 9
  Convention relating to a Uniform Law on the International Sale of Goods, 26
  European Convention on Human Rights, 208
  Hague Conference on Private International Law, 10
  New York Convention/Convention on the Recognition and Enforcement of Foreign Arbitral Awards, 18, 62, 66
  UNCITRAL 11th Multinational Judicial Colloquium, 41
  United Nations Conference on Trade and Development, 21
  Vienna Convention for the International Sales of Goods, 141
  WHO Framework Convention on Tobacco Control, 19
convergence
  Africa, 227
  Asia, 59, 227, 243
  defined, 35
  ISEAL codes, principles, 96
  methodologies, 38
  Model Law example, 43, 57
  policy and procedures, 86, 125
  reason to believe and indoor management rule, 170, 176
  regulatory, 83, 88, 102
  trade endogeneity, 126
  UNIDROIT Principles on the Operation of Close-Out Netting Provisions, 40
Court of Justice of the European Union, 142, 215
Court of the Andean Pact, 219
credibility principles, 96
cross-border contracts/transactions. *see* contract law, international trade/law

Index

data, 16, 206
decisions. *see* case studies/decisions
Delaware, 118, 123
democracy, 246
Directive 2005/29/EC, 146, 147
Directive 95/46/EC, 206
Dispute Settlement Understanding (DSU), 212
divergence
    Asia, 55, 185, 190, 231
    costs, 104, 112, 138
    duty to review, 175
    Europe, 138
    financial law, 34
    flip clauses, 40
    key factors, 45
    Model Law, 46, 57
    organisational governance, 86
    private regulators, 84, 102
    reason to believe and indoor management rule, 167, 176
    tolerances, 37
    uniform law, 13
Doing Business and Enabling Trade Indices, 194
Draft Common Framework of Reference (DCFR), 137, 142
duty to review, 176

economics
    ASEAN Economic Community (AEC), 180, 184
    ASEAN socio-economic differences, 190, 191, 194
    Asia, 246
    bureaucracy, power, wealth, 193
    contractual risks, 170
    corruption, 194
    harmonisation, 138
    integration, market-driven, 192
    law, commercial, 22
    law, exporting, 130
    law, home, 119
    law, investments, law-specific, 111
    law, model and transitions, 31
    law, rule of, 213
    law, switching costs, 122
    law, uniform, 9, 19, 132
    legislation, 15, 16, 22, 182
    national interests, 189
    network effects, 106, 125
    political stability, 192
    Regional Comprehensive Economic Partnership (RCEP), 222
    reincorporating, 120
electronic commerce, 16, 21, 30, 31
English law, 26, 118, 130, 141, 144

environmental law, 19, 21
Europe/European Union
    Amadeus database, 124
    arbitration, 76
    Brexit and judgment enforcement, 221
    British Retail Consortium (BRC), 95
    Council of Europe, 206, 208
    Court of Justice, 142, 206, 213, 219
    directives, 146, 206
    divergence rates, 135
    Draft Common Framework of Reference (DCFR), 137, 142
    economic integration, 224
    European Bank for Reconstruction and Development assessment tool, 17
    European Convention on Human Rights (ECHR), 208
    European Free Trade Agreement, 217, 219
    Eurozone markets, 119
    harmonisation, 138
    law, Asia, 210, 217, 232, 233, 242
    law, civil, 136, 138, 139
    law, company, 105, 124
    law, contract, 135, 136, 140, 148, 231
    law, Europe, 105, 130, 207
    law, rule of law, 208, 214
    law, Switzerland, 118
    sale of goods, 29, 141
    unification, legal, 228
exceptions, statutory, 49

fair trade labelling organisation (FLO), 99
fiduciary requirements, 113
financial crises, 191, 247
financial institutions, 15, 21, 40, 55
financial law, 34, 37, 39, 43, 91
flip clauses, 40
foreign direct investment (FDI), 188
Foreign Economic Contract Law, 28
foreign tax claim exclusions, 51
free trade. *see* international trade/law
French law, 26, 214, 239

Geneva, Convention and Protocol, 63
German law, 26, 244
Global Financial Crisis, 39
Global Food Safety Initiative (GFSI), 95
globalisation, 148, 188
Google, 206
government
    agencies, 15, 19, 86, 89, 128, 181
    authoritarian constitutionalism, 247
    Chinese, "bringing outside in," 238
    good/bad difference?, 226

Index

government (cont.)
  rule of law divisive, 205
Guaranty Law. *see* China (People's Republic of China, PRC)
Guide to Enactment of the Model Law, 31

Hague Conference on Private International Law (HCCH), 10, 14, 27
Handbook on Competition Policy and Laws, 187
harmonisation. *see also* convergence
  ASEAN integration, 187
  jurisdictions, 139
  law instruments, non-contract, 146
  law, consumer, 143
  law, contract, 138, 139, 143, 144, 146, 217
  law, international, 9
  possible?, 145
  trading conditions, 138
home law, 122, 130, *see also* jurisdictions
Hong Kong, 75, 135
human rights, 19, 208, 209
Hungary, 10, 28

implementation
  ASEAN Economic Community (AEC), 180, 184, 187, 198
  case law, Europe, 208
  gap, 180
  models, legislative, 18
  public policy, 183
  regulatory intermediaries, 85
  uniform law, global/regional, 13, 23
incorporating, 120
Indonesia, 135, 186
indoor management rule (IMR), 153, 157
information technologies, 106
insolvency, 21, 35, 41, 47
intellectual property, 16, 187
International Accreditation Forum (IAF), 95
International Chamber of Commerce (ICC), 20, 76
International Commercial Terms (INCOTERMS), 12
International Council for Commercial Arbitration (ICCA), 70
International Institute for the Unification of Private Law (UNIDROIT), 10, 15, 27, 40, 144, 230
international regulatory cooperation (IRC), 81
International Social and Environmental Accreditation and Labelling Association (ISEAL), 96, 99
International Standard Organisation (ISO), 90

International Swaps and Derivatives Association (ISDA), 39
international trade/law
  adoption gap, 18
  agreements, 16, 217
  arbitration, 63, 66, 74
  Asia, 27, 186, 192, 221, 238
  associations, 84
  centre of main interest (COMI), 51
  convergence, 126
  economics, 182, 188, 194
  foreign tax claims, 51
  harmonisation, 145
  international labor organisation (ILO), 90
  jurisdictions, 116, 122, 130, 221
  law, commercial, 12, 144
  law, contract, 143, 144, 148
  law, insolvency, 35, 41, 44, 54, 56
  law, sales, 26, 28, 128, 141
  law, uniform, 9, 10, 12, 41, 44
  network effects, 118
  regulations, 81, 87, 131
  Trans-Pacific partnerships, 222

Japan, 135, 231, 240, *see also* Asia
jurisdictions
  Anglo-Commonwealth, 153
  arbitration, 62, 79, 118
  Asia, 135, 139, 145
  competition, 129, 131
  Delaware, 118, 123
  Europe, 24, 124, 208, 216
  incorporating, 121
  Model Law, 31
  reform capacity, 20
  representation, 10
  specialisation, 122

Korea, 135, 207, 237, 243

language, 106, 117, 130, 191
Laos, 135
law
  arbitration, 63, 118
  authoritarian constitutionalism, 247
  bankruptcy, 37, 43
  enforceability, 93
  harmonisation, 9, 125
  impact, 16
  insolvency, 21, 35, 41, 47
  instruments, 141, 142, 144, 146
  jurisdictions, 116, 130
  language, 106, 110
  models, 21

Index

modernising, 11
network effects, 113, 115
organisational forms, 85
pluralism, 7
reforming, 15, 19, 26
specialisations, 111, 112, 115, 121, 125, 127, 130
laws. *see also* model laws, rule of law
League of Nations, 10
Legal Origins project, 234
legislation
　history, 15
　legislative texts, 11, 15, 16, 20, 141
　legislators, 16, 19, 113, 125, 134
　models, guides, 15, 21, 41, 53
Loan Market Association (LMA), 39, 59
London Court of International Arbitration (LCIA), 76
lonely organisation syndrome, 183

Macau, 135
Malaysia, 79, 80, 103, 135, 186, 193, 245
management rules, statutory and indoor, 157
markets
　ASEAN integration, 185, 198
　economics, 192
　failure categories, 108
　information tech analysis, 106
　jurisdictions, 119, 122, 129, 131, 138, 217
　network effects, 108, 111, 125
　participants, 127
　specialisations, 122
　standardisation, 114, 128
Meiji regime, 241
Middle Kingdom (China), 236
model laws
　adopting, 13, 19, 30, 42, 49
　arbitration, 10
　Asia, 55, 148, 231, 239
　attributes, 11, 41
　civil codes, 29
　convergence/divergence, 43, 57
　elements, 41
　enactment guide, 31
　Europe, 136
　indoor management rule, 154
　insolvency, 53
　interpretations, 77
　UNCITRAL, 30, 35, 41, 56
　United Nations CISG, 27
MOUs/agreements, 7, 16, 63, 89, 90, 93
Myanmar, 135

national single window (NSW), 186, 189, 193
networks, 105, 115, 126, 188, 193

New York Convention/Convention on the Recognition and Enforcement of Foreign Arbitral Awards, 18, 62, 65, 66
non-governmental organisations (NGOs), 84, 87, 94

Organisation for the Harmonisation of Business Law in Africa (OHADA), 29, 35, 227
organisations/businesses, 85, 89, 102, 183, 193, 194
organizational law. *see* company law
Orientalism, 242, 249

pan-Asian law, 239, 242, 246, 248
pan-European civil code, 136
Philippines, 135, 186, 193
pluralism, 7
politics
　Asia, 192, 236, 239, 246
　harmonisation, 139, 143
　laws, 10, 13, 19, 126, 143, 205
　legislative models, 15
PRC. *see* China (People's Republic of China, PRC)
presumption of regularity, 153, 157, 162, 170
Principles of Asian Contract Law (PACL), 148, 229, 231, *see also* Asia
Principles of European Contract Law (PECL), 137, 148, 230, *see also* Europe/European Union
property protection, 168
public policy, 72, 183
public sector corruption, 194

Regional Comprehensive Economic Partnership (RCEP), 222
regularity presumption, IMR, 153, 157, 162, 170
regulations
　conflicts and cooperation, 88, 97
　contract law, 143, 147
　mergers and acquisitions, 98
　regulators, 84, 92
　technical, 187
　transnational, 84, 131
RTB (reason to believe), 161, 162, 167, 170, 176
rule of law, 204, 206, 213, 226

sale of goods, 19, 128, 141, 146
Shanghai, 135
Singapore. *see also* Asia
　arbitration, 75, 221
　ASEAN Summit, 2007, 184
　Asia's Global Law School, 232
　Asian values, 245
　contract law, 144

Singapore (cont.)
  Doing Business Across Asia, 227
  EU-Singapore Free Trade Agreement, 217
  jurisdictions, 135
  Model Law adoption, 55, 77
  national single window (NSW) development, 186
Socialism, 10, 237
soft laws, 36, 39, 42, 77, 141, 142, 148
South Asian Association for Regional Cooperation (SAARC), 59
Southern Africa Development Community (SADC), 219
Soviet Union, 219, 237
Spain, 28, 206
specialisations, law, 112, 115, 121, 125, 127, 130
standardisation
  ASEAN competition policy, 187
  certification program owners (CPOs), 95
  company/contract law, 116, 119
  limitations, 127
  mis-/over-/under-standardisation, 109, 125, 127
  network effects, 107, 125
statutory exceptions, 49
statutory indoor management rule, 157
Studies in the Contract Laws of Asia, 230
sustainability, 84, 96, 103
Switzerland, 118, 133

Taiwan, 135, 243
technology, 2, 21, 187, 198
telephone analogy, 107
Thailand, 135, 186, 193, 246
Tokyo, 135
trade. *see* international trade/law
transnational law/regulations, 81, 91, 98, 238, *see also* international trade/law
Trans-Pacific partnerships, 222
Transparency International's Corruption Perceptions, 194
treaties, 11, 18, 19, 23, 26, 207, 241
Trento project, 136
Tribunal of the Southern Africa Development Community (SADC), 219

uniform law. *see also* harmonisation
  adopting, 10, 13, 18, 19, 21, 145
  Asia, 27, 239, 248
  conventions, 9, 26

convergence defined, 35
economics, 19, 23
Europe, 138, 228
insolvency, 41
jurisdictions, 131
model laws, 29, 44
modernising, 11
politics, 2, 13, 25
rule of law, 207, 212
single law set, 112
UNCITRAL, 14, 26
United Kingdom, 76, 95, 208, 212, 221, *see also* Europe/European Union
United Nations
  11th Multinational Judicial Colloquium, 41
  arbitration, 10, 69, 71
  commercial law, 14, 30
  drafting legislation, 10, 23
  guides, 17, 41, 56
  Model Law, 35, 41, 44, 71, 77
  UNIDROIT Principles of International Commercial Contracts (UPICC), 230
  United Nations CISG, 19, 128, 141, 147
  United Nations Commission on International Trade Law (UNCITRAL), 9, 14, 25, 62
  United Nations Conference on Trade and Development (UNCTAD), 21
  United Nations Forum on Sustainability Standards (UNFSS), 91
  United Nations General Assembly, 10, 15
  United Nations Global Compact, 91
  United Nations International Institute for the Unification of Private Law (UNIDROIT), 10, 15, 27, 40, 144, 230

Venice Commission for Democracy through Law, 206
Vienna Convention for the International Sale of Goods (CISG), 141, 144
Vietnam, 28, 135, 186, 237

Western law, 6, 230, 232, 240
World Bank, 17, 211
World Health Organisation (WHO) Framework Convention on Tobacco Control, 19
World Trade Organisation (WTO), 212

Zhejiang High People's Court, 161

Printed in the United States
by Baker & Taylor Publisher Services